Praise for *Llewellyn's Complete Book of Nort*

"A love letter to North American Witchcraft, this book is a must for folk magic apprentices, practitioners, and connoisseurs. Cory Thomas Hutcheson reminds us how the magic of the land and the people in North America is found on every corner, in your mother's blessing, at the ocean shores, and everywhere in between. This is the magic of resistance, tradition, and survival... Immerse yourself in the rich origin, history, and traditions of folk magic in North America guided by local experts, folklorists, and magic practitioners, such as H. Byron Ballard, Brandon Weston, J. Allen Cross, and more."

—Rev. Laura González, Pagan educator and creator of the English/Spanish podcast *Lunatic Mondays (Lunes Lunáticos)*

"This new and exciting tome covers many of our major American folk magic traditions on topics such as divination and spirit communication. Each section is presented by a recognized authority and/or scholar within the tradition. Traditions like Conjure and Powwow are treated in a respectful, thorough manner to provide an insider's perspective that will be accessible to the novice as well. Anyone who wants to explore these often hidden, magical sides of American folk culture would do well to immerse themselves in *Llewellyn's Complete Book of North American Folk Magic.* I have been involved in American folk magic academically and personally for almost fifty years, and I find that I have benefited greatly from reading it. The chapters are exciting, affirming, and will expand your knowledge and vision of our world and your life within it."

—Jack Montgomery, author of *American Shamans*

"Rich, engaging, and incredibly diverse, this book gives us irreplaceable and enlightening glimpses into every folk magic you can imagine, from the South to the North and all the way out west. A must-have book for any folk practitioner."

—Frankie Castanea, AKA Chaotic Witch Aunt, author of *Spells for Change*

"This collection of American folk magic is so expansive and so diverse, it's a must-have for every practitioner...I love the many authors with different backgrounds whose voices share their history, their practices, their magic within this tome without crossing the boundary into closed cultures. Many Americans feel somewhat lost trying to get in touch with our ancestry across vast oceans, but that's not always necessary. So many of these ancestors brought that magic with them here, and it changed and adapted to new lands. This book is a platform for these legacies to be carried on in a single publication and gives the opportunity for readers to seek more from the contributors within."

—Marshall, the Witch of Southern Light, cohost of *Southern Bramble: A Podcast of Crooked Ways*

COMPLETE BOOK OF

NORTH AMERICAN FOLK MAGIC

ABOUT THE AUTHORS

Stephanie Rose Bird is the author of seven books: *The Healing Power of African American Spirituality: A Celebration of Ancestor Worship, Herbs and Hoodoo, Ritual and Conjure*; *A Healing Grove: African Tree Remedies and Rituals for the Body and Spirit*; *Light, Bright, and Damned Near White: Biracial and Triracial Culture in America*; *Four Seasons of Mojo: An Herbal Guide to Natural Living*; *Earth Mama's Spiritual Guide to Weight Loss*; *365 Days of Hoodoo: Daily Rootwork, Mojo & Conjuration*; and COVR award-winning *Sticks, Stones, Roots & Bones: Hoodoo, Mojo & Conjuring with Herbs*. Bird holds a BFA cum laude from Temple University's Tyler School of Art and an MFA from the University of California San Diego as a San Diego Opportunity Fellow. A former Professor of Fine Art at the School of the Art Institute of Chicago, she has been interviewed on PBS Wisconsin, ABC7 News, BBC London, WNPR, WBEZ, various podcasts, and at venues. Her innovative workshops that blend Gaia-based Spirituality and Hoodoo are held across the country. Her writing on Hoodoo, green witchcraft, shamanism, holistic health, herbalism, complementary therapies, and herbal lore, focused around African diasporic healing ways, has been featured in *SageWoman* (where she also has a column, "PanGaia") as well as other periodicals, almanacs, and more. She contributed to the *World Folklore and Folklife* encyclopedias published by Greenwood Publishers and the online anthology *Nobody's Home*. She is passionate about folklore and mythology and is a member of the American Folklore Society. Bird is a practicing healer, Green Witch, Hoodoo, and Shaman while also being a mother, wife, author, and artist. Bird works as a magickal herbalist and aromatherapist and is co-owner of SRB Botanica with her daughter. Their products include organic herbal soap, herbal salves, and balms, as well as elixirs (http://www.srbbotanica.com). To book an appearance or engagement, visit Bird's website at http://www.stephanierosebird.com.

H. Byron Ballard, BA, MFA, is a western North Carolina native, teacher, folklorist, and writer. She has served as a featured speaker and teacher at several festivals and conferences, including the Sacred Space Conference, Pagan Spirit Gathering, Starwood, HexFest, and many others. She serves as senior priestess and co-founder of Mother Grove Goddess Temple and the Coalition of Earth Religions/CERES, both in Asheville, NC. She podcasts about Appalachian folkways on *Wyrd Mountain Gals*. Her essays are featured in several anthologies, and she writes a regular column for *SageWoman* magazine. Find her online at www.myvillagewitch.com.

Starr Casas was raised in the Southern culture of the Deep South and holds onto the values of her ancestors. She is a traditional Conjure woman with *four* living generations of workers and two generations that have passed on. For over forty years, veteran Rootworker Starr Casas has been helping folks through her ancestral heritage of Old Style Conjure works from south of the Mason-Dixon line. She is the best-selling author of *The Conjure Workbook Volume 1: Working the Root*, published through Pendraig Publishing, and *Old Style Conjure* and *Divination Conjure Style*, published through Red Wheel/Weiser. She is also the author of many best-selling self-published titles on Old Style Conjure such as *Working with the Bible*. Mama Starr is a teacher and offers hands-on teaching to folks; contact her for more information or check out her events calendar.

Ixtoii Paloma Cervantes is a full-time Curandera, Mexican Shaman, and an *Abuela de la Tradición* (elder that teaches Curanderismo). She was born and raised in Mexico into the tradition and started working as a Curandera and a Shaman in the 1980s. Although she is from Northern Mexico, she spent most of her life, until her early thirties, in the Yucatán Peninsula. This allowed her to learn different styles of Curanderismo from her family and mentors. Running away from her destiny, she went and studied biological science, though her mother foretold that she would return to Curanderismo as her main career. Now she applies her educational background to find the science behind the remedies and rituals of Curanderismo. She moved to Europe in the '90s. There she learned other spiritual and complementary/alternative techniques for well-being. In the late '90s, she moved to the United States, where she deepened her studies with local medicine people and Native American elders. She currently lives in California, where she offers private consultations and has her school, the Ixtoii Institute of Shamanism and Curanderismo. She teaches in California and in other states and countries. Her mission is to train amazing Curanderismo practitioners who can adapt the tradition to modern times and who can restore their lives to live fully in harmony with themselves, others, and Mother Earth. You can reach her at https://www.palomacervantes.com/ or at hola@palomacervantes.com.

Kenya T. Coviak is an African American folk magician/Hoodoo practitioner from Detroit, Michigan. Her magical training includes oral traditional teachings, magical studies in American Modern Neo Pagan witchcraft, and magical herbalism. She specializes in workshops and lectures on these subjects, as well as runs a teaching grove. She is co-owner of the Michigan Witches Ball, hosts the podcast *My Magical Cottagecore Life*, and owns Detroit Conjure LLC.

J. Allen Cross is a practicing Witch of Mexican, Native American, and European descent whose magic is formed by his mixed family culture and Catholic upbringing. Through his writing he hopes to bridge the gap between things like culture, religion, magic, and the paranormal. In 2021 he authored the best-selling book *American Brujeria*, which serves as a guide to modern Mexican American folk magic. Nowadays, he lives in his home state of Oregon, where he works as a Witch, author, and paranormal investigator full-time.

Dr. **Alexander Cummins** is a contemporary cunning-man and historian of magic. His magical specialities are the dead (folk necromancy), divination (geomancy), and the grimoires. Along with various publications for occult and academic publishers, he is a frequent speaker on the international circuit, co-hosts the podcast *Radio Free Golgotha*, and is a founding editor of Revelore Press' Folk Necromancy in Transmission series. Originally from the Midlands in the UK, Al now makes his home in New England. Dr. Cummins' work, publications, classes, and services can be found at www.alexandercummins.com.

Morgan Daimler is an author, teacher of esoteric subjects, witch, and priest of the Good Folk (aka fairies). A prolific writer, Morgan has published more than three dozen books, both fiction and nonfiction, and presented workshops on fairies and Irish mythology at various events and conferences.

Lilith Dorsey, MA, hails from many magickal traditions, including Celtic, Afro-Caribbean, and Native American spirituality. Her traditional education focused on plant science, anthropology, and film at the University of Rhode Island, New York University, and the University of London, and her magickal training includes numerous initiations in Santeria, also known as Lucumi, Haitian Vodun, and New Orleans Voodoo. She has been a professional psychic for over three decades. Lilith is a frequent presenter at festivals and gatherings, including the Sirius Rising festival, Sankofa Fest, New York City Pagan Pride Day, and the Earth Warriors Festival. She is a regular guest on several Pagan blogtalk radio shows. She is the author of numerous books on magical and African Traditional Spirituality, including *Orishas, Goddesses, and Voodoo Queens*; *Water Magic*; and *Voodoo and African Traditional Religion*.

Morrigane Feu is a witch and a priestess in the province of Québec, Canada. She has been on an ever-evolving Pagan path since 1996 and now facilitates public rituals in Montréal. In the last few years she has channeled her lifelong interest in folklore, folktales, and mythology into the study and revival of French Canadian folk magic. Sorcellerie now permeates all of her magic and rituals as she strives to share it with as wide an audience as possible.

Mario Esteban Del Ángel Guevara was born in Monterrey, Nuevo León, Mexico, where he obtained his bachelor's degree in bilingual education at the Universidad Autónoma de Nuevo León. Del Ángel Guevara is a PhD doctoral candidate in Hispanic linguistics at the University of New Mexico Department of Spanish and Portuguese, where he has taught courses in Spanish as a second language, heritage language, medical Spanish, and courses on Curanderismo: Traditional Medicine of Mexico and the Southwest. Doctoral candidate Mario Del Ángel Guevara has translated a number of books on traditional medicine from English to Spanish and serves as an interpreter for Mexican healers who participate in the Curanderismo courses at the University of New Mexico. He has apprenticed with Rita Navarrete in Mexico City and has researched the contributions and lives of other curanderas such as Teresita Urrea from Sonora, Mexico, and El Niño Fidencio in Nuevo León, Mexico.

Via Hedera was born in Southern California but currently lives in the Pacific Northwest on Salish territory, where she is a writer, folklore enthusiast, sculptor, and practitioner of American folk witchcraft. Having grown up around the commonplace spiritual mysticism and superstitions of her large, diverse family and community, she dedicates her time to the study of folklore as it transmits across the land and between people. Wherever there is the merging of magic and connection between spirits, Via is sure to haunt. She is author of *Folkloric American Witchcraft and the Multicultural Experience: A Crucible at the Crossroads* and spends her time collecting American folklore, sculpting altar statuary, and dancing with the dead. Find out more at www.viahedera.com.

Cory Thomas Hutcheson was raised in Tennessee and grew up surrounded by family lore about Ireland, Poland, and Scotland. After a few overseas excursions in parts of Europe, he returned home eager to dive into the folklore and folk magic of North America. He started a research website and podcast with his friend and magical partner Laine called *New World Witchery*, which has been examining North American folk magic practices since 2010 (www.newworldwitchery.com). He has also authored a book on the folklore of playing card cartomancy called *54 Devils*, as well as the Llewellyn title *New World Witchery: A Trove of North American Folk Magic*. He has a PhD in American Studies with specializations in folklore, ethnography, ethnic studies, and religion from Pennsylvania State University, and he teaches classes in the humanities as well as online about folklore. He continues to look for more wonder in the world and is grateful to all the contributors to this book for helping him see so much of it all around him.

E. F. E. Lacharity lives in Ottawa, Ontario, Canada, with his wife Chantal and two daughters. He has been a Frankish Heathen (Thia Frankisk Aldsido) since 2011 and is an active member of his regional Pagan community, principally with Rúnatýr Kindred and Raven's Knoll. He has had a lifelong interest in the folklore and folk beliefs of his heritage and has absorbed all he can from his parents and grandparents and the elders who have passed on much of their old ways. These teachings are primarily focused on folk wisdom gained from rural living. In the 2010s Erik became interested in witchcraft and quickly took to the ways of his French Canadian ancestors, supplementing what he could from available ethnographic works. A few years ago, he began researching, collecting, and collating information along with Morrigane Feu, and the work in these pages—as well as the *Courir le loup-garou*—are the fruits of that passion.

Melissa A. Ivanco-Murray is a writer, artist, and musician with bachelor of science degrees in Russian and International Relations from the United States Military Academy (2011) and a master of arts in Slavic Languages and Literature from the University of Virginia (2020). She is currently a PhD candidate in the Slavic Department at UVA. Melissa has been a member of Ár nDraíocht Féin since 2015 and served as the Distinguished Faith Group Leader for the Fort Bliss Open Circle from 2016–2017. Melissa is the creator of the *Slavic Tarot* deck as well as the author of a fantasy series, *Circle*, which is loosely inspired by Slavic folklore and mythology. For more information about her past, present, and future works, see www.maimurray.com.

Dee Norman is a witch who grew up in her family's Italian American magical tradition and is the author of *Burn a Black Candle: An Italian American Grimoire*. She has been a student of cartomancy since the mid-eighties and is the creator of the *Emblemata Lenormand* oracle deck. She is also a card reader with clients around the globe. Throughout the past twenty years, she has been using her professional experience as an adult educator to develop and present workshops on Tarot, Lenormand, and a variety of magical topics. When not tending her household altar or paging through grimoires, she likes to play creepy video games and explore amateur cryptography with her daughter. Find out more about her projects and read her blog at www.blackcandlecottage.com.

Aaron Oberon is a folk witch, print relief artist, Florida fanatic, and author of *Southern Cunning: Folkloric Witchcraft in the American South*. They have been practicing folk magic for over half their life and grounded their witchcraft into the sandy soil of Florida for almost twenty years. Aaron lives in Southwest Florida and can often be found hidden in the mangroves speaking to lost and forgotten gods (and is often lost themselves). You can hear Aaron gush more about Florida and folk magic on their podcast *FolkCraft*, co-hosted with Temperance Alden. To see Aaron's art, musings on magic, and read jokes only they find funny, find them on Instagram @aaronoberon.

Robert Phoenix was born and raised in Pennsylvania and currently lives in south-central Pennsylvania and works for the state of PA. He has always been interested in folk magic and has studied many different systems over the years. He is a member of the Reformed church, known nowadays as the United Church of Christ, and an enthusiastic supporter and champion of Pennsylvania German culture. He loves Powwowing because it's a Christian-based system that really does work, and it connects him to the traditions, beliefs, religion, and folklore of his ancestors. He is the author of *The Powwow Grimoire*, *The Powwow Guy: A Memoir of a Pennsylvania Dutch Braucher*, and the website https://www.pagermanpowwow.com/. He was featured in the film *Hex Hollow: Witchcraft and Murder in Pennsylvania* (2015, directed by Shane Free).

Jake Richards was born and raised in East Tennessee and holds his Appalachian-Melungeon heritage close in his blood and bones. Jake has practiced Appalachian folk magic for over a decade and is the creator of the *Conjure Cards* deck and author of *Backwoods Witchcraft: Conjure & Folk Magic from Appalachia* (2019), *Doctoring the Devil: Notebooks of an Appalachian Conjure Man* (2021), and *Ossman and Steel's Classic Household Guide to Appalachian Folk Healing: A Collection of Old-Time Remedies, Charms, and Spells* (2022). He is also a member of the Phoenix Line of Braucherei practitioners and runs the *Holy Stones & Iron Bones* blog on all things Appalachian.

Sandra Santiago is a radical educator, activist, and poet. Sandra is initiated in various branches of African spirituality; she is a Lucumi Priestess of Obatala as well as a Yaya Nganga in Palo Mayombe. She does integrative light work via reiki and intuitive divination. She is a certified Reiki Master and is accredited by the World Metaphysical Association and the Accreditation Council of Holistic Healers. Sandra is a medium in the Afro-Caribbean tradition Espiritismo and has been offering consultations and readings since 2010. Her work can be defined as decolonization therapy. It is a healing process where wounded spirits and souls from disenfranchised groups can work to recover from historical trauma, racism, and other collective social ills caused by the long-term negative effects of colonization. Sandra's work has been published in various anthologies, including *Shades of Faith: Minority Voices in Paganism* (2012) and *Shades of Ritual: Minority Voices in Practice* (2014), and she has contributed to the *Wild Hunt*, a daily online news journal. She has also taught at many gatherings, conferences, and venues across the United States.

Robert L. Schreiwer is the president and founder of the Urglaawe tradition within Heathenry, which is a Pennsylvania Deitsch term that means "primal faith." He is currently the president and CEO of the Troth, which is the oldest and largest Heathen organization in existence. He is the manager of Heathens Against Hate, a Philadelphia area–based outreach organization, and a prison chaplain for Heathens.

Eliseo "Cheo" Torres, retired as a Vice President of Student Affairs from the University of New Mexico, is now part-time faculty teaching traditional medicine, Curanderismo courses year-round. Cheo regularly lectures and offers a two-week summer class and two online courses on the history, herbal remedies, and rituals of Curanderismo to audiences ranging from scholars and students to people hoping to become knowledgeable about alternative and traditional medicine, including lay people and medical professionals alike. Before coming to New Mexico, his most recent role was Vice President for Student Affairs and professor at Texas A&M University–Kingsville. He had various roles throughout his twenty years there. He has published seven books in his subject area. His most recent books are *Curanderismo: The Art of Traditional Medicine without Borders* and *Curandero: Traditional Healers of Mexico and the Southwest*, published by Kendall Hunt Publishing Company, and previously published books include *Curandero: A Life in Mexican Folk Healing* and *Healing with Herbs and Rituals: A Mexican Tradition*, both available from the University of New Mexico Press.

Benebell Wen is the author of *I Ching, The Oracle* (2023), *The Tao of Craft* (2016), and *Holistic Tarot* (2015), published by North Atlantic Books. She is a Taiwanese American occultist with deep family ties to Buddhism and Taoist mysticism. Wen has also practiced law in California and New York, primarily in the areas of venture capital, mergers and acquisitions, intellectual property, and securities law. Her academic background is in critical race theory and intersectional feminism, having focused her legal education in social justice law.

Brandon Weston is based in Fayetteville, Arkansas, and is a healer, writer, and folklorist who owns and operates Ozark Healing Traditions, an online collective of articles, lectures, and workshops focusing on the Ozark Mountain region. As a practicing folk healer, his work with clients includes everything from spiritual cleanses to house blessings. He comes from a long line of Ozark hillfolk and is also a folk herbalist, yarb doctor, and power doctor. He is the author of *Ozark Folk Magic* and *Ozark Mountain Spell Book* from Llewellyn Publications.

COMPLETE BOOK OF

NORTH AMERICAN FOLK MAGIC

A Landscape of Magic, Mystery, and Tradition

Edited and Compiled By

CORY THOMAS HUTCHESON

LLEWELLYN PUBLICATIONS
Woodbury, Minnesota

First Edition

First Printing, 2023

Cover design by Cassie Willett

Interior art by Llewellyn Art Department

Rabbit Spirit image on page 314 by Andrew Jimenez

Zodiac Man on pages 118 and 194 by Mary Ann Zapalac

Library of Congress Cataloging-in-Publication Data (Pending)
ISBN: 978-0-7387-6787-1

Llewellyn Publications
A Division of Llewellyn Worldwide Ltd.
2143 Wooddale Drive
Woodbury, MN 55125-2989
www.llewellyn.com

Printed in the United States of America

This book is dedicated to all those who have carried magic forward through dark times like a lamp under a basket, and to those carrying it now so that the future can know light.

Contents

Disclaimer

This book is presented solely for educational and entertainment purposes. The author and publisher are not offering it as medical advice. For diagnosis or treatment of any medical condition, readers are advised to consult or seek the services of a competent medical professional.

While best efforts have been used in preparing this book, the author and publisher make no representations or warranties of any kind. Neither the author nor the publisher shall be held liable or responsible to any person or entity with respect to any loss or damages caused, or alleged to have been caused, directly or indirectly, by the information contained herein. Every situation is different, and the advice and strategies contained herein may not be suitable for your situation.

In the following pages, you will find recommendations for the use of certain herbs, essential oils, and ritual items. If you are allergic to any of these items, please refrain from use. Each body reacts differently to herbs, essential oils, and other items, so results may vary from person to person. Essential oils are potent; use care when handling them. Always dilute essential oils before placing them on your skin, and make sure to do a patch test on your skin before use. Perform your own research before using an essential oil. Some herbal remedies can react with prescription or over-the-counter medications in adverse ways. Please do not ingest any herbs if you aren't sure you have identified them correctly. If you are on medication or have health issues, please do not ingest any herbs without first consulting a qualified practitioner.

Acknowledgments

A work attempting to span a continent—and several centuries of history—is by necessity a group effort. This book would not exist without the magical folk who took the time to share their knowledge, experience, and wisdom through these pages. Our immense thanks to Stephanie Rose Bird, H. Byron Ballard, Starr Casas, Ixtoii Paloma Cervantes, Kenya T. Coviak, J. Allen Cross, Alexander Cummins, Morgan Daimler, Lilith Dorsey, Morrigane Feu, Mario Del Ángel-Guevara, Via Hedera, E. F. E. Lacharity, Melissa A. Ivanco-Murray, Dee Norman, Aaron Oberon, Robert Phoenix, Jake Richards, Sandra Santiago, Robert L. Schreiwer, Eliseo "Cheo" Torres, Benebell Wen, and Brandon Weston. We are grateful to each of you for lending us a bit of yourselves, your traditions, your time, and your magic on this project.

We are also thankful for our editors, Heather Greene and Nicole Borneman, who have labored long and deserve much rest after bringing this ship into the shore. Appreciation is also due to the art department at Llewellyn, who have helped to translate many of our ideas into visual language.

Finally, and perhaps most crucially, we are grateful to those whose lives and stories have brought this magic down to us through the generations. We acknowledge that to keep magic's flame lit is a tireless task, especially when so many forces seek to quench that fire. We recognize that we have played a part in both sides of that task at various times, but we hope always to do better and bring magic from many places and many voices to many ears and many hands. The more who can carry this fire, the greater the chance it lasts. Here's to a flame eternal, fueled by the folk and their magic.

INTRODUCTION

If you were to set out walking across North America, you might pass through every landscape with wide-eyed wonder and potentially never see another person, so unfathomably huge is the territory you'd travel. Yet it is the people in connection with the place that can offer you a totally new kind of wonder. What many people fail to realize about North America is that it is very, very enchanted.

Picture a land stretching five thousand miles across, bound by two of the world's great oceans. Within that space, nearly twenty-five million square miles, you find frozen tundra and enormous glaciers (albeit ones that are receding now more rapidly than we'd like). You encounter scrub pine forests, deciduous rainforests, blooming deserts, vast prairies, and towering redwood groves full of trees so mighty and ancient they make you believe in the power and presence of giants. Some of the world's oldest mountains roll through one side of the landmass, while newer and more dramatic peaks stretch over the tops of thunderstorms on the other. And the *people*. Millions and millions of them. A land that has housed hundreds of Indigenous nations for millennia, until invaders from lands across the sea violently eradicated and displaced them. The children and grandchildren of those invaders have now exploded to even greater numbers, contending with their dark legacy while also trying to forge a bright future of their own in the vast, richly diverse landscape (and, one hopes, working to forge that future in more cooperation than their ancestors were).

The robust continent of North America is a fusion of space, landscape, and inhabitants. We have here a biodiversity to rival or surpass many continents, with a wild proliferation of flora and fauna that can shock someone who has never seen a creature like a moose, or delight them as they see prairie dogs popping from burrows in curious bursts of fur. The people here are both cosmopolitan and uniquely individual, representing the fusion of dozens or more lineages in any given family while also asserting a sense of purpose and destiny.

The magic of this continent resides in the people, informed and shaped by the landscapes they inhabit and the forces of history that have guided them. For some, the magic is in the wonder of those prairies, mountains, and forests—and rightly so, as they are fundamentally bewitching on their own! But there are other kinds of magic here, derived from the people's way of living in this land. They carry traditions from elsewhere into new nooks and crannies, where old stories about weather-predicting bears become transformed into celebrity groundhogs, or an ancient fairy race unmoored from its home in the hills of Ireland must suddenly slip into the old stones of Appalachia to hide. The revels of Chinatown during the New Year's Lunar Festival are different than those one might find in the towns around Beijing, but they speak to those traditions and the way they have been transformed here.

These transformations, the ways that the traditions of distant lands are reshaped in North America by the people who dwell here, are at the heart of what we call "folk magic." What exactly do we mean when we say that term, then? As a professional folklorist, I could certainly offer some academic-sounding explanations using terms like "vernacular belief structures" and "performative behavior." But while I appreciate the scholarly side of things, I also recognize that when we talk about folk magic, it's something that comes from the heart and the gut as much as the head, and so I'd prefer to use that language here instead.

Folk magic is the way that ordinary people shape the world with the uncanny, otherworldly, or wild power they have access to. Mostly, that power comes from an interaction between the landscape and the person doing the magic, and there are plenty of people who don't envision folk magic as "magic" at all. A Baptist woman praying down the blood of Jesus to protect her favorite department store layaway clerk would be horrified by the idea she was doing magic, for example (and if this example feels oddly specific, it's because I speak from direct experience here). Yet her act of invoking protection through divine or supernatural means is not particularly different than an African American man putting down a line of salt or brick dust powder around a home to protect it from harm, or a Jewish American person installing a mezuzah on a doorway to provide blessings and keep the household safe. They are all what we might anthropologically call apotropaic charms—ones designed to ward away evil—and each practitioner might not call what they do magic, but for an outsider looking in, they would seem very much the same.

Folk magic is the magic of the people, so who are those people? We often think of the "folk" in a sort of sepia-colored way, a nostalgic image of rural "salt of the earth" types using old-fashioned ways. In truth, the folk are you and me and everyone around us. Everyone belongs to folk groups of some kind—families, religious communities, classrooms, or military companies. All of them have unique folk bonds, as well as rituals and traditions that connect them. And in most cases, these folk groups have magic that they tap into in times of crisis, need, or want.

To tell the story of folk magic in North America, then, we must meet the folk. In order to understand the folk and their magic well, you need to hear about it from them directly.

And so this book puts in your hands a map of sorts. It will take you to a number of stops from coast to coast, through Canada, the United States, and Mexico. Most importantly, at each stop you will get to sit down with the people who practice the magic and hear about it from them. The contributors in this book all have experience doing the magic they discuss as a member of their folk communities, and in most cases, teaching and sharing their magic with others as well.[1] As you pull up to each new spot on the map and knock on a new proverbial front door in this book, I ask that you listen to what the contributors have to say. Absorb what they tell you about their folk magic, even if it's not folk magic you yourself might do, and listen to the stories and spells they weave.

What Is Folk Magic?

Of course, listening to all the folk magicians in the world won't help you if you don't know what they're talking about. The words "folk" and "magic" seem familiar to most who have heard them, and we may have a vague sense of what they mean when joined together, but it might help a bit to clarify what the authors and contributors in this book mean when we say "folk magic."

For one thing, it has to be derived from the folk. Already we've talked about who those folk are and why it is so important to make sure we are turning to people within folk communities to understand and listen to what they say about themselves.

But what about the "magic" bit? There are a lot of definitions that float around out there regarding magic, ranging from a century-old chestnut attributed to Aleister Crowley stating that it is change in accordance with will (to paraphrase). That essentially means a person's guiding purpose or intention can be used to coax change in the world, and it's a pretty good definition. From a more academic perspective, magic is often thought of as rituals, objects, performances, beliefs, and behaviors that influence the natural world in supernatural ways (again, to paraphrase). People do magic all the time, even if they don't call it that. Someone avoiding walking under a ladder is following a superstition to avoid bad luck, changing their potential future. Another person sharing a dream they had with a friend and asking, "What does it mean?" is participating in a very old tradition of divinatory magic, attempting to glean messages from the great beyond (or at least their subconscious). Hanging horseshoes in the home, carrying a rabbit's foot, or even making a wish on a shooting star all have magical connotations. Even people who consider magic to be something sinister and dangerous might be surprised at how much of it they do in their daily life from an anthropological point of view, from making the sign of the cross when they are frightened and need protection to writing down prayers in the hopes that they will come true (a form of petition-writing magic).

1. With one notable exception in the section on folk mysticism and Mormon tradition, which I wrote and take responsibility for any errors therein.

We often think about magic as coming in essentially two flavors. The first is a ceremonial form favored by people practicing from old books of magic (called grimoires) or using highly involved rituals to effect complex changes in themselves or the world around them. They often wind up working with foreign languages, following detailed instructions on inscribing figures and sigils onto particular materials, and doing their magic in precise ways at particular times to make it work. And it is very effective for them. This is sometimes referred to as "high magick" because of its emphasis on elevated spiritual states and the requirement for a kind of education and a depth of knowledge from practitioners.[2]

The second is built upon the back of what everyday people do and believe. They inherit their rituals from family or community members and often use very simple, easy-to-get ingredients. The purpose of the rituals they do is to alleviate some immediate need: an illness, a financial or legal problem, or finding love / money / sex / work as soon as possible. It is urgent magic, driven by necessity and shaped by culture, and while it can be enhanced by working at particular times, it really comes down to doing what is needed to get a result right now. This is folk magic, which is also sometimes called "low magic," although virtually no practitioner I've met ever thinks of it as a "lesser" magic than the ceremonial kind.

Both magical forms are valid, and they are not strictly exclusive. Folk magic often incorporates seals from grimoires or abides by astrological rules that would be very familiar to ceremonial magicians. But there is something about folk magic—its rootedness in place and people and need—that makes it appealing and effective in unique ways.

Folk magicians may go by a wide variety of names, too: witches, conjurers, cunning folk, Hoodoos, *traiteurs*, *curanderos*, *hechiceras*, rootworkers, Brauchers, sorcerers, fairy doctors, and more. In some cases, their communities see their work as necessary, vital, and worthy of support and praise. More often, the communities around folk magicians tend to be more circumspect. They may recognize the value of the magic they do but keep a wary distance, because anyone who can use magic to help can use magic to hurt too. In some cases, folk magicians can be seen as a menace, and they may even experience great persecution because of their talents and abilities.

In the pages of this book, you'll meet folk magicians from a wide variety of backgrounds. Some are open about their practices with the communities around them, and some tend to keep their power carefully hidden from prying eyes, only revealing their connection to the world of the unseen to those they trust. What you will find, though, is that all of them love both the magic they do and the communities whence that magic comes. They see the whole tree, with roots in their home culture or cultures, a sturdy trunk of practice and knowledge, and branches spreading out among the folk they live with and love to share magic with them all.

2. If this sort of magic(k) interests you, you might look at *Llewellyn's Complete Book of Ceremonial Magick: A Comprehensive Guide to the Western Mystery Tradition*, edited by Lon Milo DuQuette.

A brief but important note: Throughout this book you will be hearing from folk practitioners dealing with a variety of cultural practices that may not be supported by medical science or which could cause you other sorts of problems (such as legal entanglements). The contributors of this book make no warranties as to the effectiveness of any of the material presented here, and nothing in this book should be taken as medical or legal advice. Please consult a licensed medical professional for all medical issues, and consult with professionals in other fields as needed. This book is expressly about folklore and folk belief, and thus the material presented here is to be understood within its cultural context and as a part of that system of folk belief only.

The Journey: Where This Book Takes You

There are a lot of stereotypes about how witches travel on flying broomsticks or even the backs of soaring goats (in kind of a Halloween-ish Santa Claus way). But really, one of the great metaphors for living in North America is the road trip. We set off on a journey with a destination in mind, but the ways we travel and the things we see or encounter along the way wind up being far more the point of the trip. In some ways, the hit TV show *Supernatural* seems a more accurate representation of the traveling folk magician, as the main characters get around in their 1967 Chevy Impala. And so, we shall head out into "the field," as we folklorists call it, on a trip to learn all we can about the fascinating topic of North American folk magic.

If you were to hit the open road in search of folk magic, you'd likely find you need only head down the block to bump into some kind of everyday sorcery. That, however, would only give you a small sliver of the much larger magical picture you can find here. So instead, as you read through this book, I will be traveling with you as we visit more than two dozen different folk magicians throughout the reaches of North America. You'll get to sit down with each of them and hear them talk about their particular branch of folk magic, including its history and contemporary practice, and then learn a bit about how they got involved with that path in the first place. They'll talk about what it takes to become a part of the practice (including whether or not the practice is considered "closed" to those without proper initiatory or cultural backgrounds) and offer some first steps to learning more. There will even be practical experiments along the way that you can try out to see what interests you.

You will probably notice that while several of these folk practitioners discuss their Native American ancestry or family connections, and a few pieces of the lore in the book do touch on Indigenous information such as historical tribal lands and legends, we have not focused on the Native experience of folk magic here. Why? In the simplest terms, this is just not the right book for that topic. Native American cultures and practices comprise over two hundred distinct nations in North America alone. Trying to shoehorn two or three Indigenous writers to speak on their folk magical practices is reductive and will only serve to exoticize people who already experience that sort of "othering" in so many places. Ideally, someday there will be a book—or hundreds of books—written by Indigenous authors about their spiritual and folkloristic worlds and ways. But that is not what this book can do, especially not under the editorship of a white person who does not belong to any of those communities.

This book will offer you a lot of folk magic to think about, though. And a lot of places to dig deeper, find out more, and better understand the folkways of the magic-users of North America. Throughout the book, I'll share some field notes about relevant subjects of interest or traditions from the region we are visiting. I include an expansion at the end of each section called "Traveling On," which offers additional key sites or points of interest, magical terms you might want to know, and further reading on some of the traditions discussed. I'll also pause to offer my own reflections as we move between these different areas and try to provide context, commentary, and companionship along the way.

The experience of folk magic is one of movement, journeying, and encounter. Meeting the people who are the "folk" behind each practice is absolutely vital to understanding the magic. I'm honored that you've chosen to come along with me, and I hope that I will be a good guide along the way. I promise you'll meet astounding people, learn something new, and end up seeing a much more enchanted place than you did before (even if you only look out your front door).

Happy travels, bon voyage, and *buen viaje* as we begin our journey!

CHAPTER I

New England and the Maritimes

Chapter 1

The Witch's Bridle: An Introduction to the Folk Magic of New England and the Maritimes

Where do you start a journey that involves witchcraft? And how do you travel? How will you get from point A to point B—or in the case of the crooked, twisting path of witchery, likely point A to point Q by way of point X-Y-Z.

I had thought very seriously about doing this book as a regional folk magic guide that didn't follow a particular path, or that went from West Coast to East Coast as a way of unsettling and breaking the "westward expansion" mindset that seems embedded in the colonialist story we get told about the United States. It's also worth noting that starting at the eastern shoreline and working west winds up ignoring the fact that there were literal nations of people already living in all those spaces. In the New England area alone, the Iroquois Confederacy had enormous influence over a number of tribes in the region.

I have three reasons, however, that I decided to start our journey into North American folk magic here, in the northeastern part of the landmass. Firstly, our journey will take us along in the direction of the sun and the moon on their travels through our skies. Since celestial objects—these two in particular—have such a rich connection to folk magic in these lands, it seemed reasonable to take their lead, and to use the extra hours of daylight we get from going that way to cover more ground, so to speak.

Secondly, I was able to start us not at Plymouth but in places like Montreal and Newfoundland, Acadie and Quebec City, breaking the mindset that "American folk magic" is purely "US folk magic." You will see very clearly that is not the case in this book. The first people I get to introduce you to, in fact, are a pair of French Canadian *sorcières* who will take you into a land deeply haunted by tricky devils, flying canoes, white beasts, and magical traditions that go back four or more centuries in this place. They will tell of *fées* and *revenants* (two types of magical creatures) as well as show you the haunted marionettes—the dancing northern lights that can be beautiful, but also a bit scary in magical estimations.

Thirdly, I love New England. One of my favorite places to visit is Boston, for example, because it is both historically engaging (the Freedom Trail), intellectually innovative (MIT and Harvard), and stuffed full of people from so many walks of life (amazing Irish pubs and also some of the best Italian antipasti I've ever eaten in North Boston), as you will see in Morgan Daimler's excellent section on the Irish American folk magic traditions we find in this part of the country (and further abroad in places like Chicago). Additionally, it's full of folklore, and that folklore is full of witchcraft and magic.

We often associate areas in and around New England with some of our best-known witch stories. Salem is here, of course, a place that has captured our imaginations for better or worse since 1692. Another favorite tale of mine is that of Maine witch Betty Booker, who rode a skinflint boat skipper all over the state after turning him into a human horse with a magic "witch's bridle" when he treated her poorly. There are stories of witch sheep in Rhode Island, along with dozens of witch stories in places like Connecticut and New Hampshire. Plus the long history with life on the sea in this part of the continent has always involved folk magic as well. This is part of the grand tour of folk magic that can't help but burst at the seams with witchery and enchantment.

To that end, you'll be meeting someone in this section who very much embodies that sort of overflowing folk magical persona. For now we'll call him Dr. Coelacanth, and I'll tell you he's a New England cunning man with an eye for charms that feel like they came from the dusty grimoire of a Lovecraftian Innsmouth wizard, but which hum with magic as soon as you read them. He'll be pulling on many threads of folklore and helping mingle old worlds and new as he shows you how to use a sieve and shears to know the future or speaks of magical engraved washpots. If you could sit down to tea with a sorcerer like that as you begin your journey, why wouldn't you?

In the end, I can try to justify my travel choices all day long. (And because we're following the sun, we could use those few extra hours for me to do my justifying.) The choice was mine, and we had to start somewhere. Frankly, I'm delighted we're starting here on the rocky coasts, hearing the sounds of *loup-garous* in the distance, the roar from Fenway Park, and the quaint creaking of boat timbers and old gabled roofs straining with magic.

Let us begin.

Habitants *in Flying Canoes:* Sorcellerie and the Magical World of French Canadians

E. F. E. LACHARITY AND MORRIGANE FEU

We undertook the journey into Sorcellerie as two separate voyages, as we were both interested in connecting with the magical traditions of our people in a bid to move away from the influences of more modern paths. E. F. E. developed a love for the oral culture, focusing primarily on the *contes* (stories), while Morrigane was drawn to the roots of French Canadian practice. After meeting at a Pagan gathering, we soon put faces to names, as we had already been following each other's work for some time.

Our separate voyages thereafter came together in the project known as *Courir le loup-garou*, a blog on traditional French Canadian Sorcellerie with the mission of reviving the old ways and presenting them to the modern witch community. This work has had us pouring through the handwritten notes of many ethnographers, which are preserved in various archives. In order to make this work widely accessible to the witch community, the work on our website has been published in French and English. We write in French to rekindle the old ways in those within the culture, and we write in English to reach a wider audience and to reconnect anglicized French Canadian descendants with the magic of their people. The work we present here is one small part of the greater story being told.

The First Settlers

The first attempts at French settlement in North America were begun in 1541 by Jacques Cartier. However, his colony at Fort Charlesbourg-Royal, modern Québec City, did not last. It wasn't until the efforts of Samuel de Champlain in 1608 that the settlement began in earnest with the founding of Québec City proper. Settlers came by sea, primarily from overcrowded, poorer areas of France, namely Aquitaine, Northern France, and Burgundy. From there, they went on to found colonies in Acadie (1604), Canada (Québec: 1608), Pays d'en Haut (1639), Terre-Neuve (1655), Pays des Illinois (1675), Louisiane (1682), Île-Royale (1713), and Île-St-Jean (1720). The largest influx came from the soldiers sent to fight in the Beaver Wars (1603–1701), who made up the Carignan-Salières Regiment (1659–1794). These soldiers, once their service was completed, were granted lands to settle by the king. In an effort to grow the population of a fledgling New France, the king sent *filles du roi*, sponsored young, underclass women, to marry the colonists (1663–1673).

Many descendants of these first settlers took up work in the fur trade, becoming *voyageurs* and *coureurs des bois*, while others farmed and set up small industries. This brought French descendants into contact with Indigenous people, from whom they learned the ways of living on the land. Later, as other industries grew, so did the French presence. It didn't take long for the French in New France to develop their own distinctive character. As new settlements are always precarious and fraught with daily challenges, oftentimes life and death, the people depended on their faith and time-honoured magical techniques. As the church and medical institutions were oftentimes far and few between, age-old charms, divinations, treatments, and the intercession of powerful folk saints were the trusted recourse for these people.

Diaspora

Several factors led to the vast dispersal of French settlers throughout North America. These pressures to move broke down into three broad categories. The first was primarily exploration, such as attempts to find a navigable western route to China. This was the impetus that drove Jacques Cartier, and later, Samuel de Champlain, to establish trade routes and settlements on behalf of the king. The second was founded on exploitation and economics, with the fur trade front and centre. Although spice and precious metals were the original goal of the exploration, it became apparent that beaver would be the prime commercial resource of New France, causing many companies to soon establish themselves. Thirdly, we have the constant presence of warfare between European powers, Indigenous peoples, and settlers.

It can be said that these same motifs were repeated at numerous times in later generations, where the fur trade pushed French explorers further south, north, and west (into Pays d'en Haut and, later, Pays des Illinois). The exploitation of lumber also began to take over once fur became scarcer. As industries moved into the future United States, many French Canadians followed suit. However, there was no single more horrific event that impacted the diasporization of the French of New France than the Grand Dérangement (the Expulsion of the Acadians: 1749–1750). After prolonged conflict between the British and the French along with Indigenous allies, the Acadiens were subjugated and made to give oaths of allegiance to the British Crown and, thus, the Church of England. As Roman Catholics, this was unacceptable, and as a result the French in Acadie, Île-Royale, Île-St-Jean, and Terre-Neuve were deported en masse to British colonies to the south, in Europe, and in then-Spanish Louisiane. Over 85 percent of Acadiens in Nova Scotia were displaced, with 54 percent from Acadie in total.

Quiet Revolution

The *Révolution tranquille* (Quiet Revolution) was a time of socio-political and religious upheaval in Québec during the 1960s. At its core, it was a culmination of over a century of oppression on French Canadians in Québec (who took on the national identity of Québécois) by not only the old British regime, but the institution of the Catholic church. Throughout this period, the education system—which was controlled by the church—was overhauled, and a public school system was established. This further led to a period of *laïcité* (secularism), which slowly turned the minds of the average Québécois away from older folk beliefs, magic, and superstitions.

Although there was a great boon for the preservation of the French language, older elements of French Canadian folk culture—especially in terms of Sorcellerie—were buried away in archives and largely discarded. The proverbial baby of French Canadian folk magic was tossed out with the bathwater of a corrupted Catholic church bureaucracy. This is where we now pick up the torch and move things forward. All the history mentioned here has made it apparent that our tradition is a recovery mission above all else. That is to say, Sorcellerie is a revolutionary cause to reclaim our magical roots.

The Sorcellerie Tradition

French Canadian folklore has been enjoying a revival since the early 2000s. Before that, most articles had been written either in the 1920s or in the period adjacent to the Quiet Revolution in an effort to safeguard the practices that were quickly being abandoned. It is worth noting that the articles from the 2000s often relied on other authors' work, not firsthand accounts. These benefited from a general subject overview, cross-sourcing, and decades more research. The former body of work is mostly built on firsthand accounts, providing a closer look at original practices with little interference or interpretation. However, we must warn readers that these older sources often hold very racist views and should be approached with caution. An exhaustive bibliography can be found at the end of this book.

Historical Practices

Early practitioners did not consider their practice to be Sorcellerie. Rather, there was a great tolerance of folk beliefs within Catholicism for traditions around healing and inducing luck. *Dons* (gifts) of healers were an important part of life in the colonies where doctors were few and far between. Divining future spouses by eating specially confected *galettes salées* (salt cakes), reading the future in egg white's *fantasmagories*, or using a needle and thread as a pendulum were all generally tolerated. However, what was considered acceptable and what was not—in the eyes of the church—varied greatly throughout New France. What is clear is that desperate times called for desperate measures. In the folk Catholic belief of the *habitants* (French inhabitants), their *Dieu*

(God) was inherently good but could be swayed. In those instances, the favour of certain beings, be they saints or *malices*, could be justified.

These folk beliefs and customs were deeply rooted in the populace as a matter of necessity. In a world where knowing your future husband could be a matter of life or death ("Is he from a good family?" or "Can he provide for his future family?"), making a *galette salée* (salt cake) and eating it before bed, allowing you to dream of your future husband, was necessary. If the young woman had foresight in this matter, she could seek means to avert such a fate if he turned out to be a good-for-nothing. Therein lies the root of the word *Sorcellerie*—sort. That is to say, your lot. Through these time-honoured practices, the everyday *habitant* could sway their lot in this life. Likewise, through the art of *jeter un sort* (casting a lot or curse), a practitioner could sway the lot of another, oftentimes negatively in retribution.

Certain festivals and days of observance were considered to be *jours* (or *temps*) *forts* (strong days or times). They could be Catholic holidays or agrarian tides that brought portents or required certain rituals to accompany routine activities (planting, harvesting, etc.). Some of these *temps forts* were:

- *Jour de l'an* (January 1): Receiving the paternal family blessing
- *Jour des rois* (January 6): Eating a cake where a keepsake was hidden
- *Mardi Gras*: Eating crêpes
- *Dimanche des Rameaux* (Palm Sunday): Home blessing with palms
- *Vendredi-Saint* (Good Friday): No planting
- *Pâques* (Easter): Collecting *l'eau de Pâques*, water which cured everything
- *Fête-Dieu* (sixty days after Easter): Processions to bless the fields
- *Saint-Jean* (June 24): Gathering healing herbs at the height of their power
- *Toussaint* (November 1): Visiting family graves
- *Jour des morts* (November 2): *Criée des âmes*, where all sort of things were auctioned to pay for masses for souls in purgatory
- *Réveillon* (December 24): Family feasting
- *Saint-Sylvestre* (December 31): Beating the old year and making room for the new one
- *Les douze jour de Noël* (twelve days of Christmas) (December 25–January 6): When each day prognosticated the weather for the month it was associated with

- *Le temps des sucres* (when the maple sap runs): A time when families came together to boil the sap into maple syrup; it was also a time when *la Chasse-galerie* (the Wild Run, often depicted in a flying canoe) was known to take flight

These are but a few examples of some *jours forts*. In practice, each segment of society and each practitioner had their own observance days set, which they kept due to familial or regional traditions.

Tools

French Canadians didn't use complex tools for their magic; they used what they had on hand. One of the most powerful tools was the use of simple *aiguilles* (pins) for countering hexes. If someone put a spell on you, you could boil *aiguilles*, causing pain to the hexer until the curse was lifted. This practice was ubiquitous, with regional variations, and everyone used it: ordinary people, self-proclaimed witches, and even some priests. *Aiguilles* could be boiled in plain water, vinegar, milk, or even in the blood of a hexed animal—or person! Sometimes they were stuck in balls of yarn or pieces of red flannel before boiling. There is an account where the *aiguilles* were placed in a bottle of urine, the hex dissolving as the *aiguilles* rusted. Today we can use them to undo someone else's magic, or our own, by boiling them in the liquid we deem most appropriate. They may also be carried on oneself for everyday protection.

Sacred waters, such as collected rain that fell on May 1 or water drawn from a running body of water at dawn on Easter Sunday, were used to heal all sorts of ailments and as protection. Blessed water also had a similar power. It was, and still is, applied on the body, on animals, and likewise sprinkled around the house. Nowadays, this water can replace any liquid in a ritual or spell. Other magical tools found in *contes* (stories) and folklore were wooden sticks, cards, scissors, cloth, whistles, bottles, musical instruments, and other typical household items. Although offerings were predominantly made to saints, mostly rosaries and money, we found that spirits and other beings were receptive to them. Spruce beer, tobacco, and various cooked or raw grain were well received. At times, a meal may also be shared. In our personal practice, coffee and chocolate are given to the ancestors.

Malices

The first step we took in this practice was to establish relationships with some beings that we call *malices*. They are magical spirits that can be found in folklore or folktales interchangeably. To give you a starting point, here is a list of beings that seem to have been present and important in every French Canadian community.

Le Bonyeu: The Bonyeu (dialect form of *Bon Dieu*, Good God) is how French Canadians understood the Supreme Being, the font of all worldly power, natural or supernatural. Bonyeu was most often viewed as a judge who recorded one's deeds, a witness to all events. With his hand, he not only shaped earthly events but could also intercede as he so desired. Although he and Jesus often show up as distinct beings in stories, they were understood as one trinitarian person. However, Jesus was viewed as a compassionate healer, whereas the Bonyeu is far more in line with a judging notion of God.

Le Yâbe: The Yâbe (*Diable*/Devil) is a ubiquitous figure in the anecdotes. He is willing to make deals in exchange for offerings or, more frequently, by putting conditions on his help. If any condition is broken, your soul will be damned and sent to Hell. These conditions always seem straightforward, but of course prove to be difficult to abide by. The Yâbe is a devious, dangerous creature, but he can be outsmarted. Quick thinking may get you out of your deal or tip the balance in your favour. Witches often sell their soul to the Yâbe in exchange for power. The Bonyeu can force the Yâbe to help humans, shielding them from the Yâbe's cunning, but men will invariably break the Bonyeu's instructions, resulting in that help disappearing. Even when made with God, a deal is a deal.

Sainte-Anne: First a folk saint, the strength of Sainte-Anne's cult forced the Catholic church to adopt her as the grandmother of Jesus, but nowhere in the Old Testament is her name mentioned. She came to Canada with the first French colonizers, and her cult followed them wherever they went. She's a healing saint and has different pilgrimage sites, the most popular being the basilica in Sainte-Anne-de-Beaupré, Québec. Relics and publications from the basilica are said to heal people who have never been to the basilica and have the power to break curses.

Ancestors: In addition to your own ancestors, there are cultural ancestors that you can build relationships with such as Jos Montferrand, a man whose legend was akin to Paul Bunyan's; La vieille Gardipy, an incredible freethinking woman and healer from les Hauts; or the Dulac family of witches, who were open about it and can be used as stand-ins for the few other witches who dared to be public.[3]

***Fées* (Fairies):** *Fées* are as common in the tales of *conteurs* as they are absent in everyday life. In French Canada, *fées* are the *malices* mostly mentioned in relation to *trous de fée*, a grotto or cave where they are said to dwell. They are never really seen or heard—with one exception, where a fairy was said to protect draft dodgers during the Second World War.

3. See the translation from Barbeau on our blog: https://courirleloupgarou.org/.

Lutins: There is no direct translation for *lutin*. They are pixie-like creatures that lived mostly in stables. Seldom seen, a sure sign of *lutin* presence was finding horses exhausted in the morning with braided manes. These *malices* took care of the horses, feeding them either the owner's oats or their neighbour's if none were to be found in the stables. To get rid of them, you caused them to spill oats or ashes. The *lutin* would have to count each speck, thereafter to never return.

Loup-garous (Were-Beings): One became a *loup-garou* either by making a pact with the Yâbe, by falling victim to a hex, or by forgoing one's religion (such as no confessions, sacraments, communion, or observing the Eastertide) for a long time, often seven years. A *loup-garou* could be freed from its form by striking their forehead or drawing a drop of blood. Although there is the word *loup* (wolf) in this *malice*'s name, they could take many forms: wolves, bears, dogs, cats, oxen, and even balls of hay or yarn.

Revenants: In this category, we place every kind of human returning from the dead. These *malices* could be spectres haunting a place, a house, or even objects; people coming back to warn of an impending death in the family or amongst friends; souls needing something from the living; souls trying to fulfill a promise; or even souls appearing to friends or family at the moment of their deaths. French Canadians were surrounded by echoes from the once-living.

Marionettes: This is the name given to the northern lights. *Marionettes* are thought to be inhabited by the souls of the damned or by imps, the souls of unbaptized children, or those dancers that the Yâbe caught. They're attracted to music and will descend lower and get closer to the musician or singer. The *marionettes* are said to sometimes abduct people, break a musician's instruments, or maim a person, especially if the lights turn red. They can also predict wars to come. There is some overlap between the French Canadian folklore surrounding the *marionettes*/northern lights and some of the First Nations' cultures. It's safe to assume that an exchange of beliefs took place here.

Feux-follets: Feux-follets are fast little flames that could be the souls of sinners, wandering souls waiting to be liberated, or even the souls of *loup-garous*. They're mostly malevolent—people following them were being sent to their deaths—but they are also known to have helped lost travelers find their way. The most effective way to get rid of them is to stick a needle or a pocket knife into a post, making sure to create a triangle between the blade, handle, and post. The *feu-follet* will have to pass through the eye of the needle or the triangular gap until they hurt themselves, effectively freeing the soul from that flame.

We strongly encourage you to discover which spirits, if any, French Canadians brought with them to your area, and go out and meet them.

Voyages and Practices

French Canadians are inherently a storytelling people. They also possess a travelling spirit, from their journey across the ocean into unfamiliar lands to the further journeys they embarked upon once they settled New France. We have hundreds of narratives by *conteurs* (storytellers) who would weave tall tales of encounters with magical beings as the *voyageur* (traveller), often the hero Ti-Jean, voyaged into strange far-off lands. These tales mimicked the life of many occupations held by *habitants*, such as *coureur des bois* (fur traders), lumberjacks in far-off winter camps, fishermen out at sea, or any itinerant occupation that carried them across the continent.

These tales recounting the marvelous have been revived as a spirit-engaged practice as a means to travel the spirit world. The practitioner will make certain offerings to guiding beings, then take a physical journey (ex: a walk in the woods) where each step is spiritually significant. Spiritual tools or power items may be received from the beings, which can help the practitioner grow in their craft. In this way, the witch becomes the hero of their spiritual voyage, becoming like Ti-Jean in those tales we have come to know and love.

Neuvaines

Neuvaines were a tool traditionally used to thank saints for their help. In the Catholic church, you would say a prescribed prayer for nine days in a row, sometimes accompanied by prescribed actions. However, in our practice, we use *neuvaines* to thank any spirits who have offered their help or guidance, and there are no set prayers. We had to come up with our own, and we encourage others to do the same. This tool can be used at any time of the year and can be promised in exchange for any assistance or favour. If you make this promise, make sure you follow through with it.

Our largest *neuvaine* was held in honour of our ancestors. We began with a simple candle lighting on October 24 and wrote and then recited part of our yearly prayer. We wrote, recited, and lit the candle daily until November 1 (*Toussaint*/All Saints' Day). This prayer is personal to our own relationships with our ancestors and is reused every year on the same dates, with a few tweaks. We have also used this prayer in a time of dire need after we received our ancestors' protection. If the candle hasn't completely burned out, we keep it for a subsequent *neuvaine*. Just like our ancestors did, we strive to not waste anything while keeping the sacred character intact.

Divination

The most prevalent form of divination was omen reading. The French Canadians constantly read signs in nature and everyday life, trying to figure out the weather and important events. Some of these observations became rules; for example, if pigs have an elongated spleen at the autumn butchery, winter will be hard.

There were also many forms of divination used to discover who would be your spouse. We do not have examples of these methods being used for anything other than love and marriage, but it's easy to expand on them in a modern practice. For example, a woman would write the names of all her *pretendants* (potential beaus) on pieces of paper, which were then tightly rolled and placed in water. The first paper to unroll would bear the name of her future husband. Nowadays, this method could be used for any choice to be made and/or figuring out the most likely outcome.

The only method we found of general divination was to drop an egg white in a glass of water, leave it in the sun for half an hour, and scry the egg white for images, called *fantasmagories*, and interpret them. This is a simple and efficient method that still resonates today.

Conclusion: Where the Voyage May Lead

We are always reading and learning more, scouring obscure sources and archives to distill what practices are still relevant today. We will keep sharing our discoveries with the witch community. What we hope for the future is that stories from French Canadians and their descendants will be added to these more academic sources. We hope that by putting this work out there, old stories, habits, and superstitions will resurface and will be given a second life in the practices of those our work resonates with. Somewhere out there, someone—perhaps you, the one reading this now—is waiting at the shore of Sorcellerie, getting ready to step into the Flying Canoe. It is our fervent wish that you take this journey and see where it may lead.

FIELD NOTES
Seaside Sorcery

Given the heavy involvement with and dependence upon maritime occupations in New England, Newfoundland, Nova Scotia, and other areas in the North American Northeast, it's little wonder that a vast number of folk magical practices and bits of lore became embedded in the region. Here follows a brief sampler of some of those magical tidbits:

Weather Lore

- "If Candlemas day be fine and fair, The half of the winter's to come an' mair [more]."
- "Mackerel skies and mare's tails, Make lofty ships carry low sails."
- "A rainbow in the morning the sailor's warning, A rainbow at night is the sailor's delight."
- "Heavy winds kick up a rain."[4]

Buying the Wind

The practice of "buying the wind" sometimes occurred in dire straits. Captains and crewmembers on becalmed ships would often be tempted to throw money overboard in order to purchase a quantity of wind from God/nature/the sea/etc. The problem arose in that the quantity purchased was always vastly more than one expected to buy. As one sailor put it, "Never buy wind when you're on a boat. You're daring God Almighty, and he won't stand for that. You'll get all the wind you want."

In one tale, a captain tosses a quarter overboard. Immediately, such a gale rises that it tears the sails and mast from the ship and pushes the ship into shore, where it barely holds together as the crew disembarks. The captain remarks that if he'd known God sold wind so cheaply, he'd only have got a nickel's worth.[5]

Cauls and Wind Knots

Many tales exist of sailors buying cauls (the membrane that sometimes covers a newborn's head after emerging from the womb) from dockside witches to prevent drowning at sea. And those same dockside sorceresses sometimes sold knotted cords to help sailors call up wind as needed—each knot, when undone, would release an increasing amount of wind.

4. Fraser, *Folklore of Nova Scotia*, 107.
5. Dorson, *Buying the Wind*, 32–37.

Crafts of the Cunning: Cunning-Folk Practices in New England

ALEXANDER CUMMINS

This essay forms a survey of some of the core components of early modern British cunning-craft, which may seem strange for an anthology on North American folk magic. There are, as far as I could glean, two main reasons for inviting me to do this. Luckily, neither of them are traps.

Firstly, the historical: that is, pertaining to the dead. Early modern European settlers and colonisers brought not only their families, tools, diseases, expectations, and preconceptions with them on the ships over to the so-called "New World"—they also brought their magic. Sixteenth- and seventeenth-century cunning-craft in the forms of sorcerous techniques, perspectives, and—yes—"little Witchcrafts" certainly informed such New English magics and those of modern America more broadly, and it is therefore absolutely worthy of both celebration and critical analysis as an ancestral source and influence in the great melting-pot cauldron-wealth of all American folk magic.[6] Fortunately, like many cunning-men before me, when not talking to spirits or removing *maleficia*, I teach. Specifically, I teach about the history of early modern magic, so I feel we have this base covered pretty well.

Secondly, the living. I am a professional magical worker born in the Midlands of England, currently at large in North America (New England, no less) doing the crafts practiced, taught, and inspired by these pre-modern forebears. I feel the living yet also historical nature of cunning can be aptly introduced to you via a pub anecdote. Once, while sitting in a pub after a folk magic conference with a dear friend—amidst the collegiate hubbub of professional magicians drinking and comparing powder recipes and so on around the table, as cunning-folk have done for centuries—he paid me the compliment of (albeit jokingly) referring to me with a proper conjure doctor's animal nickname, Dr. Coelacanth, connecting me to that rediscovered fish by remarking he hadn't thought they made cunning-folk anymore and yet here I was.

Now, I make no claim about being the last cunning-man left—indeed, I rather like this analogy because it shows a thriving spiritual ecology and real communities demonstrating that cun-

6. Mather, *The Wonders of the Invisible World*, 67–68.

ning from a range of practitioners is still useful to folks. I also like that this framing highlights that cunning-craft study can be something of a haunted museum as well as a living consultation room. As such, you are welcome to think of this essay as "Dr. Coelacanth's Cabinet of Curiosities and Cunning Cures."

This essay will thus offer comparisons and case studies for those curious about these folk magics and their cunnings, both old and renewed. As a cunning practitioner, I take no umbridge with anyone trying to get something efficacious out of the approaches and techniques I share in this essay; in fact, I encourage it. We'll consider the crafts of folk from English shores into North American chowder houses and taverns to see just what sorts of practices were found in the early American colonies, as well as the practical workings I, and others of my ilk, still do today.

Terms of the Art (or, Cunning-What Now?)

Our survey of the crafts of the wise women, village wizards, and local spiritworkers collectively referred to as *cunning-folk* can begin with historian Emma Wilby's summation of the great and rich variety and range of titles—and contexts of labelling—for such service-magicians:

> Wise man or woman, cunning man or woman, witch (white or black), wizard, sorcerer, conjurer, charmer, magician, wight, nigromancer, necromancer, seer, blesser, dreamer, cantel, soothsayer, fortuneteller, girdle-measurer, enchanter, incantantrix and so on. These generic names...overlapped considerably and were often interchangeable. At any given time, the term used to define a magical practitioner would have depended upon the type of magic they practiced, where they lived, whether they were liked or disliked and whether the person defining them was illiterate or literate, rural or urban, Puritan or Catholic and so on. The same practitioner, for example, could be referred to as a "wise man" by one person, a "witch" by another, and a "conjurer" by yet another.[7]

Along with (so, so many) regional specificities, it is worth bearing in mind that cunning-folk are quite literally *folk who do cunning things*. Firstly, "the term that sixteenth-century people in England used most often to describe skill in magic is 'cunning'...derived from the Anglo-Saxon *cunnan*, which meant simply 'to know.'"[8] Beyond the particularities of sieve-and-shears, shewstones, horseshoes, and so on—which we will get to, I assure you—cunning is as cunning does. Secondly, focus on the actual actions, roles, functions, and meanings of such cunning work yields

7. Wilby, *Cunning Folk and Familiar Spirits*, 26.

8. Klaassen and Wright, *The Magic of Rogues*, 5.

far more useful perspective than any over-reliance on the strictures of nomenclature might. A rose by any other name may still un-bewitch as sweetly.

Cunning Works (or, Service Magicians Gonna Service)

And did cunning-folk ever un-bewitch. Such wise-guys and wise-gals "provided a range of magical services, such as love magic, fortune telling, thief detection, the finding of hidden treasure and lost or stolen property, and the diagnosis, detection, and cure of harmful witchcraft," and did so by employing "an array of tools, from palmistry, horoscopes, and astrological [and geomantic] charts, to almanacs, divination techniques, and spirit conjuration."[9] These practitioners and their tools and techniques came colonising with everyone else, and they were certainly "also present in seventeenth-century New England, specialising in fortune-telling, folk medicine, and counter-magic."[10]

Bearing in mind that the *cunning* of these folk magics described the (frequently somewhat idiosyncratic) worker themselves—and, more importantly, the effects and efficacy of their work—more than defining a dogmatic canon of some unchanging official model of any so-called traditional cunning, we may still outline three kinds of work these practitioners did for themselves and their clients to develop an appreciation of a cunning ethos or style of working: divining, charming, and conjuring.

Divining

Cunning divinations came in computational forms—that is, interpreting meaning out of datasets within closed quantifiable systems like astrological nativity horoscopes and geomantic shield charts—and non-computational forms such as dreaming, visionary prophecy, and scrying in stones, glasses, and mirrors. Then there are the object-based divinations—book-and-key, sieve-and-shears, even the pendulum—which we might consider betwixt these two categories. All forms are used in cunning detections and put to use in unbewitching work, as well as diagnosing medical pathology, finding buried treasure and lost or stolen goods, locating missing or fugitive persons, discovering guilty parties (which seems the most popular use of object divinations especially), and even finding opportunities for advancement.

Charming

The findings of divination are operationalised into the spell-crafts of remediations and apotropaic and protective charms. These include spoken, written, and gestural forms of charming: in

9. Sneddon, *Witchcraft and Magic in Ireland*, 34.
10. Sneddon, *Witchcraft and Magic in Ireland*, 34.

order to create, empower, and deploy rituals, talismans, bundles, sigils, incenses, powders, and various other magical medicaments and regimen.

Here I would also include the works of thief-compelling that could accompany detecting thieves: not only establishing who stole from you, or where they might be now, but holding out the prospect of forcing them to confess, to return said goods, or simply to suffer for having crossed you. A reputed "fear of magical reprisal itself was also hoped to induce enough of an effect to achieve a speedy recovery," and even contemporaries sceptical of magic noted that such detective sorcerers "kept thieves in awe, and did as much good in a country as a justice of peace."[11] One prominent historian of cunning-folk even stated "the deterrent effect of their reputations was, in fact, the most important asset cunning-folk had in this respect."[12] We may also include both protective "preventatives" against misfortune and curse-breaking works against malevolent witchcraft and the restless dead—such as the infamous witch-bottle—under such a category of charmings.

Conjuring

Cunning conjurations call angels, devils, fairies, the dead, and a host of other nature spirits of place and time. They conjured most commonly from their working-books: personal collections of magical operations, formulary, prayers, seals, incantations, and so on; their receipt-book of shadows, if you like. These spellbooks were patchworked from grimoiric manuscripts, highbrow occult treatises, practical astro-geomantic handbooks, a range of heresiographers' demonological surveys, as well as the ephemerides and almanacs for timing their work, and apparently whatever other potent sources these spell-hounds could get their hands on. These folk grimoiric approaches to conjuration have historically earned disapproval from stricter ceremonial grimoirists on the continent. E. M. Butler notes of such devil-may-care English conjure:

> Any adept of the school of Solomon would harbour an uneasy feeling…that English magicians, like English statesmen, must have provoked disasters by being ill-prepared. The informal and happy-go-lucky nature of the preparations includes no daunting instructions about the forging of instruments, the tanning of skins, or the mixing of inks.[13]

That we don't even necessarily forge our own black-handled knives seems to have dismayed the early modern equivalents of your favourite occult social media forum warlocks. Indeed, most

11. Reynolds, *The Table Talk of John Selden*, 130; Cummins, "Transatlantic Cunning."
12. Davies, *Popular Magic*, 97.
13. Butler, *Ritual Magic*, 236.

cunning operations require merely new, "virgin," or even just "clean" tools. While few would sensibly question the great potential to empower a self-forged blade with prayers hammered into the very metal, such a tool is not always necessary. Many cunning operations explicitly instruct you to simply buy the instrument or ingredient. At the end of the working day, results magicians have to produce results more than impressive props.

As a final note on cunning conjuring, one may observe from the operations in their historical working-books that the conjuration of spirits frequently empowers the other works of divining and charming in the first place. Conjuration was not (only) a separate practice, but a means of directing spirits to further empower all manner of work. Indeed, working with spirits was conceived as a critical means by which one could not only *do* cunning, but even actually learn it in the first place. Consider the reflections of one servant sent out by his master to secure a cunning-man, who when pressed for the source of his cunning-craft, said that he "had his knowledge by familiarity with a spirit" and had been compelled to give the spirit something in return.[14]

The Cunning Diviner (or, Cunning Means Knowing)

To speak of how cunning-folk learn cunning—mostly, it seems by paying attention, by using books, and (most crucially) by calling and keeping spirits—is also to see how they learned other things: whether your husband is cheating; whether that horrible-lady-you-try-really-hard-not-to-call-a-horrible-name at work is throwing the evil eye; when exactly to ask your landlord to fix the damn leaky roof so he'll actually do it; where little Abigail has wandered off to; who stole my linens. It's divination. It's always been divination. So let us focus briefly on two popular (dare I say, emblematic) forms of cunning divination in early modern North America: coscinomancy and geomancy.

By Peter and by Paul: Sieve-and-Shears Coscinomancy

Resorts to object divination—whether the-book-and-the-key, the apple peel, or the coscinomancy of sieve-and-shears—seem to be gateway folk magics to outright cunning. They seem mostly practiced historically by folks without access or willingness to engage with the spirits or by folks without computational divinatory skills and the resources of more established cunning-folk. As I've discussed elsewhere, coscinomancing seems to have been a particularly popular activity in late-seventeenth-century New England.[15]

The technique itself was and remains straightforward. It only really requires the said frame-sieve and shears or scissors, as well as a pal to hold the other end and a list of suspects. Here's John Aubrey giving a useful summary:

14. Klaassen and Wright, *Magic of Rogues*, 33.
15. Cummins, "Transatlantic Cunning," 166–68.

> The Magick of the Sieve and Sheers (I think) is in Virgil's *Eclogues*: The Sheers are stuck in a Sieve, and two maydens hold up the Sieve with the top of their fingers by the handle of the shiers: then say, *By St. Peter and St. Paule such a one hath stoln* [such a thing] the others say, *By St. Peter and St. Paul, He hath not stoln it*. After many such adjurations, the Sieve will turne at the name of the Thiefe.[16]

Coscinomantic instructions do not usually specify the operators *have* to be maidens, but this does happen to accord with certain magical ideas about the potency of youths and even occult conceptions of virginity. Aubrey's account also demonstrates a common trope of sourcing folk magical techniques in antiquity—whether such claims are vague homogenizing allusions to "the Ancients," affirming the ubiquity of the practice "all around the world," or specific citations such as namedropping Dante's psychopomp here, all of which are worthy of further study.

By Stick and by Dirt: Geomancy

To offer an excellent snapshot of how cunning-craft was actually practiced, and the social and legal responses from communities and authorities (never mind presenting a specific instance of my favourite system of divination), consider the case of Philip Jr. and Robert Roman, cunning brothers of late-seventeenth-century Chester County, Pennsylvania. There, Quaker leaders questioned the Romans—first as religious elders, and then as serving magistrates—regarding their use of "astrology, geomancy, and chiromancy," in particular the "divineing by sticke" method found in the work of John Heydon; that is, making marks in the dirt to form geomantic figures and set a chart. The authorities claimed that in addition to finding lost objects, the Romans were also responsible for coaxing away the wife of one Henry Hastings. When their premises were searched, they found Heydon's book (*Temple of Wisdom*), Reginald Scot's *Discoverie of Witchcrafte*, and a book allegedly by Agrippa "teaching negromancy."[17]

There is a lot to pick out from this brief account. We get a sense of the popularity of geomancy in the reference to an infamous geomantic author like Heydon by name as well as various specific details of the practices. We also see the consolidation of religious and legal authorities against such practices in listing the black magic of Agrippa and in the legal escalation of the prosecution. The other cunning books listed in Roman's possession are also worthy of brief note, especially Scot's *Discoverie*, a text written to discredit ignorant witch-hunting that ended up democratising access to the spells, charms, and conjurations it criticized by including an entire cunning grimoire in its pages, thus proving indispensably popular with cunning-folk themselves.[18] The Romans'

16. Aubrey, *Three Prose Works*, 213.
17. Butler, "Magic, Astrology, and the Early American Religious Heritage, 1600–1760," 333.
18. Davies, "The Reception of Reginald Scot's *Discovery of Witchcraft*," 381–401.

cunning little library offers further context for the interrelation and cross-pollination of different occult disciplines, especially the way divination and sorcery can be elided both in suspicious popular imagination and literally in working spells out of divined findings, such as with thief-work. Who knows what Robert was actually doing for Mrs. Hastings, but I suspect she was not happy in that marriage. I've gone into a little more detail on this case and its contexts elsewhere if you're interested.[19]

To start with divination for now, geomancy is said to apply the "use and rules of astrology"—that is, astrological categories and correspondences as well as certain techniques—to data generated by making marks. Originally, the marks were made in the earth or sand with a stick, although by the early modern period, they were often made on paper with a pen.[20] There are no ephemerides and no astronomical interest in the heavens at all, but rather in what the astrological bodies and forces have already imbued into the earth, stones, plants, animals, and so on. Interest lies in how planetary influences and spirits interact here on Earth. Geomantic divination thus relies upon discerning and analysing various guiding forces and inertias of the cosmos, not from detailed measurement of the relative positions of the stars, but in the fall of dice or the scratching and tallying of marks upon a page made "without counting" and while "pondering in your heart" the question you are inquiring about.[21] In other words, rather than plotting the movements of sources or harbingers of particular influence and affect, one is directly communicating with an aspect of the divine.[22]

I employ the geomancy I practice for myself and for my clients to explore remediations to rebalance disarray, secure blessings, repair dysfunctions, and avoid obstacles as well as to simply describe or map the client's situation or options. The characters and sigils of geomantic figures, considered "betwixt images and characters," present unique opportunities to cohere, stabilise, and deploy their virtues, spirits, and influences in order to aid one in achieving the intended goals.[23] I think of geomancy as a foot-track magic of the Wandering Ones across material spaces, a bottom-up cosmology of dirt sorcery concerned with reminding "elementated" and planetary parts of nature that they already possess their dormant so-called astral virtues. Ultimately, the geomancer sorcerer works such chthonic humoural-planetary magical solutions from the grassroots up. I am sure there are astrologers and Neoplatonists pursing lips at this brief summation. I'm happy to talk it out over a pint.

19. Cummins, "Transatlantic Cunning," 169–72.
20. Agrippa, *Three Books of Occult Philosophy*, 412.
21. Heydon, *Theomagia, or the Temple of Wisdom*, 2.
22. Cummins, "Transatlantic Cunning," 171.
23. Agrippa, *Three Books*, 397.

Charming (or, Rummaging through the Medicine Cabinets of Curiosity)

While the lifeblood of cunning might arguably be said to be in the charms themselves, this survey must content itself with only a brief summation of the complex forms and functions of such crafts. So, I present three sets of cunning charms that offer a taste of the work: the planetary, the counter-offensive, and the domestic healing.

By Starry Sigils and Substances

Planetary charms are the most easily derived from astro-geomantic divination. These could range from generalised medicaments and therapeutic regimen to bespoke astrological remediations discovered through horary or decumbiture charts, cast at the time the client or patient asked the astrologer for help or at the time they first became sick, respectively.[24] Such charting can tailor solutions from the planet antipathetic to the specific maladies the client faces. As the astrologer-physician Joseph Blagrave—who decried cunning-folk as professional rivals but certainly wasn't shy about using their techniques—described, "As instance if Saturn be the afflicting planet, then herbs must be used under the Sun and Jupiter. If Mars be the afflicting planet, then herbs must be used under the dominion of the Sun and Venus."[25]

Blagrave also employed the more generalised approach, evidenced in his deep reliance on the healing virtues of the Sun: "In the curing of *all kinds* of evils, I do usually cause the patients to wear a select number of Solary herbs gathered in the hour of the Sun."[26] These planetary charms sometimes include incantational components, as when the Wiltshire cunning-woman Anne Bodenham recommended prescribing "a Spell written in a peece of paper" to be hanged about the client's neck, and for the client to pray "to *Jupiter*, [as] he is the best and fortunatest of all the Planets, and in such a case as this we always pray to the Planet *Jupiter*."[27]

Moreover, such planetary number squares, seals, and characters could be used to empower sympathetic *materia*, such as raw herbs for poultices, "diet-drinks," steam-baths, and "sigilated" powders, which could then themselves be used to deploy those planetary virtues. So, you could "sprinkle or sow about the powder of this sigil [of Jupiter, the Greater Benefic]" at a location "that there be peace and concord in that place...with great joy," for instance.[28]

24. See Cummins, *The Starry Rubric*, especially chapter 4.
25. Blagrave, *Blagrave's Astrological Practice of Physick*, 156.
26. Blagrave, *Blagrave's Astrological Practice of Physick*, 156. Emphasis added.
27. Bower, *Doctor Lamb Revived*, 21.
28. Belenus, *De Sigillis Septem Planetarum*; Sloane MS 3846, f. 45r–49r; Klaassen and Wright, *The Magic of Rouges*.

Coaxing and grasping starry potencies out of the flora (not to mention fauna) of the earth itself was an important dimension of many cunning early-modern magics, and they were employed toward typically cunning goals. Certainly, in matters of planetary unbewitching specifically, powders, sigils, and other charms of Jupiter are employed in order to overcome enemies and witchcraft; those of Venus are used "to make peace, and dissolve wychcraft and engender love"; and those of the Moon might aid in alleviating the evil eye, "for they take away envy, and other hurtful things."[29]

By Scolding Stinking Waters

Reginald Scot presents a general and perhaps recognisable protective cunning use of the horseshoe: "Nail a Horse-shoe at the inside of the outmost threshold of your House, and so you shall be sure no Witch shall have power to enter thereinto. And if you mark it, you shall find that rule observed in many Countrey-houses."[30] However, I would like to focus on a more particular use of such iron for—that's right—removing malevolent witchcraft:

> Get two new horseshoes, heat one of them red hot, and quench him in the patients urine, then immediately nail him on the inside of the threshold of the door with three nails, the heel being upwards; then having the patients urine set it over the fire, and set a trivet over it, put into it three horse nails, and a little white salt: Then heat the other horseshoe red hot, and quench him severall times in the urine, and so let it boil and waste until all be consumed; do this three times and let it be near the change, full, or quarters of the Moon; or let the Moon be in Square or Opposition unto the Witches Significator.[31]

Cunning unbewitching frequently manipulates a patient's urine to launch counter-attacks through the magical link between witch and victim. Such are the craft-logics behind a range of some kinds of witch-bottles, usually filled with the patient's urine.[32] But such is also clearly a part of the rationale of spitting in one's "Piss-pot, where you have made water" to uncross yourself.[33] Note also the cunning use of everyday things—nails, trivets, door thresholds—which we certainly see in works of washing.

29. Klaassen, *Making Magic in Elizabethan England*, 89, 87.
30. Scot, *The Discovery of Witchcraft*, 150.
31. Blagrave, *Blagrave's Astrological Practice of Physick*, 156.
32. Lilly, *Christian Astrology*, 465–66; *Blagrave's Astrological Practice of Physick*, 154; Thwaite, "What Is a 'Witch Bottle'?", 227–51; Gordon, "Domestic Magic and the Walking Dead in Medieval England," 65–84.
33. Scot, *The Discovery of Witchcraft*, 152.

By Gauntlet's Wash Pot

Cunning-folk did not limit themselves to the aggressive counter-magic of "spoiling" witches; they also performed various works of genuine healing. Let's examine just one instance, from the working-book of Arthur Gauntlet:

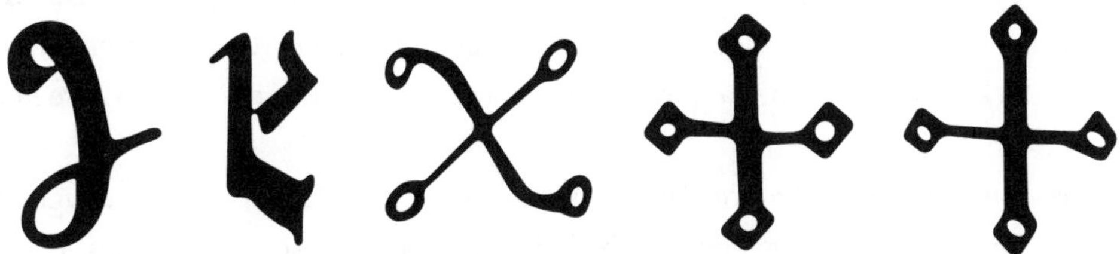

Figure 1-1: Gauntlet's Wash Pot Inscription

> If something has been weakened. Engrave this character in a new cooking pot, in the hour of the Sun, and fill it with clean water and read this Psalm [7:2] completely seven times over that water during 7 days. Upon completion of this, wash the weakened [thing] with the prescribed water & it will be made whole again.[34]

There are many features to note in this apparently simple operation: newness, planetary hours, the Sun's specific prominence, sevens, these characters themselves, week-long duration, and the making-whole from washing localized areas of acute embodied dysfunctions. Consecration of the cooking pot—as in cunning operations of the trivet, the horseshoes, the sieve-and-shears, even the-book-and-key—renders a household item a locus of spiritual potency. In this case, our everyday cooking pot is marked with magical characters in accordance with harmonising solary influences, and its contents are sacralised by durational performance of scriptural authority and sacralisation, to the ends of cleansing and empowerment. You can indeed teach a new pot old tricks.

Conjuring (or, My Grimoire Magic Is Always Necromantic)

We may arm ourselves with an understanding of how (some) cunning-folk cast their circles in both chalk and "black" (charcoal), consecrated their tools, and generally called both their holy and unclean spirits from the infamous Book 15 of Scot's *Discovery of Witchcraft*. We could easily detail the ritual trappings of all the whats and hows. But we are perhaps better served in this brief survey by considering some of the whos and whys of cunning spirit conjuration.

34. Rankine, *The Grimoire of Arthur Gauntlet*, 264.

The most important cunning call, answering both who and why, is to familiar spirits: those personal spirits that work directly for (or even with) the practitioner. Such spirits bring their cunning-folk information as well as imparting, empowering, and delivering spell-work. They also facilitate a variety of engagements with other spirits. Cunning familiars were not just spirits called to do particular works of magic, but familiar spirits worked in order to do one's cunning in general. From long-standing biblical appeal, a magician (especially a practical magician) was often literally defined as one who trafficked familiarly with a spirit. For instance, in Deuteronomy 18:10–12 we find:

> There shall not be found among you any one that maketh his son or his daughter to pass through the fire, or that useth divination, or an observer of times, or an enchanter, or a witch, or a charmer, or a consulter with familiar spirits, or a wizard, or a necromancer. For all that do these things are an abomination unto the Lord: and because of these abominations the Lord thy God doth drive them out from before thee.[35]

In such spiritworking models, that is how you do magic: outsourcing.

By Familiar(ity with) Spirits

We should note that the term *familiar spirit*—at least in this cunning context—thus describes a function and working style of a spirit relationship more than a particular typological taxon of spirit. Many workers sought their personal guardian angel in a "shewstone," and it is not uncommon to find operations in working-books for calling "thy owne proper goode Angell…which of god appoynted unto thee for a guyd all thy life."[36] Beyond a personalised guardian angel, many appealed to popular archangels as a direct guide in their work. The astrologer-physician and talisman-maker Dr. Richard Napier famously consulted with the archangel Raphael.[37]

Even less well-known figures such as Wolverhampton cunning-man William Hodges "resolved questions astrologically; nativities he meddled not with; in things of other nature, which required more curiosity, he repaired to the crystal: his angels were Raphael, Gabriel, and Uriel."[38] Familiarity could be very formal and very religious as well as a matter of practical sorcery. Conversely, as we saw in the discussion of Nash of Cirencester's familiars earlier, it was well understood that many

35. Authorized King James Version.
36. MS Rawlinson D 253, f. 21–33.
37. MacDonald, *Mystical Bedlam*; Hadass, *Medicine, Religion, and Magic in Early Stuart England*, especially chapter 3.
38. Lilly, *William Lilly's History of His Life and Times*, 116.

workers employed more mercenary—even devilishly "unclean"—spirits, requiring the worker to sacrifice to or otherwise feed their familiar in exchange for its cunning aid, teachings, and power.

The familiar spirits that most fascinate me are—perhaps unsurprisingly—the dead. For a start, ghost familiars are found across the spectrum of holy and unholy spiritwork. On the angels-in-glasses end, we have reports of cunning-folk maintaining "that the spirits which appeare vnto them in the Christall, or in the glasse, or water, or that any way do speake, and shewe matters vnto them, be holy Angels, or *the soules of excellent men*, as of Moses, Samuel Dauid, and others," and specifically "deale by them against devils."[39] On the witches-suckling-black-cats end, it is occasionally posited that "it be supposed that the Imps of Witches are sometimes wicked spirits of our own kind and nature, and possibly the same that have been Sorcerers and Witches in this life."[40] The prospect of familiars as a sort of Mighty Dead of sorcerous forebears who serve rather than are served suggests some fascinating possible implications concerning power and pact in conjuration…That should probably wait for a more dedicated and less tangential study in the future.

What these examples show in their various ways is commitment. You don't just sometimes or even regularly call a familiar spirit; you *have* a familiar spirit, as when "some of the cunning men say, they have Moses or Elias, or the Spirite of some holy man."[41] More to the point, if you want to keep your spirit (as it were) familiar with *you*, odds are you must either live in holiness routinely or somehow feed it or give it something it wants. Agrippa reported that "those that Invoke the Souls of dead Bodies…carry about with them certain Pocket-Daemons; and who, as they say, nourish little Spirits in Glasses, by which they pretend to Foretel and Prophesy."[42] Especially by likening such practices to those of Socrates's time, Agrippa also confirmed an articulated and operable connection between archaic Greek and ancient Hellenistic *goetia* and the early modern Goetia of the very grimoires that cunning-folk were using.[43]

The natural inclinations of the individual deceased soul should never be forgotten. Such agency and influence on the work can most obviously be observed in accounts of cunning-folk summoning the souls of those who knew and loved them in life. We find just such an example of personal connection—indeed, impassioned grief—amplifying such works of necromancy in the case of London cunning-woman Mary Parish successfully summoning her executed friend (and

39. Gifford, *A Dialogue Concerning Witches and Witchcraftes*, 22. Emphasis added.

40. Joseph Glanvill, *A Philosophical Endeavour towards the Defence of the Being of VVitches and Apparitions*, 21. Glanvill considers "this supposal may give a fairer and more probable account of many of the actions of Sorcery and Witchcraft, then the other Hypothesis, that they are always Devils."

41. Gifford, *A Dialogue Concerning Witches and Witchcraftes*, 22.

42. Agrippa, *The Vanity of Arts and Sciences*, 116.

43. See Stratton-Kent's *True Grimoire*, *Geosophia*, and *The Testament of Cyprian the Mage*; Cummins "'In the Manner of Saint Cyprian,'" 83–116.

possible suitor) George Whitmore to become her ghost familiar.[44] But there is another way certain dead may be "sympathetical" to the works of the necromancer: the professional interest of dead magicians.

By Dead Magicians: Retired but No Less Vocal

Tutelary ghosts, while not necessarily the most common spirits historical cunning-folk were associated with, were certainly summoned. More broadly, such spectral tutors were absolutely a feature of the milieus of early modern magical practices in which cunning-folk engaged. The sixteenth-century *Excellent Booke* records the magician and seer involved in its reception, Gilbert and Davis, visited by a host of dead magicians—including Solomon, Agrippa, Adam, and the fourteenth-century occult philosopher and rumoured "nigromancer" Roger Bacon.

These spectral teachers offered very practical and apparently successful advice on working techniques: what to wear, how to behave—all advice for how to conjure and command spirits that could deliver more magical knowledge, understanding, and power. Gilbert and Davis were certainly not professional cunning-men or service-magicians, and far closer to (indeed, colleague rivals with) courtly magus Dr. John Dee. But we certainly find versions of their methods and calls—in form, content, and even specific "unclean" spirits—in the working-books of cunning-folk.[45]

While the current evidence cannot attest to, for example, our cunning-man of Greys Inn Lane, Arthur Gauntlet, regularly summoning the ghost of, say, Albertus Magnus *directly*, his working-book does open with the "Instructions of Cyprian," a patron magician of magicians. Gauntlet's book also includes excerpts from the *Thesaurus Spirituum*, a work attributed to Roger Bacon, who was said to have written versions of this text under a patronage of Cyprian. Grimoirists resurrect the relic bodies of deceased magicians' works to jumpstart and grandfather their own endeavours, if not to outright circle dance in dead wizards' cross-topped Solomonic kicks. Are the old pacts and protocols not still honoured? This necromancy is *inter alia* a necromancy of text and the performances such texts instantiate, and no less enspirited for it.

Beyond our haunted books of magic, our magical practices themselves may be haunted too. Our Rosie-crucian geomancy tutor, John Heydon, outlines a certain folk eschatology in which (some aspect of) certain deceased souls remain at places they loved in life, and they are even sympathetically allured to attend to the living who are working what the dead once worked. Crucially, Heydon considers such souls may be "not meer spectators, but abettors," and likens them to "*old men* or *Country Parsons* that are past *Wrestling*, *pitching the Bar*, or *playing at Cudgels*"

44. Timbers, *The Magical Adventures of Mary Parish*, especially 58–69, 71, 78, 91, 94, 102, 113, 121, 123–25, 157, 159, 162, 168.

45. Legard and Cummins, *An Excellent Booke of the Arte of Magicke*.

who nevertheless "will assist and abet the young men of the parish at those Exercises."[46] Moreover, some of these professionally invested souls may be elevated to be able to provide even more divine assistance:

> The better sort of Souls, who having left the body, are *ipso facto* made *Genii* instead of men; that besides the peculiar *hapinesse* and *blisse* they reap thereby to themselves, they are appointed by God, and have a mission from him, to be Overseer of humane affaires: but that every Genius does not perform every Office, but as their natural inclination and customes were in this life.[47]

Dead magicians, if properly called and attended, may certainly fulfill such an "old boxing coach" overseer role in a necromancer's work. This understanding of what I find myself calling the Retired Dead facilitates a more casual mediumship of, say, hearing advice (or, more often, *criticism*) over your shoulder as you process ingredients, conjure plant allies, and otherwise work your crafts in front of your Cunning Dead. In my experience, magicians, whether alive or dead, have never been the sort to be shy about expressing opinions—especially about other people's magic.

Conclusions for Modern Cunning (or, Apples for Teachers)

So, given that I divine, charm, and conjure in traditionally cunning manners through familiar spirits—including dead cunning-folk—and am employed to apply traditional solutions to modern problems on a professional basis, I am occasionally referred to as a contemporary cunning-man. I do not consider myself a reconstructionist, but I am a necromancer. I certainly do not seek to pretend the present is the past, taking us backward in an escapism of modernity (tempting as that might be some days). Rather, at least on a good day, I can bring the wisdom of the dead into the living world through my work here and now. Such an ancestral practice nourishes me as I nourish it in my days and ways. So, let me end by telling you how I might start a typical working day.

I place an apple and a cup of tea before the statue I use to represent the cunning dead who come forth to share professional advice and spiritual empowerment. They sit amongst a few tools of the trade: a set of shears, a blackthorn cane, a Bible that I definitely didn't steal from a hospital (I swapped it out with one I brought with me, *actually*), a wrought-iron trivet, divining sticks, fox bones, prayer-gear, geomantic charm-bundles, and so on. They gather beneath a shrine dedicated to the Three Magi and next to the blessed dead of my ancestors. I top up a shot glass of gin, offered a few days ago in thanks for work successfully resolved. I say a good morning from over

46. Heydon, *Harmony of the World*, 189–91.
47. Heydon, *Harmony of the World*, 190–92.

my own first tea of the day, sprinkle something floral, offer a quick prayer, and outline the day's couple pieces of work with them. Solary herbs destined for a charm-bundle for a client's business success are to be placed on chalked geomantic sigils before them to charge in the third hour of the Sun.

The ritual ink I am preparing, for the construction of a particular Pentacle of the Moon for another client's dream incubation work, is to be opened in the third lunar hour and have certain prayers muttered into it. I decide that—if I have enough time today—we'll run divination on a couple of ongoing projects: some admin, a few check-ins, even a personal matter or two. But, you know, really only if I do that other thing today, and get these orders out, and respond to those emails, and proof that draft, and book that class, tend to that spirit, practice that incantation, finish that chapter, dispose of that offering, fold laundry…Thoughts cohere, suggestions arise, options are weighed, resolve percolates. With a rough order of the day's business assembled, I give some thanks, slouch off to an altar or laptop, and—after putting the kettle back on of course—work begins.

This is far from my only engagement at their space or with these spirits. There are occasionally rites of great formality and solemnity; I assure you I am also very spooky when the need arises, thank you very much. But I want to end quite deliberately on this personal, domestic, and unassuming work of these quotidian morning rites: these everyday ceremonies, offerings, communications, attendances, and helping habits of working with these spirits. For it is with these kinds of engagements *inter alia* that I continue to work—on the good days and the bad, to the best of my abilities and understandings—my craft out of theirs.

FIELD NOTES

Was There Witchcraft in Salem?

Very few people grow up in North America without at least hearing about the Salem witch trials. From February 1692 until the late spring of 1693, fourteen women, five men, and at least two dogs were all executed on charges of witchcraft, with more than 150 investigated. Another dozen or so were convicted but thankfully spared the noose before the end of the trials. A number of historians have helped narrow down the causes of the trials, with everything from a now-dismissed theory it was caused by ergot fungus hallucinations in a bad harvest of rye to the more likely conflicts between economic classes and rival families.[48]

While it's a grim and horrifying chapter in Colonial American history, very few people take seriously the idea that there were actual witches in Salem. None of those accused or executed were practicing either the diabolical and phantasmagoric version of witchcraft that Salem accusers like Abigail Williams, Elizabeth Parris, or Anna Putnam described in their testimonies or the contemporary, nature-based form of witchcraft religion that was popularized in the late twentieth century.[49]

What might be worth noting, however, is that while people in Salem weren't necessarily practicing any religious forms of witchcraft, many were using folk magic on a regular basis, and those practices were sometimes *seen* as witchcraft. Some examples of folk magic found in Salem and other parts of Colonial New England at the time:

- **Elizabeth Morse** practiced a version of cunning craft and performed healing charms for her neighbors.
- **Samuel Wardwell** operated as a sort of psychic, predicting things like future lovers and children, and was reportedly fairly accurate. He once told a woman she'd bear five daughters and then a son, which then happened.
- **Dorcas Hoar** of Beverly, Massachusetts, was arrested several times in the decade prior to the famous trials for owning books of fortune-telling and divination.
- **Rebecca Johnson** and her daughter used a method known as coscinomancy—divination by means of a sieve and shears—to find out if her son was still alive.
- **Sarah Cole** of Lynn, Massachusetts, noted that she and her friends used a method known as the "Venus glass," which involved breaking an egg into a glass of water

48. Boyer and Nissenbaum, *Salem Possessed*; Karlsen, *The Devil in the Shape of a Woman*; Norton, *In the Devil's Snare*.
49. Boyer and Nissenbaum, *Salem Possessed*; Karlsen, *The Devil in the Shape of a Woman*; Norton, *In the Devil's Snare*.

to divine the identities of future husbands. (This is very similar to contemporary sleepover fortune-telling games.)

- **Mary Sibley** asked Tituba to make a "witch cake" of ground meal and urine from one of the afflicted Parris household girls, then feed it to a dog. It was thought this might break the spell and cause the witch casting it tremendous pain, thus revealing her identity.
- **Tituba** herself came from Arawak and Taino ancestry and may have brought in some of her peoples' folk practices, although most testimony focuses on forms of witchery that resembled European sources.
- While Tituba is sometimes mislabeled as "The Black Witch" of Salem, she was one of several people of color accused of witchcraft. A Barbadian slave named **Candy** and the Putnams' slave **Mary Black** were also both accused of witchcraft; they later went free. Candy *may* have used some rag dolls for folk magic, although it is just as likely she was coerced into presenting them as magical charms when they were simply toys. Mary Black was one of the victims accused through "spectral evidence," and no particular folk magic is ascribed to her.
- **John Brown** of New Haven, Connecticut, claimed (while likely inebriated) that he could make the devil appear by drawing circles and "strange figures which he called the lords of the second, third, tenth, and twelfth house."[50]

None of these instances were examples of the "grandmothers you couldn't burn" so often alluded to in the early twenty-first century (which is wrong on many counts, not the least of which is that New England victims weren't burned, but hanged). But while we may be relatively sure that the Salem trials were a disaster on many fronts, we can also be just as sure that magic—specifically folk magic—was very much alive and well in the area long before and after those trials.

50. For more on each of these individuals, see Hall, *Worlds of Wonder, Days of Judgment*, 97–101. See also Boyer and Nissenbaum, *Salem Possessed*; Karlsen, *The Devil in the Shape of a Woman*; and Norton, *In the Devil's Snare*.

An Enduring Awareness of Things Unseen: Irish American Folk Magic

MORGAN DAIMLER

Magic is a wide-ranging and fascinating subject, and especially when we dial in to specific veins of folk magic. These inevitably have their own tone and flavour that is shaped by the community these forms of magic are rooted in, and this is just as true with Irish American folk magic as it is with anything else. I grew up in the northeast US in an Irish American community, and while I have found instances where what I was taught aligns with things that can be found in Ireland, I have also found cases where what is believed or practiced here differs from the Irish versions. This creates a fascinating and complex group of folk beliefs that are connected to their Irish source but have grown and adapted as well.

Romanticizing the Past: Immigration and Ireland in the American Imagination

To understand Irish American folk magic, we have to begin with an understanding of both the immigrant communities that have formed this approach and the original Irish folk magic that is the predecessor of it. Irish American communities, in general, have a strong sense of their roots in Ireland, although they are prone to romanticizing it and creating an image of the place that is generations out of date; for Irish Americans, Ireland becomes a kind of holy land, but one that is imagined very differently than the reality. This idealized Ireland is based on memories and stories that were passed down in families and reflect an Ireland decades past.

There is an emphasis on the importance of remembering where we came from and preserving the traditions that can be preserved, even when those represent things that are outdated or old-fashioned now. This distorted understanding creates a culture here that is similar to Irish culture in some ways and includes some shared beliefs, but is also different in some ways and reflects both older Irish cultural views as well as Americanisms, forming a unique synthesis of the two. It is from this synthesis that Irish American folk magic has grown.

Irish American and Irish folk magic, like most folk magic, is at heart practical. The beliefs are meant to explain both common and uncommon things around us and empower us to have some control over them. To this end, most of the practices focus on getting and maintaining luck. Luck is a key factor in these beliefs because luck was seen as something that underpinned and supported life itself. To have luck was to have everything else good in life, while to be unlucky meant being unable to obtain or keep those things, including health, wealth, and home. Some people are inherently lucky and others are inherently unlucky, but for many people, luck is an ephemeral thing that can be either nurtured or broken.

Clovers, Horseshoes, and Second Sight

The luckiest object one could find was a four-leaf clover, which then had to be carefully preserved and kept, for to lose it meant losing the luck it represented. In the US, this would specifically be *Trifolium repens* or *Trifolium pratense*, while in the original Irish practice it could be either of those clovers but may also have been *Trifolium dubium*. There is no agreement on which clover the shamrock was, as *shamrock* is just the anglicized form of *Seamair Óg* (literally, "young clover"), and *Seamair* is the Irish name for at least eight distinct types of clover.

I was taught that when such a clover is found, it should be pressed, dried, and carefully stored so that it won't be lost or decay. My trick after drying was to use clear tape in carefully cut segments to provide a permanent double-sided cover for the clover. I did this by first laying strips of tape on one side, then on the other, so that the tape sealed to itself around the plant.

Besides the superlative four-leaf clover, lucky items were those that were difficult to find or unusual, including things like a horse's tooth.[51] Found pennies were also lucky, but only if they were found faceup, taken, and kept; in contrast, it was bad luck to take a tails-up penny.

One staple of folk practice for bringing both luck and protection was to hang an iron horseshoe over a doorway, generally the main entrance to a home. There is an ongoing debate about whether the horseshoe should be hung with the open side up or down, with one view arguing that a points-up horseshoe holds the luck in while the other side says that a points-down horseshoe is figuratively pouring the luck out on those who walk beneath it. Growing up, we had a horseshoe over the front and back doors of the house, always points-up, and I have seen similar in a home in Sligo, Ireland. With that being said, I have several friends who are adamant that it should be points-down. Ultimately, I don't think either view is right or wrong—the presence of the horseshoe is what matters.

A seventh son was thought to be lucky, and the seventh son of a seventh son especially so; such people had the power to see spirits. This ability, sometimes called *an Dara Sealladh*, a Scottish Gàidhlig term literally meaning "second sight," allowed a person to see spirits, including ghosts and fairies, and also to have a precognitive or clairvoyant sense. It was something that certain

51. Quinn, *Irish American Folklore in New England*, 214–15.

people were born with, but it was also something that may be gained through certain actions, such as possessing a four-leaf clover. Beyond its previously mentioned qualities, a four-leaf clover also disperses enchantments and allows a person to see the unseen just as well as looking through a naturally holed stone.

Just as luck is a vital factor in folk practice, unlucky things are a factor in Irish American folk magic, particularly the idea that certain actions or encounters can create or portend ill luck. Some unlucky things, like having red hair (which is often seen as unlucky in both Irish and Irish American belief), a person has no control over, while others, like putting shoes on a table, a person can be sure to avoid in order to bypass the unlucky consequences. In a similar vein, there were many folk beliefs that offered protection from negative consequences—or, alternatively, promised them if the action were taken—such as being taught never to burn hair or to throw hair clippings or the hair pulled from a brush to the wind, lest birds nest in it and the person it belonged to suffer from headaches afterward. This is also a practical thing, as human hair can be a health hazard for birds, cutting off circulation to their legs if they become tangled in it.

A lot of Irish American folk magic is rooted in what might be labeled as superstition. A superstition is the idea that certain things should or shouldn't be done, or that certain things are omens. For example, there are superstitions that if your right palm itches, you will get money, while if the left hand itches, you will lose it. Or, if your right ear is ringing, people are praising you, while if your left ear itches, you are being gossiped about. This is mentioned in Barone's article on Irish folk beliefs; however, she switches the meaning of the palms itching.[52] I have presented the superstition here as I grew up with it.

Omens are abundant in folk belief and offer a person a chance to prepare for or alter a possible outcome. To drop cutlery on the floor meant visitors were on the way, for example, while cows lying down in a field meant rain was coming; both of these allowed a person to potentially prepare for what was to come. This awareness of things that might seem trivial or inconsequential were ingrained as a means to predict events and influence outcomes when possible.

So, for example, if your left ear itches (meaning someone is talking about you), then you should spit on your thumb and pointer finger, tug three times on your left ear, and say aloud that the person must bite their tongue.[53] As with the earlier note about palms itching, the academic source for this reverses the meaning of which ear signifies what; I have presented the superstitions here as I grew up with them. It's worth noting that this source and Barone both offering different meanings perhaps indicates variations in belief between communities, which is common with folk beliefs.

52. Barone, "Luck of the Irish."

53. Quinn, *Irish American Folklore in New England*, 228.

An Enduring Awareness of Things Seen and Unseen

Fairies can play a large role in Irish American folk magic, just as they sometime do in Irish folk magic. As scholar E. Moore Quinn says in the book *Irish American Folklore in New England*, "The Irish brought to the new world an enduring awareness of things seen and unseen and they were more than willing to honor both."[54] There is an idea that while there were and are spirits native to the Americas, there are also Irish beings who came along with or followed after the communities and people that immigrated, including a variety of fairy beings found across Irish folk belief.

I have encountered anecdotes and material dating back to the early nineteenth century describing fairies, *púcaí* (pookas), leprechauns, *leannán sidhe*, and *mná sidhe* (banshees) in the United States, usually following the same patterns that we would see in Irish accounts. While there are undoubtedly beings native to the Americas as well as a variety of beings that have been imported along with various cultures, we can certainly find evidence of Irish fairies in the mix, and the folk beliefs about them can be just as strong.

Growing up, I was told that if we were outside, we must always pour out the first of any drink (particularly alcohol for adults) onto the ground as the fairies' due, something that is echoed in Irish folk beliefs. There is a long tradition in Ireland of the first portion being the fairies' portion, and there are some anecdotal accounts of a practice of pouring out a bit of your drink onto the ground for them. This is probably for the best, as this was also the portion most likely to be dangerous to drink.

In practice here in the US, the custom often was to leave a bit of fresh water or a small amount of food, often a portion of what the family had eaten, out for the fairies. I was told that any food that fell to the ground was for the fairies—that, in fact, it fell because the fairies wanted it, and that once it fell it shouldn't be eaten by humans, something that I found echoed in an anecdotal account from *The Fairy-Faith in Celtic Countries*.[55]

In the same way, there was a belief in Ireland that any fruit (particularly blackberries) left after Samhain—or, alternately, Saint Martin's Day in some places—was not to be touched, as it belonged to the fairies. In the US, this idea transferred to apples. In both cases, the core premise was that after that date, any fruit that remained no longer belonged to humans but had become the property of the fairies, and to take it would earn retribution.

One significant difference between Irish folk belief about fairies and the same beliefs among Irish Americans has to do with the home. In Ireland, it was generally not a good thing to have fairies in the house, and many beliefs and protections are based on warding them out, from keeping an iron horseshoe over the doorway to not bringing certain types of plants or trees into a

54. Quinn, *Irish American Folklore in New England*, 212.

55. Evans-Wentz, *The Fairy-Faith in Celtic Countries*, 70.

house lest the fairies enter as well. This is because the Fair Folk were seen as potentially dangerous influences who could and would cause harm to a family's luck, health, and prosperity.

In contrast—perhaps as a way to keep these beliefs closer in a new country—among Irish Americans, there was a belief that it would be bad to drive the fairies out of a home through poor housekeeping or lack of hospitality. While I grew up with a horseshoe over the front and back doors of the house, I also grew up with the idea that it was all right for fairies to be in the home, and it was even expected to some degree. This is in line with wider Irish American beliefs noted by folklorist Quinn, who says, "Steps were taken to ensure [the fairies] would remain within the home and surrounding areas."[56] This has been one of the hardest things to unlearn as I have moved more into studying and incorporating Irish beliefs.

Keeping Iron Close: Protective Magic

Protective magic often focused on averting potential harm from otherworldly sources, both the Good Folk (fairies) as well as more malevolent powers, usually embodied by the Devil. A variety of these protections focused on children and fairies—for example, attaching a steel safety pin to a child's clothes. This was a more modern adaptation of the older practice of keeping iron near where a child slept, which would most often have been iron scissors, fire tongs, or similar fixed above a child's crib or bed.

Iron is seen as a superlative protection against not only the fairies but also any malevolent powers, and it is often used in protective charms and magic. Several different protective folk practices involve iron, from wearing it to using it as jewelry to carrying it in a pocket. Iron fire pokers were used in several different ways for protection, including casting an iron poker out the door after a person left to ensure their safe return. I have used a fire poker myself to protect a building by placing it standing up behind a door.

Iron was not the only method of protective magic. When a person sneezed and we said "Bless you," I was told it was because otherwise, the fairies might steal the person or their soul; the "bless you" was a protection against that happening. And in Ireland, it was said that if you were being pursued by an angry or dangerous spirit, you should cross running water; this is another belief that transferred to the US. In the US, if you were being chased by a dangerous spirit (especially at night) and could cross running water, you would be safe from harm.[57]

56. Quinn, *Irish American Folklore in New England*, 219–21.

57. Quinn, *Irish American Folklore in New England*, 215–22.

A Bad *Cess* to You: Healing and Cursing Lore

Another major theme in Irish American folk magic relates to cures, or methods to treat or address health issues. One simple method relating to this, for example, was using an apple to cure warts. I was taught that if one had a wart, you should take an apple and slice it in half, then rub one half on the wart, close the apple back up, and bury it whole. As it decayed, the wart would fade away. This sort of simple sympathetic magic is common and very effective.

Seventh sons were thought to be lucky and to have a magical quality to them. They could cure with a touch, as could certain people who were born with curing ability. There were also actions that could be taken by anyone to effect some cures, such as placing a bed so that the person's head was to the north. Growing up, I had been told that this was the way beds should always be placed, if possible, and that one should never have their head to the south or they would suffer from insomnia.[58]

Just as healing was a significant folk practice, so was cursing, although the method is very different. Spoken curses were far more popular than curses that required action. Spoken curses were often aimed at a person's luck or health, such as saying "Bad *cess* to you" (or "Bad luck to you") with the idea that the words were more than just an angry expression and were a literal curse on the person.[59] While *cess* literally means taxes or dues, it is also understood to mean luck and was used in phrases relating to bad luck, like in the example just given.

The Devil was often invoked against people to curse them, and sometimes a curse could be laid by withholding an expected blessing, such as not saying "Bless them" when a person was being talked about. More active forms of cursing might involve putting your left side to a person or walking counterclockwise around them or their property, as this was thought to take their luck *and* invite negative things to them.

Inviting Fairies In

Although fairies are always warded out in Ireland, the approach to these beings can differ significantly in the Irish American diaspora. In my childhood, steps to welcome fairies into the home to increase luck and health included not only keeping the house clean and tidy, but also the creation of small fairy houses in the yard. The exact history of this practice in the US is muddled and hard to trace—I was certainly doing it in the 1980s, and there have been books published about it since 2001—but I believe it does represent a genuine folk practice. While the idea has now become trendy (one can buy a fairy house online!), the original practice as I knew it was to create a small replica of any kind of house using found natural materials. When I was young I would

58. Quinn, *Irish American Folklore in New England*, 215.

59. Quinn, *Irish American Folklore in New England*, 216.

use stones, twigs, flowers, moss, and acorns to fashion little one-room homes, complete with beds and dining tables, for the fairies. The idea with this gesture was to show that the fairies were welcome and had a place within your space. This was acknowledging them as a kind of house spirit or being similar to the Roman Lares, who acted as guardian spirits of homes and public places.

Irish American folk magic is a wonderful, powerful, and unique thing that draws on Irish folk magic as a source, but it has adapted and been filtered through the lens of those who are now separated from the culture. While we can trace many beliefs back to Ireland and see the original practices there, we find a rich array of material in Irish American belief as well—from gaining luck to cursing to protection to healing—that represents unique versions of these magical practices. Simple actions, simple words, and a belief in the unseen forces moving behind all things underpin Irish American folk magic. The most important aspects might be an understanding of the need to connect to and observe the world around us and to be on good terms with the fairies who so strongly influence luck, which is the primal force being nurtured in this approach.

TRAVELING ON

New England and the Maritimes

As with any guidebook, there is always much more to experience than can be neatly fit into a chapter. To that end, we offer you this addendum to the map that will provide you with some tools to explore New England and the Maritimes further.

The glossary shares some keywords that might be useful. The places to visit will point you toward locations of interest that we think you might find valuable, and the reading recommendations provide you with some top-tier texts that can help you dig in and learn more about this region.

Glossary

aiguilles: Pins boiled in water or placed in bottles and covered in urine to counter witchcraft or curses.

an Dara Sealladh: A Scots Gaelic term meaning roughly "second sight," which implies a gift of prophecy, divination, or visions.

"bad cess to you": An Irish American cursing phrase used to wish ill on someone by way of their health or luck.

charms: The body of written or spoken verbal magic.

coscinomancy: The use of a sieve and shears (or scissors) as a way of divining information.

cunning folk: A term imported from England for the group of people who would perform local magical services, including divination, charming, or unbewitching.

familiar spirit: A spirit thought to abide with a witch and serve her, or to provide aid and service to a working magician through conjuration or divination.

galettes salées: Salt cakes use to perform dream divinations, usually about future lovers or spouses.

geomancy: The use of markings or marked objects and the interpretation of their placements for divination (as with dominoes, dice, marked sticks, etc.).

Good Folk: A colloquial term for members of the fairy world, used as a way of avoiding naming them directly for fear of attracting their attention.

grimoire: A magical textbook containing spells, rituals, diagrams, names of spirits, or other occult material.

malices: Otherworldly spirits in French Canadian beliefs that were earthly or not associated with the heavenly court of the saints, including shape-shifting *loup-garous*, the *fées* (fairies), the pixie-like *lutins*, and the dancing *marionettes* (northern lights).

saints: Spiritual allies associated with Heaven and good deeds in the Sorcellerie tradition. Sometimes these are official Catholic saints, sometimes folk saints.

sidhe: A Gaelic term referring to otherworldly entities as a broad category, including but not limited to fairies, *púcaí* (pookas), leprechauns, *leannán sidhe*, and *mná sidhe* (banshees).

Sorcellerie: The practice of folk magic and reconstructed folk spiritual practices of French-Canadian colonists.

unbewitching: The practice of lifting or reversing witchcraft or curses, often practiced by cunning folk.

Yâbe: The Devil figure in French Canadian folklore, often more of a trickster than a biblical Satan.

Places to Visit

Find Magic in Montreal, Canada: Montreal has a long history of witchcraft and folk magic, and it has served as a cosmopolitan intersection for folk traditions of many backgrounds. There are a number of places catering to the larger witchcraft and magical community of the city. Bar Datcha, a Russian-themed watering spot, has historically hosted an event called "Jazz and Tarot Thursday," and there are groups catering to a wide variety of spiritual practices including Haitian Vodun and Neopagan Witchcraft in the city as well. Events like the *Fête des neiges* offer an opportunity to get into seasonal folk celebrations, including guising as winter animals and ice sculpture.

The Collections of Memorial University, Newfoundland: One of the few universities in North America to offer a doctorate in folklore, this institution also houses an immense folklore collection. If you request permission to access it as a researcher, you can find a trove of folk magical information here. There are also some good bits of archaeological material found at the L'Anse aux Meadows site, thought to be one of the first footholds for Viking explorers on the Atlantic coast of North America.

Go Beyond the Trials in Salem, Massachusetts: While there's a lot of tourist hype around the infamous Salem witch trials (and the city has more than its share of contemporary witchcraft wares for sale), there are a few spots within the town that are worth visiting for those who want to explore its folk magic side. The Witch Museum offers a good bit of historical overview for the trials, but then spend some time at the Salem Historical Society, the Peabody Essex Museum, and Phillips Library to get a more well-rounded picture of what the belief systems were like at the time, and to discover how little bits of folk magic crept into everyday life in places like Salem.

Recommended Reading

Where the Hawthorn Grows: An American Druid's Reflections by Morgan Daimler
A personal and well-researched look at Irish reconstructionist practices in North America.

Worlds of Wonder, Days of Judgment: Popular Religious Belief in Early New England by David D. Hall
A scholarly but accessible look at historic folk magic and popular belief in Colonial New England.

Tel que dit: Select French-Canadian Folktales Collected and Transcribed by C. Marius Barbeau by E. F. E. Lacharity
This collection of French Canadian tales includes several with magical lore, including tales of Ti-Jean and the Devil (Yâbe).

Irish American Folklore in New England by E. Moore Quinn
This academic text by an anthropology professor looks at the roots and the development of Irish American folk beliefs and practices in New England.

Making Witches: Newfoundland Traditions of Spells and Counterspells by Barbara Rieti
While this is definitely an academic book, Rieti shares a number of stories about witchcraft and folk magic in Newfoundland that will definitely interest readers of this chapter.

CHAPTER 2

New Holland and Deitscherei

Chapter 2

Doing More than Eating Bread: An Introduction to the Folk Magic of the Mid-Atlantic Region

Philadelphia has a character that is at once rough-edged and big-hearted. If you've ever seen the violent-but-lovable Philadelphia Flyers mascot, Gritty, that is very much the energy of the city. The mixture of history, progress, urban advance and decay, cultural crossroads, creativity, and need—all of that makes Philadelphia deeply vibrant.

Then, as soon as you leave Philadelphia proper, there is a palpable shift. The last few curves of concrete on the Lincoln Highway out of town begin to reveal a bright edge of green to the horizon, just beyond the West Chester suburbs. The ground rises and falls like breath, and as you pass over a hill, you look down on a wide sea of farmland, dotted with picturesque barns and farmhouses, verdant pastures, and rows of crops, the earth tilled to a ruddy deep brown as it was prepared for a new round of seeding.

This is a portion of the landscape that had been shaped by the presence of the "Pennsylvania Dutch," a misnomer applied to the German-speaking (*Deitsch*) immigrants who arrived in the area during the eighteenth and nineteenth centuries. Prior to European colonization, the land was the home of the Lenape Tribe and affiliated Susquehannock tribal groups. The area had long been an ideal one for agriculture with its rivers and rich soil, and when German speakers fleeing religious and social persecution in the Palatine region of Central and Western Europe arrived in Quaker-run and religiously tolerant Pennsylvania, their background as farmers helped them transform the land. They had a few quirks, especially in the eyes of their British neighbors: bank barns built into the slope of a hill (or with hills built around them, to make driving wagons into the hayloft easier); the publication of numerous German newspapers and a high literacy rate; and houses built with two front doors set side by side. Perhaps nothing so set them apart, however, as their magic.

The combination of religious experimentation, literacy, agricultural backgrounds, and ethnic isolation led to a number of interesting bits of folk magic. Pennsylvania Germans drew upon a mixture of Christian and pre-Christian influences, although they themselves were almost universally Christian in practice (albeit occasionally very heretically Christian by the reckoning of outsiders). They developed manuals of folk healing "for man and beast," as seen in the subtitle of one of the best-known of these publications, *The Long-Lost Friend* by John George Hohman (an anglicization of his *Deitsch* name, Johann Georg Hohman), published in 1820. These magics treated ailments that were unique to the Pennsylvania Germans: being "liver-grown" (*Aagewachse*) or having "the fire" (*Wildfeier*, a rash caused by *Streptococcus pyogenes*). They also treated goiters in humans and cattle, reduced fevers in children, helped stop bleeding wounds, or eased the pain of a burn. Those who could do this sort of folk magic were colloquially known as those who "know how to do more than eat bread," according to a regional proverb.

In the coming essays, you'll meet a pair of men I've known for many years now, both of whom practice versions of Pennsylvania German folk magic. Rob Phoenix is a Powwow healer, one drawing on a long tradition of Christian folk charms. These charms come from European grimoires and oral tradition, and they involve moving divine power through the one providing aid and into the ailing patient. Rob Schreiwer works within the Urglaawe tradition and practices a version of Braucherei. His system builds and reconstructs the magical worldview of the pre-Christian German peoples—often called Heathenry, although in North America the Urglaawe version of Heathenry is distinct and specifically works against many of the racist tropes that have plagued some other branches of that faith. He incorporates a mixture of old charms and new, building on conversations he says he's had over the years with several Pennsylvania German people. Both Rob Phoenix and Rob Schreiwer offer a glimpse of their systems, providing snapshots of the sort of work they do. They also provide us a road map to further discovery through their published and shared works on their respective traditions. Theologically, they are separated in some ways, but in both practices the emphasis on healing and connecting with a spirit of divinity is deeply present.

Of course, there's also the infamous Sleepy Hollow found in Washington Irving's classic tale. Incidentally, that's an actual place (sort of) and an actual legend (also sort of), and it's worth a little side trip to the Hudson River Valley to encounter a bit of the spooky magic still lingering in Tarrytown—just make sure you cross the bridge before dark. Hints of old Dutch belief and folkways still linger, even in a much more progressive and modern New Holland (one of the Colonial-era names for New York).

And of course, how could we forget New York? New York City is an absolute smorgasbord of magical practices and traditions. It would be unthinkable to miss out on the distinct flavor of magic that comes along with a double slice of New York–style pizza. City magic has a character that reflects the cosmopolitan nature of crossroads upon crossroads upon crossroads.

We'll also venture down into New Jersey to visit with Stephanie Rose Bird, who will show us a bit of how traditions like Hoodoo have taken root in this landscape, in cities like Newark as well as further down in cities like Baltimore, where a long tradition of candle shops has kept African American folk magic available for many years. Bird's childhood experiences demonstrate just how much fusion takes place in these mid-Atlantic spaces, as she connects the Hoodoo of her ancestry and community to her love of plants and green witchery as well.

The landscape of the seaboard is fascinating, full of sweeping farmland vistas and bustling urban hubs like New York, Baltimore, and Philadelphia. Wherever you look, there is also magic. Just don't look too hard at Gritty, though. We don't want any trouble.

A Nameless Tradition: Italian American Magic from New Jersey

DEE NORMAN

There are times when it feels like Italian American folk magic is more easily defined by explaining what it isn't rather than attempting to describe what it is. To make things simple, let's immediately eliminate some potential misconceptions. It can't be described by a comprehensive list of spells, practices, or rituals due to the Italian peninsula's patchwork of cultures. The magic of Lazio is influenced by the cosmopolitan nature of Rome, while people in Trentino-Alto Adige may have strong German influences on what they do, and Sicilian practitioners are likely to have methods unique to their southern climate and slightly more isolated geography. Meanwhile, the entire southern coast of Italy has historically been heavily influenced by Greece. The loose group of beliefs and practices that make up Italian American folk magic do not create a coherent, standalone religion from this riotous mix. Its traditional practitioners are primarily Roman Catholic and do not draw a line between their Catholic beliefs and their magical practices. In fact, the belief systems blend, creating techniques that incorporate both magical and religious aspects.

It is also important to realize that while Italian American magical and folk practices are like Italian magic, they are not exactly the same as Italian magic. Over the course of many years, the rituals and behaviors that arrived in the US from various parts of Italy have mixed together. Some magical components that were common in Italy are nowhere to be found on these shores because they were gradually replaced. Italian immigration to the US began in earnest in the mid-1800s, so Italian American practices have had a couple hundred years to evolve separately from purely Italian practices.

So now that I have told you what it isn't, let's talk about what it is. We can start by saying that Italian American folk magic is a collection of pragmatic magical and spiritual practices centered around the home, family, and both spiritual and physical health. Honoring ancestors and working with Catholic saints both play a significant role. Some of its practices, such as evil eye preventatives and cures, can be traced back to pre-Christian times. Other practices, like reciting a charm upon first sight of the full moon, are of a more recent origin because the tradition is constantly evolving with a keen eye for what works. There are practices that are performed solely in private and others that are enacted right out in the open—some of them even take place in church.

The magic I have learned from my mother and grandmother is a magic of family and household. It is a flower that blossomed in the Garden State of New Jersey, fed by the Italian American community there: How to honor and work with ancestors. How to make sure your family is safe. How to protect and improve the atmosphere of your home. What to do to make sure you have enough money in your pocket to pay your bills. How to eliminate your worries. It may sound pedestrian, but the magic is ever-present, gleaming under the veneer of the everyday, and it is always within reach.

The Old Country: The Source of Italian American Magic

Ours is a tradition that is passed down through our extended families from generation to generation. As I mentioned, the primary sources of my Italian American magical know-how are my mother and grandmother. From childhood onward, I learned first by watching them and later by peppering them with questions. However, I don't have to go back too many generations before finding my family in Italy, specifically Southern Italy, in and around Naples and Benevento.

My ancestors arrived in the US with the 4.2 million Italians that immigrated between 1891 and 1920.[60] The Italian peninsula had always been a fragmented area, with very strong regional differences. In fact, Italy did not unite into a single kingdom until 1861. Even after unification, there was a vast divide between wealthier northern and poorer southern parts of the country, but no matter what region an immigrant came from, they were faced with the same challenges. They each had to struggle to assimilate into the culture of the United States. Along with their worldly possessions, they carried their spiritual and magical possessions—the source material for the magic I practice today.

You may wonder why immigrants, who were working hard to survive and make the most of the opportunities presented by their new homeland, would cling to what could be considered old-fashioned ideas about magic. The very uncertainty of their new lifestyles and their frequent inability to get help through official channels kept them living on the edges of mainstream society and gave them cause to resort to magic to help them accomplish their goals.

The magic of Italian immigrants was fueled by the hopes, dreams, and desperate needs of their daily lives.

60. Tirabassi, "Why Italians Left Italy," 233.

"Back Home"

By the time I was born into my Italian American family, they had been living in Kentucky for years, but they still called West Orange, New Jersey, "back home." My mother was born in West Orange and most of our family members still lived there. When I was a child, it was a place of story and legend: where great-grandma hid the family in the closet and prayed the rosary when it stormed, where great-grandpa made his own wine with the wine press in the basement, and where my grandmother had to break the ice on the top of the barrel of olives to scoop out a cupful in winter.

West Orange was the geographic heart of our family life, and it was where we traveled for important life events like christenings, weddings, and funerals. When we visited, I would sink into a soundscape of raised voices talking over each other in what we called "Italian" but what is really a dialect of Neapolitan. I would be repeatedly fed to bursting by ancient-seeming great aunts who would produce dish after dish out of their inconceivably small kitchens.

My memories of West Orange are a series of vignettes, most of them taking place in kitchens. I was in one of those kitchens the first time I understood the impact my spiritual practices could have on my family and me. We were visiting West Orange to bury my grandfather. I was heartbroken at losing him, but my grandmother had summoned me to the kitchen table to "do the cards" for Cousin Twinkie. Her real name wasn't Twinkie, and she wasn't actually related to any of us, but she was part of the extended group that my mother grew up with, and therefore she was part of the family. She had lost her husband the year before. I knew it was going to come up in the reading. I was twenty years old—still young enough to be nervous about reading on such a serious subject. She looked apprehensive as I shuffled the deck. Family members were streaming in and out of the kitchen, but when my eyes met Twinkie's the noise and activity around us faded away. I could recognize a sadness there like mine, tempered by the passage of time but persistent.

It was at that moment I became fully conscious of what I was doing. Here in the heart of the home, I was performing a sacred duty in the service of my great big, boisterous family and our wider community. I wasn't reading cards to give her advice or entertainment or even something to contemplate; I was providing comfort and reassurance, and if I was lucky, helping Cousin Twinkie heal herself a little bit. My pain and loss could reach out to her pain and loss, and the cards would build a bridge to help us come together to find relief from our separate griefs.

This is the heart of Italian American folk magic and spirituality. The sublimely spiritual taking place amid daily life. A small act that takes place in the present, creating a sacred connection between past and future.

A Nameless Tradition

Though similar practices in Italy are called *Benedicaria* ("Way of Blessing"), my family's magical tradition does not have a formal name.[61] When I got old enough to try to pressure them into admitting our family did magic, they would laugh at me and say, "This stuff is just the things we do!" From their perspective, the magic I could so clearly see seamlessly blended into all the other tasks they performed while running their households, like doing the laundry or tending the garden. This was incredibly frustrating to me as I was growing up. How could I be sure I was really participating in a tradition if it had no name, no formal set of practices, no center to hold on to? Of course, what I didn't realize at the time was that while it may not have a name or a codified set of practices, it certainly had a center. The center is my heart and my personal relationship to my ancestors, the good spirits around me, and my deity. However, that center expands to include my household, my family, my friends, and neighbors. Practicing Italian American magic allows me to perpetually walk through a spiritual landscape that is so finely woven into my daily life that the two cannot be separated.

Another difficulty that I struggled with growing up is that though I now gleefully call myself an Italian American "witch," my mother and grandmother never used that term to describe themselves. In this way, they are like most traditional practitioners who don't identify themselves as magic users, witches, or anything of the like. They consider themselves good Catholics if they consider themselves anything. In more recent generations, practitioners have made an effort to claim words like *strega* ("witch") and *stregoneria* ("witchcraft"). Historically, both terms are laden with negative connotations and were used to indicate someone who practiced harmful magic. Some modern practitioners have rehabilitated these words and bear them as a badge of cultural pride.

Throughout the history of Italian American folk magic, there are practitioners of all sorts to be found: male and female, old and young. There is no formal process for entering into the practice—you simply learn the methods and incorporate them into your life.

A Special Place? (Psst! It's an Altar!)

There is a place in my mother's home where a candle burns all day long. She lights it in the morning when she gets up, and it isn't extinguished until she goes to bed. Statues of saints cluster there, prayer cards propped up at their bases. Saint medals are scattered in between pictures of family members and beloved friends. Fresh flowers bloom in a vase near mementos that represent special people or occasions. It is the place in her house that I love best. It is the heart of her spiritual practice and where she prays for people. Its peaceful influence permeates her home.

61. Taumaturgo, *The Things We Do*, 10.

She doesn't call it an altar, but it certainly is. If I were to press her, she possibly would admit to it being "a special place," and that is as far as she would go.

I have a similar place in my home, situated, like Mom's, near the dining room. On my altar that is not an altar (it's totally an altar) are pictures of ancestors and statues of St. Expedite, the Three Wise Men, St. Anthony, and other entities I work with. I also do my practical magical work there, burning candles or creating charm bundles to accomplish my goals. This space is the physical center of my spiritual and magical life. It serves the dual purpose of honoring my ancestors and protecting and caring for the living. Whenever I need to feel the support of my ancestors or the other good spirits around me, I turn to my altar. It is a sacred space that generates peace and prosperity for my household.

Each morning, I light what I call the altar candle, which is simply a general-purpose candle meant to honor my ancestors and the other entities I work with. Every day, I check the state of my altar. For example, I make sure any gifts I have given to my ancestors (water, flowers, etc.) are fresh. If I burned incense there, I make sure I have cleaned up the ashes. My altar tends to collect things. My daughter likes to put cool stones she finds or crafts she makes on it. That means I occasionally must do a declutter.

I reset my altar around three times a year. I don't have predetermined times to do so; I just do it when it feels right. To reset, I start by removing everything from my altar and thoroughly dusting everything, including the cabinet I use. After that, I wipe down everything with holy water. I often use holy water that I make myself, but I always keep some holy water that was blessed at my patron saint's shrine for important occasions, like resetting the altar. I take some time deciding what needs to be on this new iteration of my altar. I listen to my intuition throughout this process, and I often receive feedback from family members (living and dead) about what needs to be there. Once everything is on the altar and arranged to my liking, I light a fresh altar candle and some sandalwood incense, which I use because it was one of my grandmother's favorite scents.

This style of altar is very personal, and while I can refer to books or online resources to determine what colors to use or what incenses to burn, I feel it is always more powerful to use associations that are significant to me and my family. Doing so, I am taking advantage of the powerful emotional correspondences that are built into my life experiences. For example, I use old arcade tokens to symbolize joy because my father managed an arcade when I was a child, and we spent many happy days there.

If you haven't tried building an altar in your home, I highly recommend it. Setting aside an area of your dwelling for the sacred will change the atmosphere of your home and replenish your soul. The altar doesn't have to be elaborate, and you can construct it from items you already have at home. Choose a quiet corner of your house, dust it, and fill it with things that are sacred to you: family photos, items from nature, drawings, or statues—the possibilities are as endless and varied as there are people in this world. It can be as small as a windowsill or bookshelf. Once you have built the altar, make sure to spend time with it on a regular basis. Take the opportunity to listen there and you will receive comfort and sustenance.

Working with Ancestors

Everywhere I turn in my house, there are reminders of family that have passed from this world. I find my father's books interspersed amongst mine on my bookshelves. A stick my great-grandfather used to make wine rests in a corner of my office. Some of my grandmother's jewelry is tucked away in my jewelry box. And, of course, there are photos of my ancestors on my household altar. The family is constantly with me, and with their presence comes a feeling of continuity. My connection with my ancestors provides inspiration during good times and support during bad times. They are the support upon which I build my spiritual life.

When I work with my ancestors, I do mostly very simple things. I give them clear fresh water. I burn candles for them. I share with them things they would have enjoyed in life. For example, any time I get a pretty crystal, I leave it in front of my grandmother's picture because she shared my love of crystals and tumbled stones. After a few days, when it feels right, I remove the stone and use it for whatever purpose I bought it for. Though I started out doing this to show my grandmother respect, I have noticed that I don't need to cleanse the crystal if I leave it in front of her picture.

I also spend a lot of time just talking to my ancestors. I let them know what is going on in the family, though I feel they are well aware of everything we do. Before I do any magical work, I usually bring my problems or worries to them. Sometimes all it takes is some quiet time explaining my concerns to them and then waiting to receive a response. I may receive some intuitive nudges or a message in a dream. Or the issue may resolve itself, without any seeming effort on my part! However, though my ancestors may occasionally swoop in and solve my problems, they like to see me develop and grow. So, I am always ready to put in the work, both magical and mundane.

One of the most common questions about ancestral work is where to start. The first step is easy: If you have a household altar, make a place for them there. If not, set aside a small area where you can arrange some photos and a candle. If you don't know who your ancestors were, you are not excluded from this party! Replace the photos with a framed art print that says "Family" or a piece of paper on which you have written "my ancestry." Feel free to include people who have strongly influenced or cared for you but who are not related by blood, like Cousin Twinkie. The concept of family is a broad one and should spread far and wide and throughout your community. Once you start to connect with your ancestors, you might find yourself drawn to genealogy so that you can start finding out more. Or you may find out that one of your relatives has traced the whole family tree. If you are adopted, you can reach out to the ancestry of your adopted family in whatever way you feel most connected. Family is family and that doesn't change even in the world beyond this one.

Once you have created a sacred space for your ancestors, they will start making themselves known to you. That is all it takes because they have been there all along, watching over your shoulder and giving you advice. The only difference is that now you will actively be listening for it. As your conscious relationship with them grows, you will start to get ideas about how to honor them with gifts of water, food, or things that they enjoyed while they were alive. You may feel moved to add statues of saints or other entities or flowers or any number of decorations. Follow your intuition.

If you establish contact with an ancestor that makes you uncomfortable or that seems negative, never fear. Your other ancestors will rush to your aid and help the troublemaker move on. Focus your efforts and attention on those that wholeheartedly support you. They will perpetually be on your side, and they have your best interests at heart. They will help guide you in your earthly and spiritual development.

Working with Saints

When I need something that falls under the purview of one of the saints I work with, I turn to them for help. My patron saint, the one I work most closely with, is Saint Expedite (also called *San Expedito* in Italian American communities). He is the patron saint of procrastinators and urgent causes. Patron saints are known for helping people living in a place (like a city or country; for example, St. Anthony of Padua), performing an activity (like a hobby or profession, like how St. Andrew is the patron saint of those who fish), or born on the saint's feast day (a day the Church has picked to honor them, like how St. Sylvester is honored on New Year's Eve). Patronages are assigned to saints based on their life stories. You can find out information about saints by doing some research online or consulting a book like Butler's *Lives of the Saints*.

Though I am not much of a procrastinator, I have built a relationship with Saint Expedite because he is also the patron of getting things done quickly, and because he entered my life in a way that could not be ignored. While I was living overseas, I wanted to move back to the United States with my partner. He was an Australian citizen, and we had a lot of paperwork and red tape to manage to get permission for him to stay in the US. On one of our several trips to Sydney to visit the US Consulate, we stopped by St. Mary's Cathedral. There was a table located in the entryway, covered with pamphlets about the building. On one corner of the table, I saw a small stack of prayer cards. I picked one up and was shocked to see an image of Saint Expedite. It was printed on flimsy paper and cut out by hand. I instantly realized what I was holding. Saint Expedite had helped someone, and in return, they were publicly thanking him by printing and distributing his cards. The cards are left in public places with the hope that they will be seen and taken home, encouraging others to build a relationship with the saint. This is a typical way of working with the saints. When you ask them to intercede on your behalf, you also promise to do something when you receive what you have asked for. I often promise public thanks to the saint, like the homemade saint cards I found in the cathedral. If you have ever seen a classified message that reads "Thanks to Saint Jude for prayers answered," you have seen the public thanking of a saint. Other traditional ways to thank a saint include donations to shrines or charities, praying to them regularly, or giving the saint gifts like fresh flowers.

As we took the train back home, I thought about Saint Expedite. Despite his importance to the Italian American community, I had never worked with him before. I knew he was the patron of getting things done quickly, so when I got home, I created a small altar for him. I put the prayer card I took from the cathedral on a table and burned a red candle in front of it. I prayed to him and asked him for help with the immigration process. From that point on, we didn't have any delays in completing the immigration paperwork. In fact, we managed to submit everything we needed just in time to take advantage of a law that was soon to be changed, but which allowed us to complete the process in three months instead of five to nine months. It wasn't until later that I realized I had found Saint Expedite's prayer card and started praying to him on April 19, which was his feast day. Since then, I have considered him my patron saint, and I have worked to build a relationship with him. He is not the only saint I interact with, but he is one of the few whose statue stays on my altar all the time. And he is certainly the saint I turn to in times of great need.

I feel it is important to mention that you are not required to be Catholic to work with the saints. If you feel drawn to the practice, you should experiment with it to find out if it works for you. To get started, find out about their histories. Eventually you will feel drawn to one or more based on their story or appearance, or maybe even something that you can't fully articulate. Once you know who you want to work with, get an image of the saint and start building a relationship with them. Learn more about their history and patronages, and learn some prayers that are associated with them. If you need to tweak the language of the prayers to feel comfortable using them, do so! If you want to burn candles in front of your saint's image, white is always appropriate. Or you can choose a candle color based on the color of the saint's clothing.

Here is a short overview of a few popular saints and their patronages.

- **St. Anthony** is the saint of lost items. The next time you lose something, pray to him for help finding it. You can pray from your heart, or you can say, "Saint Anthony, please come around. Something is lost and can't be found."
- **Mary, Untier of Knots** is one of my favorite names for the Virgin Mary. She is the patron of marital conflicts and can help with resolving them but also assists with solving any difficult or impossible problems. Prayer is the key to working with

her, so pray the Hail Mary while meditating on a picture of her serenely unknotting the difficulties of the world.

- **St. Mary Magdalene** is the patron saint of women and can be called upon for assistance with any problem that a woman may experience. She is also known as the patron of those who are penitent of their sins or who struggle against temptation. She is an understanding listener and a saint of great practicality. Burn red candles while you tell her your problems and ask for her help.
- **St. Roch** (Italian Americans call him **St. Rocco**) is the patron saint of bachelors and dogs. He protects people from epidemics and other illnesses, so call on him when someone needs healing. He is often depicted with a dog that is bringing him a loaf of bread. When you work with him, promise him bread if he comes through for you.

Once you have started working with a saint, it is important to watch and listen for their guidance. You will need to listen to and trust your intuition to do so, but be prepared to receive hints and nudges that will help you stay on the right path in life. Sometimes the messages can come through loud and clear, through dreams or during meditation. Other times, you may see a color or item significant to the saint to let you know you are on the right path.

To ask for help, write what you need on a piece of paper. It doesn't have to be fancy, but it does have to be clear. Leave the paper in front of the saint's image, light a candle, and ask for what you need. Burn candles in front of the image until you have what you have asked for. Then find a way to thank the saint. You can give the saint gifts like flowers or water, contribute to charity, or publicly thank the saint by posting a thank you on a message board dedicated to the saint or distributing their prayer cards. Feel free to be creative with how you give thanks. As part of my effort to publicly thank Saint Expedite, I teach classes about him so that others can learn about how to work with him.

When working with the saints, it is best to be consistent, ask for what you really need, and to avoid asking for anything that might harm yourself or anyone else. However, feel free to ask for protection or the prevention of harm.

Dealing with *Malocchio* (Evil Eye)

As I was growing up, *malocchio* was a perpetual concern. Got a headache? Stomach upset? Feel like things just aren't quite right? You probably have "the eyes" on you. The basic concept of *malocchio* is that people—wittingly or unwittingly—beam disruptive influences at you when they look at you with envy. The influences can do anything from afflict you with symptoms, cause you to lose or break things, or cause all kinds of delays and mishaps in your personal life, and that's just to name a few! Upon closer investigation of this apparently simple concept, it unfolds into a complex and ancient belief system stretching back all the way to 700 BCE.[62]

Most of the general protection magic I have learned is associated with preventing *malocchio*. Throughout my life, I have discovered that these specific protective practices do an amazing job of keeping me safe from all kinds of harm—*malocchio* itself, general bad luck, and purposeful psychic attack.

One anti-*malocchio* charm has become increasingly popular since witchcraft author Raven Grimassi wrote and spoke about it. It is called the *cimaruta* ("top of the rue").[63] These pendants are usually cast in sterling silver and depict a twisting branch of rue upon which is hung an assortment of protective charms such as a toad, a dagger, a sacred heart, a fish, and a rooster. Though the symbol itself was not used in our household, the idea of wearing a grouping of charms for protective purposes and warding off *malocchio* is something very familiar. Try out the following method to construct your own protective charm bundle.

Charm Bundle for Protection

There are two different ways to wear these charm bundles: pinned inside your clothes or on a long chain around your neck. Either way, no one should be able to see the bundle while you are wearing it. If you choose to wear it on a chain, select one that is long enough to allow the group of charms to be tucked inside your shirt. I prefer using a safety pin to pin it to my bra strap. You can also choose to pin it on the inside of your waistband or the inside of one of your pockets. You might even want to try pinning one to the inside of your purse or backpack if you carry one. When the bundle is not being worn, it should be kept in a special place such as a jewelry dish on your bedside table or in front of a statue of a God/Goddess/entity that is significant to you. You can make this bundle for yourself or for someone else. The instructions here are written as if you are making it for yourself.

Plan to use three, five, seven, or nine charms. (Depending on the size of the charms, the bundle can get bulky, so keep that in mind.) An odd number of charms is used because odd numbers represent mobility and change, so the charm will be lively and capable of combatting *malocchio* at every turn.

1. Select your method for wearing the charm bundle. Find a chain or pin that suits your method.

62. Hand, "The Evil Eye in its Folk Medical Aspects," 170.
63. Grimassi, *The Cimaruta and Other Magical Charms from Old Italy*, "The Cimaruta."

2. Gather the protective charms you want to include in the charm bundle. You can use anything that speaks to you of protection or other good intentions: a protective symbol like a *cornicello* ("little horn," a traditional Italian protective charm), a charm with a precious stone with protective properties, a saint medal, or (if you are using a safety pin) a small black or red ribbon.
3. Once you have collected the items you need, find a quiet place to work. You can do this work nearly anywhere. If you have a household altar, you can do it there. Or you can sit comfortably in a chair or on your bed.
4. Take some deep breaths to calm your mind. Once you feel ready, focus on what you intend the charm to do. See it happening. I usually picture the charm protecting me on all levels—spiritual, mental, and physical.
5. When you feel ready, thread each charm onto the pin or necklace one at a time. As you do, state why you chose each charm. For example, "This jade is to give me long life. This St. Christopher medal is to keep me safe while I travel. This *cornuto* is to protect me from the evil eye."
6. Once you have threaded all the charms on, hold the bundle in your hand and again visualize yourself surrounded by peace and protection.
7. If you choose to, you can ask a particular entity (like a saint or angel) to bless the bundle and maintain its efficacy.
8. Wear the bundle daily, especially if you leave the house. When you are not wearing it, keep it in the special place you have chosen.

Advice from Mom and Grandma

I learned the ethics of our family practice by observation and extrapolation. My grandmother only explicitly told me one rule: to always tell the truth while performing divination. She said it wasn't fair to hold back or change what I saw. I have followed this rule throughout my life, both when reading professionally and for loved ones. Though it has not always been the easiest rule to follow, finding ways to deliver difficult messages has pushed me to pay attention to how divination is handled and helped me see how a reader can choose where to put the locus of control when doing a reading. There is a large difference between telling someone "That plan isn't going to work," as though the future is set in stone and the situation is hopeless, and asking them, "That plan isn't going to work out, but the following options will get you where you want to go. Which one appeals to you?" The first method strips the client of their agency, and the second strengthens it.

The other, implied rules I've learned from my family are as follows:

1. Before specific work is done, take it to the ancestors or the saints. Their intervention usually provides the easiest solution with the best outcome.
2. Most of the work you do should be for the good of yourself and those around you. Working against others is not forbidden; it is only accepted in the direst of circumstances, usually when the well-being of loved ones is on the line.
3. Purity of heart and intention are the two best tools you have. Make sure you wholeheartedly desire what you are seeking when you are planning and performing your work or asking ancestors or saints for assistance.

Be honest with yourself and others, trust in your ancestors and the saints, and realize that the magic you do ripples out from you, changing and assisting your family, your home, and your community.

Magical Tools at Your Fingertips

One of the best parts of getting started in Italian American folk magic is the simplicity and ubiquity of some of its tools. If you want to start building a magical tool kit, you likely will find that much of what you need is already in your home. The following are just a few examples of the supplies we use.

- **Salt** is used for banishing and cleansing as well as casting your influence upon an area. Thrown under your doormat, it will keep unwanted guests at bay. If you want to change the atmosphere of your house, tell a handful of salt what you want it to do and scatter it around your dwelling. For example, I could take a handful and say, "Salt, lighten up the mood in my home. Bring in good cheer!" Then I would visualize the end result before scattering the salt around.
- **Colored string or ribbon** make easy protective charms. Red ribbons will protect any item they are tied to. Wearing a black string will keep you safe from the evil eye (in general, wearing any kind of black is considered protection).
- **A supply of nice paper and a pen you like to write with** will come in handy when writing requests to your ancestors or saints.

Some common herbs can help round out your supplies.

- Smoke from **bay leaves** will drive unwanted influences from your home. Set the dried leaf on fire, blow it out, and waft the smoke around your home. Carry a saucer to catch the hot embers.
- **Garlic** will protect and purify any area. You can carry a clove of unpeeled garlic as a protective talisman, or you can grow garlic in your yard to keep negativity away.
- A sprinkle of **oregano** in your wallet or purse will draw money.

As you can see, it is likely that you have magical tools that you didn't even know about scattered all over your house! They are waiting for you to pick them up to make some magic, because magic is in everything that surrounds us, and it permeates every fiber of our being. It is the life force rushing through us and the gentle breeze that caresses us, it is in the warmth of the fertile earth under our feet, and it is the fuel for the dreams that inspire us to reach dizzying heights. All of us are magicians—or witches, if you prefer—just by the very nature of being born on this planet. Consciously or unconsciously, we channel our energy along with our efforts to make our dreams come true. It is my sincere hope that what I have written here helps you see the magic in the simple things around you so that you can pick them up and wield the power that is inherent in you.

Interested in Learning More?

If you come from an Italian American background, or if there is an Italian American community near you, you can start with talking to the people around you. Avoid the terms "magic" or "witchcraft," and instead ask questions about how things were done. "Did Grandpa do anything to make sure the house was safe from storms?" is the type of question that can yield interesting responses.

Try the "give something to get something" approach. Mention a folk magic practice of your own and see if they do anything that is similar. If you are talking to people outside of your family, realize that it might take some time to build rapport with them before they are ready to share their traditions with you. They don't want to appear backward or silly, and they don't know what background or perspective you are coming from. Pulling out a notebook or otherwise attempting to record the conversation might make some people nervous, so work up to asking for a formal interview, if you're up to doing that kind of work.

As for books, there are a handful of popular books that address the topic from a practitioner's perspective, and there are some useful academic sources. They can be found in the further reading section at the end of this section and in the bibliography at the back of the book. I have recommended books on both Italian American practices and Italian practices because I feel that information on Italian magic informs and provides background for what we do here in the United States.

I hope you, too, will come to love Italian American folk magic as I have, and find your way "back home."

FIELD NOTES

The Big (Charmed) Apple

Cities have their own magical feel, and each city is uniquely different, of course. The way that Boston does folk magic and witchcraft, with its legacies from nearby Salem and its Irish and Italian populations, is going to feel a little different than the way Chicago does folk magic, with its strong Central and Eastern European influences and the immense impact that the Great Migration of African Americans had on it.

New York City, too, is entirely unique and offers a massive number of ways to manifest magic for anyone who wants to practice. For example, the city is home to a large Jewish American population, which ranges from ultra-Orthodox to progressive Reform practices. Among Jewish practitioners, one might find all sorts of folk magic, including the use of *tichels* (ritual head coverings), especially when performing any spiritual action like lighting Shabbat candles.[64] They might also incorporate *segulot*, or personal protective amulets. These might include amulets made of coral designed to protect children against the evil eye or the folk demonic figure of Lilith, a list of angelic names, or a longer letter-like text written in Hebrew and sealed with the *Magen David* (Star or Shield of David). The use of thread worn on a person's body, or even wrapped around graves, is another form of protective charm in Jewish practice (and one that gained some notoriety when celebrities like Madonna began wearing them while connected with a modern Kabbalah group).[65]

Other groups also practice a number of folkways within the city. Catholic communities, often ethnically aligned with Spanish/Latinx, Polish, Irish, and Italian groups, have many folk spiritual rituals, involving evil eye charms (like little amulets of a pair of horns, or a hand making horns with its fingers) or body parts cast in wax or metal that are offered to saints to seek aid for specific ailments. The use of holy water and candles is common as well (and not limited to Catholic practitioners, as many Eastern Orthodox people also used them). Huge festivals are also used to honor particular saints and parade their images through the streets while providing a sort of "pop-up" market for charms, saint cards, and other folk magical items. And of course, many of these groups wove practices in and out of each other. One account tells of a huge Catholic festival for the Madonna of Carmel on 115th Street in the 1920s at which "an old Jewish man wandered through the crowd with a Yiddish-speaking white parrot on his arm; the parrot had been taught to say in Italian, 'Come Italians,' and predicted fortunes by drawing cards from a deck."[66]

Today, New York is host to dozens of candle shops and botanicas that cater to the spiritual folk communities around them, providing candles, charms, and more for the urban folk magician.

64. Z, "A Short History of Tichels and the Modern Resurgence."

65. Trachtenberg, *Jewish Magic and Superstition*, 133–35.

66. Orsi, *The Madonna of 115th Street.*

The Power of Faith in Action: Pennsylvania German Powwow

ROBERT PHOENIX

Growing up in Pennsylvania with rural German-speaking grandparents who were members of the Reformed church was an amazing experience. From them I learned a love and appreciation for both my family history and our religious beliefs and traditions, alongside a deep-rooted respect for our cultural ways. Everything from my grandmother's kitchen-side garden tomatoes to my grandfather's work ethic has both colored my upbringing and helped make me the man that I am today.

When I first began exploring folk magic in the late 1980s, I was young, and I didn't have a teacher to set me on a direct path. Like most seekers, I read as much as I could on various folk magic traditions and alternative religions. Over time and through various forays into differing traditions and practices, I found my way into the Pennsylvania homegrown tradition of Powwow. I soon realized that this was the most religiously and culturally appropriate path for me and, to this day, it remains the most personal and powerful means of connecting me to both my family history and the cultural and religious foundation from which I came.

Powwow is a simple tradition of faith healing that is empowered by my personal relationship with Christ. It is a means for me to bring the healing power of Jesus into the world while still holding fast to the inherent religious values of Pennsylvania German folk Christianity. In other words, the Christianity *of the folk*, which varies by region and culture. It is a cultural translation of Christianity that allows for tradition such as Powwow to come into creation alongside and within the practice of the local church that satisfies the cultural and spiritual needs of the people. Pennsylvania German Powwow is, by its very nature, a less rigid and ritualistic tradition by comparison to some of our more modern folk magic and New Age brothers and sisters. Indeed, the word "magic" is often frowned upon by practitioners of Powwow in favor of a more reserved definition of "faith in action."

Bits and Bobs and Belief: The Basics of Powwow

Powwow requires very few tools or props. Your faith in Christ is your strongest asset in Powwow. A Bible might be your constant companion, as it is for me. In addition, some bits of string, a few stones you find on the ground, and even some coins you have in your pocket can serve as your most powerful allies in your healing work.

To be a Powwow is to manifest the healing power of Jesus in the world. It is to give others the gift of your faith so that they may be well. It is a simplistic tradition in that it largely requires nothing more than the recitation of a spoken charm while making a few gestures over the person in need of healing. If you think of Powwowing as *active prayer*, then you have a good understanding of what the tradition is.

It is often stated that Powwow is not for everyone, and I would agree. In order to effectively practice the tradition, one must have unshakable faith in the Holy Trinity, which is no easy thing in this day and age. This prerequisite demands that one has absolute belief in the Christian worldview. In addition, some folks in the culture believe that one must also be of Pennsylvania German descent. Pennsylvania German culture is diverse, with descendants from Switzerland, Austria, France, Germany, Bulgaria, and other German-speaking cultures that came to Pennsylvania and merged with the existing communities. We are a unique culture not found anywhere else in the United States. Personally, I do not believe that one must be of the culture to become a Powwow.

I have also come across a few other somewhat-obscure requirements that include being over the age of thirty-five, having been taught Powwow by a member of the opposite sex, and even being born the seventh son of a seventh son. It's a rather common method of learning Powwow to be taught cross-gender (male to female). I've had a few teachers of Powwow over the years, mostly female, but also a few that were male.

But in all seriousness, all one really needs to become successful at Powwowing is a desire to do so with an understanding that you are carrying on a very specific cultural tradition, and therefore are willing to respect that culture within your practice. And that means adhering to the religious foundations of the tradition, as I stated earlier. Powwow is historically, culturally, and religiously a Christian tradition based on a Christian worldview. Modern interpretations based on Neopaganism are not accurate to the culture from which Powwow originated.

Who Is a Powwow and What Do They Do?

Powwow is a solitary practice. If you can imagine a desperate mother visiting the local recluse Powwower late in the night, begging for them to heal her colic-fussing baby, then you have an idea of what Powwowing is like. It is a practice that is used on an as-needed basis. In other words, a Powwow is a regular person who just so happens to use their faith in God to bring healing when and where it is needed most.

Throughout history, Powwows have often lived on the fringes of society, enjoying a reputation of both respect and fear. I believe this is the by-product of both the mysterious nature of faith healing as well as the result of intentionally withdrawing from society for both privacy and Godly purposes, which is so common within the Powwow tradition. In my experience, too much stimulation from the outside world can cause me to lose focus on my spirituality, which is the very foundation of my healing skills. I imagine it was much the same for my cultural predecessors.

A majority of the work of Powwow is, as mentioned earlier, healing. However, we do not limit ourselves to just works of faith medicine. In fact, it's been my experience that clients are more likely to seek some form of protection against an unseen enemy or force. A look at some of the source materials for the tradition will reveal that at least some of the Powwow's work was devoted to protection against malevolent witchcraft, which is in keeping with early Pennsylvania German settlers' beliefs about forces they did not fully understand.

In addition to protection from witchcraft, handmade charms made of paper or metal in the form of *himmelsbriefs*, or talismans, were not uncommon. *Himmelsbrief* translates as "letter from Heaven," which is a letter written by a Powwow that allegedly carries the power of God within it; it is most often used to protect the bearer from harm. I've personally made many talismans out of silver and iron over the years that were designed to attract various forces into the bearer's life while also making herbal charms, or *brauch bags*, to protect from negative energies or attract specific blessings. A *brauch bag* is a cloth pouch filled with specific herbs and paper charms and/or metal talismans designed to protect or attract specific energies. The word *brauch* comes from the German word for Powwow, *Braucherei*, meaning "to use." Powwowing is a diverse tradition in this regard.

Some Powwows, such as myself, are schooled in astrological studies. This knowledge aids us in both agricultural pursuits (proper planting and harvesting times) as well as magical work (the timing of talismanic creation, etc.). Indeed, astrology plays a huge role in my personal work and I regularly consult my ephemeris or gardening almanac when I'm planning to make herbal salves and other home remedies.

Gardening, farming, herbal remedies, and the like can also play a role in Powwow. We seek to live in harmony with our land, as God intended, and to use plants as both food and medicine. We cultivate these natural gifts to help heal ourselves and others who come to us. If you've never experienced the mystery and spirituality of planting your own herbs and vegetables, tending to them as they grow, and harvesting them when they are at their peak, then I urge you to give it a try. My connection to my land only adds to my faith, and these things make my Powwow much more effective.

There have been times when a client has come to me with a mysterious condition that they could not determine the root of. In these situations, I may do a card reading for them to help unveil more questions that lead to a better understanding of what is going on. I prefer to use an old deck of playing cards. I was taught many years ago to diagnose a client using playing cards, and my readings are always spot-on.

The idea behind reading playing cards is rather simple: The cards are shuffled by the client seeking the information. Then the reader begins throwing out the cards, faceup, on the table. As each card is laid out, the reader prays (whether silently or out loud) for guidance from God. One by one, the cards are laid out on the table, sometimes in three or four rows, sometimes in a haphazard pile, while the reader receives the needed wisdom from God and imparts this to the client.

It can be somewhat unnerving for a client the first time they experience such a reading. The method calls for the reader to go into a nearly trancelike state of meditative connecting with God in order to receive the most useful information for the client.

When all cards are laid out on the table, the reading is ended, and no further information will be provided to the client.[67]

It is often stated in folk magic that the items you use should be of the everyday variety, meaning no object other than your Bible should be viewed as sacred. Coins used to rub away warts should be of the common type found loose in your pocket or purse, and they should be spent when you are finished using them for Powwow. Stones for relieving pain are to be picked up off the ground as needed and discarded in running water such as streams or rivers after your work is complete. Cards for divinatory purposes should also be used to play games such as gin rummy or bridge. In other words, nothing used in Powwow should be kept solely for such purposes. All objects can and should be a part of your everyday life. This, in my opinion, builds a familiarity with the object and can therefore make it more trusted in the eyes and mind of your client. It also keeps the sacredness of your work in God's hands, rather than your own. If we begin to assign a sacred value to everyday objects, I believe we overstep ourselves and take power away from God, in a manner of speaking.

"On Earth as It Is in Heaven": Keys to Powwow

The real key to understanding the power behind Powwow is your faith in the Holy Trinity. Powwow is an extension of your Christian faith. It is the next step of your religious tradition in that it allows us to manifest the power of Christ in the physical world. It follows the biblical teaching of "on earth as it is in Heaven." In other words, if we can pray for it, we can help manifest it in the material world. We need not purposely attempt to direct any form of energy or force any sort of power toward our work. When a client comes to us for healing, we simply recite the appropriate healing charm with full confidence that God will manifest the healing. It really is that simple.

67. If you wish to learn more about this card-reading method, visit my blog page at www.pagermanpowwow.com.

Some of the most common Powwow source works include *The Long-Lost Friend*, written in 1820 by John George Hohman, a German immigrant who settled in southeastern Pennsylvania; *Egyptian Secrets of Albertus Magnus*, written by an unknown author in the 1700s in Germany and reprinted in Allentown, Pennsylvania in 1869; and the *Romanus-Buchlein*, dated around 1788 in Germany, which was the foremost inspiration for John George Hohman's work.

One of the most well-known Powwow charms for healing is the removal of warts or lesions using a coin. The coin is rubbed on the blemish while reciting something along the lines of: "What I see is growing, what I rub is going. In the name of the Father, Son, and Holy Ghost." The coin is then given to the client with the instruction to spend it right away.

A variant of this charm utilizes a potato cut in halves. The wart is rubbed with the potato half while reciting the above words. The two halves are then tied together, and the bundle is buried at the corner of your property.

A general protective talisman used frequently in the Powwow tradition is known as the SATOR square. This is a series of letters that are arranged in such a way as to read the same both forward and backward. The earliest uses of this charm were believed to occur during the first days of Christianity, when it was illegal for the followers of the "Christ cult" to gather. The SATOR square was said to have been marked on the outside of meeting places so believers knew it was safe to gather there. An example of the SATOR square was found in the ruins of Pompeii.[68]

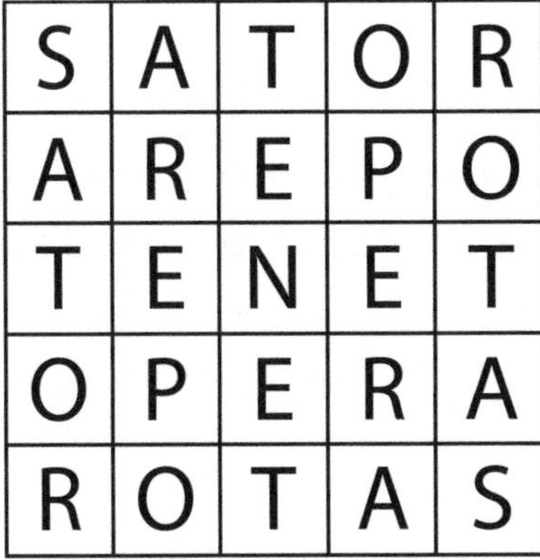

S	A	T	O	R
A	R	E	P	O
T	E	N	E	T
O	P	E	R	A
R	O	T	A	S

Figure 2-1: SATOR Square

The letters of the square are believed to represent a scrambled version of the words PATER NOSTER, which is Latin for "Our Father," a popular Christian reference to God and also a very popular Christian prayer. The square is used as a protective talisman in Powwow and can be

68. Mitchell, "The SATOR Square."

etched on any material or drawn on paper to offer protection against negative entities, energies, or occurrences (such as accidents) when carried.

String is sometimes used to "tie off" an illness. The client is seated in a chair facing east, the direction of sunrise, while the Powwow takes the measure of the client by measuring from head to toe, the length of the left arm from shoulder to tip of middle finger, the length of the left foot, and the measure of the head. Knots are tied to mark each measure. The string is then burned to remove the malady.

The Bible can be used to remove illness or evil from a client by using it to "sweep" the body from head to toe. With the client seated in a chair facing east, the Powwow would sweep the Bible from the head to the foot of the client, as if wiping away the influence, while reciting the following:

> *This water and this fire* [one sweep downward]
> *This water and this fire* [a second sweep downward]
> *This water and this fire* [a third sweep downward]
> *This is a good thing* [touch client's forehead with the Bible]

Repeat the above for a total of three times. After the third repetition, slap the Bible once on the floor to release the influence into the ground while saying, "In the name of God the Father, God the Son, and God the Holy Ghost."

"A Powwow on Every Street Corner": Celebrating the Powwow Tradition

For me, Powwow is how I celebrate my spirituality. It is the work that I feel called by God to do in this lifetime. Rather than devoting myself to a particular church or weekly worship service, I use my connection to God to bring healing and peace of mind to those who request it. I can think of no purer expression of faith than to use it to bring at least a little good into the world.

The tradition of Powwow was once extremely common amongst the Pennsylvania Germans. As J. Ross McGinnis states in the 2015 documentary *Hex Hollow*, at one time in Pennsylvania there was "a Powwow on every street corner."[69] Nowadays, Powwow is less common but still well-known and well respected. In fact, there is a resurgence of interest in preserving traditional Pennsylvania German Powwow, and a number of younger practitioners have begun training in

69. Free, *Hex Hollow*.

the older traditions. The danger of Powwow passing into the realm of obscurity is not as grave as we once thought it was, thanks to the work of those of us who help keep the tradition alive.

Pennsylvania is my home. It is where my ancestors immigrated to from Austria and Germany in an effort to find religious freedom and economic opportunity. It is where my family built their homes and their lives and their churches and where I was born and raised. It is fitting that my spiritual and magical life is aligned so directly with the land my family is closely tied to. I cannot imagine a practice more appropriate than Powwow for a Pennsylvania German son such as myself.

May God bless you in all that you do.

FIELD NOTES

The Magic of the Chain Letter

If you've ever been annoyed by an uncle forwarding you an email claiming that copying and pasting it and sending it along to ten friends will bring you good luck (but failing to do so will result in some vague, ominous, and terrible fate like being eaten by Chihuahuas), you've actually been handed a digital artifact of a very old folk magic tradition!

In the Pennsylvania Dutch area, the use of the *himmelsbrief*, or "heaven letter," goes back centuries. These were literally thought to be letters dropped down from heaven, often inscribed in elaborate calligraphy and promising that those in possession of the letter would be protected from harm—especially fire and violence. Some also promised luck and good fortune for sharing the letter and intimated that failing to do so might (just like your uncle claimed) get you nibbled by various house pets. (Well, they weren't quite *that* specific.)

One of the best-known examples of this is the Koenigsberg Letter of 1714, which read:

> I command thee, fire, by the power of God, that thou wouldst allay the flames, as true as Mary remaineth so chaste and pure; for this cease thy rage, oh terrible fire. This I count to thee, oh fire, for ransom's sake in the name of the Holy Trinity. I command thee, fire, thou wouldst thy violent heat allay, for the blood which he shed for our sins and his death. All this I accept as a ransom for thy sake, in the name of God the Father, the Son, and Holy Ghost. Jesus Nazarenus, King of the Jews, help us out of these dangers of fire, and protect this land and its borders from all epidemics and from pestilence. Whoever keeps this letter in his house, he will not suffer from conflagrations, and if any pregnant woman carries this letter on her person, no sorcery, apparition, or witchcraft can harm her. Also everyone who keeps this letter at home or carries the same on his person will be secure from dire epidemics and pestilence.[70]

While the history of these letters goes back centuries, possibly even as far back as the latter days of Ancient Rome, sharing these letters became much more common as the postal service became standardized—and of course, Philadelphia is the home of the first federal post office in the United States.

Over time, these letters began to take on new elements, including stories of those who either shared the letters and found unbelievable rewards or those who didn't share them and…well… Chihuahuas. In the internet age, email became the new means of transmitting both the stories

70. Bilardi, *The Red Church or the Art of Pennsylvania German Braucherei*, 311–12.

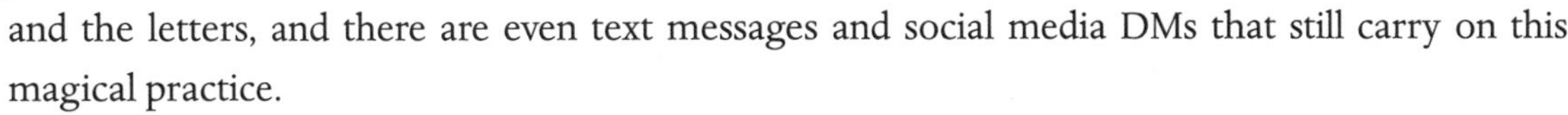

and the letters, and there are even text messages and social media DMs that still carry on this magical practice.

So, if you want to try out a slightly obnoxious but definitely pedigreed form of folk magic, you could always send along a chain letter or email. Or text message. Or just skip the hassle and attach a note to a Chihuahua before leaving it on your neighbor's doorstep.

A Heathen History:
Braucherei in the Urglaawe Context

ROBERT L. SCHREIWER

Long the front line of folk medicine for the *Deitsch* (Pennsylvania Dutch) people, Braucherei is pre-Christian at its core and features overlays from Gnostic, Judeo-Christian, and Lenape traditions. The heirloom healing Deitsch practice of Braucherei (also called Powwow in English) and the related magical practice of Hexerei serve as tremendous folk resources for the Heathen denomination of Urglaawe.

Practitioner communities retained a large volume of oral lore in the form of myths, "superstitions," charms, etc. The Urglaawe movement, which I founded in November 2007, arose from these living Heathen traditions as well as from the wider Deitsch folk religion. Urglaawe features the Heathen elements still living within the Deitsch culture, drawing much of its knowledge from Braucherei and Hexerei lore.

The Urglaawe community is now working to make this knowledge more accessible to the Urglaawe community inside and outside of the *Deitscherei*, the noncontiguous areas in multiple states and provinces that form Pennsylvania Dutch Country.

While there are plenty of writings on the topics of Braucherei in the past, there is a significant amount of oral lore that I have collected over the past fourteen years. I am sharing some of this information here for the first time. Subjects include not only the healing and magical practices, but also historical perspectives that are unique to the Deitsch culture. In some cases, the Braucherei masters' or mentors' lore was passed on by their apprentices, thus becoming part of regional iterations of the oral tradition.

Definitions and Terminology

One of the biggest challenges in defining Braucherei and Hexerei stems from the fact that there is no central authority making the determination between the two. Indeed, depending on where one is located in the Deitscherei, the terms refer to distinct yet related practices, or one term or the other is used for the whole of the practices. For simplicity in description, some people have referred to Braucherei as "white magic" and to Hexerei as "black magic," but neither of these terms is accurate, and each is inappropriate for the Urglaawe context because often magic for "good" purposes still takes place at the expense of another being or idea. For example, if I use Braucherei to heal a client of ringworm, it appears to the client as though I am doing a "good" work. However, from the ringworm's perspective, I am most definitely doing harm.

For the sake of this writing, the term *Braucherei* is being used to describe the traditional healing practice, often called Powwow in English, as identified through much of southeastern Pennsylvania. This is the more socially acceptable and well-documented of the two practices. It is generally seen as beneficial to the client or to the community.

Although I shudder to have to draw this separation, I use the term *Hexerei* in this writing to describe the magical and healing practices of the more remote areas of the Deitscherei. These are often the traditions of the poorer and more marginalized segments of the Deitsch society. In many cases, Hexerei is equated with evil and magic that serves the self, though this is an incomplete and very biased perspective. Perhaps the largest difference is that more Hexerei practitioners retained old ways that were consistent with the elder lore from Europe—with less of the Christian overlay, which is likely why they were branded Satanists by the Christian establishment. It is important to note that anything that can be done in Braucherei can also be done in Hexerei and vice versa.

Der Urglaawe, simply called Urglaawe in this writing, is a modern expression of the ancient Germanic religion as seen through the lens of the modern Deitsch, or Pennsylvania Dutch, culture.

Where I grew up in Berks County, Pennsylvania, the two practices were viewed as two sides of the same coin, with Braucherei being "of God" and Hexerei being "of the creature," or evil. Throughout the course of my lifetime, I have lived in other parts of the Deitscherei and have experienced the old-world elements of Hexerei that are more common in the remote areas of the Deitscherei in central and western Pennsylvania, parts of Maryland, Virginia, and West Virginia. Many of the practitioners in this region were referring to their actions as Hexerei when they were performing the functions that would be called Braucherei in other parts of the Deitscherei. Their practice was often more holistic, though, because it lacked the Christian dualism that is so common in the well-described practice of Powwow in eastern Pennsylvania.

In 2008, when I started my own Braucherei training in the Three Sisters Center for Healing Arts, I was already looking at the practice alongside Hexerei from a more holistic perspective. My mentor, Jesse Tobin, had done extensive research into the history and lore of Braucherei, and her instruction included many of the things that hardcore Christian Brauchers will deny exist, such as the fact that many Brauchers continue to practice in syncretic contexts that feature a multiverse cosmology, and that some of the old deities continue to be called by name in workings. Frequently, the practitioner does not recognize the being as a deity but lists them among the saints or helpful entities that can assist them or their clients in healing or achieving goals. Tobin published some of her findings in the Center's quarterly publication *Hollerbeier Haven*, which is currently known as *Hollerbeer Hof*.[71]

Similarly, many self-described practitioners of Hexerei have been left out of (or avoided completely) the academic discussions about their traditions due to a fear of being labeled as evil or Satanists by the mainstream Deitsch establishment. Indeed, there is some historical basis for this fear, stemming from attempts to disrupt the culture, particularly during the interwar period of the 1920s and '30s. Additionally, many Deitsch people have refrained from sharing information outside of the culture due to stereotypes of the Pennsylvania Dutch being backward or superstitious.[72] As we shall see, the "Dumb Dutchman" portrayal played a role in weakening our culture, including the healing practices, well into my lifetime.

Although Pennsylvania Dutch history is described in many books, the historical locations, actions, and influences of the Palatine settlers are often overlooked, even by present-day Deitsch scholars. This is to our own detriment because we Pennsylvania Dutch have always had our ways. The exploration of our lore, whether written or oral, can deepen the understanding of our culture, including our magical and healing practices.

A Brief Pennsylvania Dutch History

Throughout much of Pennsylvania history from the Colonial era, the "Palatine Boors"—as Benjamin Franklin referred to the earliest Deitsch forebears—pursued their own interests and established their own institutions.[73] They were welcomed by William Penn, caught up in the confusion of the Maryland-Pennsylvania border disputes, and carried on their own relations with the Native Americans, including an oral tradition claim that "When the Conestoga abandoned their lands west of the Susquehanna, they did not do so to the government of Pennsylvania or even to their brethren in the Iroquois Confederacy. They left the land to the Palatine settlers who lived freely among the Conestoga. It was not the Confederacy's land to sell or Pennsylvania's land to buy."[74]

In the early 1600s, the Dutch and other explorers and settlers first encountered the Lenape. It is noted that early on, the Lenni Lenape were considered by other tribes to be the "grandfathers." However, by the 1640s, the Lenape were referring to the Conestogas, who are better known in English as the Susquehannocks, as their "uncles," and were, by 1645, "subject and tributary" to them.[75] This is likely due to a war that took place between the Lenape and the Susquehannocks circa 1630

71. All issues of *Hollerbeier Haven* and *Hollerbeer Hof* are available as free downloads on www.braucherei.org.

72. Shyrock, "The Pennsylvania Germans in American History," 262–63, 268.

73. Franklin, "Observations Concerning the Increase of Mankind."

74. "Edna C.," personal communication, October 2013.

75. Jennings, "Glory, Death, and Transfiguration," 19.

over access to trade with the Dutch at New Amsterdam. The Susquehannocks pressed eastward and northward, forcing more of the Lenape into what is now southern New Jersey and Delaware.

Ultimately, by 1635, the Susquehannocks had defeated the Lenape, whose numbers were also depleted by smallpox, and the relationship between the two tribes continued to evolve outside of colonial interference once the Pennsylvania Colony was established in 1681. During the 1660s, the Haudenosaunee and the Susquehannocks engaged in conflicts that ended with Susquehannock defeat in 1675.[76] However, the Susquehannocks retained land along the Susquehanna River.

By the 1730s, some Palatine Boors had settled on the Susquehannock lands, and all indicators point toward the Susquehannocks welcoming the settlers and the increased trade, which they desperately needed after the wars and smallpox epidemics had drastically reduced their numbers. Importantly, Boors were not settling on Pennsylvania or Maryland land—they settled on Susquehannock/Conestoga land.

Eventually, there were border skirmishes with the Calverts of Maryland. This series of skirmishes is known as Cresap's War (1730–1767) or the Conojocular War, which was fought primarily over the Conejohela Valley on the south bank of the Susquehanna River. The conflict arose because Maryland and Pennsylvania each had errors in their land grant charters. Maryland's charter granted land north to the fortieth parallel—roughly where the Tacony-Palmyra Bridge crosses the Delaware River—way north of Old City Philadelphia. This would have put Philadelphia into Maryland. Eventually, however, corrections resulted in Pennsylvania holding land claims deep into Maryland.

In 1724, the Crown issued a proclamation instructing the two colonies to work the problem out. The proclamation banned new migration into the area until the land had been surveyed. Neither colony ceased making new settlements; actually, each felt pressure to stake a claim before the other could get to the land. On May 10, 1729, Pennsylvania created Lancaster County, which extended well into the Calverts' claim. Maryland responded by sending land agent Thomas Cresap north into the Susquehannock land of Conejohela to build a settlement. Meanwhile, Pennsylvania Quakers settled on the east side of the Susquehanna and established the village of Wright's Ferry.

Ironically, Palatine Boors had preceded both the Quakers and the Calverts and were already present for several years on the Susquehannock lands on the west side of the river—with the Susquehannock welcoming them and actively engaging with them in trade. Thus, some Boors were already there prior to midsummer 1730, when Wright's Ferry began to carry Pennsylvania settlers to the west side of the river. As far as the Boors were concerned, they were subject to the Conejohela Susquehannock, not to Pennsylvania or Maryland.

The Boors had come through Pennsylvania primarily, although Baltimore was a port of Palatine arrival. However, they were not interested in taking sides between Pennsylvania and Maryland,

76. Wallace, "Indians in Pennsylvania," 103–4.

so they traded with all parties, including Cresap. It was at this time that the Susquehannock, who continued to suffer losses due to disease, quit the Conejohela area, moving into Conestoga or Conestoga Town, which is near present-day Millersville, Lancaster County, Pennsylvania. There was no clear Crown charter over the territory, nor clear rulings on Susquehannock territory from the Iroquois Confederacy.

Eventually, conflicts over taxes, territories, and boundaries resulted in a spiral of legal and political conflicts. When Cresap tried to cross the Susquehanna on a ferry in October 1730, some Pennsylvanians fired on it and sank the boat, although all on board managed to get to shore. Additional flare-ups—armed in many cases—led to Lord Baltimore stepping in to try and ease tensions while setting clear boundaries. Cresap and the Maryland Militia engaged in terrorist campaigns against any existing Pennsylvanian settlers as well as the Boors, with whom he also violated several land agreements.

By 1736, the Iroquois Confederacy was rising in power, and it was wooing the Pennsylvania Colonial government for more trade and interaction. As part of this courting, the Confederacy expressed interest in selling a stretch of land to the Pennsylvania Colony. However, it was not the Confederacy's land to sell. A large portion of it had been Iroquoian Susquehannock land, but the Susquehannock were not part of the Confederacy (although many of them joined the Cayuga once abandoning the land in what is now Pennsylvania), and the Confederacy had never claimed this land in the past.[77] Still, this conflicted zone and in-between space on the map was the home that the Boors carved out for themselves and became the regional basis for the lasting legacy of Deitsch culture.

Foreigners in Their Own Land

Benjamin Franklin despised the Boors, partially because his interest in establishing a German-language newspaper failed due to the popularity of the newspaper of rival Christoph Sauer. Wrote Franklin: "Why should the Palatine Boors be suffered to swarm into our Settlements, and by herding together establish their Language and Manners to the Exclusion of ours? Why should Pennsylvania, founded by the English, become a Colony of Aliens, who will shortly be so numerous as to Germanize us instead of our Anglifying them, and will never adopt our Language or Customs, any more than they can acquire our Complexion."[78]

Franklin goes on to say that the English and Saxons—not other Germans—make up the principal body of white people. The Palatines were considered "swarthy" (an identity I have embraced). This leads one to realize that bigotry toward the Pennsylvania Dutch population existed from the Colonial era. In some cases and contexts, particularly when it came to the language, this bigotry

77. Weslager, *The Delaware Indians*, 196–208.

78. Franklin, "Observations Concerning the Increase of Mankind, 1751."

persisted through the Civil War, at which time our numbers were needed among the "white" population to keep the establishment in power.

From the Civil War on into the early twentieth century, the Deitsch culture, including its magical and healing practices, enjoyed the peace and freedoms afforded to it by the US Constitution. It wasn't until international tensions with Germany—which the Pennsylvania Dutch population had no loyalty to, as it had not existed as a sovereign entity during Palatine emigration—began to increase that anti-Teutonic sentiment and bigotry flared up again. World War I brought about discomfort for many Pennsylvania Dutch and German Americans, but it was really during the interwar period that efforts were undertaken to weaken the Deitsch culture.

The Suppression (*Die Unnerdricking*)

Throughout my life, I have heard myths and legends about how the Pennsylvania Dutch language formed a protective barrier around our culture. The barrier helped maintain our unique ethnic identity, but, as the German Empire began to strengthen, that barrier also helped fuel the fires of anti-German hysteria through World War I.[79]

Oral tradition carries this sentiment, which I hereby use to paraphrase scores of relatives, Brauchers, Hexes, and even teachers: During the 1920s and 1930s, a body could cross one of the most populous states from Philadelphia to Pittsburgh without needing English. This made some leaders nervous, particularly since Pennsylvania was an industrial powerhouse and the Deitsche have always been major producers of food on the national level.

These large, unassimilated sections of Pennsylvania that were dominated by a distinct Germanic culture and language worried many authorities on the local, state, and federal levels, and efforts were made to shut down the central practices in order to strip the people of their identity within a generation or two. The causes and the methodologies used during the Suppression were many, but the sad fact is that one segment of the Deitsch population was often used against another segment. This boiled down to the very core of the culture, including Braucherei and Hexerei, wherein Braucherei became more acceptable as part of the establishment while Hexerei became associated with evil and Satanism.

I have conducted over seventy interviews with people who identified as Hexes, Hexers, and Hexerei practitioners, and not a single person interviewed worshiped Satan. Most revered nature and utilized the world around them to practice their magic, which mostly consisted of protection spells and spells that increased bounty. Some did call to one or more of the old deities, although few recognized them as gods or goddesses. Thus, the aspersions cast toward Hexerei practitioners often victimized them because they tended to be on the margins of society.

79. Wenger and Bronner, "Communities and Identities: Nineteenth to Twenty-First Centuries," 53–76.

Idisi and Quilting Bees: Sexism and Christian Hegemony

Outright persecution often fails, but making the elder traditions look backward and stupid is an effective means of undermining a minority culture. The stereotype of the Dumb Dutchman was pervasive in the Deitscherei from the time of entry into World War I well through the 1940s, and the "Hex murder" in Rehmeyer's Hollow in 1928 set the stage for the Hexerei traditions to be sensationalized and mocked, not only by the rising mass media but also by the Southern Baptist and other evangelical churches that were expanding into Pennsylvania at the time.

Blue laws, which are restrictions placed at the state or local level on activities generally frowned upon by church authorities, disproportionately targeted women, partially due to the sexism innate in the wider American culture. The notion of empowered or equal women made it that much easier to whip public opinion up against the traditional practices. Ironically, even today, we see the Deitsch establishment pushing back against syncretism and feminism in the practices in order to maintain an unnatural patriarchal, hardcore Christian hegemony that certainly never pertained to Hexerei and that dismisses the different streams that influenced the development of Braucherei over the centuries.[80]

Take as evidence a comparison of the First and Second Merseberg Charms, used in historical and contemporary Braucherei. The First Merseburg Charm ascribed to women the power to loosen fetters. In some translations, the term *Idise* is carried over from the *idisi* of the first line of the Charm and is used instead of "women."[81] The Idise are the matriarchal spirits who watch over the family lines, and it is from them that the concept of the fairy godmother is derived.[82] The Second Merseburg Charm refers to several Germanic deities by name.

First Merseburg Charm

Eiris sazun idisi, sazun hera duoder;
suma hapt heptidun, suma heri lezidun,
suma clubodun umbi cuoniouuidi:
insprinc haptbandun,inuar uigandun.[83]

Translation

Once sat women,
They sat here, then there.
Some fastened bonds,
Some impeded an army,
Some unraveled fetters:
Escape the bonds,
flee the enemy![84]

80. Kreibel, "Medicine," 341–60.
81. Bilardi, *The Red Church*, 74.
82. Paxson, "Matronæ and Dísir."
83. Griffiths, *Aspects of Anglo-Saxon Magic*, 173.
84. Giangrosso, "Charms," 111–14.

Second Merseburg Charm

Phol ende uuodan uuorun zi holza.
du uuart demo balderes uolon sin uuoz birenkit.
thu biguol en sinthgunt, sunna era suister;
thu biguol en friia, uolla era suister;
thu biguol en uuodan, so he uuola conda:
sose benrenki, sose bluotrenki, sose lidirenki:
ben zi bena, bluot zi bluoda,
lid zi geliden, sose gelimida sin![85]

Translation

(The modern Deitsch/Urglaawe deity names were placed in by the author.)
Voll and Wudan were riding to the woods,
and the foot of Balder's foal was sprained
So Mariyeschtann, Sunna's sister, conjured it;
and Freid, Volla's sister, conjured it;
and Wudan conjured it, as well he could:
Like bone-sprain, so blood-sprain,
so joint-sprain:
Bone to bone, blood to blood,
joints to joints, so may they be glued.[86]

Many Braucherei practitioners of the past and present will state that they view Braucherei as a legacy of these charms, yet, somehow, the old deities and the matriarchal spirits were cast aside and the practice became strictly of patriarchal Christian origin. This, of course, is a dissonance of absurdity that the Urglaawe community rejects completely.

Based on oral tradition, I can say the following is true from my observations: *Braucherei can be practiced within the context of any spiritual system except for the lack of one.* Neither Braucherei nor Hexerei is a religion, though both practices include many elements of the folk religion of the Pennsylvania Dutch. While it is true that most practitioners historically would identify as Christian, particularly Lutheran or German Reformed (now UCC), their practices in the home would often contrast starkly with church canon.

It is widely known today that, in order to make the Christian religion more acceptable to the people of Europe, the Germans in particular, the religion had to undergo some changes, resulting in "a Eurocentric particularization of Christianity epitomized by the concept of Christendom."[87] The attributes of many of the deities of various European countries were thus grafted onto Mary or one saint or another. For example, attributes of the goddess Frouwa were set into St. Gertrude of Nivelles, who, as a Catholic saint, is still revered by the heavily Protestant Deitsche on the feast day of March 17. On this same date, Urglaawer hold the Frouwasege (Frouwa's Blessing).

Attributes and lore associated with the goddess Zisa were similarly absorbed into Mary, Undoer of Knots, whose Catholic feast day coincides with the date that the goddess saved the city of Zizarim from Roman invasion.

85. Griffiths, *Aspects of Anglo-Saxon Magic*, 174.
86. Fortson, *Indo-European Language and Culture*, 325.
87. Russell, *The Germanization of Early Medieval Christianity*, 190.

Many of the features associated with the goddess Holle, who is viewed as the chieftess of Urglaawe, became embedded with St. Walburga.[88] This led to her association with May Day, which for Urglaawer, begins at sunset on April 30. This is referred to by many Christians, Heathens, and Pagans as *Walpurgisnacht*. Urglaawer refer to that night as *Wonnenacht* ("the Night of Joy") or *Hexenacht* ("the Witches' Night"), thereby separating the celebration of the return of Holle to the physical realm from the Christian overlay that is intended to diminish the power of the goddess by casting an evil light on Her actual self while elevating the Catholic saint in Her stead.

Indeed, strong females and feminine energies pervade both Braucherei and Hexerei. The Oley-Pikeville Freindschaft (or, roughly, "guild" of Braucherei practioners), of which all Three Sisters Center practitioners are a part, was founded by none other than *die Barricke Mariche*, or Mountain Mary, who is perhaps the most-renowned folk legend in all of Pennsylvania Dutch lore. The power of women and of feminine energies does not diminish the power of men and of masculine energies but, due to the sexism at the root of the patriarchal system, balance has often had to be maintained using alternate means.

Another bit of oral tradition, which was uttered to me personally by an elderly family member, is, "The only thing more powerful than a deacons' meeting is a quilting bee." This little quote reveals a lot about the nature of the Deitsch culture, even in Plain sectarian communities. For all the power that men appear to have, when the women get together and come up with ideas, they then can express their thoughts to their husbands, thereby flexing their power to have a say in the evolution of their community. It's not optimal or fair that they have to do this, but at least the culture has found a way around the restrictions placed on women by the Christian overlay. There are, after all, plenty of indicators of more balance between/among genders in earlier Germanic tribal societies than there was once Christianity became ensconced. Maybe this is why Martin Luther hated Holle.[89]

Our oral tradition, as expressed to me by many people including Braucherei and Hexerei practitioners, carries the following sentiment: "During the Colonial era, the English were shocked to see Deitsch women working plows and Deitsch men preparing meals. Perhaps even more scandalous was that Deitsch women were able to practice medicine in the form of herbalism as part of Braucherei and Hexerei practice." This last part always confounds me because there is plenty of evidence of women in England historically engaging in similar practices.

Historian Jean Soderlund describes some social mores that might have influenced the perspectives of the oral lore. She writes, "The primacy of New England and its conceptual framework has made Pennsylvania women seem oddly tangential to the course of American women's history, when in fact their diversity places them at its center...Three basic themes in women's his-

88. Chisolm, *Grove and Gallows*, 63; Pennick, "The Goddess Zisa," 107–10.

89. List, "Frau Holda as the Personification of Reason."

tory have left Pennsylvania women outside the story: 1) the cultural dominance of New England; 2) the middle Atlantic experience of women as generalized from Quaker women's lives; and 3) the Revolution as bench mark in women's experience."[90] This meant that the dominant perspectives were from outside the Pennsylvania Dutch culture, so one could imagine how a woman working the fields could be interpreted as making "slaves of their women" by the English culture, in which women seldom worked the fields.[91]

Allgschlecht and *Ungschlecht*: Gender Interpretations in the Twentieth and Twenty-First Centuries

Gender and gender identity are topics of social discourse in the current era, but it is interesting to note that, among at least a handful of Hexerei practitioners whom I interviewed, some of the questions related to the practice and to gender have been settled. The following information comes from a cluster of seven Hexerei practitioners located in Snyder, Northumberland, Schuylkill, and Columbia counties.

Four of these practitioners were trained in the 1950s by the same mentor, whom they referred to only as Howard J. The other three were less confident in the terms they provided, yet the consistency of twelve genders was solid among all informants. Five of them shared which gender they identified with; per their request, I am not citing their names. They all expressed a fear of mockery or some other reprisal should their gender identity be exposed outside of the confines of their Hexerei practice.

At first blush, some of these terms sounded horribly offensive to my Deitsch ear, but that is not how they were intended when given to me. I am sharing these terms as they were presented. The translations might sound harsh, but, as the oldest generation passes, it is up to the current practitioners to decide what to do with these. All of these terms relate to gender, not physical sex, and it is noteworthy that the concept of this difference was even developed. The terms also do not relate to sexual orientation.

- *die Fraa*: Woman
- *der Mann*: Man
- *es Allgschlecht*: "The all-gender"
- *es Ungschlecht*: "The un-gender" (none)
- *der Buweschmaga*: "Tomboy"
- *es Mannweib*: "Man-woman" (manly woman)

90. Soderlund, "Women in Eighteenth-Century Pennsylvania," 165.
91. Shyrock, "The Pennsylvania Germans in American History," 268.

- *es Iwwergschlecht*: Transgender (literally)
- *der Gwaer or es Gwaerschlecht*: Queer or "lateral gender"
- *es Drittgschlecht*: Third gender
- *der Zwill*: Twill; two threads wrapped around each other
- *die Dunde*: Womanly man
- *der Kuyoon*: Like a "tomgirl"

The practitioners see some differing abilities among the genders, including some of the following:

- Those who identify as *Drittgschlecht* are said to be particularly clairvoyant.
- Those who identify as *Zwill* are said to be particularly mechanically inclined.
- Those who identify as *Dunde* are said to be strongly empathic.
- Those who identify as *Ungschlecht* are said to be the most prophetic.

In the context of the sexism discussions, it is important that practitioners of Braucherei and Hexerei recognize the complexity of the differentiations between one's physical sex and one's gender. This topic has arisen within our Urglaawe community in regard to the Deitsch language, and this is still a subject that is actively evolving.

The Rise of Allopathic Medicine

The rise of allopathic modern medicine is also a turning point for the practice. As an industry, it pretty much started as a white man's institution and quickly became politically well connected. Medical roles traditionally held by women, such as birthing, increasingly fell under the medical protocols and laws devised by white men. Meanwhile, in this unassimilated German culture, women continued to practice a competing form of medicine on a widespread and equal basis with their male counterparts.

The American Medical Association has taken on what it defines as "quackery" since its founding in 1853.[92] Indeed, not all medical practices are necessarily legitimate or correct, and there was value in standardizing practices and shutting down the "snake oil salesmen." In the twentieth century, though, the AMA set its eyes on Braucherei.

Several reasons for this are cited in the oral tradition, including sexism, bigotry, and a preoccupation with money and power. For example, a newspaper article from the February 19, 1932,

92. Kao, "Medical Quackery."

Reading Times titled "Fortune Telling Frauds Stir State Hexerei Probe" describes the arrest of two women for fraud related to Hexerei practice. The article describes their practice as a "ring" centered in Palmyra, Allentown, and Reading and levies charges that more than $20,000 was defrauded from clients for tasks ranging from curing health woes to helping chickens lay eggs. The reporter frequently mocks the superstitious nature of believers, places Hexerei alongside fraudulent psychics, and considers them a threat to established medicine.[93] Not exactly balanced journalism.

Notice also that the ones targeted for arrest were women.

I will note, though, that if these reports are correct, then there is an underlying problem that could not have happened if guilds' policies were followed: the use of cash to pay a Braucher is forbidden, and most Hexerei practitioners follow the same rule. One may theoretically donate cash, but it is supposed to be done in a place where the Braucher cannot see what is being given. Brauchers are not supposed to charge for the practice, though they can charge for materials if purchasing is required. It is a gift from the divine (in whosoever's context).

This is due to the fact that we, like the Christian practitioners, view our ability to use the power as a gift. In the case of Urglaawe, it is a gift derived from the cosmos or from the force of Wurt (creative life force and possibly a Maker deity) itself, and it is our return gift to Wurt to pass it on. Requesting payment for our services is an insult to Wurt, which does not seek compensation from us for this gift.

However, since a central tenet of Heathenry is that a "gift demands a gift," Urglaawer practitioners will frequently instruct a client to pass a good deed or a donation on to another recipient. In both the Urglaawe and Christian contexts, the absence of a demand for money does reduce the level of scrutiny into the healing and magical arts by the states' governments. We Heathens often say "a gift for a gift," but there are very clear "pay it forward" exceptions that allow the gift to be passed to another in need instead of to the original giver.

There is also concern when the things the people are asking for are shady or outright immoral. I would never curse another for someone, for example. I would never ask the cosmos to have a hen lay an egg every day (everyone needs a break sometimes, even hens!), and the responsibility for finding a treasure is on me.

Another article, from December 24, 1928, states that, due to the death of a child who was under the care of a Powwow "doctor," a watch would be kept on local Powwow operators to ascertain whether violations of the law were occurring.[94] Interestingly, the charges against the doctor were dropped, but the article goes on to list, in a sensationalized matter, other cases that involve Powwow. The newspapers of the era were not reporting on the Braucherins who used

93. "Fortune Telling Frauds Stir State Hexerei Probe," 16.

94. "State Official Here Concerning Death of Fredericksburg Child," 1.

eclectic herbalism to create a palliative remedy that, anecdotally speaking, led to a decrease in Spanish flu victims in their region. They don't carry reports of the good works done for the community. Why? Because good news may fill up a couple of square inches in one day's paper, but oddities and bad news can occupy the news for months. Add in the anti-German sentiment of the time and you had a perfect storm for pushing the Dumb Dutch stereotype. Public sentiment made it easier to prosecute the most vulnerable practitioners, and the Suppression drove many of them underground.

The blue laws that were put on the books as part of the Deitsch Suppression could, theoretically, still be activated. Some of those laws are still out there but are not being enforced. In 1998, for example, a law against fortune-telling was activated against a shop in Lebanon that advertised Powwow. The practitioner was, according to oral tradition (as cited to me by other practitioners in the Lebanon area), "not charging for Powwow practices but would charge for other occult services beyond the practice." The practitioner, Marie May, was shut down for fortune-telling based on a 137-year-old (at the time) law.[95]

Oral tradition, as cited by the same local practitioners, stated: "The real target was specifically Powwow because people were complaining about it being 'Satanic,' even though anyone who knew her knew she did not believe in Satan. The closest she might have been guilty of would be calling to Wudan or Dunner, which is still Satanic in the eyes of the fire-and-brimstone churches. The blue law on fortunetelling was simply an expedient method of terminating the problem."

Kitsch Culture and Romanticizing the Past: Recovery Begins

Anti-German sentiment led to more suppression during World War II, and herbalists were in direct opposition to the rise of Big Pharma, so they went way underground. After the war, though, the suppression mostly faded out, and the "kitsch" culture arose. Kitsch culture was very tourism-friendly; it romanticized the culture and seemed to take special enjoyment in the English dialect we call Dutchified English, which has many markers of Deitsch while using mostly English vocabulary. The kitsch culture lent itself well to the Kutztown Folk Festival, which was established in 1950. The kitsch culture was very popular though the 1960s, and many of us remember the same kitschy items (e.g., the little iron Amish figurines) in the homes of friends and relatives.

Kitsch culture has never gone away. The most common and well-known hex signs that you can find at tourist traps are a product of that culture, even if the symbols themselves existed long before. The artist and the style of those signs are distinct. They are no more nor less meaningful or legitimate.

95. Rouvalis, "Psychics Have Trouble Foretelling When a State Law May Be Used Against Them."

Honestly, kitsch culture sustained and advanced the Deitsch culture in the public's mind, and it also associated the culture with happiness, and family, and love rather than with Hex murders and scammers. Had the kitsch culture and the Folk Festival not arisen, I do not know what the state of our cultural identity would be, and Braucherei and Hexerei might be just a memory. So much was lost during the Suppression that we will never be able to recover it all: lore, charms, herbal remedies. Despite the pressures on the Pennsylvania Dutch from the dominant society to assimilate, the kitsch culture helped us hold on to some pieces of our culture's folklore, foodways, and healing ways.

Allopathic medicine is a wonderful thing, but it has its dark sides too, as we all know. The pairing of politics and medicine has been a burden on the people of the United States since about the time the Brauchers (actually, since they were mostly women, it would be more correct to say Braucherins) were targeted as being problematic. Knocking them out served as an example to others. The effects of this continue today. Many of the Hexerei practitioners I interviewed were only willing to speak with me because I had a voucher from someone they trusted. They wanted none of their personal information to be shared, and they were very concerned about my notes because their energy was on the paper.

And, sadly, the vast majority of them did not pass on their knowledge to the subsequent generation (my parents' generation) because the Deitsch culture, like so many other "ethnic" cultures, did not fit the vision of the Space Age. Ours were the ways of the past: decrepit, backward, foolish. However, the 1980s saw a slight reversal in that trend, and that reversal grew stronger and stronger. Currently, there is so much interest in the language, culture, and heirlooms that there are not enough of us to meet the demand.

Der Urglaawe and the Future

The Heathen denomination of Urglaawe is growing rapidly, and within its ranks are many who are interested in learning the practices of Hexerei and Braucherei. While I could list off some spells and charms, the meat of the culture is in the daily living practices that embrace the world around us. This means there are elements of animism in the way Urglaawer practice the traditions.

For example, a *Ruckschtee* is a stone whose spirit is awakened in order to turn back incoming forces, whether they are human in origin or the result of acts of nature. In the current era, a *Ruckschtee* is frequently a stone of quartz, which is sacred to the god Dunner. A circle of quartz *Ruckschtee* can create protected space within corrals, and a rectangle of *Ruckschtee* can be placed at the corners of the rooftop in order to discourage lightning from striking the house. Some people wear a *Ruckschtee* as a pendant or carry it with them in order to keep their courage in times of stress, or to dissuade anyone who wishes them ill from attacking, whether physically or energetically.

The charm for activating a *Ruckschtee* utilizes runes, which appear in a Deitsch context but have required heavy research, investigation, and theorization due to breaks in the lore. The rune used for this charm is named Antwatt.

Figure 2-2: Antwatt Rune

Take the stone and hold it in your application hand. If you are not sure which hand that is, go with your dominant hand. If you are ambidextrous or ambisinistrous, just choose one, but have that choice be permanent.

With your other hand's thumb, draw the Antwatt rune over the stone three times (sort of like a thumbs-up sign, with the thumb angled to reach the stone as needed) while telling it that Dunner has need of it: "*Der Dunner braucht dei Graft*" (dah DOON-ah browkht dei GRAHFT).[96]

Continue to draw the Antwatt rune over the stone in multiples of three passes while you say the following chant. After you have completed the first utterance of the incantation, you can either continue using Antwatt or switch to other runes if you know them (again applied in multiples of three). Repeat the incantation two more times, for a total of three.

Wach dich, Wach dich, schloof'chi Seel
Ruckschtee, Ruckschtee, kennscht dei Deel
Schpiggel, Schpiggel, Dunnerkeil
Sicher, Sicher dei Meeschder ruft
Zu b'schitz' uns halt' uns heel.

VAHKH dich, VAKH dich, SHLOHF-khi SAIL
RUUK-shtay, RUUK-shtay, KENSHT dei DAIL
SCHPEE-yel, SCHPEE-yel, DOON-ah KAIL
SEEKH-ah, SEEKH-ah dei MAYSH-tah ROOFT
TSUU beSHITZ uns UN halt uns HEEL

96. The transliterations are approximations of the Deitsch pronunciation.

The cadence of the first four lines is much like "eenie meenie miney moe." The fourth line brings about the consecration, so the rhyme changes, and the fifth line is the conclusion.

A Rough Translation
Wake up, wake up, sleepy soul
Ruckschtee, Ruckschtee, you know your part
Mirror, Mirror, Dunnerkeil [a reflection of the Hammer]
Safe [or certain], Safe, your Master calls
To protect us and hold us hale.

After you have completed all of the utterances and rune drawings, make that same "thumbs-up" with your application hand and draw Gewwe over the stone to "close" the connection.

Figure 2-3: Gewwe Rune

Assuming your application hand is your right hand, the process would go like this:

- The first step (opening) would be done with your left hand in the thumbs-up position while the right hand holds the stone. The left thumb draws the rune on the stone in multiples of three.
- The last step is to move the stone to your left hand and to close and seal using your right hand in the thumbs-up position, drawing/chanting Gewwe (geh-veh).

A Note on Runes

The presence of runes in the Deitsch culture has long been an open question. There is some acceptance that some hex signs, or barn stars, have runic elements to them (Yoder and Donmoyer), but the most extensive use of runes that I have come across in my research has been among self-identified Hexerei practitioners. While the rune forms they shared with me are unique, there is enough similarity to the Elder Futhark that I believe their use appeared within the last 100 years but then got altered (and broken) as the information was handed down from one practitioner to the next.

In November 2021, the Urglaawe community finally completed its first set of runes, or *Deitsche Raane*, and the history of the development and use of our runic system will be published in an upcoming book. It is important to underscore that we do not believe this rune system to be of antiquity, but we are reconstructing the theories and practices that were provided to us by the prior generation of Hexerei practitioners.

Conclusion

There is no requirement of Deitsch ancestry in order to participate in Urglaawe in any form. The Deitsch culture is the lens for this particular expression of modern Heathenry. The Deitsch culture nurtured and shielded the knowledge, philosophies, and living, evolving practices that served as the building blocks of Urglaawe. Thus, elements of one's evolving consciousness are far more important factors than ancestry. We build our communities on common values and compatibility. We share a journey through this life, yet we each have sovereignty of our own consciousness and responsibility for our own deeds.

There are many differences between the Urglaawe and the Christian ways of practicing Braucherei. The differences stem from the very basis of the religions: the concepts of whether humans are an integrated part of creation or have dominion over it, and whether there is a separation between the divine and the mundane. These topics are covered frequently in Urglaawe publications and forums online. As Braucherei, Hexerei, and Urglaawe are all living, evolving traditions, please expect to see more publications, artwork, music, and fiber arts creations coming from the Guild of Urglaawe Practitioners of Braucherei and Hexerei.

FIELD NOTES

The Candle Shop

While Braucherei and Hexerei get a lot of attention in terms of mid-Atlantic folk magic, it's important to note that there are a number of other traditions heavily represented here as well. A late–eighteenth century influx of refugees from Haiti (prompted by a revolutionary outbreak) filled Philadelphia with a number of free Blacks who brought with them traditions like Vodun, and Hoodoo has also long had a home in places like Baltimore and Philadelphia.

The cosmopolitan crossroads in these big cities led to the establishment of magical communities who needed access to magical products. Businesses opened that catered to these clients, often under names like "candle shops," selling candles (of course) as well as incenses, oils, and books on occult magic. Here are some examples of historically important shops that provide materials and magical guidance to city-dwellers.

Harry's Occult Shop: This Philadelphia shop served the city as a local pharmacy when it opened in 1917, but a number of the city's Black residents turned to shop owner Harry Seligman to help supply them with the ingredients and tools they needed for their magical work. Many were practitioners of Hoodoo, and Seligman, a white man, quickly worked to learn just how to supply and use the various products being requested.[97] Harry insisted that the shop's products were to be used to "Light a Torch for the Good and Cross Swords Against Evil," and the shop became a hub for people interested in learning not just African American folk magic, but methods derived from Spiritualism, Espiritismo, and Western Mystery Traditions. The shop changed hands several times before eventually closing at its original location. It has since relocated to South Street in Philadelphia and reopened under the name Harry's World.

Grandma's Candle Shop: In Baltimore, a "candle shop" is another name for a store selling supplies for African American folk magic, as well as materials for other traditional folk magic (such as candles and herbs that might be found in a botanica catering to practitioners of Lucumi or Vodun). Grandma's Candle Shop is located downtown, where it has been serving the Baltimore folk magic community since 1978. Over time, it has become more of an all-purpose metaphysical shop that caters to a variety of traditions including Wicca and even Christian folk magicians. In 2020 Grandma's Candle Shop closed its physical doors, moving online as the shop Crystals & Craft, although they do still wrap candles and other fragile purchases in pages of the local newspaper.

97. Long, *Spiritual Merchants*, 156–57.

Lucky Star Candles, Home of Old Grandpa: Another Baltimore staple of Hoodoo supplies, Old Grandpa is not related to the "Grandma" of the previous candle shop. Instead, Old Grandpa builds his recipes and formulas based on ones learned from his own grandmother. This shop hews much closer to the old-school candle shops of yesteryear. Old Grandpa has been writing and producing his own Dream Book (a type of manual used to determine lucky numbers for things like lotteries) and a magically oriented almanac for decades. His shop primarily serves Baltimore clientele, but also people from as far away as Washington, DC. Like Grandma's shop, it largely seems to be an online-only presence now, but it is still run by its original owner and produces unique products you won't find anywhere else.

A Solitary Nature: My Hoodoo Story

STEPHANIE ROSE BIRD

Hoodoo is a colorful collection of folkloric practices gathered from across the United States with emphasis on Southern states. However, I'm living proof it can be found anywhere! It encompasses many folk practices and beliefs originating in Sub-Saharan African countries, prominently West African. These Africanisms were preserved traditions that then collected influence from Native American, Appalachian, European, and Asian traditions.

The early informants of Hoodoo were from the Deep South but also Virginia, from which my ancestors hail. Today, there is an urban orientation within Hoodoo coming out of Detroit and other cities like Chicago, where I currently live. Hoodoo's rural origins can be seen in the heavy use of plants, animals, and natural components. Urban Hoodoo is adapted to reflect the urban environment. While there are specialists who dedicate attention to a specific type of Hoodoo, my focus is often on the intersectionality of cross-cultural, regional, and interfaith beliefs that are incorporated. My historical specialty is the Deep South, but I also pay close attention to happenings in the Midwest, Pennsylvania, and New Jersey, where I grew up and became so inspired. Hoodoo is a form of justice, a way of balancing the scales between those who have too much power—and abuse it—and those who have little or no power, in the mundane sense of the word.

As a Green Witch, artist, and Shaman, I strongly ascribe to and appreciate the power of plants through the practice of magical herbalism and aromatherapy. In fact, I was drawn to Hoodoo as an eclectic Pagan and as a part of my heritage simultaneously. I was raised in the Christian church as a Methodist, like many. Christian elements such as the psalms, angels, saints, and perhaps even candle burning have origins in the Abrahamic faiths. When I downplayed or chose to look past Christianity in my earlier works, such as *Sticks, Stones, Roots & Bones: Hoodoo, Mojo & Conjuring with Herbs*, and chose to champion Paganism instead, the path where my passion lies was prioritized. In some ways, this is because I see Hoodoo as deeply tied to place, connected with the land, and so respect for the land must be a part of Hoodoo's practice. However, Hoodoo adapts to both people and land over time, as I've seen in my years. With age and maturity, I have come to recognize religion's esoteric nature and have incorporated snippets of Christianity into my contemporary work. In my more recent work, *365 Days of Hoodoo: Daily Rootwork, Mojo & Conjuration*, I include psalm, angel, and saint workings, and, of course, the cross-cultural and interfaith (though largely Pagan-rooted) candlemancy also referred to as candle magick. I pay the most attention to the Pagan underpinnings and pre-Abrahamic aspects of Christianity in this work, and in all my work.

Hoodoo can coexist as a powerful practice regardless of the presence of a religious belief system. I have often said that *Hoodoo is not a religion*. It is personal by nature, and even its name is subject to change. According to Hoodoos, it goes by various names, most notably Conjure, Conjuration, and Rootwork, or simply Roots. Just as we aren't tethered to a specific region or type of individual, we aren't bound by strict dogma. There aren't typically hierarchical positions like priests or priestesses, nor is there a sacred book or text that outlines our practices.

This is not to say that religious beliefs aren't folded into Hoodoo, or that we don't have luminaries. Historical figures like Dr. Buzzard of South Carolina and Aunt Caroline Dye of Arkansas, whose Hoodoo practices stand out, remain steadfast resources. Still, as a solitary Green Witch and Shaman, I was immediately drawn to Hoodoo not only for its apparent connections to my ancestry, but also because you can be a solitary practitioner.

I am primarily a self-taught writer, as my formal degrees are in fine art, not literature. I have liaised with many herbal and aromatherapy organizations. Bless them all. While I am grateful to places like the American Botanical Society and the National Association for Holistic Aromatherapy for their treasure troves of botanical and aromatic healing information, I am not a certified anything—though some would say I'm certifiable, hopefully in jest.

An attractive feature of Hoodoo is the opportunity to teach yourself, at your own pace, in your way. Yes, you can read books, take classes, and attend workshops or conferences, but spending time in nature; listening carefully to your clients' concerns; conjuring the ancestors, nature, and ascended spirits in sacred spaces; and using specific types of tools and materials remains the best bet for becoming a powerful Hoodoo.

Hoodoo is rich, varied, and inclusive. Yet, it is undeniably associated with the Deep South, Black Americans, and our migrations—so, by extension, it also encompasses elements from Africa, and its tenants are alive in the African diaspora; I'm speaking most notably of the Caribbean Islands, Brazil, and parts of South America. For this reason, Hoodoo is not limited to a specific region or type of person. Hoodoos' African connections are to be honored, and its interconnectivity between cultures and faiths deserves exploration.

Before closing this discussion about Hoodoo and religion, there are a few essential points to consider. As Hoodoos, we don't just draw from Abrahamic faith. The age-old African Tradition Religions (commonly referred to as ATRs) and their offshoots in the African diaspora (such as Candomblé, Santeria/Lucumi, and Umbanda) couldn't help but enjoy a healthy relationship to Hoodoo. Hoodoos notice and incorporate what is around us and what emanates from inside, especially our ancestry. Hoodoo, the practice that mainly originated with Black folk and folds in our ancestral beliefs, is flexible and open-minded enough to look back to the heyday of the practice in the early– to mid–twentieth century. It embraces our views and neighbors, and it deeply honors our kinfolk. The easiest way to define Hoodoo is as a collection of folklore and folk beliefs.

Call of the Wild

While on the topic of origins, let me share my Hoodoo origin story. I have shared a bit about how I practice as a solitary, but there is much more to it. When someone is born with second sight, also referred to as being psychic, we refer to that person as being born "with the caul" in the Black community. My elders never told me I was born with the caul, but I've always marched to an inner drummer. I've been attracted to the weird, strange, and, in some cases, that which is considered dark or mysterious.

I grew up in Salem, New Jersey. Half of the area was devoted to farming. The landscape is home to marshlands, lakes, rivers, ponds, and woods. I've always been fond of trees, often climbing them to hang out among the branches as a child. One tree in particular had an impact on me: the Salem Oak. We used to take field trips to see the Salem Oak. Can you imagine that? A field trip to see a tree! It used to be one of the most famous landmarks—a legend of sorts, at between 500–600 years of age. Salem, which was established in 1675, was home to an English Quaker named John Fenwick who was said to have signed a treaty with the Lenni Lenape tribe underneath that very tree.[98] The white oak, which is a symbol of integrity and strength, finally became the largest of its kind in New Jersey before collapsing under its own weight in 2019.

I recall eating with my mother in the diner named after the Salem Oak; it feels like a fresh memory even though it has been decades. The tree certainly impressed and inspired me with possibilities. The Salem Oak was more than just a tree. As memory serves, it had an energetic field around it. Its broad boughs seemed to suggest pride. Its presence healed the spirits. Visiting the tree solidified a deep appreciation for nature and a firm belief that trees (and other parts of nature) resonate with the human spirit and are alive with spiritual energy.

I was devastated to learn that the great white oak of my childhood had died. Their usual lifespan is 200–300 years, but the Salem Oak was thought to have been 565 years old when it uprooted itself, as if to say, "Enough of this world." It lives on in countless people's memories, stories, furniture, and art, and its progeny, scattered across the country, still bear acorns every year.

This feeling of gratitude for and fascination with nature was reinforced in many ways throughout my life. I grew up in a wetland, on a lake, with a house facing the water, nestled by trees

98. Franklin, "'It Was a Part of All Our Lives.'"

and plant life. Neighbors were more of a thought than a reality. The landscape of my childhood allowed curiosity and discovery in the natural world. Though people lived nearby, my primary company was nature. Most activity was centered around the landscape: swimming during the warmest months, ice skating during the coldest, seeing different tree formations along the water, eyeing wildlife that frequented the area, and hearing eerie sounds when the lake was frozen provided amusement. Walking amidst the trees, sometimes with moss beneath my bare feet, smelling wild laurel blossoms, gazing at sassafras trees, and poking myself with holly was what interested me and brought me joy.

The wonders of nature moved me. I grew to attempt to capture nature's energy as a young painter and eventually as a healer. My creative practice crossed over from aromatherapy, writing, and art-making to healing when my parents' health became a concern. Through a desire to cure them of their health ailments, I began searching for what I could do. I found a copy of Jethro Kloss's herbal *Back to Eden* and became hopeful when I learned that the trees and plants in our nearby forest, on some of my relatives' property, and that I passed on my daily walk to the school bus, were not just splendid visions, but could also offer valuable support to treat my parents' daunting ailments. Through Kloss's extensive knowledge, I found light in an otherwise scary and confusing situation that had left me feeling powerless.

The Healing Power of Plants

This new knowledge was empowering. A light went off in my head—healing was possible through the power of plants! The healing power of plants has become the theme of my work and fine art. Indeed, it is a mantra that fuels my life's work.

In Kloss's work, I noticed many of the Native American origins of herbal remedies, which made me curious about what African Americans and other people of color added to the healing mix. At the same time as my immersion in the plant world, I became increasingly passionate about magick. I noticed some herbs like hops, chamomile, pasque flower, and skullcap not only made it easier to fall asleep because of their nervine and calmative qualities, but also, while sleeping, I could fly and undertake other seemingly impossible feats (like shape-shifting) under the influence of the herbs. I was smitten. Plants were not only healing to physical health—they had another dimension: they were magical and uplifting to the spirits.

As a teenager, "mind, body, spirit" wasn't in my daily lexicon, but it was a trilogy taking root in my soul. In short order, a cousin of mine introduced me to the alchemist Albertus Magnus. This cousin confided to me that he was a warlock. I had a friend at school that claimed she was a Witch, even inviting me to her circle a few times. My mystical environment, readings, and acquaintances coalesced to reinforce my interest in plants, magick, and spirituality. By my early teens, little did I realize, I was paving my path to being a Witch—a Green Witch, at that.

Being open to my environment, hearing the voices of my ancestors, and welcoming the guidance of nature spirits allowed me to notice other mysteries in my midst. Near the summer place my uncle sometimes resided in, I saw what seemed to be altars and various sculptural figures featuring cowrie shells and coconuts. I was not afraid of these things. Instead, they drew me in. Their appearance made me want to understand them more.

My uncle, looked upon by some as eccentric, was more than happy to share. He was involved in an offshoot of an ATR called Santeria. He told me, "I am a child of Shango, and you, my sweet niece, are either of Oshun or Yemaya-Olukun."

Hmm, I thought, *What on earth is he talking about?*

My journey began with *Back to Eden* and reading about herbal remedies. It thickened into shamanism and alchemy through Albertus Magnus studies, then took a sharp turn into African-Derived Religion (ADR) through my uncle, who was on his pathway to Santeria priesthood (becoming a Babalawo in Yoruba). I found that nature was alive with entities, beings, and characters—who knew? This made a strong impression on my very creative mind and fed my need to see my people in my spiritual practices.

I have included some practices that were created as part of my Hoodoo journey. They pay homage to the vastness of Hoodoo. These are practical workings, offered here as original and open exercises.

A Note on Rare Plants: We Are Earth Mama's Stewards

I learned at an early age that it's important to honor source—our dear Gaia, our Earth Mama. We must work in concert with her and conserve her bevy of healing delights. As a Green Witch, Hoodoo, or Pagan practitioner, be mindful of the fragility of plants and roots: grow your own, forage with care, or purchase well-sourced, non-endangered herbs for your magickal workings. Remember, plentiful substitutes for rare and endangered plants abound. Just do some research.

Mama Bear's Dream Pillow

I maintain connection to my Green Witchcraft and Shaman's journey through my dream pillows. They are easy to make and very effective at aiding sleep and cultivating prophetic dreams. Working creatively with Earth Mama by using natural ingredients, her gift, helps us enjoy Earth's soothing embrace before we drift into the land of dreams.

Gather:

- Spanish moss
- 2 teaspoons Queen Elizabeth root powder
- ⅛ teaspoon chamomile

- ⅛ teaspoon rose otto essential oil (or quality rose fragrance oil)
- ¼ teaspoon lavender essential oil

1. Crumble bay leaves, chamomile flowers, French lavender buds, hops, lemon verbena, mullein, and rose petals into a bowl until small and relatively fine. While doing so, recite the appropriate chant for each herb:

   Geb, help me (bay leaves)
   Inanna, relax me (chamomile flowers)
   Isis, keep me safe (French lavender buds)
   Gaia, direct my dreams (hops)
   Geb, I thank thee (lemon verbena)
   Inanna, guide me to the truth (mullein)
   Isis, shield me (rose petals)
   Thanks be to Earth Mama for sharing your healing gifts
2. Break Spanish moss into one-inch pieces, then add to other ingredients.
3. Stir in hops.
4. Sprinkle essential oils over the bruised herbs and stir to mix well.
5. Sprinkle Queen Elizabeth powder over the mixture and stir.
6. Mature by placing in a dark jar away from direct light. Shake daily for four weeks. Each time you shake, reactivate the magical quality of the herbs and flowers by reciting this invocation:

   Geb, help me
   Inanna, relax me
   Isis, keep me safe
   Gaia, direct my dreams
   Earth Mama, I thank thee
   Geb, guide me to the truth
   Inanna, shield me
   Thank you, Isis, for sharing your precious gifts!

   While waiting for the mixture to mature, rub the herbs with your hands and make sure to breathe on them each day.
7. During this time, make a small pillow to place within your pillowcase. Use two nine-inch squares of the fabric of your choice (I recommend gingham, linen, hemp, mud cloth, adire indigo, or kente) and purple cotton thread to sew a pillowcase. (Purple is a sacred color.) You can insert a small scarab or Thet into the

pillow at this point, or it can be tied to the outside later. Once you've finished sewing your pillowcase, make nine knots with the thread to fortify your stitchery magically and physically: two knots near the middle of the top; two knots on each sides; three knots at the bottom.

8. Once the mixture has finished maturing, add it to the dream pillow. This dream pillow is designed for protection, strength, restful sleep, and prophetic dreams. It can be recharged in four to six weeks, when the aroma is no longer evident.

Note: Allergy sufferers should wear a dust mask for this project. You may want to replace the hops with jasmine flowers if you are in recovery from alcohol addiction.

Yemaya-Olukun Bath Ritual

To the Yoruba people of Nigeria and other followers of Ile-Ifa, Yemaya-Olukun is a most benevolent entity that embodies the spirit of creation. This ever-present being lives in natural bodies of water. Yemaya is the Great Mother or Cosmic Womb. This powerful mother figure is beloved by many for her deep understanding and generosity. Olukun, her partner, is the androgynous entity representative of the depths of the water. To invoke Yemaya-Olukun, try this bath ritual, written from the perspective of an eclectic Pagan (me). Note: this not a closed practice as far as I am concerned.

Create an altar in your bathroom on a window ledge, table, or in the tub by following these steps:

1. Clean the designated surface (ledge, table, or tub) by lightly brushing with a foraged feather.
2. Lay down a white satin or white silk cloth.
3. Arrange cowries and conch shells (or other available seashells) on the cloth.
4. Put a sea stone in the center of the shells.
5. Put a glass of rum surrounded by coins facing north, south, east, and west next to the circle of shells.
6. Dip a charged crystal or aquamarine stone in the glass of rum, and then set it on top of the sea stone.
7. Set out a few tropical, leafy plants or ferns.
8. Light frankincense and myrrh incense, or burn tobacco or a blue candle on a fireproof plate as another offering.
9. Add bath salts under running water in a plugged, clean bathtub.
10. Get in the tub. Relax and enjoy!

• • • • • • • • • •

Hoodoo Herbs: Five Faves for Workin' the Roots

The word *roots* is used frequently in Hoodoo. The word carries many connotations for Black folks in particular, and everyone generally. Roots are about origins, and as a word it speaks to the ancestors and evokes visions of the Motherland. Roots is another name for Hoodoo, and Hoodoos are referred to as Rootworkers. Roots are a Hoodoo's herbs, and that is the focus of this section.

Roots are worked for matters of the mind, body, and spirit. They set the tone in ritual and help in conjuration work of a spiritual nature. Here are what I consider Hoodoo's five faves:

1. **Frankincense (*Boswellia sacra* and *Boswellia carterii*):** Intertwined with Christianity as one of the gifts for baby Jesus. In Hoodoo, frankincense is a precious, readily available, easy-to-use, high-frequency resin that conjures spirits and creates a peaceful and positive vibe in the home.
2. **Adam and Eve Root (*Aplectrum hyemale*):** This is a type of orchid that can grow in many gardens. As its name suggests, Adam and Eve root is used as a love-draw plant and is prevalent in love mojos and relationship magic. This holistic root is also a pain reliever and is macerated to use for the treatment of boils.
3. **High John the Conqueror Root (*Ipomoea jalapa*):** This root is one of Hoodoo's most popular and influential. High John represents the spirit of surviving enslavement. High John is believed to have been an African prince who was captured and sold into slavery, yet, as a trickster, he evaded his potential owners and survived as a free man. Emblematic of sympathetic magic, High John's appearance, sensual qualities, elements, and use coordinate with the type of magick it is used to perform. You can make an excellent bodyguard mojo for your personal protection featuring this root.
4. **Five-Finger Grass (*Potentilla* spp.):** Five-finger grass goes by many names. I like five-finger grass because it employs a sympathetic magic outlook—after all, it resembles a hand. This popular Hoodoo plant yields wisdom, power, health, prosperity, and love. It grows readily. Associated with the third eye, or ajna chakra, you can steep the grass in a cauldron of spring water. Strain out the herb and use the tisane to bathe your third eye, opening the way to luck as well as its other gifts.
5. **Devil's Shoestrings (*Viburnum opulus* or *Nolina lindheimeriana*):** Used to trip the devil up and to gain the upper hand in a romantic relationship gone off the rails. It is laid in the path of the intended loved one or a lover you want to get rid of to

yield powerful results. If you're after a job, create this Job Fixin' Toby (another type of mojo bag). This is a traditional blend from an original Hoodoo informant from Algiers, Louisiana. Combine a bit of snakeroot, devil's shoestring, a High John the Conqueror root, and cinnamon chips in a chamois skin, along with a silver dime (a dime minted before 1964). Sprinkle it with Van Van oil. Carry in your front pocket. Squeeze it as you focus on your money-making opportunities.

Jack the Diviner

Hoodoos dig divination. We notice the signs in dreams, numbers, and symbols in life. Prophecy is important. By activating and stewarding a deep relationship with a specific collection of items wrapped into a ball shape, you can build a conjuration and prophecy aid called a Jack. A Jack is similar to a mojo bag, one of Hoodoos' most vital tools, but is primarily a divination device. According to an informant from Virginia, here's what you can do with your Jack:

- Hang it around your neck and whisper your wishes to it.
- Use it like a pendulum. Notice the direction it swings to determine whether the answer to your question is yes or no.
- Hang it around your neck, but hold it out and away from your neck to ask it questions so you can observe its movement.
- Use a Jack to find money. Stick nine pins into it to activate the money-finding power it holds.

Finding My Mojo

Santeria, Ile-Ifa, ADRs, and ATRs are freeing belief systems practiced by the ancestors and some of my family. While there's something profoundly soulful and connected about ADRs and ATRs, I get stuck on the prominent R representing the word *religion* in each of them. I was once very religious, but religion has left me. In its place is a healthy dose of spirituality: Earth-based spirituality, or eclectic Paganism. The answers I seek, in terms of spirituality and healing, are rooted in the practices of my Black ancestors, and they are held in the annals of Hoodoo.

Just as I am a solitary practitioner in Green Witchery, I can also practice solitarily as a Hoodoo. There are classes and apprenticeships out there, but I learned the old-fashioned way—empirically. I studied it for myself, just as I advise those who reach out to me to do. Information is widely available in excellent books and on various websites. More valuable even than those sources is *the* source. When people write to me and say, "I've tried several books. I've studied at XYZ place, but I still don't feel like a real Hoodoo," I tell them it's because they haven't tapped into their magical potentiality yet—their *ashe*—our source. Magic can be all around you, and the resources can pile up in your library, but ultimately you are the driver of this trip! You alone have the power to become a Hoodoo and do with it what you desire.

Sure, there are traditions in Hoodoo—we have our favorite herbs for rootworking and incense and candles for conjuration, but you, as a modern person, can also be a driver of sorts. You can sort out what is helpful to you and what role you as the practitioner want to play in your community, family, or society at large. At the same time, Hoodoo can be a deeply personal spiritual practice for individual healing and empowerment, and it is a tool to address various issues in everyday life.

TRAVELING ON
New Holland and Deitscherei

As with any guidebook, there is always much more to experience than can be neatly fit into a chapter. To that end, we offer you this addendum to the map that will provide you with some tools to explore New Holland and Deitscherei further.

The glossary shares some keywords that might be useful. The places to visit will point you toward locations of interest that we think you might find valuable, and the reading recommendations provide you with some top-tier texts that can be used to dig in and learn more about this region.

Glossary

ADR: An acronym for African-Derived Religion.

ATR: An acronym for African Traditional Religion.

Benedicaria: Italian name for a tradition of magical healing, mostly unnamed in North America.

Braucherei: A healing tradition found among the Pennsylvania Dutch community.

cimaruta: An Italian-rooted charm made from a sprig of rue, or a charm designed to look like a rue plant, made out of a material like silver.

cornicello: An Italian-rooted charm designed to look like a small horn and intended to avert the evil eye (*malocchio*).

Hexerei: The practice of witchcraft or morally ambiguous magic.

hex signs: Decorative signs found on the sides of barns (and some homes) featuring geometric designs and incorporating iconography such as the distelfink (goldfinch), rosettes, or acorns and oak leaves.

hexenmeister: Literally a "witch master" who was able to repel curses and deal with other forms of witchcraft on behalf of clients.

himmelsbrief: A "heavenly letter" designed to bring protection to the one carrying it.

Hoodoo: An African American traditional folk magic relying on the use of natural materials, often influenced by religious traditions but not under the control of any specific denomination.

malocchio: The Italian term for the evil eye, a form of harmful magic frequently caused by jealousy or envy.

Olokun: Partner/consort of the Yoruban orisha (holy figure) Yemaya, with dominion over the waters of the earth.

Powwow: Another name for Braucherei (possibly derived from early associations with Native American healing practices or, alternatively, from a dialect pronunciation of the word "power").

roots: A term used in African American folk magic and Hoodoo for most plant-based magical ingredients, or the specific spells and workings done to influence an outcome.

Ruckschtee: A stone whose spirit is awakened in order to turn back incoming forces, whether they are human in origin or from the result of acts of nature.

strega: Italian word for a witch, a practitioner of stregonaria (witchcraft, usually with a connotation of potentially harmful magic).

Urglaawe: A reconstructed Heathen practice drawing on the traditions of the Pennsylvania German people and incorporating much of their folklore and magic.

Yemaya: A Yoruban name for the orisha (holy figure) of the sea and motherhood.

zauberzeitl: Abbreviated prayers or Bible passages (often reduced to a string of letters and punctuation) that could be worn, carried, or posted to elicit an effect.

Places to Visit

Browse the Bookshops and Botanicas of Bushwick, New York: While there is no shortage of places in New York City that are occult-connected, the little area of northeast Brooklyn that houses witchy shops like Catland Books (as well as the esoteric record shop known as Heaven Street Records) has also become a hub of contemporary witchcraft. Add to that the botanicas in the area, like Botanica San Miguel or Botanica San Antonio, and you've got a very active spot for finding folk magic ingredients, groups, and individuals. You can also hop on the subway and head up to Harlem, which has its own collection of candle shops and a deeply rooted history of folk magic supply stops.

Visit Headless Horsemen Haunts in Tarrytown, New York: This is the famed real-life setting for Washington Irving's story *The Legend of Sleepy Hollow*. While it very much capitalizes on its famous connection to the author, this little hamlet just north of New York City also has a full array of folkloric points of interest. A trip to Philipsburg Manor offers a hint of the storied past of Dutch settlers and haunting legends, or you can visit Patriot's Park, where there once stood a tree used to hang Benedict Arnold's traitorous compatriot Major Andre. The tree was later struck by lightning, making it a veritable "lightning rod" for legends and ghost stories, and a source of folk magic as well, since both sites of hangings and lightning-struck wood have powerful magical uses.

Wander the Candle Shops of Baltimore, Maryland: Some of the oldest shops, like Grandma's or Lucky Star (mentioned earlier), are only available online now, but if you are in Baltimore, it's worth wandering around to see if there are any places open that call themselves "candle shops," as they likely carry a number of folk magic supplies and can be incredible sources for learning magical history and tradition.

Explore the Pine Barrens of Southern New Jersey: The Pine Barrens is home to the famous Jersey Devil, a cryptid (folkloric creature) who has been reported as far back as the early nineteenth century. One legend states that the creature is the thirteenth child of a witch named Mother Leeds, who cursed her child to become a monster.

Attend a Folk Festival in Kutztown, Pennsylvania: Kutztown is home to of one of the largest folk festivals in the country, where you can try Pennsylvania Dutch food, see live demonstrations of barn star painting, and even visit the Pennsylvania German Cultural Heritage Center to hear the Deitsch language and learn about a number of the magical traditions in the region.

Look at a Legendary Rock in Leonardtown, Maryland: Leonardtown is the site of the famed witch haunting of Moll Dyer. Moll was blamed for a particularly bad blizzard, and the townspeople in the area ran her into the woods and set fire to her home. She died frozen to a rock that still bears her handprints. For years the area experienced ghostly hauntings and poor harvests that were considered her curse. The stone with Moll's handprints is kept at the town's Tudor Hall as a memorial to Moll and her legend (which, incidentally, was partly the inspiration for the hit cult horror film *The Blair Witch Project*).

Celebrate the Sea Witch in Rehoboth, Delaware: A local legend tells of a British ship, the De Braak, which sank off the coast of Delaware. Rumors claimed it was laden with treasure but protected by a sea witch. For nearly two centuries, any attempt to find or raise the ship brought storms (even hurricanes!). When the boat was finally raised in the 1980s, no gold or silver was found, but the sea witch has become a celebrated figure in the town of Rehoboth, which has an annual parade and festival in her honor.

Recommended Reading

City Witchery: Accessible Rituals, Practices & Prompts for Conjuring and Creating in a Magical Metropolis by Lisa Marie Basile
Basile's guide to urban folk magic combines her New York City environment with practical exercises to give the reader a chance to create magic in their own urban spaces.

The Red Church or the Art of Pennsylvania German Braucherei by Chris Bilardi
Bilardi's book is a very detailed guide to the fundamental practices of the Pennsylvania German Braucherei system.

"Hex Signs: Sacred and Celestial Symbolism in Pennsylvania Dutch Barn Stars" by Patrick Donmoyer
This little booklet from Donmoyer's work at the Pennsylvania German Cultural Heritage Center outlines a number of Deitsch practices and beliefs (and dispels some notions about the magical nature of barn stars).

Hex and Spellwork: The Magical Practices of the Pennsylvania Dutch by Karl Herr
While it is a bit general and slim regarding some of the Deitsch-specific practices, Herr's book does offer a brief overview of relevant folk practices from the region.

Spiritual Cleansing: A Handbook of Psychic Protection by Draja Mickaharic
Mickaharic presents a variety of folk magic traditions that represent the many influences found in places like New York City, all aimed at keeping a person safe and spiritually hygienic.

The Powwow Grimoire by Robert Phoenix
Phoenix has created a modern version of a traditional Powwow magical book for the twenty-first century that combines established workings with modern needs.

The First Book of Urglaawe Myths by Robert L. Schreiwer
In this short collection, Schreiwer provides a number of folktales and myths that have influenced historical and contemporary Pennsylvania Dutch people.

Jewish Magic and Superstition: A Study in Folk Religion by Joshua Trachtenberg
This book, originally published in 1939, is sometimes outdated but still provides an excellent overview of many Jewish and Jewish American folk traditions and magical practices.

Honoring Your Ancestors: A Guide to Ancestral Veneration by Mallorie Vaudoise
This guide to working with ancestors incorporates folk traditions and practices from Italian American magic while also connecting to Vaudoise's New York landscape.

CHAPTER 3

The Upland South

Rise Like Chimney Smoke: An Introduction to the Folk Magic of the Mountain South

The Blue Ridge Parkway running between Virginia and North Carolina is an impressive stretch of road. If you happen to drive it on a slightly cool morning when the low-sitting clouds curl around the dark green tops of the mountains and their mix of pines, poplars, maples, oaks, and more, you'll quickly understand why a large chunk of this area is called the Smokies. If you visit during rhododendron blooming season, you'll gaze with wide-eyed wonder as the bushes turn scarlet pink all around you. At sunset, you'll have to stop at one of the lookouts and watch until the last rays of violet, rose, and tangerine slip behind the horizon.

Whatever you do, you're going to have a pretty good day if you're driving this road. The Appalachian Mountains form a sort of "backbone" to the region we can call the Upland South—a range of states that generally includes Virginia, West Virginia, Kentucky, Tennessee, and North Carolina (with bits of western South Carolina and northern Georgia usually included). It's an area where a wide number of people have put down roots: the Indigenous Cherokee, Creek, and Lumbee tribes, the Scots Irish, African Americans, Portuguese settlers, Latin American peoples, Kurds, Ethiopians, and even a misunderstood group of people known as the Melungeons.

This is the region I called home for most of my life, and there's a definite pride in being from the South in some ways. There's plenty of painful history, too, including a legacy of slavery, Jim Crow, and the Trail of Tears, all of which are still sending ripples through time today. We can walk that line between our shadows and our shine because we know that no one is all light or all darkness. While many think of "the South" as a single homogenous entity, it's not. Instead, enclaves and pockets of many cultures exist here, frequently intermingled but also with distinct characteristics that set them apart. The Upland South has a very distinct "flavor" from the Deep South (which we'll visit in the next section), and even within this region there are hollers and hills and plateaus and lowland plains and cities and unincorporated communities and—well, the variety of people you would find anywhere, just with a Southern twist.

And, of course, magic dwells here. This region is and long has been rife with powerful magical traditions including faith healing "fairy doctors" and cunning folk who arrived from the British Isles, Powwows and Brauchers who drifted down from the upper Appalachian regions in Pennsylvania, Indigenous medicine keepers who know the local vegetation better than anyone, Rootworkers and Hoodoos who can heal you or make you sorry for what you've done lickety-split, faith healers and snake handlers from charismatic and spirit-filled churches, and of course, witches.[99] There are always witches. Here, sites like Roan Mountain, North Carolina, or Adams,

99. For more on the wide range of cultural fusion that happened in the Appalachians, see the excellent study on the merger of German, Irish, Scottish, English, African, and Indigenous (usually Cherokee) cultures through magic called *Signs, Cures & Witchery* by Gerald C. Milnes.

Tennessee, may lay claim to particular witch legends, but stories of witches that can steal milk or take off warts or blight cattle or switch bodies with a deer are everywhere. Some witches go flying about at night, using "witch's grease" to rise out of their houses like chimney smoke and visit (or steal from) their neighbors. Some are water witches, not really considered "witches" in anything but name, who help find underground springs and wells with forked branches or copper rods (a practice called *dowsing*).

The magic of the Upland South is always a little double-edged; it's mostly friendly and does you good if you treat the land and people around you well, but if you cross them then you'll quickly feel how sharp it can be. The people bearing that magic are also of that tenor, with a lot of hospitality and kindness to offer you but unafraid to get their hands dirty when the work requires it.

In the following pages, you will hear from two Appalachian-based folk magicians who will show you that the same hills produce distinct flavors of enchantment that can complement or even contradict one another, all while adding to the overall salt and seasoning of the South. You'll meet H. Byron Ballard, the "village witch of Asheville," as she escorts you through her garden and her land, teaching you how the roots she has bear wildly witchy fruit. Then we'll sit down with Jake Richards, whose folk magic comes from the backwoods and contains everything from the Psalms to the Devil, and who draws upon a diverse set of roots of his own to keep magic vibrant and thriving today. I'll also share my own brief introduction to a few of the stories and spells that make up my practice.

If I had the time, I would try to show you everything magical about this region, but even ten lifetimes wouldn't be enough. So instead, spend time with me here in the hills and valleys, along the riverbanks and in the woods, in Music City and "Hotlanta," and let the enchantment draw you in for as long as you can stay.

• • • • • • • • • •

Bark, Fruit, Root, Seed: The Homely Folkways of Old Appalachia

H. BYRON BALLARD

It is not possible to talk about the folk magic of this region—the southern highlands of the Appalachian Mountains—without learning about the land itself and the people who have inhabited it, including those who continue to do so. The herbs, the recipes, the tonics, and the poultices—all of that is the set dressing. To walk the land and bide near the people will reveal wisdom more surely than a cursory reading of any text, save the one written on the faces of the people and the ridges and valleys of the land itself.

I'll be focusing on the southern edge of coal country down to the black soil of northern Alabama; we will set aside the northernmost part of this long mountain range, as it hosts different sets of cultures. The portion of the overall region that we are considering has enough interlocking cultures to hold our attention.

The stereotypes of Appalachian people hold kernels of truth, as most stereotypes do. Coal miners, liquor makers, subsistence farmers, and mill workers are all part of the historical peoples of the region. Storytellers, quilters, dancers, and music-makers: these, too, populate the area, enlivening dull, repetitive lives, and beautifying harsh ones.

But stereotypes fall short and mask the richness and diversity when it comes to the cultures living within and attached to the broader culture of the region. These relics that linger in a modern and electrified world come from all educational backgrounds, in all colors, from all classes, and worship all manner of gods—or none at all. The roots of the basic folk magic we practice came from ancestral immigrants, for we are a place of ramblers, of wanderers. Even the Cherokee came to these mountains from somewhere else, building townships and farms on land that was home to earlier tribal people, settled folks, nomads, and mound-builders from long before.

What binds us—beyond religion, music, or food—is the land itself: old hills and rivers, deep mines, and back roads that whip through the mountains like copperhead snakes. There are lakes here that cover drowned villages as well as ski slopes that attract outsiders for a sport the Native people never knew.

I grew up in a rural cove and both participated in and observed practices that were common with my extended family and neighbors. Like many people of my generation and the generation before, I left home after high school and came to live in more urban areas, going to school there and claiming a career. The country ways were left behind in daily practice but demanded my attention again in my middle years as I reclaimed some of what it meant to be a modern Appalachian woman. I talked to relatives, racked my memory for old places and old ways, and tentatively (at first) added some of these bits and bobs into a twentieth-century American life. Now I serve as a bridge between the old practices and how they can come to have meaning in a modern context. I am also surprised and delighted to find myself a repository of others' stories and remembrances, and a link that allows members of the vast Appalachian diaspora to come to a different way of thinking about the folkways of their Ancestors.

As a gardener and forest farmer, I am happy to say that I love the plants that people our diverse region. Every season brings new lovers into the hilly world around me. Chickweed and creasy greens pop up in the earliest spring, and ramps soon follow. Dandelion greens are sautéed with fresh eggs, and the flowers make a nice tonic. Juneberries and sweet, tiny, wild strawberries usher in the early summer jam season. Sang root is next, and the second coming of stinging nettle. Every season and all year long, under the savage sky, beneath the snow—there is always a simple plant for food, for medicine. Bark, fruit, root, seed. Spending the necessary time to learn their ways brings infinite rewards and a connection through time and space to the Ancestors and First Residents of the land that you call home.

My Sovereign Herbs and Some of Their Uses

If you are interested in working with the green goodness of Appalachia, I recommend that you begin with a few plants and learn what each is used for rather than deciding to learn every possible plant and always having to turn to a book for reference. Your knowledge will be deeper and broader, and you will find that there are several useful plants for any one condition or ailment.

The plants I use most often are very few, and some of them are not native to the region. The five plants in this section—bloodroot, mugwort, ginseng, black walnut, and rabbit tobacco—will give you a good idea of the diversity and the range of practice in the region. Four of these plants are native, with mugwort being a gift from European immigrants.

In such a biodiverse region, it is vital to know the Latin (botanical) name of the plants you are studying. Do not assume that the local name is universally used. You will also need to check plants' leaves, stems, flowers, growing habits, and so forth when wandering through a region different than your own. The devil is in the details, and starting with a few plants helps you know them so well that you can pick them out wherever they present themselves to you.

Bloodroot (Sanguinaria canadensis)

Bloodroot has a dear early-spring flower that is bright white with a yellow center, belying the fat root (technically a rhizome) that lies beneath and holds a bloodred secret. The fluid from this root is extracted in the fall, past the bulk of the growing season, and has been used in a variety of ways. It is known to induce vomiting but is most often used to remove warts, moles, and other skin growths. In these cases, bloodroot is applied topically, often as a black salve. A tincture of the root is also used on skin growths. It is a dangerous plant and caution should be exercised when handling it.

Mugwort (Artemisia vulgaris)

This big, crazy weed is everywhere and is terribly useful. It is in the same family as wormwood (*Artemisia absinthium*). Mugwort is not native here, but it is found throughout much of the region. It was used in Europe as a bittering agent for beer before hops replaced it. It can be a mild abortifacient, so handle with care. It is used most often now as a tea to remove intestinal parasites and as a dream tonic. It can be used to tone down nightmares and night terrors, to help you remember your dreams, and to aid in lucid dreaming and deep meditation. The simplest way to use mugwort is to cut fresh branches of it and insert them into the pillowcase (but under the pillow). The pungent but pleasant smell is released all night.

Ginseng (Panax quinquefolius)

In my first book on Appalachian folk magic, *Staubs and Ditchwater*, I refused to write about this sacred and terribly endangered plant. American ginseng has been harvested here since time out of mind and is believed to be a cure-all for almost anything that ails you. But it is legendary as a purveyor of long life—a soil-encrusted Fountain of Youth—and Asian medicine practitioners and their clients swear by it. You can certainly buy Chinese ginseng, and I suggest you do that. Unless you have the sort of conditions American ginseng requires and can plant it for your own use, please leave it be. This plant has been overharvested for generations and is poached in national parks and state-maintained forests. Let it be a legend. Think of it as the stuff of myth.

Black Walnut (Juglans nigra)

My father's ashes are buried under a stand of black walnut trees that he planted on the land where I grew up. This tree is wonderfully special to me for other reasons, too. It grows straight and tall, and every fall during the mast season ("mast" being all the nuts and seeds that drop to the ground for animals—including humans—to feast upon), it drops heavy green-and-black husks on the unsuspecting. Black walnut is different from its tame cousin, the English walnut (*Juglans regia*): it is smelly and hard to bust out of its woody shell. Black walnuts are often raked out onto a driveway and driven over to remove the outer husk. In addition to being a delicious protein that keeps well, black walnut has been used to treat intestinal parasites and to dye cloth. It will also stain whatever it touches (including skin) and should be handled with garden gloves. I smooth black walnut oil on candles as a dressing; it is a way-clearing magical oil because the tree roots release a chemical called juglone that suppresses the growth of other plants within the tree's canopy. And I use the nut meats in a buttery poundcake.

Rabbit Tobacco (Pseudognaphalium obtusifolium)

This plant has been used in many ways by the Native peoples here—as a decongestant, among other things.[100] It is sometimes called sweet everlasting because of its delicate scent and easily dried flowers; others call it field balsam because it tends to grown in the waste places around fields. Most country kids have smoked it at one time or another, and many folks don't give it a second glance, but I knew there was more to it than met the eye. Rabbit tobacco has gray-green leaves and tiny pale flowers, and it isn't particularly impressive as a specimen. It turns out the Cherokee consider it a sacred plant and have used it in ceremony because of its spiritual power.[101] I use it dried as sacred smoke, along with mugwort and the native mountain mint (*Pycnanthemum virginianum*).

Working with Waters

There are many types of waters that can be used to treat various conditions, both physical and spiritual. Here is a sampling of the diversity that is found throughout the region.

Dishwater

Dishwater is the cold, greasy remains of cleaning up the dishes after a family meal. It contains bits of food, and through the meal scraps and plates it carries the signature essences of both the dishwasher and the family. Dishwater is used to remove warts by soaking a rag in the water, touching the affected area with the wet cloth, and then burying the cloth away from the house. There are other methods, but this is a common one.

For the reasons outlined above, dishwater can be used to remove "troubles" from a household. In many cultures, there is a sense that misfortune can visit not only an individual but an entire family, and that this misfortune can travel through the generations of the family unless it is banished from the house. One way this banishment is imposed is by loading a rag with dishwater, taking it outside, and whipping it against a large rock or stout tree. This act may need to be performed three times for maximum effect.

100. Duke, *Handbook of Medicinal Herbs*.
101. Duke, *Handbook of Medicinal Herbs*.

Ditchwater

Ditchwater is almost always gathered in the spring, following the deprivations of a mountain winter. It is rainwater that has settled in a ditch or other low area. It is mucky, but not dirty in the same way as dishwater. Ditchwater is filled with life, invisible and visible, and is used as a sovereign remedy for freckles and fertility. A woman wishing to become pregnant can rub ditchwater onto her belly, thighs, and breasts to hasten the process. Anyone longing for blemish-free skin can dab it onto their freckles. A baby's urine is used the same way and I suspect is just as effective. Better to choose willow-water.

Willow-Water

Willow-water is sometimes called "stump water" and is rainwater that has pooled into the scooped-out base of a tree stump or, in the case of true willow-water, it is found among the fat and twisted roots at the base of any willow. As we now know, willow bark contains salicin (which becomes salicylic acid, an active ingredient in aspirin), and water that has steeped in such a naturally occurring bowl at the base of a living tree would have some of those same properties. It was traditionally used to treat headaches and skin eruptions such as acne and rashes. For skin care, willow-water was dabbed onto the skin with a clean rag or the face was bathed in the water. A headache required a cool compress over the forehead and eyes. Willow-water was sometimes ingested if the head pain was too much; in that case, the water would be gathered in a glass and the sediment allowed to settle before it was sipped.

Mill-Race Water

The water gathered from the stream below the mill's wheel was often given as a drink to members of the family that were considered "no account" or lazy. Many a pot of coffee contained this sympathetic magic ingredient; it may have been a combination of caffeine and magic that got that teenager up and out the door.

Dollies and Sachets

Poppets are not unusual in this old magic, but we call them dollies or baby dolls. Made from a variety of available materials—rags, paper, corn shuck—they are used for healing, focusing fertility, or taking the wind out of somebody's sails. The doll is tied to the person who is to be affected by giving it the person's features or name, or by attaching bits of hair or a personal object to the dolly. When the intention is firmly placed, the dolly is then kept safe or disposed of by fire or burial, depending on the work intended.

Sachets (pronounced *sa-shett*) function in much the same way as dollies. A sachet can be made from folded paper or old sacking, and it holds talismans for health, luck, or drawing resources. An asfidity bag is a kind of sachet, and these were very popular during the Great Influenza epidemic of 1918–1920. It held a chunk of solid asafetida, which was believed to have the power to repel disease from the wearer. A bag might also contain a bit of broken glass, a silver dime, or a lock of the wearer's mother's hair—all designed to keep the wearer safe and healthy.

Tinctures and Tonics

Most people are familiar with the idea of a spring tonic, a drink that revives the spirit (and the liver) after a long, dark winter. These liquid medicines are an important tool in a healer's bag. They are made of special herbs and minerals that have soaked in alcohol, milk, or spring water for a proscribed amount of time.

I do my best tinctures in what I jokingly call "Appalachian heritage alcohol," when I can get it. I am referring, of course, to corn liquor (which is also called white liquor or moonshine, though I never heard it called "moonshine" when I was growing up). Family lore has it that my great-grandparents were the middlemen in a corn liquor operation in the early part of the twentieth century. Corn liquor has long been an important part of the regional economy and deserves more respect than it usually gets.

I stuff a canning jar about three-quarters full with plant material and then fill the rest of the jar with the alcohol. I tighten the lid and leave the jar for one moon cycle, shaking it when I think about it. After a month, I pour the tincture off the plant material using a strainer and then bottle it, usually in another canning jar.

Some Jobs of Work

The word "spell" was rarely if ever used in my part of the mountains. Instead, we referred to these sorts of workings much the way we talked about any chore to be done: a job of work. The particulars were often left unspecified because you needn't explain how to milk the cow—you only needed to say you were going to do it.

Bright Glass Shards in the Window

Many old mountain homes have a peculiar decoration in the kitchen window: a canning jar containing bits of broken and brightly colored glass. It's an old bindment that traveled over from the homelands and is designed to keep mischievous spirits from the hearth (which is also the heart) of the home. But most women explain the jar by mentioning the practicality of keeping children's bare feet uncut and the whimsy of the pretty light shining through the colored glass.

Egg Binding

There are many sorts of bindments available to the wily householder. The use of a plain chicken egg inscribed and wrapped with string gives the householder some control over the bad habits of family and neighbors. Written on the egg is the name (and sometimes the deeds) of the miscreant, and the words are covered entirely by being wrapped in something as readily available and common as binding twine. Into the river it goes, or down the hole of the outhouse.

Burn Spell

I've encountered so many variations of this spell to remove burns over the years, and I am always delighted to find a new one. I have used it on many occasions, and it is poetic as well as effective. The verse I learned was:

Come three angels from the North!
Take both fire and frost!

These lines are spoken three times as the speaker's hand hovers above the burn and moves in a circular pattern. Another variation is:

Come three angels from the North!
Take fire! Leave frost!

In some parts of the region, the angels become brides, and they arrive from the east:

There were three brides come from the East.
They took the fire. They left the frost.

White Potatoes

We call them "Arsh" (Irish) potatoes here to contrast them to sweet potatoes. White potatoes are used as a poultice on skin eruptions such as a rash or fungus. They are peeled, grated, and applied directly to the skin. As the air touches the poultice, it begins to darken and becomes almost black, which no doubt inspired people to believe in the drawing power of this tuber.

Warts and Healing Touch

In rural places, there are people who perform various healing tasks, and their position is based on how well they do that work. There is hands-on healing, of course, but there are also people who are believed to have special abilities based on accidents at birth. A child that has never seen its father is expected to be able to blow the fire out of a burn or blow into a baby's mouth to cure thrush. The seventh son of someone who was also a seventh son is supposed to have special abilities, often related to healing and prophecy. Likewise, the seventh daughter of a woman who was also the seventh daughter is supposed to have unique abilities relating to midwifery and general healing. A child born with a "caul" or "veil" (a piece of placenta) over the face or head is believed to have great gifts of prophecy and to have a special connection to the divine.

Hands-on healing has been a parlor game for charlatans and medicine shows for a long time, but there are members of mountain communities that seem to have extraordinary healing power just by placing their hands on the person who is sick. My great-aunt could see spirits and heal warts, and there were plenty in the family that were suspicious of the spirit gift but grateful for the removal of warts. She claimed no real power—as do many mountain healers—but claimed she was only a channel for the Divine Will to do its work.

That Woman in the Apron

Popular culture likes to refer to these practices as "Appalachian granny magic," but I don't know any serious practitioner who calls it that. Most would be suspicious of the word "magic" (as many are of the word "witch"). And "grannies" are certainly not the only workers in these healing fields. Best to give it its academic name—Appalachian folk magic—when speaking outside the region, and within the region it is mostly a craft with no name.

This old, troubled, and spirit-haunted land evokes many iconic images: the rolling and expansive hills reaching to the endless horizon, the bright quilts sewn by many hands, a cast-iron pan filled with corn bread. But my favorite image is an old woman in an apron, standing for a moment's rest as she surveys the work still to do in her garden. She leans against a thin-handled hoe, its edges deadly sharp, a devilment to weeds and snakes equally. The hem of her apron serves to wipe the sweat from her upper lip and then she bends, veined hands gripping the hoe with authority, and returns to her work.

FIELD NOTES

Planting by the Signs

In a landscape where small farms often struggled to produce enough food for everyone, being able to time the planting, growing, and harvesting of crops was essential. One common practice to maximize the outcome of a crop was to link it to lunar astrology, a practice known as "planting by the signs."

The basic idea is that each of the twelve zodiac signs rules a different aspect of planting, connected to the way it also rules the body. Many almanacs printed (and still do print, as this practice continues today) the figure of the "astrological man," with indications that Taurus rules the neck, Cancer rules the chest, etc.

By tracking the combination of moon phases and astrological placement, which changes every three days or so, a person can determine the best times to plant, grow, and harvest. It is best to sow seeds that produce edible fruit when the moon is "on its back" (with the "horns" up), particularly when it passes through the "fruitful" signs of Scorpio, Taurus, or Cancer. Similarly, a person might want to avoid planting during the last days of a waning moon in a sign like Leo or Gemini, as those are considered "barren" signs that won't produce good food.

Theories about the moon and its astrological dance through the zodiac go well beyond just planting: a person might choose not to cut their hair on a day when the signs aren't favorable to avoid having it grow back too quickly (or not at all!). Similarly, some Appalachian folks don't pickle or make kraut when the moon is in Pisces, the sign of the feet, for fear their batch will become rancid or overly smelly.[102]

The following list is a brief summary of some of the signs' associations in folk magic and folk astrology:

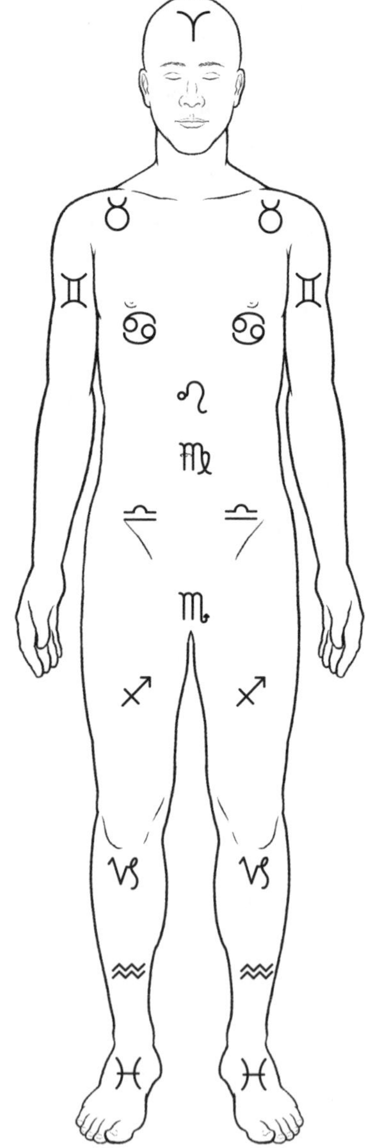

Figure 3-1: The Zodiac Man

102. For more on these practices see Milnes, *Signs, Cures & Witchery*, and The Foxfire Series, edited by Eliot Wigginton.

Aries: Weeding, clearing land, tilling soil, and harvesting; barren sign

Taurus: Planting, watering, transplanting; a very fruitful sign

Gemini: Weeding and harvesting, especially tubers and roots; barren

Cancer: Planting and transplanting, especially above-ground crops; fruitful

Leo: Weeding, cultivating the soil, and some harvesting; barren

Virgo: Tending to land and thinning crops, cultivating soil, weeding; barren

Libra: Fertilizing or watering, planting; very fruitful

Scorpio: Planting, transplanting, nurturing, enriching soil; very fruitful

Sagittarius: Good for some root crops, tolerable for planting; somewhat fruitful

Capricorn: Clearing land, tilling soil, harvesting; somewhat barren

Aquarius: Good for enriching soil and some planting and cultivating; somewhat fruitful

Pisces: Planting, especially root crops or tubers; fruitful

Each almanac may have slightly different interpretations of the fruitfulness or barrenness of these signs, and some will give different advice based on region. I recommend picking up an almanac specific to your bioregion, not just for its astrological advice but because it will usually tell you a good bit of folklore about your area, too!

The Poor Man's Play: Appalachian-Melungeon Folk Magic

JAKE RICHARDS

I was born and raised in the southern Appalachian Mountains of east Tennessee. I grew up in a household system that straddled two worlds: ours and the spiritual. I was reared on stories of haints and panthers in the woods, and I watched many times as our lives were shaped or directed by the dreams and visions given to my elders after they "talked with God." From a young age I learned the spiritual taboos that many now call superstitions; they guided almost every moment, word, and action in the homelife. To us, superstitions weren't ignorant or simple—they were wiser and more precautious than they seemed to others.

How It's Taught

Growing up and learning workings for hard times isn't as cut-and-dry as having a few sessions explained to you. It is a lifelong learning process that demands patience, caution, respect, and ease. Nothing in nature can be forced. For this reason, you have to listen to the elders the first time they speak, and always listen to them. The most magical information can be gleaned from a conversation over morning coffee in a Waffle House. The elders give small bits of information every now and then, as if slowly tilling the soil of spiritual wisdom for the next generation. It is handed down like an old family toolbox to help guide you in life, hidden in plain sight.

This toolbox is filled with the knowledge of how to cook the most ridge ingredients into a hearty meal, the satisfaction of working by the sweat of your brow for hard-earned money, the wisdom to know your finite place in this world, and the comfort of knowing that the trailblazers of yesteryear guide you now. Usually, in the past, this information was inherited within the family, but some things may be taught to others outside the family, usually from man to woman and woman to man, ensuring an equal gender dynamic within the folk practices of magic and medicine.

Appalachians are a hardy, stubborn, and independent people. We have no middleman between us and our neighbor, us and our environment, nor us and our Maker. The Mountaineer has just enough courage to go before the Throne standing as he does humility to go with his eyes closed.[103] The Appalachian terrain can be treacherous and harsh, and when the first settlers came, they quickly learned this. But they learned more than survival from the mountains themselves—they learned their strengths. As such, throughout Appalachian history, neither has been able to tame the other. The mountains and the people lived in as much an equal way as they could, and amongst the progression of the world, we are still trying to hold on to those ways.

Whether this magic is passed down by family or friends or learned from the spirits themselves, a respectful mind, a strong will, and a humble spirit is needed for this work. Connect with the land and learn your place in it. You need respect to approach the ancestors, a strong will for them to recognize you, and a spirit humble enough to sometimes kneel and accept that a bigger Will is at play regarding your needs or requests. Most importantly, you need trust. You must trust the spirits enough to lead you into madness without the promise of return. This work demands all from you. Whether you're willing to sacrifice is up to you.

Whence It Arose

This strong independence and coexistence with the land has influenced every aspect of our lives here: in our social and romantic lives, our communities and spiritual groups, in the way we pray or eat, and in the way we hold ourselves with dignity and pride. Like the mountains, we are fine standing alone and braving life's storms, firmly holding our ground on the bedrock of our deep roots, but we also know the strength of community is like the strength of the mountain ranges linked together: strong enough to avert disaster and change the weather of life for us all.

The magic of this land has roots in many places, over land and water: from Europe, to Africa, to the Indigenous peoples who still call this land home. It was influenced by Ireland, England, Scotland, and many other areas in Europe; by West Africa through the Atlantic slave trade, which arrived west of the Appalachians from the colonies of Virginia and the Carolinas; and from the local tribes here, such as the Cherokee. Folk magic, much like our architecture, agricultural practices, social taboos, history, and way of life, is shaped and flavored by the land on which it developed. The tools available, the beliefs behind magical acts, and even morals are all shaped by the natural world here.

Sounds complicated, but once the basics are known, the rest is as simple as riding a bike. Because of its simplicity, all this work can be done with a Bible, a glass of water, some dirt, and a candle. Throughout the long history of Appalachia, until the last one hundred years or so, we were labeled "isolated" and "secluded." But when looking at our culture, dialects, folklore, and practices, I personally prefer the term "secured." Being cut off from the rest of country in the advent of Western medicine and industrial progression, we may have been left behind "in

103. Going with eyes closed is the belief behind the old Appalachian burial practice of placing quarters on the eyes of the dead (and to keep them closed out of respect).

another era," as people describe us, but because of this, we are a people not of this current world. We live simple, eat simple, and pray simple.

How It's Done and Who Does It

Appalachians lived with just enough room as we needed and nothing more. But this didn't come without challenges and struggle. Our weather can be unpredictable, as can the promise of crops or jobs. The only constant is the tried-and-true wisdom of our elders before us, guiding our hands to plant crops by the moon, empowering our breath to make death bypass our homes, and sanctifying our prayers for safety and salvation on the mountain winds. It was a time when the mountain knew our names and the creeks bathed us in broken laps of cleaning water.

We use the plants, stones, bones, and feathers of the mountain to move the hand of God in our favor. This can be as simple as praying psalms for protection from evil while traveling a dark back road or placing a photo of a grandchild in the King James Bible at Mark 10:16 ("And He took them up in His arms, put His hands upon them, and blessed them") or Matthew 18:10 ("Take heed that ye despise not one of these little ones; for I say unto you, That in heaven their angels do always behold the face of my Father which is in heaven") for whatever the child may need. We may also fill our oil lamps discreetly with dirts, dusts, hair, or herbs to effect change in a situation, whether for the survival of crops or livestock, the reunion of lovers, or salvation from devils. We do this by the movements in the firmament of the heavens: the phases and signs of the moon, the times of the setting or rising sun, and the opening and closing of the vault of heaven. Likewise, we are no strangers to divination, whether it be bones, playing cards, or apple seeds; we have no reservations against asking future or past things of God through such methods, as our folk religion allows it.

Because of our seclusion and our resulting clannishness, we relied on our local mountain communities for what we needed in any area of life, especially spiritually and medically, due to the lack of churches, pastors, hospitals, and doctors. When someone had an accident or illness, there was usually at least one person to turn to—someone who either had knowledge they learned or a gift they were given at birth. With the lack of medical professionals and even religious institutions, one fellow man or woman in the community held the power to navigate you away from the chilling grips of death with a lead, secure your fresh soul into this world with a dime, or guard you from devils with a simple breath. They were called many things: conjure folk, yarb doctors, midwives, or witches. As with any practice, there were degrees of expertise that some folks were assigned by their communities, either as a love conjurer, a healer specialized in burns or warts, a healer specialized in healing beasts more than men, etc.

The most common degree of practice was the midwife, who knew the ins and outs of childbirth and aftercare. Each midwife approached birth differently: a midwife might only employ the latest medicine, paying no heed to superstitions or old wives' tales; she may or may not use herbs to comfort the mother or "jump the child down" (a Melungeon term), herbs which she may or may not believe held any sway with the spiritual affairs of human life; or she may do it all, with the addition of knowing just when the little soul is ready, how to guard it from lurking spirits, when to turn vessels in the home to keep the child from struggling, when to place the axe beneath the bed to ease the mother's birthing pains, and when to lay the Bible, open to the story of Christ's birth, on the mother for aid. The same degrees of this work occurred with every other title holder in the community.

The other most common degree or field of work was the folk witch, a person made almost entirely of stories. They were usually an outcast for being "other" or due to some variant of disgrace that justified their exile from the social life of the community. The mind of the mountaineer can be a wonderful place, full of innovative thoughts and stories about life, but it can also be filled with overactive imaginations and fear of the unknown—even when that unknown is a living, breathing person. Such thoughts can put people in danger, and at the very least, brand them for a long time as monstrous and witchy.

The Melungeon Witch

In the Appalachians, a whole class of people were feared and cut off because of their mixed race—my people: the Melungeons. So who were they? And what does a small, mixed ethnic group have to do with the Appalachians and folk magic? I'll tell you just that!

Many have been led to think that the era of slavery, segregation, and Jim Crow simply lent a hand in the blending of folk magic in America by empowering the disempowered, like in the Deep South with Hoodoo. Many people don't know that such racial beliefs held by whites made their way into the magical folk mind of this region as well as others, but they did. Such things, as horrible as they are, I cannot name here, but they are well documented.[104]

The Melungeons are a triracial group of people, hailing from mainly Black, white, and Indigenous roots. The term *Melungeon* was thought to come from the French *mélange*, given to us by French Huguenots who settled in the Tennessee valleys. The word could also have come from the Kimbundu word *Malungu*, which originally meant "watercraft." In Colonial America, Malungu came to mean "those from the same tribe" and further evolved to mean "sibling" or "family"; we still use it to refer to other Melungeons as "melungo/malungo," for a cousin or sibling.[105] The same etymological evolution of the word also occurred in Brazil, where many people stolen from their homelands in Kimbundu-speaking areas of West Africa lived.

104. See Cavender, *Folk Medicine in Southern Appalachia*.

105. Hashaw, "MALUNGU."

No one has ever agreed on what our origins are or how our "little race" started, whether it began with the lost colony of Roanoke, with indentured and free Black and white servants in Virginia, or with the Spanish and Portuguese expeditions of Juan Pardo, Hernando de Soto, and Lucas Vázquez de Ayllón. The latter is the most likely origin; each of these expeditions left behind hundreds of men, women, and slaves, and they melded into the local tribes, especially those on the Pee Dee River, where in 1754 it was reported that there were fifty families, "a mixed crew," living on Drowning Creek.[106] From there we mixed with the Lumbee, sharing core family surnames such as Oxendine, and later on, there was more admixture of Black and white. For much of our history, we have been recognized by people like Hamilton McMillan and James Mooney as being a branch of the Lumbee tribe.[107]

Either way, we know that beginning around 1760, Melungeons migrated from the coastal Carolinas and Virginia to escape the racial customs there. We moved to an area more lenient at the time: the mountains of Tennessee, North Carolina, and Virginia, where we arrived in the late 1700s, among the settlers at Fort Watauga. But soon, trouble followed us here: our ancestors encountered Major Ferguson, whose militia tried to run off the "backwater men" and "mongrels," an old term for mixed-race folks in Colonial America. They faced off in the Battle of King's Mountain in 1780, which the Overmountain Men won in one hour. Although the Overmountain Men settled at Fort Watauga, it is all too often only remembered as a place that was attacked by the Cherokee in 1776, after which little mention is made about it outside of land records. Melungeon folklore tells a story of us living west of the mountains in fertile valleys, then being ran off—up into the rough ridges—by encroaching settlers, but this did not occur at Watauga, nor any other place we settled, according to records. Regardless of the reason, we took to the rough ridges for refuge.

Up there we survived on fruit trees, sallet greens from the forests, and groundhog, wild boar, rabbit, and squirrel as our main meats. These staples are still with us today in recipes for rabbit sausage, groundhog patties, and fried eel and squirrel stew, and in our medicines that call for groundhog grease and rabbit hide.[108] Folk magic and folk medicine often have a blurred line here, and the two can be synonymous when dealing with injuries or disease, or simply to keep the body healthy.

Because of our isolation and anti-miscegenation laws, endogamy was also practiced. Melungeons only married within the group or those that sought refuge with us, such as runaway slaves, poor whites, Natives, etc. This occurred prior to and into the early 1800s. After that, the Melungeons denied any African admixture with claims of Portuguese blood, to explain the varied complexions

106. Pezzullo, "The Malungeons According to Joanne."

107. McMillan, *Sir Walter Raleigh's Lost Colony.*

108. *Appalachian Melungeon Heritage Cookbook.*

from fair to tan, brass to dark; the gray and dark brown eyes; and the straw- to coal-colored hair that varied in texture from relaxed to wavy to tightly curled. This was a defense technique, called "masking" by Mark Groover.

Groover noted that the strategies of the Melungeons, Cherokee, and Lumbee were armed resistance, cultural conservatism, and masking; the Melungeons used portions of all three, but the one that had the biggest effect (aside from armed resistance) was masking by curating elusive tales about our origins, from shipwrecks off the coast to being descended from the Lost Tribe of Israel.[109] All this cultural juggling was to avoid having our rights disenfranchised due to new laws in Virginia and Tennessee, and to avoid the threat of being enslaved. This is why we moved with our Melungeon neighbors en masse from place to place: to avoid being picked out and sold further north or south.[110] We also clung to our Native blood—that is, until the Indian Removal Act, at which point we reverted back to the Portuguese claims to avoid being sent away by the government.

Some Melungeons did their best to be recorded as white during segregation, while others didn't care either way if they were allowed to vote, what schools they went to, etc. Some who stayed on the Pee Dee kept with it and fought for recognition, such as the Lumbee, who until 1885 called themselves "Malungean."[111] There were others who saw no problem in being labeled Black and soon assimilated into that community, as did those Melungeons who easily passed for white, leaving those in between isolated still. However, this isn't as cut-and-dry as it sounds because there was more to legal "whiteness" than skin color. Yet again, we need to recognize that the Upper South (specifically the mountains) lacked a plantation economy as well as clearly marked racial categories and a well-developed racial vocabulary.

As much as we would've liked to live our lives on the ridges, given our murky history before and after 1800, we had to admit there was a society growing near the ridges, and it would soon be difficult to ignore or avoid—especially when the valley people had so much and we had so little, as much as our pride would have liked to believe otherwise.

This growing nation threatened us with laws in a society we were pushed into. Because the valley people knew Melungeons were mixed, and due to the one-drop rule, they would not hire Melungeons. No one wanted to be near us, not even doctors, intensifying our reliance on home remedies. This forced us to make our money through illegitimate means: from counterfeiting money from secret silver mines to distilling illicit whiskey from the apple trees on the rocky ridges so it could be sold. Likewise, this forced us to birth our own children, care for our own sick, and bury our own dead in the rocky soils of the ridges.

109. Groover, "Creolization and the Archaeology of Multiethnic Households in the American South."

110. Groover, "Creolization and the Archaeology of Multiethnic Households in the American South."

111. Paredes, *Indians of the Southeastern United States in the Late 20th Century*, 76.

Everywhere Melungeons gathered, we settled on or near the ridges, not only for seclusion, but also for medicine—the strongest herbs grow at higher elevations. Between the aftermath of the Civil War and World War I, the younger generation of Melungeons began leaving the ridges for better economic opportunities, leaving the elders behind at home.

Remnants of the discrimination Melungeons faced are still with us, and this can be seen in the representation we get in literature. When novels or short stories mention a Melungeon character, they are often portrayed as an evil monster, a henchman of the devil, or a diabolical witch. Or just mean and drunken. These stereotypes can be seen in the following tale.

Children of Perdition

An old Tennessee folktale says that Melungeons are the offspring of the Devil and a Native woman he took up with, explaining our often-darker skin and our disposition toward meanness. This tale is the origin of our label as "children of perdition," being born from an unholy union, which, in the literal sense of the day, was the common-law marriage between races.

In this folktale, the Devil and his wife had been fighting in hell and he left. He settled in the Blue Ridge Mountains for a time and took up with his Native mistress. They made a whole hoard of Melungeons who were as dark as their mother but as mean as their father. Soon the little Melungeon brood became too much for the Devil—they tortured him day and night; there was never a resting moment. Finally he said to himself, *This place is worse than hell* and stormed off, heading back home. As he stormed across the mountains, his footprints burned the vegetation, and nothing grows there still to this day; that is how the balds on Roan Mountain were made. In another tale, the mountain itself is called a Gate to Hell.

This tale was collected before set rules were in place for collecting folklore. As such, we do not know how much it changed over the years, or who first told the tale. It first appeared in the book *God Bless the Devil!* in the 1940s. Either way, it lent itself to Melungeon legend, for better or worse, in the local society.[112]

Tales like this told the white mountaineer that the Melungeons weren't just the children of perdition, but they were in league with their father, and as such they were a witchy and queer (with the connotation of "weird") people from then on. Preachers considered it a badge of honor to win over one of the "godless Melungeons" and preached sermons on how naturally diabolical we were, including stories of blood drinking and other witchery.

Now, remember the endogamy? Due to the limited blood in the community, polydactyl syndrome became a somewhat common occurrence. Folks were born with six fingers, and some still are, even though endogamy is no longer practiced. People, both Black and white, would tell their kids to behave or the Melungeons would come and snatch them up with their six-fingered

112. Aswell et al., *God Bless the Devil!*, 207–14.

hands, taking them away to the caves and cliffs they lived in. Some said it was to make a sacrifice to their hellish father; others said it was to eat. Since the early 1800s, beginning with the writings of Will Allen Dromgoole, Melungeons have been described as a stereotypically odd, suspicious, quick-to-violence, filthy, devilish people.[113] Whether we are cast as criminals or winged monsters from hell, it's hard to see us as we really were—and are—due to all the exotic tales that make us "exciting."

A Queer and Witchy People

Since the 1800s, other folklore surrounding us and members of our group has grown—lore that is likely based in fact. Early explorers of Melungeon history and life (such as Will Allen Dromgoole, as hated by us as she was) often remarked about our crude attachment to superstitions, charms, folk medicine, and the signs of the moon.

Knowing how the seclusion and isolation affected the folk magic practices of greater Anglo-Appalachia—and even that of Affrilachia, when referring to Black communities and families here—and that by the mid-1800s Melungeons were mostly assimilated into the growing Appalachian culture (aside from diet and dialect), it is no wonder that the same folklore, remedies, and magic would be found among them, just as it is among Black Appalachians, through cultural interchange.

Between the slurs of "ridgerunner" and "ramp" were whispers of what went on behind closed Melungeon doors. Tales abounded of what happened to people who didn't pay for illegal Melungeon liquor: within just a few days, an unknown disease would begin to devour them from the legs up. Doctors in the valley not only couldn't treat this disease, they also couldn't explain it. Similar tales were told about people who were simply going through Melungeon territory (today termed *Melungia* to account for all places Melungeons settled) at night and didn't meet the bite of the Melungeon's dogs.[114] Tales like this are told elsewhere, especially in the Deep South, where the phenomenon is known as "unnatural illness": disease caused by magical poisoning from walking over a magic powder or buried charm. It was said that magic kept law and revenue officers off Melungeon land, as well as anyone who wished to cause trouble, and that it kept our homes and kin healthy, safe, and strong. The last resort, if that didn't work, was violence, and many a revenue officer or sheriff lost their life battling the local Melungeon group.

113. Dromgoole, "The Malungeons."

114. Davis, *The Silver Bullet and Other American Witch Stories*.

The Poor Man's Play

As far as I have found, the magic of the Melungeons differed only slightly from the practices done in greater Appalachia. No matter the race or class, those who did (and do) this work share an innovative and resourceful mindset. We make it work, beyond any obstacle in our way, and overcome the oppression society pits against us, whether it is racial, classist, or economical. As such, we can do just as much with a handful of dirt and a glass of water as most can do with elaborate rituals and methods. The backbone of our work is sympathy: we affect the world by acting out what we wish to happen, whether that is by moving two candles closer and closer together to unite two lovers or by sweeping dirt out of a home from back to front to likewise sweep out the ghosts.

Appalachian folk magic is a theater where you become the director—and the characters. It is fueled by the sympathetic, parable language of the Bible, language which becomes the dialogue and monologue of the work, of the play. Whatever is acted out convinces the hand of God to move in a like manner. But in recent decades, the reason Melungeons seemed queer and ignorant for keeping our ways has been forgotten by the majority of the population as society progresses, and the mind of the mountaineer is opening up to the possibilities that lay outside the mountainous bowl that brewed this work and crafted the stubbornness of his very bones. Likewise, the power of this work is being forgotten as people move farther and farther away from the bone-filled beds of their ancestors; they forget the feel of the mountain breeze, the chills from baby haints crying inside the cemeteries, and the echoes that reverberate off the mountainside, across the river from where a baptism is being performed.

Historically, this work was passed down in the family or from one person to another. Today, as it is being revived, the same traditions are continuing, with the added benefit of inviting others into the tradition—as long as they do not alter it and still try to sell it off as traditional. So, by technicality, Appalachian folk magic is a semi-closed tradition. It was practiced by normal town folks and by the feared and revered "professionals": people who lent their services, whether that service entailed conjuring, cursing, healing, love magic, or finding the witch that cursed you to return the spell to them. Appalachian folk magic can be practiced alone or together, though usually no more than a handful of people are involved, depending on the task at hand. The professionals (yarb and root doctors, conjure doctors, and witch finders) were people whose lives were dedicated to Appalachian folk magic, whose company was composed primarily of incorporeal companions and whose time was mostly spent alone, save for the spirits or plants and animals in the mountains. Likewise, the professional needed to have a strong will; enemies, seen and unseen, could be strong and resilient. Any doubt or fault in one's work could mean the life or death of the person they were working the root or doctoring the devil for.

The Appalachian Conjurer's World

The cosmology of Appalachian folk magic reflects the religious environment here: an animistic flavor of old Baptist religion, where God is not aloft somewhere but here in the hills and valleys, keeping a careful parental eye on all, even the smallest sparrow. Appalachian culture evolved and we gained a spirit of independence tempered with humility. We are strong enough to face devils and haints and witches and death, even to go before the Throne ourselves, but all the while we know we aren't the source for that power; we know that it belongs to a Greater One.

Below God are our ancestors, those who came before us and still play a role in the communities and families they left behind. Historically, our dead were buried on family lands, in family cemeteries. It is no wonder that living near the spirits of our dead would lead us to develop a system of methods to communicate with them, which we still follow today, in the age of public, faraway burial places. Since our ancestors are no longer constantly present on our land, today we make small shrines for them that contain a Bible, white cloth, and photos/memorabilia. The shrines are on some small table or shelf in the living area of the home.

Because this work is highly based on the Bible and local folklore, many folks in the old days followed the biblical "eye for an eye" when it came to this work, meaning cursing is not uncommon among these hills, as long as it is just—an eye for an eye. As the old folks always explain, whatever you do, God's got just as much to do with it. So if it comes to fruition, then it was within the will of Zion. But it must not tip the scales of balance, or the scales will fall back in your direction.

Tools and Works

The items we use are all conveniently available to us, whether through the land, our homes, or the store down the road. We use candles, oil lamps, doll babies, dirts, and oils for our works, as well as herbs such as ginseng, bloodroot, and trillium (herbs that still provide an income through root-digging for some families, especially Melungeon families like my own). But beyond all this, Appalachian folk magic is more than a tradition to write and teach about, or to pick up and do. It's something that gets deep into the marrow of your bones and stays with you for the rest of your life as you follow certain superstitions, from what day you clean the house to the particular way you put your shoes on in the morning. It becomes second nature, and it's hard to imagine navigating life without it.

Here are a few of our methods.

Egg Cleansing to Remove Spiritual Messes, Hexes, or the Evil Eye

Take a room-temperature egg that has been washed in cold water and allowed to dry. While reciting Psalm 23, pass it over your whole body from head to toe. Pass it three times over the front, three times over each side, and three times over your back, as best as you can reach. Once done, crack the egg open and drop the white and yolk into a glass of cold water, but do not look at it from the top. Let it sit for thirty minutes. If the contents sink completely, the cleansing was successful. If a few bits of the egg white reach the top in "webs," do the cleansing once more, or however many times it takes for the egg to completely sink. Dispose of the water and yolk far from the home, "where no man will walk," like the side of a tree, a rock, or a brick wall.

Ritual to Bring Blessings and Prosperity to Yourself

1. Recite Deuteronomy 28:1–8 over olive oil seven times:

    And it shall come to pass, if thou shalt hearken diligently unto the voice of the Lord thy God, to observe and to do all his commandments which I command thee this day, that the Lord thy God will set thee on high above all nations of the earth: and all these blessings shall come on thee, and overtake thee, if thou shalt hearken unto the voice of the Lord thy God. Blessed shalt thou be in the city, and blessed shalt thou be in the field. Blessed shall be the fruit of thy body, and the fruit of thy ground, and the fruit of thy cattle, the increase of thy kine, and the flocks of thy sheep. Blessed shall be thy basket and thy store. Blessed shalt thou be when thou comest in, and blessed shalt thou be when thou goest out. The Lord shall cause thine enemies that rise up against thee to be smitten before thy face: they shall come out against thee one way, and flee before thee seven ways. The Lord shall command the blessing upon thee in thy storehouses, and in all that thou settest thine hand unto; and he shall bless thee in the land which the Lord thy God giveth thee.[115]

2. After taking a bath or shower, sprinkle new salt (salt bought specifically for this and never to be used in food) in your shoes.
3. Next, anoint your brow, breast, hands, and feet with the blessed oil.

Do this before business deals, starting a new job, payday, and so on.

115. Authorized King James Version.

Going Further

If you're interested in learning more about Appalachian folk magic and you are not in the region of southern Appalachia, or you don't have anyone to turn to in order to learn the basics, then I certainly recommend my books *Backwoods Witchcraft*, *Doctoring the Devil*, and *Ossman and Steel's Classic Household Guide to Appalachian Folk Healing* for a further understanding of just what you'll be getting yourself into. At the end of this section are a few more resources I recommend on both Appalachian folk magic and the Melungeons.

Because of its little-known status, Appalachian folk magic is becoming much like what Hoodoo has become in past decades: just another notch to add to someone's belt, whether for social, egotistical, or economic purposes. This work isn't a badge of pride or honor or anything special. If it must be worn and touted as such, then the whole point of the work has been missed. Appalachian folk magic is who you are and who you become. It is the amalgamation of the trials and triumphs of our ancestors.

If you're serious about learning Appalachian folk magic, find a reputable source—a person who you are sure knows what they are doing—and ask them to teach you. Now, here comes the manners part of it: constantly asking for someone to teach you is rude. Professionals are carriers of their familial practices and as such, they are entitled to choose whom to pass their knowledge on to and when. Often it will be a younger family member. It's nothing personal; as I explained above, not everyone comes to folks like me with the best intentions. So yes, you must gain a professional's trust and their friendship, and even then they may not teach you, because this work cannot be taught in a few classes or brief conversations—it has to be lived. It has to be endured, even during the hardest times of life. Some real sacrifices would need to be made by both parties. Appalachian folk magic shapes you, as with everything in life, and some folks will just never fit the mold to do this type of work.

FIELD NOTES

Doodlebugs and Water Witching

One type of witch has almost always been welcome in their community: the water witch. In folklore and historical documentation, that term does not apply to a witch who works seaside spells or dances naked by the riverside under a full moon. (They might well have, but it's not what they're known for, although it does sound like a good time.) Instead, the "water witch" in the parlance of the Upland South referred to those with a specific skill set: dowsing.

Dowsing is the use of extrasensory perception to locate particular resources, the best known of which is water. Dowsers—also called doodlebugs in addition to the water witch epithet—would be called upon whenever someone needed to dig a new well, which made them incredibly valuable members of their communities.

Most accounts of dowsing practices indicate that the water witch would be born with "the gift" to be able to dowse. Sometimes this came as the result of being the seventh son of a seventh son or being marked at birth with a caul (an amniotic membrane that is sometimes still around a baby's head right after they are born). In others, the gift of dowsing emerges over time and they simply find they have a skill for it.

Dowsers usually use one of two methods: the branch or the rods. The branch method involves cutting a fresh, green section of a tree—usually a peach or willow, although other trees are sometimes used—that comes in a Y shape. The dowser then holds the two shorter sections of the branch in their fists and lets the long tail of the Y point in front of them. They will walk until the branch begins bobbing up and down. Many dowsers seem to barely control the branch once water is found, with some feeling it violently ripped from their hands. The number of bobs can sometimes be used to figure out how deep the well should be dug, too.

The rods method involves taking two copper rods bent into an L shape and holding them so the long parts are pointing parallel in front of the dowser. The dowser will then walk around until the rods suddenly drift together in an X shape over the spot where the well should be dug.

While many doodlebugs do their work only for water, there are also a number who claim to be able to locate any resource, including gold, coal, oil, or other minerals. Mineral mining companies and oil drillers have been known to employ dowsers to avoid hitting underground water supplies and to find veins of their targeted substance. In a letter dated December 8, 1993, the Chevron Oil Company told Welsh dowser J. P. Taylor that "you opened our eyes to the world of dowsing…it certainly made us think there is more to it than we had previously known." The letter goes on to highlight how Taylor, with no prior knowledge of the specific geology of two regions, had been able to accurately identify subterranean oil and gas reservoirs.[116]

116. Taylor, "Oil Testimonial."

Some doodlebugs also claim to do "map dowsing" using a pendulum over a map of a particular area, although this is more in line with treasure-hunting methods than the water witching so common in Appalachia.

Because of the vital service they provide by finding water, many communities not only tolerate their local water witches, they embrace them. It's one of the few instances where someone being called a witch is almost universally considered a mark of honor!

The Clear Moon Brings Rain: Religion, Folk Belief, and Omens in Middle Tennessee

CORY THOMAS HUTCHESON

One of my favorite quotes is from the book *Sula* by Toni Morrison. In it, the town of Medallion, Ohio, has recently endured what is called a "plague of robins," in which hundreds of songbirds have started dying off in the streets, trees, meadows, and yards. Some link this to the return of the titular Sula, a spurned and cursed woman associated with wild behavior and reckless love, but even as they make that connection, most simply feel this new robin-pocalypse is not a terror to be combatted, but a woe to be endured. The intervention of supernatural forces in the natural world, the sense that *someone, somewhere* is telling them *something,* is a part of the ordered universe. It is entirely mundane magic. Morrison's passage reads:

> Evil must be avoided, they felt, and precautions must naturally be taken to protect themselves from it. But they let it run its course, fulfill itself, and never invented ways to either alter it, to annihilate it or to prevent its happening again...Plague and drought were as "natural" as springtime. If milk could curdle, God knows robins could fall.[117]

My own experience of Southern folk magic—which I sometimes refer to as Southern Conjure, something slightly distinct from other forms of folk magic rooted in the South, such as Hoodoo—has been much like Morrison's novel paints it to be. There's an order to things, a structure that underlies the flow and operation of the world. It's a world based on signs and omens, on magic that you can carry in your pocket or shoe or hatband. It's serious tales about why you hold your breath as you pass the graveyard, and comical ones that make fun of those who speed past the graves in fear.

117. Toni Morrison, *Sula*, 89–90.

I want to introduce you to the South as I know it. I hope to be honest about it because the Upland South—like all of North America—has its demons, both past and present. I hope to give you a taste of the wonder that shows up here, too, because it truly is a landscape of folktales, of hauntings, of strange creatures, and of magic. I will also tell you a bit about myself and my practice and share what I can from my own understanding of the place I lived in for more than three decades of my life, a place that is still "home" no matter how much I complain about backward politics, humid summers, or gentrification. I hope that you'll finish this essay with a better understanding of who I am, and by extension, what the South is when it gets into a person's bones and shapes them, growing in and around their soul like roots pushing into red clay and black earth. I hope, in my own Southern way, to charm you—in every sense of the word.

One Hundred Churches: A Brief Religious History

The part of the South I know best is a stretch known as Middle Tennessee. Historically the Shawnee, Cherokee, Yuchi, and Chickasaw peoples inhabited the lands I called home for most of my childhood. Tennessee's colonization by Europeans began when it was still the state of "Franklin," with settlers moving beyond treaty boundaries in Appalachia and into the Cumberland Plateau region over the seventeenth and eighteenth centuries. In 1796, the newly established United States determined a settler boundary and named the area Tennessee, apparently taking the title from a Cherokee word.

That, of course, was not all that was taken from the Cherokee, as during the nineteenth century Tennessee resident and US President Andrew Jackson signed the Indian Removal Act into law, and shortly after his term in office ended, the Trail of Tears began. While the Cherokee have managed to maintain some presence in the eastern mountain regions, the historic homelands of most Native peoples are now the homes of more recent colonizers and settlers. Some, such as the Scots Irish, came to the region because they wished to escape the governance and cultural reach of the more "Eastern" English-derived settlers. They brought with them a variety of faiths, mostly Protestantism, which was seen as fairly radical at the time compared to the Anglican/Episcopalian Protestantism found in places like Virginia. Methodists, Presbyterians, and Baptists all looked to carve out their own spaces in the area, which most viewed as a sort of "promised land."[118]

African captives were enslaved throughout the region, and over time African American religious practices began to emerge within Christian frameworks. Scholars like Katrina Hazzard-Donald have argued that many aspects of African Traditional Religion were folded into Protestant church practices, with water immersion having parallels in both West African ceremonies and the

118. Woodard, *American Nations*, 101–14, 189–99.

"dunking" or river baptisms done among frontier Protestants. Crucially, the African American experience of Christianity was never one-dimensional. Many slave-holding whites in the South actually forbade their African and African American captives from practicing any religion, including Christianity. Partly this was an effort to dehumanize them, since they frequently framed slaves as "animals" and thus outside of the scope of religion. Partly, though, there were fears that if African Americans learned about the doctrines of Christianity—which often preached that all human beings were "brothers" and "sisters" together—they would demand to be seen as equals and treated as co-religionists, even family.[119]

Of course, forbidding religion has a way of making it much more likely to take on new shapes and to survive in the shadows, gaining a power all its own. Ingenious African Americans developed ceremonies like the "ring shout," a silent circular procession that was designed to seem like a moving prayer but which echoed African group dances.[120] A wave of religious revivalism in the nineteenth century, known as the Second Great Awakening, led to a surge in charismatic religious practices, and so faith healing, possession by the Holy Spirit, speaking in tongues, multiday revivals, and more found a home in places like Cane Ridge, Kentucky, and other frontier spaces.[121] These folk expressions of religion meant there were also numerous churches formed, each with varying ways of performing their faith.

On my own road to folk magic, I've had a lot of influences. My religious background, however, was always a little askew from those around me. My mother was Catholic, and so that was largely my upbringing, but I was never deeply ensconced in the Catholic system; I was not fully confirmed, for example, and not baptized in any official capacity either. My father was a church music leader at a Presbyterian church while I was growing up; he eventually went to a Methodist congregation. My parents were divorced, so I attended both services, and I went to services with friends at Baptist churches, Jewish synagogues, and other religious houses, as I was naturally very curious and open to religion. Many members of my extended family are members of the Church of Jesus Christ of Latter-Day Saints ("Mormons," in common parlance) and so I have some familiarity with that belief system too, from attending services with them.

While all of this gave me a good background in religious education, it also illustrates the point that I was never "in" any one church. I have always been at a sort of junction of belief and practice, a confluence of these different sources. I don't always spend a great amount of energy on their differences because I see the awe and wonder that flows among all of them, but those differences can be severe. There are streaks of deep antisemitism in Southern culture, sometimes even couched in pro-Israeli sentiments. Segregation among congregations created generational racial

119. See Raboteau, *Slave Religion*, and Genovese, *Roll, Jordan, Roll.*

120. Hazzard-Donald, *Mojo Workin'*, 45–48.

121. Butler, *Awash in a Sea of Faith*, 291.

divides that have only begun to heal in recent decades (if they are healing at all). My Catholic influences have always been somewhat suspect to many Southern Protestants (although they are less of a problem in urban areas).

If you drive through a city like Nashville today, you'll quickly see the legacy of this incredible diversification of belief. It's sometimes said that Nashville has more churches per capita than any other city in the country. Or, to put it another way, you can drive ten minutes in any direction from downtown and you'll probably pass a hundred churches. If you can get around all the pedal taverns on lower Broadway, that is.

Which brings us to the other paradox of the South I know: we may look like a place of virtue with all those churches, but we have more than enough vice as well. Not far from Nashville is Lynchburg, Tennessee, home of the Jack Daniels distillery. Bourbon, whiskey, and moonshine have long been a part of Tennessee history—legal and otherwise—as have bars, taverns, and honky-tonks in which to consume said spirits. Nashville is known as "Music City," largely due to its incredibly robust country music scene and the presence of dozens of recording studios. Crucially, the music that made Nashville so prominent is built on a variety of influences. Bluegrass retains some of the lyrics and structure of the Child Ballads found in England and Scotland and brought in by Scots Irish immigrants, but one of the best-known bluegrass instruments is the banjo, which is derived from African musical traditions. Blues and country music both come from "country blues" origins, performed by African American artists like Lead Belly and Robert Johnson, and then formed the basis for later developments in the soul, rhythm and blues, and rock 'n' roll genres. "Juke joints" were dance halls with live music, loose dancing, and strong liquor, and there were more than a few people who would play all night on Saturday so they'd have something to be forgiven for on Sunday.

Devil Cats and Snake Charms: A Pair of Tales

What does all of this religious history have to do with the folk magic, though? To answer that, I'd like to tell a pair of stories. One is a folktale, and one a personal story. I begin with the folktale, which I call "The Devil-Cat":

> A man got his wages every Saturday, but before he could get them home to his wife and family, he'd take them out and drink and gamble them away. It left the family in an awful way, but there didn't seem to be much anyone could do about it. Then, one night he was playing cards with some no-account friends of his and pulled down glass after glass of whiskey. They were smoking and carrying on, and so the house was stuffy. He opened up a window and sat down next to it, and all of a sudden heard a voice come in from the dark, saying, "First warning, John. Lay

> aside your drink, your cards, your fiddle and bow, or I will return in two weeks and take you away to hell." That sobered him up pretty good, and he managed to keep away from whiskey and sin for a full week.
>
> But when Saturday rolled around again and his pocket was full of wages, he couldn't resist, and so he set to carousing and playing again. Once again, as he sat by an open window he heard, "Second warning, John. Lay aside your drink, your cards, your fiddle and bow, or I will return in one week and take you away to hell." Well, this time he made an even bigger swing to try and keep from giving in to his vices. But when Saturday came, the weight of coin in his pocket was too much, and he thought he'd have just one little old drink, one fiddle tune, and maybe one game of cards. But ones became twos, and twos became threes, and soon the money was fast converting to good times and leaving nothing to feed John's wife and children.
>
> So, as he sat by the window this time, all of a sudden a great black shape leapt in and landed on the card table. Everyone went skittering away as they looked at the enormous shadow, which they later claimed had burning red eyes. It landed right in front of John and hissed and spat in his face as he sat frozen in fear. Then with a mighty swipe of its claws, it tore old John to pieces and left him dead before charging back out of the window and into the night. Everyone said it was the Devil come for John and that it had clawed out his very soul to drag away to hell.[122]

Next, the personal story: I made a friend during my folklore studies who happened to also be a fairly successful musician. She was a fiddle player (a really good one) and she was studying Appalachian ballads and had an interest in folklore herself. Eventually she also married a successful alt-country musician. For their wedding present, I sent along some of the usual things like glassware from a gift registry, but I also made them a traditional rattlesnake charm to bring them success in their musical careers. He wound up being very successful as the headliner for his new band, which she also played in. She has her own successful solo career too, and even joined an all-women "supergroup" of alt-country performers in the years that followed.

Now, am I saying that my charm had anything to do with my friend's success? Or that someone's choice to have a drink or play cards will eventually lead to them being attacked by a devil-cat of some kind? No, absolutely not. Instead, I'm saying that these ideas are always there in the background of Southern life—devils may lie in wait for those who do wrong, for example, or a small charm might offer up a bit of extra luck or a nudge into success and fame. Even if these ideas aren't "true" in a literal sense, the belief that they could be true fuels a churning world of magic underneath everyday living. Additionally, while there may be a rhythm to all that enchant-

122. Adapted from Hyatt, *Folklore of Adams County, Illinois*, and Halpert, "The Devil and the Fiddle."

ment, it doesn't mean everything follows a straight, logical line. The devil may come to collect the souls of drinkers and gamblers, but he also figures into lore in which he teaches people how to play the fiddle or win at cards just as often. In the land of one hundred churches, there's no shortage of belief to fuel the fires of conjure work.

There's a paradox in the magic, which makes it even more mysterious, and frequently a little scary too. That's the way it works, though. Witches, conjurers, and our magical ilk all do the work that lives between wonder and fear. Some of us find lost objects, or talk out fire from a burn, or stop up blood with a Bible verse. And some of us sour the milk or drag down the fortunes of those that slight us. Some do all of the above. All do what is necessary.

The Rattlesnake Fame Charm

This is a version of the charm I made for my fiddler friend. Did it lead to her success? Well, no, since she had a successful career long before we met and she's an incredibly talented musician anyway. But it certainly didn't hurt her opportunities any, and maybe a weird gift like this added a little magic to her life that made writing that next song just a touch easier, or pulled the stage fright jitters down a peg when needed.

To make this charm, you ideally would have a rattlesnake rattle (if you can find one ethically sourced from someone who collects from already-dead rattlers). That can be tricky, so if you need to, you can use the bristly flower heads and/or roots of the plant known as rattlesnake master (*Eryngium yuccifolium*). Take the primary curio—rattle or plant—and wrap it in red flannel, along with a big leaf of five-finger grass (cinquefoil, which looks a bit like wild strawberry leaf and is thought to grant favors to the bearer). I also like to fold in a bay leaf (used to crown people in ancient times when they won a race or had other successes) and allspice (a Caribbean berry that can bring business luck). I take a coin from the year of the person's birth—usually a penny or a dime if I can find one—and add that into the packet too. I fold all of this into a square, then wrap it tightly with alternating turns of a red thread so that the final packet is wrapped both horizontally and vertically, making a big equal-armed cross around it. I bless this with whiskey or coffee as I speak Psalm 65 over it.

This charm regularly needs "feeding" with a bit more whiskey or coffee, and I will often speak the verse "Thou crownest the year with thy goodness; and thy paths drop fatness" as part of the feeding rite.[123] I feed a charm like this at least once a month, and as often as once a week if I'm working it actively for a particular goal. Its intended purpose is to bring you opportunities for increased success, particularly in fields where you need to catch someone's attention, such as art or music.

123. Psalm 65:11 (Authorized King James Version).

Bad Things Come in Threes: Living by Signs and Omens

While I do use charms and magic on an as-needed basis, much of the way that enchantment enters my life is through what I like to call "omen-ic" living. The Toni Morrison quote I mentioned earlier captures the essence of that idea: the interconnection of the world means that subtle clues, meanings, hints, and signs are ever-present, and someone with a mind for magic can frequently tap into that. On some level, it seems that many people—especially those involved in a magical lifestyle of some kind—recognize that the world is essentially "speaking" to them, if they are willing to listen.

Even Southern people without a specifically magical bent usually have some hint of this omen-based mindset. For example, the weather is a very common source of proverbial wisdom and lore. People frequently use idiomatic expressions or folk methodologies to detect patterns in the weather around them and predict potential changes that will personally impact them. In some cases, these changes are immediate: a greenish sky and hail preceding a tornado in some parts of the country; animals freaking out prior to an earthquake in another place. Some of these we accept almost as scientific fact, but we resist signs with more tenuous connections, like when wasps build their nests up high prior to a long, hard winter. Several people I've spoken to over the years have made excellent points about detachment from our surroundings, particularly nature. When we don't directly rely upon natural phenomena to feed us or make us comfortable (due to living someplace with regular access to food, climate control, and entertainment), we "unlearn" the connective language of omens in the process. However, I have also found that we tend to develop a new set of omens in place of the old ones: predicting traffic based on certain sounds or sights, for example. That seems to me a prime example of being tapped in to the world around you, no matter what environment you live in.

Are signs and omens universal or personal, or some combination of the two? For most folks, reading the world around you requires a familiarity with it, with at least some aspect of personal interpretation involved. Likewise, symbols register differently: an owl swooping across the road in front of your car may just be a raptor on the hunt. But a second owl doing the same thing may be a tap on the shoulder from the universe. For someone versed in folklore, there's a lesson in many tales that says ignoring a good omen frequently lands one in hot water in mythological circumstances, so paying attention can be more valuable than blissful ignorance.

Knowing how to discern signs is also important. A song stuck in your head may just be an infectious earworm surfacing for no reason, but if you live an omen-ic life, then frequently those sorts of little details can alter your perception enough to add enchantment and significance to everything. Taken to an extreme, however, omens can become superstition. While I tend to embrace that term, I also recognize that for most people, superstition denotes custom or tradition without substance or a fear-motivated lifestyle, and I would absolutely agree that spending seven years in fear after breaking a mirror is not a life really lived anymore. In its best form, a life can be lived fatefully, purposefully, and with a tremendous awareness of the vast interconnection of all the moving parts of existence. It will be a life in which fear becomes secondary to strength and wisdom—present, but not dominant—and which allows for a more holistic interpretation of the inherently magical and connected world.

I can't resist the opportunity to share some more signs and omens from other sources. Here are some of the more common, and some of the most unusual, examples I've found:

- A clear moon brings rain, indicating a clear night sky will be followed by wet weather the next day.
- The accidental crossing as four people shake hands together means that one of them will soon marry.
- A baby smiling in its sleep has an angel speaking to it.
- When passing a wagonload of hay, you should grab a handful; it will bring good luck if you do, and bad luck if you don't.
- If the stars are thick, it is a sign of rain.
- Lightning in the south means dry weather.
- If you find an inchworm on your clothes, you will soon have new garments.
- You should never watch a friend walk out of sight or you will never see them again.
- If two persons say the same thing at the same time, they must lock their little fingers without saying a word and make a wish.
- Dream of a funeral and attend a wedding.
- It is bad luck to tell a dream before breakfast.
- Cutting a baby's hair before it is a year old will give it bad luck. (This is also said in regard to letting a baby look in a mirror.)
- A baby born with a caul over its face will be a prophet or a seer.
- A whippoorwill that alights on a house and calls is announcing a death to come.
- Misfortunes always come in threes.
- A bride should not look at her complete wedding attire in the mirror until after she is married or else the marriage will end badly.
- If sparks from a fire favor someone (move toward them in unnatural ways or numbers), they have significant magical powers.

- Hearing raps, knocks, bells, chimes, or ticking with no apparent cause announces a death in the near future.
- The seventh son of a seventh son will be a naturally gifted healer, seer, or witch.
- A cat coiled up with its head and stomach showing means bad weather is coming; if it yawns and stretches, good weather is not far behind.
- A rooster crowing at night brings rain in the morning.
- Seeing a sun dog (a halo around the sun) indicates either a drought or a radical change in weather soon.
- Fogs in August are snows in winter.
- If you are walking or riding at night and feel a sudden warmth or chill, it is a spirit, and you should turn your pockets inside out to keep it from doing you harm.
- Stepping over a broom forward is bad luck, but you can reverse it by stepping over the broom backward.[124]

Are any of these beliefs that I ascribe to with absolutely no scrutiny? No, of course not. For me it has less to do with the idea that a curled cat or a sun dog indicate weather specifics and much more to do with the fact that I'm noticing these signs. If I'm paying attention, listening to the world, then maybe I'm getting information through these signs that adds up to something important.

Or maybe sometimes a rooster just crows at night because it's kind of a jerk. Anything is possible.

New Stories and Old Enchantments

The South remains a crossroads in many ways. Numerous beliefs collide or converge as they move through our landscape. We tell stories about fiddles and devils but take immense pride in the fiddle music playing down at the honky-tonk these days too. And the South has some massively progressive intellectual and scientific institutions: Vanderbilt University, St. Jude Children's Research Hospital, and the Raleigh-Durham Research Triangle, to name but a few. I grew up in the "Athens of the South," so named because Nashville literally has a replica of the famed Parthenon with a gold-and-white statue of Athena inside, and because that area is home to a dozen or more universities and colleges.

124. This collection of beliefs based on those found in Dorson, *Buying the Wind*; Gainer, *Witches, Ghosts, and Signs*; Hyatt, *Folklore from Adams County, Illinois*; McAtee, "Odds and Ends of North American Folklore on Birds"; Milnes, *Signs, Cures & Witchery*; Price, "Kentucky Folk-Lore"; Randolph, *Ozark Magic and Folklore*; Steiner, "Superstitions and Beliefs from Central Georgia"; and Thomas and Thomas, *Kentucky Superstitions*.

We have a checkered history, one we cannot shy away from; it involves white people dumping food onto Black protesters peacefully sitting at drugstore counters and ghettoizing the Indigenous peoples of our region into reservations. Yet we are also the home of the largest Kurdish population outside of Iraq, and our Latinx population comprises people with roots in Mexico, Guatemala, El Salvador, Costa Rica, Puerto Rico, and more.

All of these influences are shaping the ongoing story of magic in the South. The stories we're telling today will become the folklore of tomorrow. We paint porch ceilings "haint blue" to keep the wasps from building nests, but somewhere in there we also hope that it'll keep away any unwanted spirits. We put bottle trees in the yard because they're pretty with their limbs decorated in colorful cylinders of glass, but they have African American roots that keep away hurtful witchcraft as well. We run an annual St. Jude Marathon to raise money for one of the leading children's hospitals in the nation, but we are also lighting candles to that patron saint of hopeless causes when we find ourselves or those we love in dire straits.

To get to know the South, it's worth spending time here. We are famed for our hospitality, after all. You can find out a lot about us through collections of lore like the Foxfire books or the publications of the Tennessee Folklore Society, and you can read our legends, listen to our music, and eat our food.

The South I know is magic. I hope you'll see the enchantment I do, and maybe come sit a spell with us sometime.

FIELD NOTES

And Ye Shall Take Up Serpents

A widespread and often misrepresented component of Southern folk religion is the practice of snake-handling. While there are many who know (and mock) the charismatic evangelical Christian practitioners who engage in this ritual, very few understand the complex range of behaviors that go along with it. Much of the practice revolves around a specific passage in the biblical book of Mark: "In my name shall they cast out devils; they shall speak with new tongues; they shall take up serpents; and if they drink any deadly thing, it shall not hurt them."[125] Additional passages discuss faith healing by the laying on of hands, as well as going forth to preach about these experiences.

In one account by journalist Dennis Covington, he speaks of being invited into one of these churches and participating in their rituals. He finds that there's something hypnotic about it all, and that despite the rough handling of the snakes and the drinking of strychnine poison, incidents of a serious nature wind up being relatively low. Moreover, the entire experience is raucous and reverent, a blend of rhythmic gospel music, clapping, prayer, speaking in tongues, passing serpents among the crowd, and ecstatic worship. He notes, "Mystery, I'd read somewhere, is not the absence of meaning, but the presence of more meaning than we can comprehend."[126] The lived experience of handling serpents—which even Covington does in the course of his book *Salvation on Sand Mountain: Snake-Handling and Redemption in Southern Appalachia*—comes down to the sense that one is tapped into something supernatural, and any rational explanations fall short.

Those who practice serpent-handling and similar rites likely do not hold truck with the presentation of their religion as something magical. Yet it is, in their estimation, miraculous, and a miracle and an act of magic can be very closely related. The influence of charismatic evangelical Christianity on the folk magic of the Upland South cannot be understated, and the snake-handling churches (which are often not very open about what they do, as the practice is essentially illegal for several reasons) represent one branch of a nearly mythic level of mystery and magic that pervades the landscape.

I should note here that this passage does not condone the practice of snake-handling, which is often done by taking venomous snakes from the wild (which is illegal) and has led to some very dangerous and illicit activities. Even Covington's book is essentially an investigation of a preacher who used the practice of snake-handling to cover up a murder attempt on his wife. This information is presented here to add context and texture to a regional practice that shares a lot of cultural DNA with other mystical and magical practices in the area.

125. Mark 16:17–18 (Authorized King James Version).

126. Covington, *Salvation on Sand Mountain*, 229.

TRAVELING ON
The Upland South

As with any guidebook, there is always much more to experience than can be neatly fit into a chapter. To that end, we offer you this addendum to the map that will provide you with some tools to explore the Upland South further.

The glossary shares some keywords that might be useful. The places to visit will point you toward locations of interest that we think you might find valuable, and the reading recommendations provide you with some top-tier texts that can be used to dig in and learn more about this region.

Glossary

Conjure: A word used to describe several folk magical systems in the South, often ones derived from Scots Irish and African American practices blended with other material.

doll babies: Figural creations made from materials such as corn husks or cobs, apples, rags, or other available items. They could be used as toys or be repurposed as effigies for magical work.

doodlebug: A person who can detect underground water or other resources by the use of dowsing rods, or the name for the dowsing rod itself.

evil eye: A condition of harmful magic caused by a person looking at someone/something with jealousy, causing it to be cursed with ill fortune or poor health. Sometimes done inadvertently or without the conscious effort of the one casting it.

fairy doctor: A magical practitioner, sometimes also called a "power doctor," with the ability to do counter-magic. They sometimes provided magical cures and remedies, but mostly worked to reverse cursed conditions or the influence of hurtful spirits (which were sometimes thought of as a type of fairy).

haint: A common Appalachian term for ghosts, deriving from the word "haunts."

Melungeons: An ethnic group found in the Upland South, particularly the Appalachians, drawing on European, African, and Indigenous heritage.

mill-race water: The water collected from below a running water–powered mill wheel or run, thought to have a restorative or invigorating effect.

stump water: The pool of water collected in a stump, often used to enable magical curing.

tonic: A strong herbal mixture designed to reduce "sluggishness" in a person's blood. These are sometimes made from bitter greens and taken in early spring in order to shake off the torpor of winter.

witch's grease: A type of unguent or salve made from a mix of herbs and animal fats (frequently skunk, bear, or hog fat in the Appalachians). This salve could have several magical properties, the best known of which was enabling the witch to shape-shift or fly.

Places to Visit

Wander through Miller's Rexall in Decatur, Georgia: This drugstore (called a "Rexall" from the Rx abbreviation for a prescription) has been serving the Atlanta area for more than fifty years. It represents a long tradition of drugstores carrying not only the typical headache treatments and cough syrups, but a wide variety of products aimed at Hoodoo practitioners. Miller's concocts many of its own formulae, including making natural remedies alongside its magical supplies, and stopping in is a glimpse into the past and also a look at contemporary Hoodoo practice. The store moved from its original Atlanta location to nearby Decatur in recent years.

Explore the Bell Witch Cave in Adams, Tennessee: The infamous Bell Witch was more of a ghost than a magical practitioner, and most of her legend centers around the Bell family and their home in Adams, Tennessee, which you can tour. The nearby Bell Witch Cave has a history of eerie voices and strange figures, and the legends began to circulate after the famous Bell Witch haunting. Some claim that the spirit still haunts the cave. There are stories of people being cursed by taking stones from the cave, so if you do visit, it's best to leave things as you find them.

Take a Picture with the Witch's Statue in Virginia Beach, Virginia: Known as "the Witch of Pungo," Grace Sherwood was the last person officially convicted of witchcraft in Virginia in the early 1700s. She had a reputation as an herbalist, but she also had conflicts with local townspeople. The townspeople accused Grace of witchcraft and had her "ducked," or placed in a river to see if she sank (meaning innocence) or floated (meaning she was a witch). She floated and was convicted, but eventually she was released and had her property returned to her in 1714, where she lived for another quarter century. Today, a statue of Grace holding a bundle of herbs and gazing down at a raccoon companion stands near the Sentara Independence hospital.[127]

Hike Roan Mountain: If you wander up into the Smokies, which border Tennessee and the Carolinas, you can visit Grassy Ridge Bald on top of Roan Mountain, near Asheville, North Carolina. It's a locus for a number of witch legends, including one about two sisters who take in a traveler only to have him get into their witches' grease and join them on a midnight flight. Many others say they've heard strange voices or even singing on the mountain, especially on windy or stormy nights, and it has something of a reputation as a potential gathering place for spirits or witches. It's also a beautiful spot to see rhododendrons in bloom!

Recommended Reading

Staubs and Ditchwater: A Friendly and Useful Introduction to Hillfolks' Hoodoo by H. Byron Ballard
This is Ballard's essential introduction to the mountain magic she knows and lives with in her part of Appalachia.

Roots, Branches & Spirits: The Folkways & Witchery of Appalachia by H. Byron Ballard
Ballard provides an intimate, seasonal look at the folk practices, beliefs, and magic of Appalachia through her eyes.

Folk Medicine in Southern Appalachia by Anthony Cavender
This is an essential guide to the plant-based and folk-remedy healing practices of the southern Appalachian Mountains.

Witches, Ghosts, and Signs: Folklore of the Southern Appalachians by Patrick W. Gainer
Gainer's collection of stories, superstitions, and beliefs is one of the very best for understanding the West Virginian portion of the Upland South.

Backwoods Witchcraft: Conjure & Folk Magic from Appalachia by Jake Richards
This is a marvelous look at Appalachian practices from Richards, who takes the time to orient the reader to the folk stories of the region as well as the beliefs and practices.

Doctoring the Devil: Notebooks of an Appalachian Conjure Man by Jake Richards
Another guide from Richards, this time focusing more on practical works from the mountain region.

127. lcbudd14, "The Witch of Pungo Statue."

Chapter 3

Kentucky Superstitions by Daniel Lindsey Thomas and Lucy Blayney Thomas
This is an older collection, but still a rich one for understanding some of the traditions and lore "down" from the mountains.

The Foxfire Series (12 vols.), edited by Eliot Wigginton and the Foxfire Fund
This series is an absolutely essential collection of Appalachian lore gathered in the mountain regions of Georgia and the Carolinas.

CHAPTER 4

The Deep South

Chapter 4

Gonna Set Yourself on Fire: An Introduction to the Folk Magic of the Deep South

On the road to New Orleans, there's a noticeable shift from deciduous hardwood trees and evergreens lining the road to a world where rich, dripping clouds of Spanish moss cover everything. Similarly, driving down into Georgia, the ropy vines of kudzu tangle around everything from forests to power lines, looking like green topiary ruins of a forgotten civilization in some places. A trip down to Florida showcases swampy cypress and saw palmetto plants; it felt like I'd somehow slipped onto a boat without knowing it and suddenly found myself idling over living waters churned by hurricanes and tides. And all of that says nothing of the fauna: alligators and water snakes, beetles and mosquitos almost big enough to saddle, birds with bright plumes or shrill cries.

The region of the southeastern United States is a fusion of landscapes as much as it is a fusion of cultures. The entire landscape is haunted, inhabited by spirits of a tragic past: slavery, the Chinese Exclusion Act, Jim Crow, hurricanes, poverty, feuds, bloodshed. But it's also a landscape rippling with magic in every corner. Hoodoo and Vodun both thrive here, and the magical background of places like St. Helena Island, South Carolina, and Savannah, Georgia, for example, is palpable even in very public ways. Additionally, the Southern Conjure found in the Upland South spills over into this region, along with traditions brought in by Chinese and Mexican immigrants over the years. There's a strong branch of French Acadian healing magic fused with regional folk medicine picked up from Indigenous peoples such as the Muskogee. This form of magic would feel very recognizable to those in Pennsylvania German country because many of the cures share some roots, although the languages involved are quite different.

There's a gothic flavor to the Deep South, a sort of dark humor and dynastic decay that pervades the stories of the region, from ghostly women watching the shore for hurricanes to the grim tales of William Faulkner. But there are also lilting qualities, a beauty and reverie and joie de vivre, that come from hurricane parties, Mardi Gras, juke joints, and backwoods blues. There's the poetry and laughter found in the works of Zora Neale Hurston and all the jokes and jibes she recorded from the "liars" (tall-tale tellers) in her native Florida. The haunted city of Charleston, South Carolina, is alive with spirits. And if you head down into the coastal lowlands, you might bump into a Gullah Geechee woman who is holding onto a culture centuries old that is full of music, wisdom, hardship, and magic.

In short, the Deep South is a crossroads. It is a place where so many different people have met for so many different purposes, and the magic reflects that. In the coming pages, you'll hear how this land and its folk magic have shaped the lives of three people deeply embedded in the worlds of the Deep South.

Aaron Oberon guides you through Florida, which exists almost as its own special brand of "Southernness." It's a place where catfish crucifixes get sold right alongside Disney bobbleheads.

Some might balk at the influence tourism has on "authentic" folkways, but as Oberon points out, in a land of juxtapositions the truth "doesn't stop the story from being entertaining and containing a nugget of magical wisdom."

Lilith Dorsey will explore the worlds of African Traditional Religion and Hoodoo, both as an academic and as someone who practices (and plays—she spent time dancing with the famous New Orleans musician Dr. John, for example, and while she takes the work of spirit seriously, she also knows how important it is to have fun within tradition). She takes the words of Mardi Gras revel-song "Iko Iko" to heart, setting herself "on fire" with a love for the folk magic and spirituality of the African American people.

We also connect with Starr Casas, an East Texas conjure woman who has been practicing her work since before some people reading this were old enough to hold a "doll baby." Casas has lived throughout the South and now offers a uniquely Texan vision of folkways and magic that is at once deeply connected to family history and ready to "go big" to get the job done. She shares her own magical history, a slow and patient process that required listening to a number of elders in order to finally develop her own ways of doing things.

Setting off down the Natchez Trace Parkway into Mississippi and Louisiana or slipping down the A1A toward the Florida Keys, you have to keep your eyes peeled. Things change subtly over time, with kudzu giving way to sawgrass or Spanish moss, and the little twists of magic around you weaving in and out of one another as you go along. This is a space that can compel you to slow down and drink it all in—the wonder and the weirdness, the decay and the delight. Take your time. The magic here rewards patience.

Florida Folk Magic: Tourism, Tradition, and Transience

AARON OBERON

It's hard not to encounter roadblocks on a search for Florida's magical history when its crowning achievement is a theme park called "the magic kingdom." It's almost impossible to discern what is genuine tradition and what has been fluffed to make the Sunshine State appear mystical. A major example would be the Catfish Crucifix, a bone from the crucifix sea catfish that has an eerie resemblance to the crucifixion of Christ. The Catfish Crucifix is a known good luck charm for gamblers, due to the rattling sound of the bones inside the cavity being reminiscent of dice shaking, and to Christians, who marveled at God's planning to put a reminder of his Son's sacrifice into the bones of a simple fish.

Or the bone's notoriety could be the result of the "legends" cycle of Florida postcards printed from the 1940s–1980s, all of which celebrated God's carefully planned reminders throughout nature. This includes the legend of the passionflower, whose ten petals harken back to ten apostles, and the legend of the sand dollar, which has five markings just as Jesus had five wounds.[128] Outside of oral tradition, only the Catfish Crucifix postcard talks about its nature as a talisman of luck and gambling by associating the sound with dice. So, which came first, the folk magic or the tourist trap? Folk magic in Florida cannot be separated from a dense tangle of Christianity, the looming threat of nature, and tourism.

Florida is a place of incredible cultural exchange. Documentation of the rich history of Hoodoo in Florida can be found in living African American tradition and in the works of Zora Neale Hurston. The influence of Lukumi and other Afro-Caribbean religions can be found across the state, notably the powerhouse city of Miami. The Greek settlement of Tarpon Springs adapted their Epiphany traditions to place the sponge—the town's major export—into an elevated position of soaking up sacrificial blood for protection rites. Throughout Central Florida and the Panhandle, the Anglo tradition of water witching is consistently attested throughout oral history and

128. "The Legend of the Crucifix Fish."

written record. Appalachian and Ozark magical traditions have moved down as families moved and brought their hidden healing methods with them.

What little magic I grew up with comes out of Southern Baptist traditions, with some Appalachian diasporic magic seeping down from certain family members. That said, it was never anything formal, and much of the magic in our family happened without me ever hearing about it. In fact, it wasn't until I was an adult and started asking questions that certain healing traditions were revealed to have been a part of what some of my great-aunties and great-grandmothers were doing. Since those things were hidden away, much of my search for magic was born out of snippets, things I would overhear rather than be told directly.

My treasured tool was a small orange Psalter I had been given before my baptism; I even wrote my baptismal date in glittery gel pen inside the front cover to celebrate. I used the Psalter for everything from protection magic (Psalm 91), to cursing or striking down bullies (Psalm 91:121), to receiving prophetic dreams (Proverbs 31). I still remember the first protection spell I did for another person with my Psalter. I had just enough pop culture influences to know that there was a relationship between crystals and witchcraft (I desperately wanted to be a witch as a child) so I set three quartz crystals around my friend, walked around them three times clockwise while reading Psalm 91, and then crushed rose petals and sprinkled them over her head to mimic being washed in the blood of Christ for protection. This was how most of my magic went growing up: snippets of Bible magic, Christian metaphors, and pop culture–influenced ideas about witchcraft.

Prophetic dreams were one of the few things my mother did teach me about, quoting the Bible and the story of Joseph to justify the nature of the dreams. Later in life I would find out that several of my female family members purportedly had this gift, but because the dreams were oftentimes negative (showing death or injury, and always coming true if the dreamer didn't say anything), it wasn't openly discussed.

With this disconnected and piecemeal relationship to magic, I was left to really create my own way of doing things. I found the Bible passages that made sense to me, maybe had enough time to google something about Wicca, and pulled from pop culture depictions of witches. As I became an adult and had more freedom and access to information, my search for Florida's magic began—that's when I hit the "Which came first: the magic or tourism?" question posed earlier. With so many traditions across the state, sometimes getting lost in the constant shuffle of tourism-centered capitalism, Florida's folk magic is both overwhelming and almost invisible.

What does someone lost in the shuffle do? Try not to think too hard. Florida is weird—not just because of its recent history of "Florida Man" escapades, but its entire history. Folk magic as I see it is loosely defined as "magic of the common people," so when your uncle takes you to your first poker game and slips you a catfish bone to help you win, does it really matter if it was popularized by a postcard? For those of us who didn't grow up in a tradition of magical formulas or receive passed-down remedies, but rather superstitions of dubious origin, we have to focus less on the encroachment of imposter syndrome and get to the core question of folk magic: does it work?

The City of Sunshine and Necromancy

Folk magic in Florida is less about creating magical items and more about finding places of power. A famous example would be taking a trip up to St. Augustine, the longest continually occupied European settlement in the continental United States, to drink from the Fountain of Youth to keep you looking young. While almost no one believes that the sulfuric well water of this lesser-known tourist trap actually has youth-affirming properties, it does illustrate a constant in Florida's magical mindset: places are magic.

One ghost story that has captured my mind and inspired a number of spells is the ghost tile of Flagler College. Once known as the Ponce de León Hotel, a beautiful establishment that attracted the upper class of America throughout its history, Flagler College is named after railroad tycoon Henry Flagler, who is also the source of this ghost story.

According to legend, when Flagler died he had a number of strange rules established for his funeral: for one thing, he wanted his body moved from the hotel to the church, and second, he wanted all the shutters throughout the hotel to be closed. These rules were followed. However, one maintenance worker was not told about any of it, and before the casket was moved, he opened up all the windows and shutters.

As the casket carrying Flagler proceeded, a storm blew through, and the pallbearers dropped the coffin. The ghost of Henry Flagler, angered by the blatant disobedience, threw open all the windows and slammed against the walls, eventually falling through the floor tiles near a window. To this day, if you carefully scan the tiles near Ponce's front door, you'll find a tile bearing the striking resemblance of Henry Flagler himself, trapped there due to the broken arrangement.

This is one of my favorite stories, and when I lived in St. Augustine, showing visiting friends and family the fabled tile was always a good time. As with many small folktales and urban legends, this was a story told to me from multiple sources. Each storyteller changes some details, and if you go to Flagler today and ask about the ghost tile, you may very well get a different story, but you'll always be taken to the same tile.

This story inspired a particular kind of spirit trap I now make: a spirit tile. Simple square ceramic tiles are hung or placed near entrances to capture unwanted spirits, often with a colorful or eye-catching design on the front and a magical seal or sigil on the back. This is one of my more covert magical protections, as guests don't bat an eye at a pretty tile the way they might a full magical seal on the front door.

I should also note that while there is a tile in Ponce that does have a vague human resemblance, the story itself is completely fabricated. Flagler actually died in Palm Beach, and while he was buried in St. Augustine, there's absolutely no evidence to suggest his casket went through Ponce at any time. That doesn't stop the story from being entertaining and containing a nugget of magical wisdom; spirit traps are an old practice and can be found across magical traditions—this story gives them a little St. Augustine spin, is all.

In St. Augustine, there is also the legend of the marriage trees. Marriage trees are a unique growth of one kind of tree seemingly sprouting out of another. To qualify as marriage trees, they both have to normally grow traditionally, meaning that parasitic trees like the strangler fig don't count.

Kissing under one marriage tree will strengthen a relationship, while two will make it last long, and kissing under three will guarantee a happy marriage. But I'm sure aspiring couples wouldn't want to kiss under trees known for sapping the life from one another, so pay attention to the species.

The most iconic marriage tree in the city is at the Love Tree Cafe and Tolomato Cemetery, where a large live oak juts between the fences with a palmetto growing right out of it. In my time living in St. Augustine, I've found four marriage trees hidden around the city, but I've left the locations of the other three up to the happy couple.

Healing Springs and Hellish Holes

Florida was often popularized as a place to go to recover from illness, in part due to its mild climate but also because of the purported healing properties of its many springs. Again blurring the lines between folklore and tour-lore, Florida's 600+ springs have a reputation for healing blemishes, fatigue, or gout, depending on who you're asking. Since the late 1950s, southwest Florida's Warm Mineral Springs has been the most popular site, as it maintains an eighty-five-degree temperature year-round.

Something that may be considered "new" folk magic is folks going to the springs to bottle some of the water themselves so they can gift it to others, normally in small glass bottles no bigger than your thumb. The idea being that it's not the temperature or even immersion in the springs that brings healing, but the water itself, which bears a special property. When I've mentioned to those folks that most bottled water in the state comes out of our springs (often to the detriment of the springs themselves), they remain steadfast that for the water to maintain its potency, it should go from the spring right to another person.

Florida's geological history can help shed some light on the sheer number of springs throughout the state. Florida is a limestone bedrock peninsula. Limestone is a sedimentary rock made up of fossilized shells and is extremely prone to eroding when exposed to rainwater. Over time the bedrock erodes to the point where the soil above it has no support, creating sinkholes. Today, sinkholes are an ever-present concern for folks living in central Florida; they can appear suddenly and cause massive damage. Most of the springs dotting the state that are lauded for their healing properties started as sinkholes. As both saltwater and freshwater mix within the porous limestone that forms the bedrock, the freshwater rises and may eventually bubble up into a freshwater spring, while the saltwater is weighed down into the bedrock.

From an animistic view, this complex process of erosion, collapse, separation, and eventual swelling of clean freshwater makes the case for why these springs are special. They were born out of emptiness, and from the emptiness they were filled with the most valuable resource on earth. Springs exemplify rebirth, recovering from disaster, and making something beautiful out of scarred land. They are places of power, even if they are very crowded.

There is another side to sinkholes that can be noted in two particularly popular places: Devil's Den and Devil's Millhopper. Devil's Den is another sinkhole spring that is relatively small, with a natural skylight made of a hole in the ground. In the morning, steam rises from the hole like a chimney, hence the name Devil's Den. Devil's Millhopper is a 120-feet deep "miniature rain forest" located in north Florida. It's full of fossils and has two potential origins for its name. The more common story is an obvious mishmash of what Americans *think* Indigenous stories are: essentially, the devil kidnaps an Indigenous "princess" and when she escapes, the Devil creates the sinkhole. The other story states that the fossils and bones are from animals going into the millhopper to visit the Devil. Both springs demonstrate an innate chthonic quality of sinkholes as entryways to the underworld. Like most things in Florida, sinkholes can bring healing or harm.

The Possum Queen of Florida

There is one place in Florida that is perhaps the best encapsulation of how the people have honored the spirits of the land. In the small town of Wausau stands a monument to the humble possum: a simple piece of granite with an image of a possum family and an inscription about its history. The town's relationship with possums started during the Depression era, when possums became the town's only reliable source of food and fur. Wausau began celebrating the possum in the late 1960s with its "Fun Day," which would later be renamed "The Possum Festival."

My informant, who asked to remain unnamed, described the first time she went to the event as a young girl in the '70s, then gave a particularly stunning description of the Possum Queen. The Possum Queen is one of the festival's mainstays, and in order to be crowned, you need to be over the age of fifty and have an award-winning recipe that includes possum. The crowning also takes into account what outfit the Queen wears during the crowning competition. The Queen from my informant's first festival won because of a single accessory: a necklace of live baby possum hanging around her neck.

The Possum Queen may not be actual royalty, but the Possum Festival does tie into Florida politics in a very real way. Since 1982, when Florida legislature designated the first Saturday in August the official Possum Day, it has become commonplace for would-be governors to make an appearance and take part in another tradition: possum swingin'. Politicians bid on the opportunity to hold a possum by its tail in front of a crowd as a display of their desire to give back to the communities of Florida (the money goes toward the local fire department and helps fund the next year's festival) in exchange for their vote. The ethical implications of this tradition are up for debate, but it is a part of this celebration and a part of the influence the animal has here.

The relationship between Wausau and the possum is one of devotees and patron. The possum provides a means of survival and in return, it has a celebration that over ten thousand people attend. Queens are crowned in its name, and it's very difficult to become governor without participating in the possum swing. An animal often reviled as "dirty" or a "nuisance" is elevated to status of life giver, kingmaker, and patron of frivolity. The possum encapsulates aspects of not just Florida, but Southerners in general: tenacity, survival, adaptability, and honoring the dishonored.

There have been discussions of "Southern Pride" for generations that emphasize maintaining racism, abandoning queer children, and centering whiteness as the only narrative for Southernness. I'll take the possum as a symbol of something to be proud of, and a reminder that the South and Florida are not homogenous. We can maintain our tenacity and fight against the xenophobic upbringing many of us were raised with. We can adapt and push forward even when we are told to leave our hometowns for "better places." We can honor ourselves and crown our own royalty—hell, maybe one day we'll even crown a Possum Drag Queen. In a place that worships the possum, anything is possum-ible.

Florida's Folk Magic Icon: Gators and the Swamp Witch

Our relationship to animals is another thing that makes Florida so widely discussed outside of the region. Obviously, we've explored one town's patronage of the possum, but the entire state is deeply tied to another iconic animal: the alligator. A relationship we share with our siblings in Louisiana, the alligator is omnipresent across the state. Every few miles a billboard advertising "real live gators" will attempt to draw folks to a given gas station, while mini golf spots commonly have at least one or two living in a pond as an attraction. Hell, we even have our own Gatorland theme park in Orlando! Of course, the gator is also emblematic of the gnarled swamp witch that mostly lives in folks' imaginations.

The gator isn't just a tourist attraction—it is a part of daily life for most non-coastal Floridians. When I worked at a theme park in central Florida, I couldn't even tell you how many times we had to shut down a water ride because a gator climbed the fence. If you've ever done a little antiquing around the state, you'll find an excess of gator memorabilia—some made from actual gator. Heads and paws are common taxidermy souvenirs—so common that while I was growing up, we always had one or two just lying around the house. Gator tail is a must-have food staple; it's basically a slightly chewy fried chicken nugget. Gators are so second nature to us that it's no surprise when traffic gets held up because a particularly big boy took his time crossing the road.

All this love and attention for gators is ubiquitous in the magic of those of us who call ourselves "swamp witches." The term *swamp witch* is part tongue-in-cheek joking about ourselves and part art mirroring real life. While there is no one tradition for making magic in the swamp, for many of us it is the heart of the land. Or, more accurately, the kidneys. Swamps, like kidneys, act like a filter. Water pools in these areas, and plants and animals reduce contaminants before the water continues its cycle. Swamps are filled with so much life as a direct consequence of the death that sinks into the ground there. Decay and flourishing ferns go hand in hand, with the gator taking center stage.

Gator paws, abundant in tourist and oddity shops alike, feature frequently as a tool of Florida witches. The paws are often twisted and gnarled, evoking the quintessential witch's finger and immediately bringing to mind *maleficium*. Holding a larger paw toward the image of a target and speaking curses is a simple and effective way to call on the aid of the gator to devour an enemy. When it comes to baneful work, the gator is unforgiving and relatively neutral. Oftentimes gators aren't actually very aggressive at all, but they will snatch up anyone that comes within their range; if left alone and given their space, they won't bother you. This is something most witches I know would also agree with.

Alligators aren't malicious by nature, and in fact they are also known to be phenomenal mothers. So, just like most witches work with "both hands," gator paws can be used offensively or defensively. One paw may be reserved for cursing enemies while another may be placed within a baby's room to protect them from illness. One friend of mine, a fellow swamp witch, has gushed on numerous occasions about the fortitude of gators and how their immune system is one of the strongest in the animal kingdom. This is something that has been under scientific investigation as a potential tool for conservation and related fields.[129] Charms for protection against disease are especially suited for smaller paws that can be placed discreetly in windows or worn around the neck.

The protective nature of the alligator may also be expressed through their scutes. A scute is a kind of bony protrusion just under the skin; on alligators, they can be seen trailing along the back like a small ridge. The bones themselves are often almost-perfect squares that run up the back of the gator like a row of shields. The (mostly) flat backs are perfect for inscribing sigils of protection. They can also be placed around piggy banks to protect finances or included in bone-throwing sets to signify the need for protection.

129. Alston et al., "Quantifying Circulating IgY Antibody Responses."

The powerful jaws of the gator have resulted in a less-common tool found at some antique shops and gator-themed attractions: jawbone knives. The teeth are removed and turned into a handle, while the length of the jaw is carved into the familiar form of a knife. The first and last tooth can be inserted back into their holes, sometimes packed with herbs and powders to form a kind of pommel and guard.

The knife itself has no history outside of being a souvenir and is not sturdy enough for the mundane purposes a knife serves. However, the modern witch can immediately begin to develop a relationship with it and feel the palpable spirit within. The gator's hunger and power fashioned into a human weapon evoke its role in martial magic, much like the left-hand paw described earlier. Cutting, separating, and removal work takes on a ruthless quality when you hold the jaw of a creature that can bite through solid bone with little effort.

Although the cutting ability of a jawbone knife is highly limited, one could take the knife and mark the perimeter of their property by driving the knife into soft soil to ward off spirits and declare the presence of an alligator spirit within. Placing gator teeth within these holes gives an additional warding quality, recalling the sowing of dragon teeth by Jason in Greek mythology. The knife has a quality of finality, an intensity that may not be necessary for all magical purposes. It calls on the most ferocious qualities of Florida's patron reptile and takes on a holy quality, and as such, the jawbone knife is a relic that should be handled with respect and used when finality is needed.

Finally, we address the gator's iconic teeth, the ultimate magical tool of the swamp witch. Alligators have hollow teeth that they grow and lose throughout their life, which makes gator teeth the only tangible piece of a gator that doesn't result from killing them. Many gator farms, sanctuaries, and attractions featuring gators will sell loose teeth that have been naturally dropped. The teeth take on many of the qualities we've discussed already (ferocity, protection, ruthlessness) while also having a quality of renewal because they are continually replaced. Beyond that, there is a deeply functional aspect of these teeth for the magical practitioner: because they are hollow, they can be filled.

There are many traditions that create magical bags (sewn talismans or written talismans folded into silk), and the gator tooth continues this practice. The tooth can be filled with powder herbs and other *materia magica* and is then capped with wax, with its purpose spoken into life by the practitioner. A tooth packed with materials that evoke protection (like readily available rosemary, written charms, and tightly folded psalms) can be worn on the body like a necklace or buried under the front porch. To encourage fertility and a healthy pregnancy, a tooth may be packed with damiana, cinnamon, seeds, or flower pistils and then placed under the bed to aid in conception. For luck, money, and success, simply put small seeds or stones in a particularly large tooth and carry it with you during meetings. Give the tooth a shake, evoking that same "shaking dice" sound of the Catfish Crucifix, to bring that luck and money magic.

Of course, I can't go far without running into baneful work. A tooth packed with stingers, nettles, thorns, or peppers and buried near an enemy's house will bring the gator's force and the astringent qualities of the contents to torment them until your goal is achieved. To ensure that there is an actual end goal, write it down and tuck it into the tooth before sealing it. Adjust as needed. For instance, to get a particularly oppressive employer to back off, you may hide the tooth in/near the entryway of your work area so they don't enter. If they do enter, they'll feel like they're in the mouth of the gator, ready to snap shut on them if they speak out of line.

The variability that comes from a single item—from a single animal!—connects to a personal magical philosophy that I attribute to my relationship with peninsular Florida. When you form a meaningful relationship with a given entity, you have almost all the tools you need to make magic. That entity could be yourself, but it's rather healthy to ask for help sometimes. A relationship with the gator is a full affair. I respect them as a food source and ensure that nothing goes to waste. They teach me to sit in comfortable silence, to wait for the correct time to make a move, to allow most to pass, and to strike when needed.

Conclusion: Indigenous Lands, Diasporic Peoples, and Florida Folkways

Florida sits on the unceded land of the Seminole Tribe of Florida and Miccosukee Tribe of Indians of Florida and their ancestors. Any discussion about the history of Florida is colored by a history of violence, war, and the attempted genocide of Indigenous Floridians. The United States only controls the land known as Florida due to racist campaigns during the First, Second, and Third Seminole Wars. Restoring the land to the Seminole Tribe and Miccosukee Tribe needs to be done and can be done. Support Land Back initiatives by listening to Seminole and Miccosukee leaders and acting as allies rather than sitting on the sidelines. There is a thriving industry of appropriation that specifically targets occultists as consumers, and as folk magic practitioners we should actively boycott non-Natives claiming to sell "Native goods." Support your local Indigenous communities and businesses.

Florida is a place of diaspora, intersecting peoples and cultures, unforgiving nature, and an inherently liminal relationship with concepts of reality. Our magic is ferocious, malleable, true, and false. It is the stuff of fairy tales; it's always changing and tricky. I've learned to suspend disbelief, revel in storytelling, and embrace our teetering relationship with ideas of tradition. Mountain migration has led to swamp sorcery here. Tourism and necromancy have become strange bedfellows here. Possums can be patron spirits and kingmakers here. Magic has become hungrier and even more crooked, more illusory, and more hilarious here. While there is a stranglehold of oppressive political forces walking on the paved streets of Tallahassee, there are also witches and folk magicians working against them. Packing their gator teeth and rattling their Catfish Crucifix against them. We will survive with the possum's tenacity and bite back with the force of our gators. Even when the sea threatens to rise up, the magical folks of this place will welcome it like an old friend.

FIELD NOTES

The Traiteurs *of Rural Louisiana*

The Acadian migration that led to a large influx of French-Canadian colonists—Cajuns and Creoles—settling in Louisiana also created a line of folk-healing practices that are indelibly associated with rural parts of the Mississippi Delta region. Within the region, those who can do miraculous works of healing are often called *traiteurs* (although sometimes women who heal are known as *traiteuses*). These practitioners generally work on physical ailments but add in a spiritual component. Everything from boils and toothaches to nightmares and mysterious swellings is in the purview of the *traiteur*'s work. They sometimes wind up treating issues stemming from bewitchment or conjuration done by practitioners of other systems such as Hoodoo.

Within the *traiteur* tradition, some primarily use spoken charms combined with prayer, breath, and gestures. Others bring in concoctions of herbs or other medicaments of their own devising, although these practitioners often go by the name *remèdes*, or "remedy men." Remedy makers use everything from local plants to store-bought drug mixtures to bits of string, wire, or spiderweb to treat their patients.

The more spiritually oriented *traiteurs* are often relying on prayers and practices similar to those found in faith-healing systems like the Braucherei in Pennsylvania German country or the cunning folk of New England. An example of one such charm involved a woman being treated for a skin condition called erysipelas that produced a painful rash. The *traiteur* used his fingers to make the sign of the cross over the wound, then crooked his fingers into a semi-circle around the affected area several times, repeating *"Au nom du Père et du Fils et du Saint-Esprit"* and *"O resispere je te le conjure de Saint Esprit"* and making another sign of the cross. This continued until he had made a full circuit of the wound, completely surrounding it with the charm and prayer.

Some *traiteur* treatments stem from the French Canadian roots of the practice, but it is also clear that some of the methods and magic used have been exchanged between systems over time, with some *traiteurs* noting that their system stems from contact with free Haitians living in Louisiana. In virtually all cases, however, those practicing this unique branch of magico-medical healing point to one source for their power: God. Almost all profess some form of Christianity and believe that the election to become a *traiteur* is a divine calling, dependent entirely on the will of their creator. They often do pass on their knowledge to a family member or apprentice before they die, at least if they are given the chance to do so, so that the power will not die out.[130]

130. See Dorson, *Buying the Wind*, and Sexton, "Cajun and Creole Treaters."

Ashé *Everywhere:* African Traditional Religion in the Deep South

LILITH DORSEY

African Traditional Religions such as Haitian Vodou, New Orleans "Voodoo," Hoodoo, and the rest were born out of what is traditionally referred to as folk magic and folktales. Some take offense at the term *folk magic*, which has customarily been used to describe systems that were sometimes thought of as "less than." In reality, they are so much more. The religions are made up of complex origin stories, poignant teaching tales, practical advice, and everything else needed to navigate this complicated thing called life. It is high time they get the respect and attention they so truly deserve. Unfortunately, most of this knowledge has been hidden because of stereotype and persecution, but those wishing to truly understand their roots must look to the history and herstory that created them. I have been a practitioner of several African Traditional Religious practices for almost thirty years, and I have dedicated my life to providing accurate and respectful information about them.

These religions have their origins in West Africa, in systems that predate Christianity by hundreds of years. Primarily, at their core, is the concept of *Ashé*. *Ashé* is described as a universal life force, a divine energy, and a cosmic connection that unifies absolutely all things. Everything in the universe possesses *Ashé*: food, flowers, animals, people, and divine beings. Understanding and celebrating *Ashé* is at the heart of Vodou, Voodoo, Hoodoo, La Regla Lucumí, and the other African Traditional Religions.

New Orleans Voodoo and Hoodoo

Similar to the city itself, New Orleans Voodoo and Hoodoo are a spiritual gumbo representative of all the unique cultures who chose to call the city home. Many are surprised to know that the original name of the location was Bulbancha, and it was home to people belonging to the Chitimacha, Coushatta, Choctaw, and Tunica-Biloxi tribes. *Bulbancha* roughly translates to "place of many tongues."[131] It seems that many tongues were spoken in the city from its very beginning.

131. Rhodes, "The Native Roots of the French Market."

As time progressed, the land became a French colony, and later a Spanish one. Many people and many cultures come together here, and the sense of spirit and community is strong.

One important thing that deserves attention is the unique shape and sacred geometry of the region. New Orleans is also known as the "Crescent City." It is so named because it is formed along a sharp bend in the Mississippi River. The river makes several bends and turns at this segment of the water's journey, and at times even appears to go backward. This spirit of place invokes a sacred geometry that is displayed in the dance and art of the region. An artful repetition is uplifted by leaps of faith. The same effect is mimicked in the local folktales.

These tales explore the larger-than-life characters who teach us how to live. Many of the names are lost in the seas of time, but the ones that remain are epic and inspirational in their own right. Uncle Monday, Doctor John, and Annie Christmas are among many legends that have gone on well beyond their individual lifetimes. They teach us strength and resolve.

The story of Uncle Monday comes to us from anthropologist, author, and Voodoo practitioner Zora Neale Hurston. Hurston was one of the very first Black woman anthropologists in the US, studying under pioneer Franz Boas. Much of her work centered on Black culture and religion, including Hoodoo, Conjure, New Orleans Voodoo, Haitian Vodou, and other traditions. The character of Uncle Monday is seen as a fusion of African and Seminole tradition. He is said to have been a captured African who escaped slavery in the US, and he was known to have great knowledge and skill, including the ability to shape-shift into an alligator. Legend tells us that he used this power to command the local alligators, and he used them to assist other slaves seeking their freedom. It is even said he helped organize and lead a BIPOC revolt against oppressors. His inspiring story tells of hope and magick being powerful enough to help the enslaved and oppressed. Over the years his tales have found their way into children's stories and even have a place in the Museum of Florida History. His power and his magic seem to have stood the test of time, and Uncle Monday has gone on to take his place as one of Hoodoo history's heroes.[132]

Another inspirational character is Annie Christmas. Annie Christmas, like most folk legends, was about as extra as can be. It is said she stood taller than any man, perhaps even seven feet tall, and could beat anyone who dared anger her. Annie is reported to have weighed over 250 pounds. Some say she ran a steamboat; others say she was an engineer on a keelboat on the Mississippi river. Annie was known to be a widow who raised her twelve sons all by herself. The phrase "strong as Annie Christmas" is still used in the southern US today. It is said she wore a charmed pearl necklace, with each pearl representing one of her enemies she had fought successfully; in time the necklace grew to over thirty feet long. She was a brash and powerful champion who was said to love her drink. Legend says she saved a boatload of people from drowning on the Mis-

132. Congdon, *Uncle Monday and Other Florida Tales*, 55–58.

sissippi before she succumbed to a fateful heart attack. Fortunately, the spirit of her power and bravery live on.[133]

Many Black folktales center around a trickster figure. This is something we see in Hoodoo with the infamous story of Robert Johnson. Blues legend Robert Leroy Johnson burst into this world on May 8, 1911, in the town of Hazlehurst, Mississippi. The town is northeast of Natchez and is now the site of the Mississippi Music Museum. By popular accounts, Johnson was a mediocre musician who had a difficult start in life but ultimately went on to hold the title of "King of the Delta Blues Singers." His story involves a crossroads.

Magically, the crossroads has always been a location full of infinite possibility. In Haitian Vodou it is the domain of Papa Legba, in New Orleans Voodoo the residence of Papa Lebat, and in La Regla Lucumí (Santeria) the crossroads is owned by the Orisha Elegguá. In Brazil it is the domain of Exu and Pomba Gira. These are all deities responsible for communication, collaboration, opportunity, and power. Clearly, anything can happen here, be it magic, mystery, or maybe even mastery. It is what anthropologists call a liminal space, a space of power and difference precisely because it is in between. In many different African Traditional Religions, it is primarily a place to leave offerings and to receive important messages.

The power and possibility that live in the crossroads were legendary long before the famous blues musician Robert Johnson stepped onto the scene. Popular history tells us that he chose the crossroads of routes 49 and 61 in Clarksdale, Mississippi, to make an offering of his soul. The reality is likely very different; there is even a theory that someone else made the deal and Robert had nothing to do with it.[134] Deals and devils can be a tricky thing. Like most Hoodoo history, the truth about Robert Johnson's fateful time at the crossroads of routes 49 and 61 can only be speculated. So much of what went on in Black communities has been lost over time.

Haitian Vodou

Sacred tales also find a place in the religion of Haitian Vodou, which heavily influenced the practices in New Orleans today. After the Haitian revolution, the population of New Orleans doubled by the year 1809.[135] The most famous creation stories in these religions revolve around a serpent and a rainbow. Most Haitians worship a singular God called *Bon Dieu* in Creole. However they may also honor the Loa, or sacred forces in the universe. The Loa inhabit everything in creation.

Two of the most prominent Loa are Damballa Wedo and his wife, Aida Wedo. These serpents are seen as creators, a divine father and mother who help form human existence. Their origin story in a way tells the origin of the entire religion. It is said that these two sacred serpents were

133. Fee and Webb, *American Myths, Legends, and Tall Tales*.

134. Anderson, *Brother Robert*, 64.

135. Lewis, "Krewe Du Kanaval Honors the Haitian Roots of New Orleans."

forced to travel from their native Africa. Damballa Wedo journeyed deep beneath the water, and Aida Wedo arched across the sky in the form of a rainbow. They met and were reunited, intertwining themselves on the shores of Haiti in order to birth a beautiful tradition in a new land.

La Regla Lucumí

The religion of La Regla Lucumí is commonly referred to as Santeria or Santo. It is one of the most widely practiced of the African Traditional Religions. The core of its belief system can be found among the Yoruba people in West Africa, who then traveled to Cuba, Puerto Rico, and eventually across the globe to major cities like New Orleans. Like the other ATRs, this is primarily an oral tradition. Sacred stories form the backbone of La Regla Lucumí and are called *patakis*. Similar to parables or fables in other cultures, these are told in response to divination, and the lesson is always tailored to the individual practitioner. The *patakis* explain difficult situations and provide insight into one's character and the workings of the world. Spiritual consultations are a frequent part of the religion, and these stories are told eloquently and often.

The divine beings in this system are called Orisha, which comes from the words *Ori* (head) and *Sha* (which is similar to the linguistic root of the word *Ashé*.) Through divination and also initiation, these Orishas help guide an individual's head, and by extension, their lives. Elegguá is the Orisha who is said to be a trickster and functions as an intermediary, almost a translator between the worlds. Elegguá is most often seen in the guise of a young child, but he sometimes appears as an elderly man as well. His colors are red and black, and a famous *pataki* describes one of the reasons why.

It is said that Elegguá was near the edge of a village when he heard two brothers talking. The two brothers were farmers, and they lived on either side of the main road. Every morning they started their day by greeting each other and talking about their families.

"I'm so glad we can live close to each other, dear brother. I love you so much and our families are all such good friends," said the first brother.

"Yes indeed, brother. Our wives cook together, our babies play together, and we can remember all the good times from when we were young every day," said the other brother.

"Great times," they both said and began to laugh.

This annoyed Elegguá and he decided to play a trick on them. Out of his sack he pulled his special hat. One side of the hat was colored black, and the other side was colored red. He put on his hat and began to walk right down the center of the street in silence.

After Elegguá passed, the brothers looked at each other. "That was weird," said the first brother.

"What, the guy in the red hat?" said the second brother.

The first brother responded, "The hat was black. What are you talking about?"

The second brother replied, "Are you blind, fool? That hat was red."

Soon an argument broke out, and it quickly escalated into a fight. The rest of the town joined in. Soon no one was caring for their crops or their animals, and a great famine began to spread. The situation became dire, so Elegguá decided to walk the other way back through the village. The villagers the saw that the hat was two-colored and realized that perception can be everything, and truth can be anything.[136]

Like many of the *patakis*, this helps people make sense of the wider world and teaches that appearance is not always reality.

How I Came into the Religions

For many years now, my life has been dedicated to providing accurate and respectful information about African Traditional Religions and preserving knowledge for archival purposes whenever possible. My personal connection to the religions began well before I was even born. Both sides of my family had a long legacy of spiritual professionals going way back into the past. My upbringing consisted of daily information about folktales and practical magickal beliefs, even if at the time I didn't realize throwing salt or singing a song about the dead was considered unusual.

As I grew a little older, I saw society tell me witchcraft and magick were dark, mysterious, equalizing, and intense, and I knew they were something I wanted more of in every possible way. I sat too close to the screen and watched my televisual inspirations show me lots of things—ultimately, that magick meant power. I read, watched, and sought out information in every place I could think of. I grew up in New York City, and at that time there were only a handful of public places to look, and many did not welcome an unattended young Black person. The struggle was literally real. However, the more information I found, the more I realized what I already knew. More formalized training, both from spiritual and academic professionals, came later. A large part of that centered on divination. I started with simple pendulums and natural dowsing rods and moved on to tarot and astrology.

After my eldest daughter was born, I joined the spiritual family at the Voodoo Spiritual Temple in New Orleans, and then I went on to initiate and began studying Haitian Vodou and La Regla Lucumí, more mistakenly known as Santeria. I often get questioned about why I would participate in so many different traditions. Each one of these religions arrived at a time in my life when it was absolutely necessary to initiate in order to accomplish important work. Loving and caring godmothers helped me more than they will ever know. All of the African Traditional Religions function like a family, with godchildren receiving guidance and instruction from their godparents and other elders in the tradition.

136. Luis Manuel Núñez in discussion with the author, 1999.

How to Start Your Own Journey

There is a saying in the traditions that "you can't get *awo* (spiritual knowledge) from a book." Even though I write books (and I really want people to buy them), I always remind everyone about the importance of individualized study with initiated godparents. This may not be easy; the search is part of the spiritual journey. Many people write and ask me how to find their own godparents in the religion. They think there's a reference list or a directory somewhere that people can pick and choose from. Nothing could be farther from the truth. African Traditional Religions like Hoodoo, New Orleans Voodoo, Haitian Vodou, La Regla Lucumí, and others consist of practices that were persecuted, misunderstood, and even criminalized for hundreds upon hundreds of years. Practitioners have seen ignorance and stereotype paint a wholly negative picture of the religions, and very often this has left them protective and suspicious of outsiders, clearly for good reason.

The community is one of the most important components of the practices, and seeking out these communities in a respectful way is a good place to begin. If you think that you would like to learn more, I suggest you get a reading with a qualified practitioner in that tradition. Ask around in local online communities, visit your local botanica or witchy store, take workshops online from myself or others, participate in open events, and ask questions.

When you finally get a reading with a respected practitioner you trust, be sure to discuss your desires and concerns, and see what the best way for you to proceed is. Be prepared that the answers you get may not be the ones you want, but instead the ones you need. One of the beautiful things about this is that when you gain insight from a reading, you are gaining personalized information specifically for you. This information doesn't reside in any book or library, but instead in a system that has been handed down throughout the ages. Through this learning, we give thanks and strengthen our connection to the cosmic forces that guide us. We defer to our elders in the tradition. In turn, we too can become elders by following the recommendations and instructions that are given. It is a glorious lifelong process.

Rules and Regulations

In addition to being asked about practice, I often get asked about rules and guidelines in these traditions. There are far too many to list in these pages. Each African Traditional Religious system, and even each individual organization, has its own unique set of instructions. They are to be followed—pardon the pun—religiously. Within the religion, there is no unifying text or "Bible"; instead, people receive individualized instruction as to how they can have good character and stay on their proper path. Practitioners frequently honor their ancestors, the Loa or Orisha representing the *Ashé* of everything in the universe. They honor their elders and also those who have come before. Some of these have famous names, like Voodoo Queen Marie Laveau, and some, like Uncle Monday, are less well-known.

An immense amount of knowledge exists in these traditions. There are hundreds of ritual songs, dances, chants, stories, foods, flowers, herbs, medicines, and more that are all used to honor the Loa and Orisha, or the sacred energies that shape the traditions. Each approach is used in response to different circumstances, and this is one of the reasons why a community of dedicated practitioners is invaluable: they help guide you toward solutions, and in turn, you help the following generations discover theirs. The system of interplay is artful and ensures the African Traditional Religious practices will continue in the best possible way.

These Trying Times

Recent times have seen much turmoil in the form of a pandemic, racial unrest, economic struggle, and more. Because of this, many are returning to their ancestral roots for solace and courage. I hope people continue to do so in a respectful and honorable way. Obviously, these words are just the very beginning. A person could spend a lifetime learning the sacred practices that comprise the various African Traditional Religions. There is no way to provide a complete overview in a few pages. However, the more you know, the better prepared you will be to navigate these ancient worlds.

The religions were birthed into existence by enslaved and oppressed people, and they faced challenges that are a nightmarish mirror of what we face today. Over time, they sharpened their tools of resistance, both magickal and otherwise, ensuring their ultimate success.

FIELD NOTES
The Crossroads Deal

The well-known legend of bluesman Robert Johnson tells the story of a Faustian bargain made between the singer-songwriter and the devil at a midnight crossroads. The legend embellishes small details from Johnson's life that also perpetuate some racist beliefs and ideas. It also merges Johnson's life with stories of other blues singers like Tommy Johnson, and Robert's early death adds in a bit of tragedy and mystery. But in Southern folk magic, there is actually some basis for the concept of a crossroads spirit meeting.

Amateur folklorist and preacher Harry Middleton Hyatt spent several years in the mid–twentieth century interviewing and documenting folk magical practices throughout the South and Midwest. Many of his informants were African American, although some were white or another ethnicity. He recorded multiple versions of the crossroads ritual story, which seemed to largely consist of a few repeated details:

1. The person would go to a crossroads just before daybreak (sometimes midnight).
2. They would make a special wish or state their desire, or in some cases bring an object with them representing their want (such as a guitar, if one were a blues player).
3. They would repeat this ritual for a sequence of nights, usually nine Sundays in a row.
4. Various animals would appear, such as a black rooster, cat, dog, or bear (or even a whirlwind), seeming more dangerous each time.
5. On the final night, they would encounter either a "Black man" or a "man in black" who would give them the skill they sought (usually by doing something like taking the guitar and tuning it or trimming the person's fingernails). Then they would leave.

In some cases, a pact was signed with the devil. Many people who tell crossroads stories seem to think that's exactly what is happening, but that detail doesn't make it into every story and isn't consistent throughout the folklore. Most folktales of Faustian bargains, for example, eventually end with the devil coming to claim his due, which seldom happens in these tales (with the exception of Robert Johnson, who died rather young, which was attributed to his crossroads contract).[137]

137. Hyatt, *Hoodoo, Conjuration, Witchcraft, Rootwork*, vols. 1 and 2.

Crossroads weren't just for striking up deals for fame, fortune, luck, or power. They were potent locations of magical work unto themselves. Another ritual recorded by Hyatt noted that a person could take a piece of wood with a subject's name on it and bring it to a crossroads on three consecutive mornings. The spell-caster would use a horseshoe nail to write the person's name in the dirt of the crossroads, then recite Psalm 35 from the Bible. The wood would be nailed with the horseshoe nail in a place that the sun wouldn't shine on it (inside a barn or shed, for example), and that would produce a run of bad luck for the person targeted. A similar spell involved stealing a person's key, rolling it in salt and cayenne pepper (and possibly spit or urine), and burying it at the crossroads until it rusted and caused health problems for the person targeted.

Whatever the use, crossroads remain one of the strongest images of folk magic we conjure up.

The Making of a Starr: Working Old-Style Conjure

STARR CASAS

I often sit back and think of how I became the Conjure worker I am today. It all started at home with my family. I cannot pinpoint any one thing that influenced me to become a Conjure worker; I think it was my whole life growing up with people who did not even realize what they were doing had a name to it. When you live a certain way your whole life, it becomes you—or you become it, I should say.

I do not remember ever going to the doctor growing up because my mama was our doctor; she had a treatment for anything that ailed you. We went to the eye doctor and the dentist if we needed to, but she even made our toothpaste. She was a lot different than my friends' mamas since she didn't really hang out, although there were always folks around our house. If one of my friends made a remark about how different my mama was, I would always say, "She just has funny ways." Those funny ways taught me, without me even realizing it, to be the worker I am today. They were building a strong foundation for me to grow on.

I am very lucky to be born to a mother who held on to her heritage and raised us as she was raised, although at times it did bother me that she was so different than my friends' mamas and just didn't fit in with them. I now understand that all the folks that were in and out of our house when I was growing up were folks she helped; many sat at her kitchen table, yet they weren't her friends. Looking back now, I realize that even though she knew many, she had no true friends. It was all people she did works for. How lonely she must have been, yet looking at her, you would never have known it. She taught us to love ourselves, to never be greedy, and to help those who needed help no matter who they were. She taught us to never judge a person because you hadn't walked in their shoes and had no idea what life had thrown at them. She taught us with actions and stories; she made us understand that there will always be someone that is worse off, and we should be grateful for our blessings. She taught us that there was nothing that we could not do, that we were the only ones who could hold ourselves back, and that what was ours would be ours. These are all lessons money can't buy. I raised my children with these lessons and they have raised their children the same way. To be a strong worker, you have to have a strong foundation;

your spirit has to be aligned. My mama was so very special and gifted. She was my world, and even after all these years, I still miss her so very much.

Some things stick out more than others when it came to my mama's funny little habits. We always had fresh white sheets on our beds, and she dusted them with powder every night before we went to bed. I now know she did this for two reasons: the white sheets are for protection while you sleep, and she blessed the powder, I am sure. I still put white sheets on the bed when I am ill, but I don't powder my bed anymore. My daughter does, and she has passed it on to her children, who love the feel of the powder on the sheets. This is how the work is passed down within families—and that is how it lives on. Families and neighbors share their funny little ways, and each new person adds their own touch to the work. Hoodoo, Conjure, Rootwork, or whatever word you use to describe it are works that are very simple yet powerful, and they have been passed down within families since the time of slavery.

Painful Roots and an Ugly Past

This work all started with the ancestors of slavery. They did the work for protection, good health, and domination over the slavers, and to keep the law away from them. The ancestors had to have patience; they had to know when to make a move and when to stay still—their lives depended on it. They could have been killed just for looking at someone the wrong way. Everything was hidden; that is why this work is sometimes called "tricks" or "laying down tricks." This is one of the first things a young worker should learn: This work came out of a time in our history when one human thought it was okay to not only own another, but they also felt like they had the right to kill them and abuse them on a whim! We must never forget that! This work didn't come from love and light, all sugary sweet! This work came out of blood, bones, and death; a need to survive in a world that was full of hate and murder! I know today it is hard for some to wrap their heads around this, but some of our history is ugly! You have to understand where the work comes from in order to understand the work.

I have heard over and over again how simple this work is. Folks forget that back in the day, when this work was brought here, the ancestors didn't have much; they weren't allowed to have anything, so they made what they did have work. They learned to hide works in plain sight. Since most weren't allowed to have money, the work focused on protection, healing, and probably some love. Most definitely, there was "law stay away" work, but not as we know it today. The law in that day and time was mostly white folks, and they made up their own rules. Freedom was what was sought after, as well as staying alive!

Today, not much has changed where the law is concerned when it comes to people of color and poor white folks! People who stand to lose something if the law gets ahold of them have just found a different way to move around. That is why "law stay away" work is still done, and it is still a powerful work. The work is like protection work, but the focus is the law. Even though times have changed and years have gone by, we have to face the facts that our legal system was not made to support poor people and people of color. I don't mean to offend anyone; I'm just stating the truth. Let me give you an example of why "law stay away" work is still so important.

I have lived in the same house for over thirty years, married to the same man for over forty years, who lives in the same house but works all the time. He needed to get the tag for his truck, so he took my car to go get it. There was a lawman parked across the street. He watched my husband—who is Chichimecas, descended from nomadic Indigenous people who lived in Central Mexico prior to Spanish conquest—get in the car and drive away. When my husband turned the corner, the lawman pulled up behind him and put on the lights. The gist of the stop was he wanted to know who was driving my car since I was the only one they had ever seen driving it; they hadn't seen my husband in the car before. This tells me the lawman simply stopped my husband because of the color of his skin. When he got home, he told me what had happened. After I got over being furious, I did some work on my car and him to make sure neither one became a law magnet. Changes need to be made in a system that is supposed to be for the people—it should be for *all* the people, not just a few.

I had a client a long time ago who just seemed to be a law magnet, and nothing I did would work. Then one of my elders gave me a simple work to do. I'll share it with y'all. If you find yourself in this situation, you need to buy a new set of handcuffs. Take a large glass bowl, dirt from the four corners of your property, a little hair from the crown of your head, some sugar, and a white candle. Place the hair in the bowl, then the dirt. Cover it with the sugar. Unlock the handcuffs and place them in the bowl. Take the handcuffs key and place it in your wallet. Set the candle inside the bowl and light it as you call on a just judge to protect you. When the candle burns out, place the bowl on top of the icebox and leave it there. That's it. Spells don't have to be complicated—they just have to work. In some ways it's like cooking: the recipe may not be fancy, but in the end, the food tastes good and nourishes body and soul.

Speaking of cooking, my mama didn't teach me how to cook in any formal way, but she did all the cooking unless my daddy was going to cook something special for us. So I learned by *watching* her cook. She taught without really teaching, and she would do the same thing every time she cooked a meal: she always prayed over her food, and she had a certain way of stirring the pots. She would first stir going the opposite direction of the clock; she would do this three times. Then she would stir going in the direction of the hands of the clock. I never really thought anything of it when I learned to cook. I stirred my food the same way because that was what my mama did. Later on, an elder explained it to me. Stirring the opposite way of the clock removes anything negative that the food might have picked up, while stirring the way the hands of the clock move and praying over the food brings in blessings to the folks who eat it.

• • • • • • • • • •

This is Conjure work at its finest, but these tricks are being lost because new generations don't cook as much. Things are just moving too fast in today's world. Most folks want an easy fix to whatever issues they have going on in their lives—they don't realize there *is* no easy fix! Everything takes time. Now, some may think magic is an easy fix, but it takes a lot of effort and a lot of spirit to make magic work. Just because it works different doesn't mean it's not work!

Shaping the Clay

We need our elders. They hold wisdom that would be lost if they hadn't shared it with us. I am grateful for every one of mine, because no matter how large or small, each lesson has made me into the worker I am today. There are so many great works that are being lost as our elders pass on. It is important that they be shared.

When I was coming up as a young worker, I didn't have just one teacher that taught me everything. The teachers came when I needed them, or when I was ready. MiMi was one of those teachers. I was in my early twenties when I met her. She owned a ceramic shop. MiMi is the one who taught me to have patience. I didn't pay for these lessons in cash, but I did have to pay for them in labor. We made the ceramics from start to finish. The molds had to be clean, then the slip (which is a type of mud) had to be poured into the molds. Once the slip set, the mold was opened and the greenware was taken out to air-dry. Once the greenware was dry, it had to be cleaned. This is where my lesson started—the rest was just heavy labor. Anything that tests us, we remember, and I truly remember this lesson. This lesson was a hard one for me because I had no patience, and I was very heavy-handed. In this type of work, you need patience, and you need to know when to be heavy-handed. MiMi taught me well!

I'm sure you are thinking, *What in the world does this have to do with learning Conjure?* Everything! If you don't have patience and know what type of work is needed for a job, then you are just going to be a hot mess! This work takes time, and you have to know how hard to hit a target when doing this type of work. There's more to it than just throwing some stuff together and lighting some candles. Let me give you an example. It was around the holidays, and I wanted to give my mama a set of greenware canisters with pigs on top of the lids. I will never forget those canisters as long as I live! Greenware is nothing more than thin, dry clay; it is very fragile. Once it is dry, it must be cleaned because the molds leave seams on the greenware, so they have to be sanded off and smoothed out. You have to be gentle and have a lot of patience or you will break the piece. I went through about four sets of canisters before I finally learned how to have a light hand and how to take my time and move slow. I will never forget MiMi and those two important lessons she taught me; they have carried me well all these years.

Making Magic Dollies

The elements, the spirits of the land, the trees, and the plants that grow wild in the forest are all part of this work. It is not only well-known roots and herbs; it is everything in nature. Conjure work is all about doing the work with what you have. Take corn husks, for example. Where I live in Texas, they're available at pretty much any grocery store, and let me tell you, they are great for Conjure! Corn husks can be made into packets or dollies; they are both very powerful.

We need to remember that the land is full of blood and bones that feed the plants their power as they grow. Then you have the power of the ancestors and the elders that have worked with the husk behind you. Some folks don't understand that when you do a work, you call all of those who did that work before you, so you have extra help even if you don't realize it.

I first learned about the corn husk dollie in the seventies, when I was expecting my daughter. I was on bed rest for five months. My grandma asked a healer to come stay with me. We became very close; she was like my mama. She made a corn husk dollie, and I remember her placing some of my hair on the dollie. I slept with that dollie the whole time I was on bed rest. When I went to the hospital to have my daughter, the dollie was there. When I came home, the dollie was gone. I remember asking where the dollie was, and she just gave me a look and shook her head, so I knew not to ask again. Much later, my grandma told me that it was a healing dollie made in a special way to protect me and my baby. Once the baby came, the dollie was burnt. "Fire cleanses," is what she said.

Since that time, I have been drawn to working with dollies. They are very powerful and hold a spirit of their own. Later on, when I was a little older, I learned how to make corn dollies. They are all-natural, and there is no glue or tape needed to hold them together. It is an old skill and one I cherish and teach sometimes. Learning to make them takes time, so it's best if you can find an elder to show you how to do this, step-by-step.

Apple head dollies are another old-style dollie that most people don't know how to make anymore, but they can be powerful for all types of love works, especially self-love. In the old days, when I was coming up, the apples were dried naturally to make the heads. Later, I had an elder teach me how to make them "the modern way." You need a large red apple, but don't core the apple. Place the apple on a cookie sheet and put it in the oven. Set the oven to 250 degrees Fahrenheit and let the apple dry out. I was taught to shape the apple into a face as it is drying, but be careful, because it will be hot. Once the apple is semi-dry, you can remove the insides from the bottom of the apple, then finish drying it. Once it is fully dry, the bottom of the apple dollie's head is loaded with the target's personal items and any roots, herbs, or dirts that might need to be added. Then the head is closed by putting a piece of cloth over the hole in the bottom. The head can be attached to a stick and wrapped in cloth or dressed in clothes. If you really wanted to, you could probably replace an old doll's head with the apple head and it would work pretty well.

• • • • • • • • • •

Meeting Nana

I believe that spirit brings folks into our lives when we need them or when there is a lesson for us to learn; Nana was such a person.

My mama always told us it is not what you know, but *who* you know that matters. When I moved to this small Texas town some forty-plus years ago, I was looking for a job. No one would hire me because I was new to town and no one knew me. (That is how it works in small towns. They can be very clannish. I am still considered an outsider by some even after all these years, although it could be because I stay to myself.) I searched for about a week, and every time I heard of an opening somewhere, I would go check it out. Still, no one would hire me. Then a lady told me that the steak house was hiring. I didn't know anything about restaurant work. She also said there was a juke joint that went with the restaurant. Now, I'd been raised to think of juke joints as places with bad reputations. That made me think twice, but I needed a job. And I didn't know it yet, but I needed Nana.

I remember the day I walked in the juke joint and saw Nana. I thought, *Lord have mercy! I probably shouldn't even be in here, much less be asking for a job.* I remember forcing myself to walk in the door. Nana was the only woman sitting at a table full of men. I was raised by an ole Southern woman and this didn't seem right to me, but I needed work!

Nana had big hair, cat eyes drawn on with black liner, and the longest fingernails I had ever seen. She had diamond rings on every finger, and she watched me walk up to the table like she knew why I was there. She excused herself from the table and we sat at the bar. I remember she asked me a lot of questions but in the end, she hired me even though I had never worked in a restaurant in my life. I was in my early twenties. I started work that very afternoon at 5:00 p.m. Nana taught me how to cook as well as many other things. She became like my second mother and was one of my mentors up until her death.

One thing Nana really knew was her plants. I would like to share the first work Nana gave me that worked with plants, although it really was more of a test to see if I was retaining the lessons she had taught me about working with living plants. I call this lesson "Unfinished Business." I don't know all the details because Nana never told me everything; all she told me was that the work was to bring a guy back to bring her peace. This was not a love-drawing work.

Back in the 1980s folks didn't have cell phones, computers, or home printers, so to get a photo of a target you had to either take a film roll and get it developed or have a Polaroid camera that gave you an instant photo. I had a photo from a Polaroid camera to work with. Nana gave me a small flowerpot, a packet of seeds, some potting soil, and the photo. I then collected some dirt from each door of the business.

Once I had everything together, I washed my pot and let it air-dry. Because of the way the picture was made, I separated the photo from the back, since the back of the photo wouldn't have burned right. Early in the morning I got up to put the work together. I mixed all the dirts together and then mixed in the potting soil, praying that my target would come back. Then I burned the photo and let the ash fall into the pot. I mixed it all together while praying my petition. Then the seeds were added and the plant was watered. Nana told me to pray over the seeds and tell them what I needed.

I worked that pot just like she told me to, morning, noon, and when the sun was going down. I remember feeling so happy when a sprout came up, but two or three days went by, and no target showed up. Then, one day, this tall drink of water walked in the door of the restaurant. It was my target! My job was a success, and I have been working with plants ever since.

This isn't the same kind of "working with plants" you sometimes read about, where every herb matches some correspondence on a chart. No, this work is about the life force of the plant and using that power to make things happen! It also means that when you're using something that powerful, you must be careful. Remember that if the plant dies, the work dies.

The Story Behind the Work *Is* the Work

Over the last fifty years I have had many elders. Each one of them has taught me some valuable lessons. In many ways, each one of them enriched my life, not only with the work, but also with the values that I have carried with me through my life. These lessons were the stones of the strong foundation my work is built on, and they are the reason I am who I am today. A strong foundation never crumbles, though it may have a few cracks. I wouldn't be the worker I am today without them.

I feel that in today's fast-paced world, folks don't realize how important elders are. It is too easy to get information on Conjure work nowadays. What so many people don't understand is that learning this work is a lot more than spells. Elders teach us much more than the work—they teach us all the important lessons we'd miss by learning on our own.

There's a story behind every work I do, and every spell has the weight of generations of teachers, elders, mentors, and family members behind it. That is what makes the work powerful. That is what makes the Conjure work…work!

FIELD NOTES

Chinese Wash, a Fusion of Folk Magic

After the official dissolution of slavery in the 1860s, Southern plantations sought cheap, exploitable labor. Since there was already a steady influx of Chinese immigrants working on railroad lines, they often imported Chinese men to work on sugar plantations as well. Eventually this led to backlash, although not to protect the Chinese workers, but because of rampant racism against them. By the final decade of the 1800s, the Chinese Exclusion Acts took hold, and Chinese immigration was severely limited (and existing Chinese immigrants were often ghettoized and treated with brutal disdain).

Still, through the course of immigration, Chinese workers had contact with other repressed groups in places like the Deep South. One lingering effect of this is the creation of formulas within traditions like Hoodoo that depend upon Asian ingredients and often have Chinese associations in their names. Probably the best-known example is a formula known as "Chinese Wash," which involves adding plants like lemongrass, citronella, and palmarosa, all of which grow in parts of Asia. These formulae were added to wash waters for things like clothes or floor cleaners (frequently, along with things like broom straws).

Chinese Wash was used for practical purposes as well as magical ones. In addition to leaving a fresh scent after cleaning, the makers of Chinese Wash would tout its effectiveness in removing "evil mess" from a person's life.

While the original formula clearly stems from Chinese ingredients, most of the Chinese Wash sold and used—first in the South, and eventually through mail-order supply houses and Hoodoo shops as far away as Brooklyn and Chicago—was manufactured by non-Chinese people.[138]

138. See Long, *Spiritual Merchants*, and Yronwode, *Hoodoo Herb and Root Magic*.

TRAVELING ON
The Deep South

As with any guidebook, there is always much more to experience than can be neatly fit into a chapter. To that end, we offer you this addendum to the map that will provide you with some tools to explore the Deep South further.

The glossary shares some keywords that might be useful. The places to visit will point you toward locations of interest that we think you might find valuable, and the reading recommendations provide you with some top-tier texts that can be used to dig in and learn more about this region.

Glossary

ADR: An acronym for African-Derived Religion.

Aida Wedo: Sacred serpent Loa of Haitian Vodou, represented by the rainbow.

Ashé: A force pervading all living things, as described in several African Traditional Religions, which also serves as a connection to the divine.

ATR: An acronym for African Traditional Religion.

awo: The concept of spiritual knowledge, honesty, and sacredness within African Traditional Religions.

BIPOC: An acronym for Black, Indigenous, and/or Person of Color.

Bulbancha: Original Indigenous Choctaw name of the place now known as New Orleans.

Conjure: A word used to describe several folk magic systems in the South, often ones derived from Scots Irish and African American practices blended with other material.

Damballa Wedo: Sacred serpent Loa of Haitian Vodou.

dollies: Figures made from items like corn husks, rags, apples, or other household items. Used to focus magical intention.

Elegguá: Crossroads Orisha in La Regla Lucumí, known as Exú the Orixa in Candomble and Umbanda.

folk saint: A holy figure that has not been officially recognized by the church. Santa Muerte and other folk saints often have very devoted followings, despite churches' attempts to eradicate their reverence.

Hoodoo: Black folk magic practiced originally in the southern US.

Ile-Ifa: A Yoruban/West African religion that influences many of the practices found in ATRs and ADRs.

La Regla Lucumí: African Traditional Religion originally practiced in Cuba and other parts of the Caribbean.

Loa: A category of divine beings in Haitian Vodou.

mojo: A term that can refer to both a physical charm (usually a bag containing magical ingredients) or the power of magic within a practitioner.

Old Style Conjure: The system of folk magic originating in the American South and generally involving work like packet creation, wash waters, candle or oil lamp burning, and the use of dollies. This practice has some similarities to Hoodoo and Rootwork, but it is often used by a wider group of practitioners.

Olukun: Androgynous partner of the Ifa spiritual figure known as Yemoya, associated with deep water.

orisha: A category of divine beings in La Regla Lucumí.

packets: Bundled spells, usually carried as amulets or talismans. Constructed from ingredients like cloth, string, or paper, as well as herbs, stones, bones, and other curios.

Papa Legba: Loa of the crossroads in Haitian Vodou, known as Papa Lebat in New Orleans Voodoo.

pataki: A sacred teaching story in La Regla Lucumí.

Rootwork: A type of African American folk magic practice centered on the use of plants (especially roots) and originating around the Lowcountry of South Carolina and Georgia.

tricks: Spells or spell components left in a particular place to release their magical charge or come into contact with an intended subject.

Vodun: An African-Derived Religion involving service to spirits known as Loa, ritual feasting, music, dancing, and spirit contact. It is sometimes called Voodoo outside of its native Haiti (Ayti) in places like New Orleans.

Yemoya: Ifa spiritual figure embodying the Great Mother and creation, strongly associated with bodies of water.

• • • • • • • • • •

Places to Visit

Wander off Bourbon Street in New Orleans, Louisiana: There is no shortage of things to do in New Orleans, but many people wind up lost in the tourist crowds and miss a number of magical spots. You can take cemetery tours of several spots in the city (including the two St. Louis Cemeteries known for their association with Marie Laveau, or the gorgeous Lafayette Cemetery in the Garden District). You can also visit authentic Vodun temples like the Voodoo Spiritual Temple, run by Priestess Miriam, or get your fortune told late at night in Jackson Square in the French Quarter.

Stop By the (In)famous Clarksdale Crossroads in Clarksdale, Mississippi: One of the best-known folk legends in the South is that of Robert Johnson, a blues musician who allegedly sold his soul to the devil to gain his uncanny guitar skills. While there is plenty of speculation about this story (it may not even have been about Robert Johnson originally, but instead about another bluesman named Tommy Johnson), it does have some roots in Southern folk magic. Crossroads rituals often involve meeting mysterious figures (such as a "man in black") in order to gain new skills or powers, and they are well documented. You can visit the intersection of highways 61 and 49 in Clarksdale, Mississippi, which lays claim to the Johnson legend and marks the spot with a giant pole with a triad of blue guitars on it.

Take a Walk Down Beale Street in Memphis, Tennessee: Memphis aligns with the Deep South much more than the rest of Tennessee, or even Arkansas across the river. Its folk magical culture involves the presence of Hoodoo supply companies like the historic Lucky Heart Cosmetics or the strong presence of the Spiritualist Church, which was founded by Mother Leafy Anderson in New Orleans and involves a number of folk magical practices. You can still get a taste of that magic today by visiting shops like A. Schwab's on Beale Street, which sells a number of Hoodoo-oriented products alongside standard housewares, T-shirts, and other goods.

Wander in and around Savannah, Georgia: If you've read John Berendt's famous *Midnight in the Garden of Good and Evil*, you'll know that Savannah is both beautiful and suffused with Southern Gothic charm. You may also have picked up that it is host to a strong branch of Southern folk magic, usually called Rootwork (although it is sometimes also identified as Hoodoo). Savannah and the nearby island community of St. Helena were the epicenter of some famous folk magic lessons, such as the conflict between Rootworker "Dr. Buzzard" (Stephaney Robinson) and the "high sheriff" of Beaufort, South Carolina, James McTeer (who reputedly used folk magic to combat his rival on his own terms). You can still find herb and root shops in the area, and occasionally you'll see evidence of peoples' practices in places like Bonaventure or Colonial Park Cemetery. (Please do not disturb anything you find.)

Seek Sorcery in South Beach, Miami: All of Florida has a long-standing connection to folk magic (see the recommended reading for famed Florida folklorist Zora Neale Hurston's work, for example). Miami is a massive cosmopolitan fusion of many cultures, so it has a wide range of folk magic associations as well. Practitioners of Lukumi, Brujeria, and Hoodoo may wind up buying many of their ingredients from the same botanicas that dot the city. You can also make a stop at the South Florida Folklife Center to learn about the many aspects of folk culture that shape and influence the magic (and life!) of the people in the Miami area.

Recommended Reading

Old Style Conjure: Hoodoo, Rootwork & Folk Magic by Starr Casas
This book is both an introduction to Southern folk magic and a personal record of how Casas developed as a Conjure worker.

The Conjure Workbook Volume 1: Working the Root by Starr Casas
For those looking for more practical Conjure information, Casas also has this book of rituals and workings.

Black Magic: Religion and the African American Conjuring Tradition by Yvonne P. Chireau
Chireau takes an academic but accessible look at the traditions of Black folk magic in African American history.

A Secret History of Memphis Hoodoo: Rootworkers, Conjurers & Spirituals by Tony Kail
Historian Kail uncovers a number of original source materials documenting the influence of African American folk magic in Memphis, Tennessee, and beyond.

Orishas, Goddesses, and Voodoo Queens: The Divine Feminine in the African Religious Traditions by Lilith Dorsey
An excellent overview of women in African American, ATR, and Hoodoo traditions, including well-known figures like Marie Laveau and lesser-known ones like Annie Christmas.

Voodoo and African Traditional Religion by Lilith Dorsey
Dorsey provides a deeper exploration of ATRs, and Voodoo specifically, in this book.

Mules and Men by Zora Neale Hurston
An essential collection of fieldwork by folklorist/anthropologist Hurston from her work in Florida and the American South, especially focused on Hoodoo.

Chapter 4

Tell My Horse: Voodoo and Life in Haiti and Jamaica by Zora Neale Hurston
Another valuable collection of field writings by Hurston, this time focusing on her experiences with Voodoo in Haiti and Obeah in Jamaica.

Spiritual Merchants: Religion, Magic & Commerce by Carolyn Morrow Long
This is a wonderful look at the way that Hoodoo and other folk magic systems became commercialized during the twentieth century.

Southern Cunning: Folkloric Witchcraft in the American South by Aaron Oberon
Oberon explores what it means to be a "swamp witch" using a variety of folkloric tools and methods to practice Southern-inflected witchcraft.

CHAPTER 5

The Midlands

Chapter 5

Yarb Doctors on Call and Hoodoos on TV: An Introduction to the Folk Magic of the Midlands

When I was fourteen, my family and I took a cross-country road trip. I remember the smell of sassafras and pine on the hills. We visited a beautiful indoor hot springs water park in the Ouachita Mountains, putting us right at the edge of where the Ozark Mountains start. We stayed with a relative in an A-frame cabin up in the hills for a few nights, and I can recall a sunset that just about broke my heart. I wanted to learn more about that place, and I began to seek out more of its lore and legends.

Almost two decades later I was at a folklorists' retreat in Memphis where a bluegrass and roots band from the Ozarks provided some of the musical entertainment. I sat with the lead singer of the band after one performance, and we got to chatting. She told some stories about her life there, and the subject of healing and folk beliefs came up. (It was a folklorists' retreat, after all.) I mentioned Vance Randolph, who, in the mid-twentieth century, wrote some of the most definitive works on the Ozark Mountains and their people, including *Ozark Magic and Folklore* and a humor collection called *Pissing in the Snow*. Many of us in the folklore community see Randolph's work as a prime example of what we call "participant-observation," where a folklorist settles in with the people they're learning about and chronicles their traditions and practices. When I brought up Randolph to my companion, however, there was a pause.

"Yeah, he learned a lot about our ways and how we were back then," she said. "But he also left plenty out. And," she continued, a wry smile turning up the corner of her mouth, "of course we didn't tell him everything."

That feeling—that while there is a lot about the Ozarks and their folklore that we can know, there's also a lot kept hidden and away from outsiders—is echoed in Brandon Weston's work. Both in his book *Ozark Folk Magic* and in his essay here, Weston points out that Randolph's version of the Ozarks might have had grains of truth during the time he wrote, but those Ozarks "no longer exist," and the modern Midlands is "more diverse than ever."

The stretch of the continent reaching from the Great Lakes down to the Ozarks has a lot of secrets, and it's been very good at keeping them. At the same time, there's also long been a public face for the folk magic here. In the Ozarks, people were likely to know a local "yarb doctor" they could call for everyday illnesses, just as readily as they might know the number for a professional medico.

When it comes to the Midwest portions of the United States and Canada, outsiders often apply stereotypes as readily as they do to the "hillbillies" and "rednecks" of the Upland South, or to the "dumb Dutch" of the Mid-Atlantic region. People think of the Midlands as "flyover" states and provinces that are not worth stopping in, and that are essentially backward and rural. But the Midlands also include robust, exciting urban areas like Chicago and Detroit and have been the home to diverse populations for centuries now. This is the home of Motown and the location of some of the biggest and most prestigious centers of learning in the country (Ohio State, Northwestern, University of Michigan, and University of Indiana, to name only a few). Irish Americans and Black Americans make up some of the largest portions of the population in Chicago and have contributed immensely to the city's cultural landscape.

In this chapter, Sandra Santiago writes about her experiences with ATRs, specifically Lucumi, and how parts of the Midwestern landscape have played host to African spiritual forces—orishas—like Eleguá and Obatala. In her essay, Santiago also talks about the role that traditions like Espiritismo—a practice rooted in nineteenth-century Spiritualism but distilled through the landscape and experience of Puerto Rico—play in a city like Chicago.

In Detroit, African American Folk Magic circulates within a tight-knit community, but there have also been interviews on the local news and television stations with well-known rootworkers and Hoodoo practitioners, as you will see when Kenya Coviak takes you around the city in her section.

Secrets in the Midlands still exist. Even as we sit and talk with each of the authors here about the distinct shape and direction of folk magic in their communities, things change. The Ozarks are no longer what is found in Vance Randolph's work, and Detroit has undergone dramatic changes since the early 2000s. Those changes will inevitably change the flavor of the folk magic here. At the core, though, some traditions remain. Knowledgeable Ozarks can still pick out useful "yarbs," and there's been a resurgence in interest in understanding plant-based healing and magic. Even as some of the auto plants have closed in Detroit, there's been an artistic florescence. A new, vibrant generation of rootworkers like Jade Aurora are opening up magical businesses to meet the needs of the people there. And, as Coviak points out, the Detroit River still runs through the city, fueling the magic always.

I am grateful for what I learned from reading the work of people like Vance Randolph, of course. Their work provides a good snapshot of a place and a time. What I am more thankful for, though, are voices like those you're about to meet, who are a part of their communities and are sharing their magic here because they want to get it right (even if they keep a few things back, just in case).

A Living Tradition: Ozark Folk Magic, Reimagined

BRANDON WESTON

The main obstacle faced by those interested in Ozark traditional healing, magic, and folkways in a modern world is time. When we read the accounts by folklorists like Vance Randolph in his *Ozark Magic and Folklore* and Mary Parler's *Folk Beliefs from Arkansas*, readers are immediately transported to an Ozarks that no longer exists. Accounts of healers like Granny Women, Yarb Doctors, Power Doctors, and others seem to be commonplace throughout the region, but upon further investigation, we see that even these traditional titles are all but forgotten. This loss of folk knowledge isn't relegated to the Ozark Mountains alone and can be seen in many other traditions as well. Storytellers die, like everyone else. Healers fail to pass on their knowledge to younger generations, and eventually an entire corpus of beliefs vanishes.

Yet despite all of this loss, the heart of Ozark folk traditions has remained intact. Connections to the land and the power of inborn magic that once influenced our rites and practices hundreds of years ago have evolved to cope with a modern world in which Ozarkers live very different lives than their ancestors did. This evolution has seemed cruel in many cases, especially when it has allowed the seeds of certain traditions to perish or be weeded out. As an Ozarker and practitioner myself, I've seen outdated systems of belief that hold on to racist, sexist, and bigoted ideologies be allowed to flourish still, entirely disregarding the fact that the Ozark region is now more diverse than ever before. This is a far worse path to take.

My work as an Ozark witch and healer began at a very young age. I can still remember spending much of my summer vacation running around in the woods collecting moss for fairy houses and talking to trees. I remember brewing up "potions" made from acorns and dyed water that I would pretend to prescribe to family members or the birds outside. To most of my friends, I lived a very strange life.

My family has always been a strange mixture of beliefs and traditions. On the one hand, most were Christians, relatively conservative, and from hardworking, down-to-earth backgrounds. At the same time, stories abounded about ghosts, monsters, and, of course, the Little People. I was told to watch out for the legendary "hoop snake," a mythical beast able to bite its own tail and roll like a wagon wheel across the ground. It was believed that if the hoop snake caught you, it would spit poison into your eyes. And then there were stories from my great-uncle Bill, who was a wart charmer born with the ability to magically buy warts off of people for a penny or nickel. I never thought twice about this strange blending of culture; it was just my life—until college, when I found a copy of Vance Randolph's *Ozark Magic and Folklore*. Up until that point, I had no idea that my family actually had a culture.

The trail made by the folklorists who have gone before us has left us a good starting point from which to begin our own path, but these resources are ultimately limited to the age in which they were written. For example, Randolph's *Ozark Magic and Folklore* held the title of *Ozark Superstitions* when first published in 1947, a testament to how many have viewed our traditional beliefs and practices. Today, traditions of folk healing and magic in the Ozarks might seem very different to those of our past. More and more practitioners now identify with cultural and religious traditions that wouldn't have been present in the Ozark region in the past. The influx of these different belief systems has at times replaced the old worldviews of hillfolk, but not to the detriment of the tradition, in my view. If anything, they have allowed us to fill in many of the gaps in our corpus of knowledge, left threadbare by the dying off of traditional healers and storytellers. We now have a chance to be ever-diligent in sifting through our beliefs and rooting out worldviews based in sexism, racism, and bigotry.

Diverse People, Diverse Practices

The Ozark identity is really a biproduct of the Appalachian melting pot. For this reason, we can see the fingerprints of many different cultural practices and beliefs on Ozark folkways. The extensive botanical knowledge that many Ozark "Yarb Doctors," or mountain herbalists, have held by memory was for the most part formulated in Appalachia through interactions with Indigenous peoples, in particular the Cherokee, Muscogee Creek, Yuchi, and Koasati (Coushatta). A few healing plants would have been propagated in the New World by settlers, like mullein (*Verbascum thapsus*), plantain (*Plantago major*), and many kitchen herbs that we still use today. Beyond this, however, the forest must have seemed very strange indeed to those first settlers. We owe a huge debt to these Indigenous peoples who were willing to pass along their knowledge of the land to our ancestors.

This proto-Ozark amalgam of traditions included many fingerprints from across Europe, not just the British Isles and Ireland, as is often believed. Many families, including my own, can trace their ancestry back to German and Swiss settlers as well. These clans made up what were called the Pennsylvania Dutch before later moving west into the most northern stretches of Appalachia. Eventually, these families would move south into North Carolina, Tennessee, and Georgia. Around the turn of the nineteenth century, land opened up in what would come to be called the

Ozarks after the forced removal of the Osage and Old Settler Cherokee to Oklahoma. These same families would seize the opportunity to travel west as small clans and communities in search of isolation and opportunity.

Many of our folk beliefs can be traced back to the British Isles and Ireland, including the fairy faith, mixed with Indigenous beliefs in Appalachia to form what Ozark hillfolk call the "Little People." These cantankerous guardian spirits of nature are often named as the source of many a healer's or magical practitioner's "gift" or power. We can also find influence from the Cunning Folk traditions, especially with the use of certain verbal charms, prayers, and Bible verses found in the Ozarks that have direct sources in the British Isles. Likewise, another great influencing tradition has been that of the Pennsylvania Germans, namely *Braucherei* in German, or "Powwow," as it came to be called in the New World. This tradition was exemplified in the early–nineteenth century grimoire and remedy book *Pow-Wows, or Long Lost Friend* by John George Hohman. In fact, copies of Hohman's work have been found in the Ozarks amongst German families. Folklorist Vance Randolph even included a charm from the work in his *Ozark Magic and Folklore*, having heard it recited from an informant.[139]

Despite influences from a range of cultural traditions and ancient practices, Ozark folk magic and healing has developed as its own unique tradition in the isolated mountains. In my several tours of the region, the one defining feature of Ozark folk traditions is that it's almost impossible to define Ozark folk traditions—especially with closely guarded practices like folk magic and healing, which are often passed down orally through family lines. There are as many magical and healing practices as there are practitioners. While there are some common features linking traditional folkways together, for the most part these practices vary from family to family, with similarities to other practices only being found where these clans have intermarried with others with the gift.

One distinct feature of Ozark folk magic and healing is its deep connection to the land itself. Often practices, medicines, and ritual implements are derived from what can be foraged or grown out in the hills. This reliance upon nature would have first formed as a necessity amongst our ancient ancestors who lived in isolation and had to rely upon what the natural world was able to provide. An extension of this idea is found in Ozark folk magic, where household tools and items like brooms, knives, axes, lamps, string, etc., are often repurposed for use in magical and healing rites. New or highly specialized tools and medicines would have been looked at as frivolous and useless purchases, especially for poor families. This connection to nature, and in particular the Ozark region itself, and simplicity in ritual tools and medicines still hold a sacred position amongst healers and other magical practitioners today.

139. Randolph, *Ozark Magic and Folklore*, 286.

Healers and Witches

The keepers of traditional healing and magical knowledge in the Ozarks have historically been specialized practitioners with an inborn connection to not only the lineage of knowledge based in oral storytelling and the passing down of folkways, but also a deep connection to the spirit world. These practitioners often took on the name of "doctor" as a sign of respect from the community. Folk names that were once commonly used included the Yarb Doctor, Power Doctor, Goomer Doctor (also called a Witch Master), and the all-encompassing position of the Granny Woman, who was often the sole source of healing for women in the community. Few use these traditional terms today outside of tall tales, and modern practitioners now have a host of alternative terms for themselves and their work.

Traditional healers were historically the lifeblood of the rural community, which was often isolated from any other forms of medical care. Many held long lineages of knowledge, passed down from healer to apprentice, often inside closely protected family or clan lines. Others took their training from dreams, encounters with ancestral spirit-teachers, or through a close working relationship with divine figures like saints, angels, or the Little People. Healers were almost always viewed as individuals set apart from the community as a whole. The ability to manipulate the spirit world for healing or harm was seen as a path few were able to take if they weren't born with the gift. For this reason, much of this knowledge has now been lost due to the lack of willing apprentices to carry on the work. Traditional taboos surrounding the passing of magical power have fallen aside in the modern Ozarks, where practitioners now choose their apprentices from those who simply have a willingness to learn, as opposed to those born under certain "tokens" or omens.

Most magical practitioners today find themselves the holder of many different practices and traditions, as opposed to the past, where individuals often specialized in only one form of healing. Some modern practitioners choose to connect to mountain herbalism, traditionally the domain of the Yarb Doctor. A "yarb" in mountain speak refers to a medicinal plant. Many modern Yarb Doctors have a vast amount of knowledge about plant and mineral medicines, much of which was passed to them orally from an elder teacher. One woman I met humbly told me she reckoned she knew about five hundred different healing plants and fungi. These folk herbalists also have a vast number of recipes for various concoctions, brews, and salves locked away inside their heads, some of which can include a staggering amount of individual yarbs.

Herbal healing in the mountains is still often geared toward "tonifying" the body using strong, plant-based tonics, taken for only a short amount of time so as to not damage our fragile constitutions. The most famous of these tonics has to be sassafras tea, made from the roots of the sassafras tree (*Sassafras albidum*) and drank in the springtime to "clean the blood," as the old-timers say. This euphemism for a laxative was often applied to tonic brews aimed at aiding the digestive system after a long winter of eating dried, salted meats and canned vegetables.

Practices of folk magic were once the expertise of the Power Doctor, who specialized in prayers, amulets, and rituals for magical healing. Today, this work has been picked up by mountain herbalists and modern Ozark witches alike and added to a vast repertoire of practices. The Power Doctor of the past never prescribed herbal remedies, but instead relied upon their innate gift and connection to the magical forces of the land to heal, and in some cases harm, others in the community. In traditional Ozark culture, a witch was always associated with using malign magic, gifted to them by demons or the Devil himself, in order to harm or steal from the people around them. Today, we use the word *witch* in a very different way, even in the Ozarks. While in rural areas there remains a suspicion against any notion of magic or witchcraft, I've encountered many healers who have taken the name "witch" to describe their work in a way no other title can. Because the Power Doctor of old used magical means themselves, they were often the first target of witchcraft accusations in the community. For this reason, many Power Doctors were very pious individuals, even preachers or ordained clergy.

Removing curses and hexes was once the task of the Goomer Doctor or Witch Master. In the Ozark dialect, "goomering" refers specifically to witchcraft. Therefore, someone who has been "goomered" has been hexed. Both the Goomer Doctor and Witch Master specialized in removing curses and sending the magic back to kill the witch who originally sent it out. There are many humorous Ozark stories related to the battles between magicians, and while Goomer Doctors have claimed to have killed many witches in the Ozarks, there is almost no actual evidence to verify their stories. Today, the work of the Goomer Doctor has faded into history, and while there are still those who use many of the traditional methods for removing hexes and curses, the idea of the witch as an actual evil presence in the community has been relegated to fireside stories and sermons from the pulpit.

Ozark Magical Theory

Ozark healing of the past often made no distinction between "physical" and "magical" remedies. A traditional herbalist was often just as likely to include a set of specialized prayers or verses from the Bible, with the understanding that the words would add their own benefit alongside the medicinal plants. Separation was instead made in the origin of the illness itself. Sickness could then come from a "physical" source, like illnesses, or from a magical source, like witchcraft. Hillfolk often first consulted traditional herbalists, who were able to properly diagnose the source of the sickness. Physical medicines based in herbal preparations could then be employed, and the patient was observed for a certain amount of time. If the illness persisted, the herbalist might then suggest looking for a healer who specialized in removing curses.

Healing and folk magic in the Ozarks are based primarily on the concept of the Law of Sympathy, sometimes referred to as the Doctrine of Signatures. This theory supposes that medicinal benefit can be drawn from plants and minerals shaped or colored like certain body parts and organs. For example, the Ozark-native cutleaf toothwort (*Cardamine concatenata*) is used for toothaches.

A similar concept called the Law of Contagion describes an invisible connection between a magical practitioner or healer and their intended patient (or possibly victim.) This connection is created by possessing certain identifying materials from the target of the work. Common Ozark materials include hair, fingernail clippings, blood, or clothing scraps. By possessing this material, a healer can heal a client without being in the same room as them; likewise, one could also curse a person from a distance. This is exemplified in the Ozark spite doll, often made of cornhusks, paper, or wax and filled with identifying material from the target victim. Once created, the magical practitioner would then be able to manipulate the doll in any way they saw fit, including but not limited to filling it with pins or nails, burying it, burning it, or leaving it under a waterfall. It was believed that the victim would become sick or feel pains from such work.

A curse made by such a connection could only be removed by a healer who was skilled in severing this magical cord. This act was often the focus of magical healing in the Ozarks. Once such an illness or curse was diagnosed, the healer would first cleanse their client, either in water or smoke, the idea being that this cleanse would be able to remove the cord. Other times, certain ritual acts could be performed, such as using scissors or a knife alongside prayers to magically cut the cord.

Diagnosis and Healing

Methods of diagnosis differed from healer to healer. In the case of physical illness, a healer might simply collect a list of current symptoms from their patient. The remedy then included plants meant to cure the illness at hand as well as heal any other factors that might have contributed. For example, a remedy for a fever derived from heatstroke might help break the patient's fever and also act as a tonic to bolster their system for when they had to return to work in the heat.

Magical illnesses were commonly diagnosed using divination. Common rituals used dowsing rods or a pendulum along with questions asked by the healer about the source of the illness. How the rods crossed or the direction the pendulum spun was then observed for an answer. Another common method of divination involved floating a leaf in a bowl of spring water. The healer would name a direction as "yes" or "no," then ask a question and observe the way the leaf spun. Fire was used in a similar manner: Coals were scraped out of the hearth and into a metal skillet. Then the healer would ask certain questions while slowly dropping plant material, commonly tobacco, onto the coals. The smoke and noises produced by the material was observed for answers.

Regardless of the origin of the illness, remedies and rituals often took many factors into account apart from just the physical items used. Hillfolk historically looked to the moon and astrological signs to determine the "best days" for many aspects of their lives, and this included healing and magic. Much of the corpus of Ozark healing knowledge comes from European systems ingrained in the minds of hillfolk. Still to this day, healers utilize the system of the four humors as well as the hot/cold, wet/dry characteristics of illnesses and plants in their work.

The "growing," or waxing, of the moon was seen as a time when power was not only growing inside the human body, but also in the natural world. Medicinal plants were harvested at the Full Moon in the case of aerial parts, like flowers and leaves, or the New Moon in the case of roots, the idea being that "power" flows down into the roots of the plant as the moon wanes. Rituals for magically "growing" health, love, or wealth were traditionally performed during the waxing moon. Likewise, work to strengthen the body of a sick patient was also done at this time.

As the moon waned, work seeking to banish, remove, or lessen could be performed with great success. Many wart charms and remedies were enacted during this time so that as the moon waned, so too would the warts. This was also a traditional time for removing hexes and any magical illnesses. A healer might connect the power of a curse to the fading of the moon with the understanding that by the time of the New Moon, the curse would be completely destroyed.

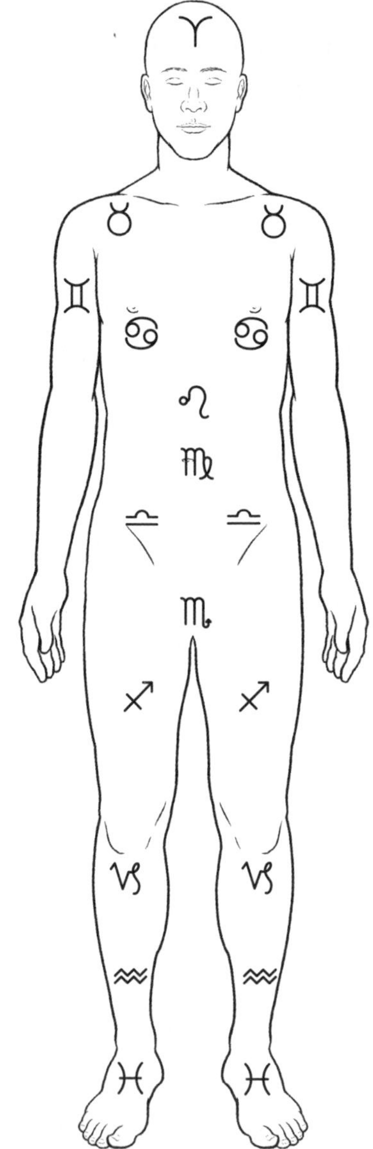

Figure 5-1: The Zodiac Man

As with the phases of the moon, healers also consulted zodiac moon signs for each day. According to the Zodiac Man, or Man of Signs, each part of the body corresponds to a specific zodiac sign. Illnesses were seen as being strongest when the moon sign was in that corresponding spot and at their weakest in the opposing sign. A headache or strong fever, for example, are in the head, represented by the sign Aries. Ritual work for healing these conditions was best performed on a day when the moon was in the opposite sign, Libra.

Cleansing Body and Soul

Cleansing is a common trend amongst both practitioners of the past and the modern Ozarks. This work most often involves washing the body, either with water or smoke, as a way of magically removing both physical and supernatural contagions. With water cleanses, the healer will often create a specialized bath for their afflicted client. This bath is sometimes as simple as fresh spring water that has been blessed with a prayer, or it might include any number of yarbs. The key with water cleansing is the movement over the body, which is why these cleanses often take place in a creek or river. At home, a client is cleansed by pouring the water over their head and letting it run down the body. If the rite takes place in a river, the afflicted patient is usually dunked under the water three times, hailing back to the baptismal rite of Christianity but also connecting to a much more ancient belief in the power of moving water to carry away illness and curses with its current.

Cleansing with smoke is another popular method. The most popular Ozark fumigant has to be red cedar (*Juniperus virginiana*), a fragrant evergreen related to common juniper and said to have magical powers by the Indigenous peoples of Appalachia as well as the Scottish and German settler families. This smoke can be used as a fumigant for illness as well as evil spirits, wandering ghosts, and demons alike. When wafted over the body, usually accompanied by certain prayers, it can act in the same way as running water to cleanse off many physical and magical afflictions, the idea being that the smoke magically adheres to the hex or illness and then carries it away as it drifts into the atmosphere.

An easy cleansing rite I always like to suggest to practitioners wanting to incorporate some Ozark magic into their own work uses some red cedar and salt. If you can't get your hands on true red cedar, don't use common cedar as a substitute. Instead, use the foliage or dried berries from one of the many other varieties of juniper. While inside your house, burn the red cedar or juniper on a hot coal; you could also work in true Ozark fashion by heating up a cast-iron skillet and dropping the red cedar into the pan. You want to use something mobile because you are then going to carry it throughout your house in a counterclockwise direction, starting at the front door. Make sure to get every room! You can do one pass or the traditional three. At the end, take the holder out the front door. Mix the ash from the red cedar with some salt and then, starting at your front door and moving in a clockwise direction, sprinkle the ash and salt mixture at the foundation of your house. Make a single pass around the entire house, then end at the front door.

Lucky Charms, Amulets, and Talismans

Physical amulets and talismans are another common element in Ozark folk magic of the past and present. In the old Ozarks, amulets were made from natural materials like animal bones, feathers, or certain nuts, as in the case of the buckeye (*Aesculus glabra*), which was carried in the pocket to ward off many different illnesses as well as curses. Teeth were also a popular item to wear or carry, in particular a boar's tusk, worn to help strengthen the wearer's own teeth. Hag stones, or hole stones, which are river rocks that have a naturally occurring hole somewhere on the surface, were and still are strung on a string and hung up outside a cabin to protect the home and family, or worn as a necklace to ward off evil influences.

One tradition I'm encouraging the return of is the crafting of house charms, or charm bags. These are small cloth bags filled with various symbolic items that are then hung up inside the home, usually near the front and back doors, to ward off all manner of evil and illness. Often these bags will contain a page with handwritten prayers or charms as well as items like buckeye nuts and nails or thorns (sometimes used to symbolize the nails of Jesus's cross and thorny crown). Once the items are added, the bag is sealed up with knots and hung where needed. Sometimes these bags are made when a home is being built and are then left inside the walls themselves, around the four corners of the foundation, or in the attic.

Make Your Own House Charm

Here's an easy recipe to make your own house charm. This is one I always like to make with workshop attendees, and it's always been very popular. You're going to start by taking a small square of paper, about five inches across, and writing the names of everyone who lives in your house one on top of the other. Write the names horizontally down the center of the paper. First, middle, and last names are best.

Then write Psalm 23 in a circle around the names: "The Lord is my shepherd, I shall not want. He makes me lie down in green pastures; he leads me beside still waters; he restores my soul. He leads me in right paths for his name's sake. Even though I walk through the darkest valley, I fear no evil; for you are with me; your rod and your staff—they comfort me. You prepare a table before me in the presence of my enemies; you anoint my head with oil; my cup overflows. Surely goodness and mercy shall follow me all the days of my life, and I shall dwell in the house of the Lord my whole life long."[140] An alternative charm I like to use reads, "May we be blessed! May we be protected! From fire and flood. From pestilence and malice. May our plates never be empty! May our cups never run dry! May our hearts always be open to love!"

After you've finished writing on the paper, fold it up into a smaller square, then put it inside a little cloth bag along with these ingredients: three new nails, three new needles, and a pinch of salt. If you have any other protective items like buckeye nuts, silver dimes, red cedar berries, etc., you can include them as well.

Once filled, tie the top of the bag closed with some string and three knots (or tie closed the drawstring of the bag with three knots). Hang the bag on the inside of your house near the front

140. New Revised Standard Version.

or back door. Some people like to make several to hang near all of the doors that lead outside the house.

Traditionally, these bags should be recharged with magical energy, or "fed," on the New and Full Moon. You can do this by putting a few drops of alcohol, camphor essential oil, or perfume on the bag.

A Modern Path

Over the years I've devoted my life to collecting everything I can about lore, remedies, and magic in the modern Ozarks. One thing that struck me about Randolph's work was that it was published so long ago. Where were the stories from today? What I came to discover is that there has been very little interest in the Ozarks for quite some time now. My goal has always been to change this. Every day, storytellers are dying off without passing down their knowledge; healers go to the grave with no one to inherit their remedies and power. But with this loss has come an evolution of Ozark folkways and traditions. Many people are now collecting stories from their families before it's too late. Others, like me, are traveling around collecting from old-timers and younger generations alike.

The best part of my journey as an Ozarker has been collecting new and interesting magical techniques, healing recipes, and mystical gleanings from the young and old alike, people who love and appreciate these mountains for what they are and seek not only to preserve the past, but also to help it evolve into something even more beautiful.

Ozark folk magic isn't like it was when Randolph and other folklorists ventured out into the hills collecting material, and it never will be. That's an idealized picture of the Ozarks that is actually harmful to the people living here. By pigeonholing Ozarkers into the hillbilly stereotype, we're simultaneously preventing actual social change from occurring in rural areas while at the same time complaining about how "backward" these rural areas are.

As with many other areas of the country, the folk traditions that remain in public view today mostly include herbal remedies, some passed down through families, but many others bringing in systems like Western Herbalism, Ayurveda, and Traditional Chinese Medicine. For many modern Ozark herbalists, training in these other complex systems of healing only adds to the foundational work they might have inherited from family members and local healers.

The grocery store and pharmacy are still centers for traditional healing in the Ozarks, although in a little bit different form. Bottled tinctures, salves, balms, and herbal teas, once relegated to creation in the home kitchen, can now be easily picked up in stores, even in rural areas. This has led to a bit of an issue, though, one that I often speak about in my workshops. I'll be brief and just say this: plants contain chemicals, and chemicals can interact with chemicals. That's to say, self-diagnoses, even of simple herbal remedies, can lead to some disastrous results, especially in cases of mixing remedies (which contain chemicals) with prescription medications (which also contain chemicals). In the old days, before people had easier access to modern medicine, the situation would have been different. People wouldn't have had to worry about mixing their prescription medicines with home remedies. This is absolutely something anyone interested in herbalism should be concerned about, and I highly recommend having a copy of an herbal interactions and contraindications book on hand for reference.

Many people today have very strict ideas about what constitutes a tradition or culture without realizing that the cultures they're talking about didn't always look the way they do now. Ozark folk magic and healing has always been a mixture of practices, remedies, and rituals. As one old-timer told me, "If it works, use it." This of course might get us into some trouble, living at a time when a seemingly endless amount of information is now available instantly at our fingertips. Cultivating a deep respect for other cultures, especially those that are at risk for extinction, is necessary when approaching any research into traditional folkways. The love and care I've seen with many Ozark practitioners when dealing with other systems of healing and magic truly exemplifies this message. It's not always the case, of course, but there seems to be something inborn in the Ozarker's spirit to seek information from the source. Like the Ozark herbalist and Granny Woman I met who wanted to add diagnostic methods from Traditional Chinese Medicine to her work with Ozark plants, so she saved up every penny she could to fly to California to study with a healing master. She returned home not with an appropriative notion of some other culture, but with actual training that she could then add to her own vast knowledge.

This isn't always doable for everyone, myself included. Sometimes we have to rely on internet searches and reading through library books. Now more than ever, though, I want to stress the importance of studying with actual cultural representatives. Even if it's just for a weekend, make the effort to reach out and talk to someone who has lived the tradition, not just read about it in a book. In the Ozarks we have many practices that are considered "open" to those not from around here. These spells, remedies, and rituals, many of which have been mentioned here, can be added to any practice with ease. There are traditions, though, that I'm much more protective of. The use of secret verbal charms, traditionally passed down orally through family lines, is one of these areas. That's not to say that these charms are unavailable to outsiders, but receiving this power, which is seen as something tangible, requires actually interacting with someone who holds the magic themselves.

The Ozarks have always been labeled as "backward," with the image of the hillbilly burned into the minds of almost every generation. The truth of the matter is that the region is as complex and complicated as any other in the country. We have our tragic shortcomings, our demons we haven't yet faced, and our lingering prejudices. We've, at times, suffered our own cultural destruction. The hillbilly stereotype has given rise to generations of Ozarkers who are ashamed of their own culture. This is particularly destructive as storytellers and healers die off without anyone in their families interested enough to take their knowledge. One man I met told me his grandma was a healer and could identify and use vast amounts of plant species from the hills and hollers around her home. He always regretted not learning from her when he still could and reckoned she took all her knowledge to the grave with her. Sadly, this is not an isolated story—it is happening more and more as rural areas are abandoned for bigger towns and cities.

But as each year passes, I see more growth, and it gives me some hope for the future. I'm always surprised at how many people attend my workshops and are interested in Ozark folkways. There's a renewed energy amongst younger generations to reconnect to their roots, both cultural and of the land itself. People are starting to move back out to the "boonies" and are making their own homestead farms. Herbal and "natural" healing methods are perhaps more popular now than they ever were. All of this gives my own work a new life as I do my part to help save the Ozark identity from the curses of the past.

FIELD NOTES

Cures of the Illinois Egyptians

Near the intersection of the Ohio and Mississippi Rivers, there's a triangle of country in southern Illinois that goes by the colloquial name of Egypt. While there is some speculation about why it earned this sobriquet, two popular explanations tell of the naming of Cairo, Illinois (the southernmost city in the state), and the close association with the Nile Delta. This, along with later place-names like Thebes and Karnak, led to a general association of the region with Egypt. Another story mentions a failed corn harvest in the early 1800s that left upper Illinois without much food but somehow didn't affect lower Illinois, which reminded many people of the biblical story of Joseph.

The people of this area, however, are not primarily Egyptian, but a fusion from a number of different cultures: Illini Native Americans, Cherokee caught in the Trail of Tears, French, Scots Irish, Black, German, and English colonials. As such, a wide variety of folkways fused in the area. Some of the most prevalent beliefs are focused on the supernatural, with omens and signs being widespread. Some include beliefs in witches that could bespell guns and transform into animals like cats or hares, or the presence of a feather "crown" in a pillow indicating a tragic death coming soon (or bewitchment as the cause of said death). Ghosts and monsters also appear, including the "chat garla," a large, catlike specter with rattling chains, and stories of a banshee.

There are beneficial aspects of folk magic and belief too. For example, "water witches," or dowsers, are frequently consulted to help find good places to dig wells. There are also a number of home remedies for everyday ailments found in this area, largely due to the independent and self-reliant nature of those who settled here (and their frequent distrust of city doctors). Some examples:

- Carry a double cedar knot in your pocket to ease aching feet.
- Put a drop of buttermilk in your ear to ease earache.
- Kill a black chicken and press it against the soles of a person's feet to help relieve a fever.
- Use sheep manure to make a tea and give it to a patient to cure measles.
- Tie a coin around your neck to stop a nosebleed.
- Send a stye away with the rhyme "Stye, stye, leave my eye, catch the first one that comes by."
- Cure rabies by getting the "mad stone" from the stomach of a deer.
- Cure tonsillitis by wearing a dirty sock around your neck (the grimier the better!).

- Tie a knot in a string for every wart you have, then bury the string at a crossroads to get rid of them.
- Place an ax under the bed of a patient to cut their fever.[141]

Remember that these examples are folkloric only and are not intended as medical advice. Consult with a doctor for any ailments you may have.

141. See Dorson, *Buying the Wind*, for more.

Lucumí, Espiritismo, and the Windy City: African Diaspora Magical Faiths

SANDRA SANTIAGO

There is much fear, stigma, and myth surrounding indigenous African spirituality in the Americas and the diaspora, even with countless devotees scattered across the globe. Lucumí, or Santeria, is one of the most widely known of them. Preserved by enslaved African people, Maroon communities, and their descendants in Cuba, it has become widely integrated into the lives of millions of practitioners. According to a 2020 report by the Pluralism Project at Harvard University, it is estimated that between 250,000 and one million people around the world practice Santeria.[142]

As a result of the transatlantic slave trade, the vitality, power, and evolution of this religion are now expressed in practices that have shaped diasporic, Afro-Latinx cultures. These spiritual practices include Santeria/Lucumí, Umbanda, Trinidad Orisha, Candomblé, Shango Baptist, and Palo Mayombe, just to name a few. One noteworthy aspect of this religion is the fact that Santeria has no scriptures and is passed through oral tradition. Until about the 1940s, there were few, if any, published scriptural texts connected to the Yoruba or Lucumí traditions. Lucumí was once a muted and hidden practice, relegated to ceremonies taking place in cloistered spaces. It has now gained worldwide notoriety. Practitioner-scholar Raul Canizares writes:

> Santeria is growing in the United States beyond its traditional ethnic boundaries. Numerous African Americans, non-Hispanic West Indians, and European Americans are embracing Santeria.
>
> The advent of non-Cubans to this traditionally Afro-Cuban religion is bringing about the transformation of a religion that was in many ways primal to one that can be characterized as universal in scope.[143]

142. The Pluralism Project, "'Santeria.'"

143. Canizares, *Cuban Santeria*.

In a Eurocentric world that places so much value on the written word versus the spoken word, the permanence and presence of the Lucumí faith is indomitable. The survival of the songs, prayers, and practices themselves is a testament to the power and strength of the spoken word that has been able to pass knowledge across oceans, across continents, and across generations without writing. In the following pages, I want to introduce you to several of the systems that have come together through me and in me and have taken root with me here in my Chicago home to become a living tradition of spirit and folk magic.

African Origins

Santeria can be traced to the Yoruba people of modern-day Benin and Nigeria. During the transatlantic slave trade in the seventeenth century, people from varying tribes and ethnic groups in West Africa and other African nations were captured and imported to Cuba, Puerto Rico, Brazil, Trinidad, Tobago, Haiti, and other Caribbean areas. They were stripped from their land, their money, their family, and their possessions. Tribes had differing spiritual practices focusing on one exclusive African deity. However, once captured, they were forcibly baptized into the Catholic faith. The enslaved Africans were prohibited from practicing their religion. To practice anything else would have been considered heresy and witchcraft, punishable by death.

Despite being stripped of all familial connections and material possessions, the enslaved people brought with them their religious cosmologies, spiritual technologies, and cultural traditions. Africans from differing city-states scattered and mixed with other ethnic groups. Under the circumstances, they created new, secret communities where spiritual practitioners taught each other to work with their deities, unbeknownst to their slave owners. Their religious deities were called Orisha.

The practitioners disguised their Orisha as Catholic figures and continued to pray to them. This is how Santeria became a syncretic religion. Enslaved Africans found commonalities within the African and Catholic deities. Using similar elements—including representative colors and physical and spiritual attributes—between the various pantheons allowed for the Catholic saints to be the facade for the continuation of their traditional spiritual practices. Enslaved Africans came to understand that honoring their Orisha was safer and easier to do if their owners believed they were worshiping Catholic saints; the name Santeria in and of itself means "Way of the Saints." This secrecy ensured the survival of the practice up to and through modern times.

God and the Orisha

Orisha worshipers believe in a creator who is called Olodumare (God). Olodumare is the creator of heaven, earth, and the universe. Santeria is perceived to be a polytheistic religion. However, this is a misconception based on non-practitioners mistaking the Orisha for gods. The Orisha are not gods. They are all representatives/manifestations of Olodumare, who placed the Orishas on

Earth to support, supervise, and guide humankind. Orisha exist in the Great Beyond/Heaven (*òrun*). Some are entities/energies representative of elemental forces. Others are said to have lived as human beings on Earth (*ayé*). Those who were human were deified due to their actions of physical or spiritual courage and good character while on Earth.

Each Orisha is connected to a set of human characteristics and elements of nature. There are four hundred Orisha. Many of the Orisha survived the transatlantic slave trade. However, some did not cross over the Middle Passage to the New World. The Orisha who were able to be conserved had to be adapted to ensure survival. This adaptation was connected to syncretism. As a result, the Orishas were and are still referred to as "santos" or "saints."

Orisha are deities sent by Olodumare to guide all creation, specifically to help the development and evolution of good character in humans. They are present to guide the head and emotions of their particular chosen devotees. The fact that Orisha have divine virtues juxtaposed with human weaknesses helps create a relationship between practitioner and deity. Through divination (spiritual reading) by a group of elders, practitioners are connected to the Orisha that has chosen to be their guide for life. This is the beginning of a bond between practitioner and deity that is built through the cultivation of a personal relationship with their Orisha.

Each Orisha has likes, dislikes, taboos, and corresponding *elekes* (prayer beads), colors, foods, numbers, and days of worship. Each Orisha has their sacred stories, known as *patakis*. *Patakis* are the narratives of their trials, tribulations, successes, and losses. These stories can be likened to parables, created to teach practitioners how to navigate life. The significance of these stories is for practitioners to learn from the experiences that the Orisha have undergone in order not to suffer as the Orisha did, and to deviate from things that may harm one's destiny.

Here is a list of the most commonly worshiped Orisha, along with the Catholic saint syncretized to the Orisha.

Eleguá

The energy of opportunity. He acts as the connecting agent in this world because he is the messenger between Orisha and humans. Eleguá is the owner of the crossroads and the witness to fate. Eleguá is often portrayed as a trickster or child who tests our integrity and our patience. Chicago—situated as a sort of "midway" city, and one where a number of African American people migrated in the early twentieth century—functions as a sort of giant crossroads.

- Saint: Holy Child of Atocha
- Colors: Black and red
- Number: Three

Obatala

Obatala is the energy of creativity, inner peace, harmony, and purity. He is the oldest of the Orisha. Because he is symbolic of purity, he is known as "Father of the White Cloth" and is the owner of one's head (*ori*). He is the father of peace, balance, logic, and wisdom. Obatala was tasked with creating the human body from clay. This is why he is considered the father of humankind. Obatala is the representative of consciousness. He is an extension of patience and truth. He reminds us of our journey on this plane, how we accumulate knowledge and wisdom, and how we exercise them through good character.

- Saint: Our Lady of Mercy
- Color: White
- Number: Eight

Oyá (Yansa)

Oyá is the energy of change, courage, and speed. She creates motion like the wind and brings swift changes to situations. She is as unbridled as her multicolored skirt, and her cutlass of wind ushers in necessary shifts in life, dismantling situations that are no longer of service. She is the owner of the cemetery, and there is no shortage of those around Chicago. However, contrary to popular belief, she does not live in the cemetery. She resides in the marketplace, and this city began its life as a major marketplace for trading and shipping. She is portrayed as a powerful warrior woman wearing a skirt of nine different colors. Shango, the energy of thunder, is her husband. Although he had many wives, Oyá was his foundation and his true partner. Together they are a dynamic warrior team. It was Oyá who stole Shango's secrets of the magic of throwing lightning from him. Oyá is the lightning and Shango the thunder that follows soon after.

- Saints: Saint Theresa or Our Lady of Candlemas
- Colors: Brown, dark red/burgundy
- Number: Nine

Yemayá (Yemonja)

Yemayá is the mother of all living things. She is the energy of motherhood and maternity and is associated with the womb. She is also the mother of the Orisha. She resides in the oceans and is an aggressive protector of her children (initiates). Yemayá is loving and filled with generosity. However, if anyone crosses her or her children, her anger knows no bounds. She can be destructive and violent. Yemayá can cause tidal waves and floods. She can create waves that drown a ship.

(Many don't know this, but there are so many shipwreck stories from the Great Lakes.) Her symbols are all the creatures that reside in the sea. Sometimes she is depicted as a mermaid. At other times, she is a matronly woman rising from the sea, her dress becoming the waves of the ocean.

- Saint: Virgin de Regla
- Colors: Blue and white
- Number: Seven

Ogún

Ogún is a primordial warrior, the blacksmith who has mastered iron and fire, creating tools and weapons. Ogún is the agent of the organization of human society. He is the father of civilization. He is also the father of technology. His symbols are the anvil and the machete. The anvil is symbolic of how iron and fire can transform, bend, and tame metal. The machete is the most versatile of tools: it cuts through forests, kills in the hunt, and can be used in farming. Ogún is the force that keeps things in motion with the gift of determination.

- Saint: Saint Peter
- Colors: Green and black
- Numbers: Three and seven

Oshún (Ochún)

Oshún is the energy of sweetness, love, fertility, and beauty. Oshún is the youngest of the Orisha, daughter of Obatala. Oshún is the embodiment of feminine grace and the power of creation. Beauty in all forms comes through Oshún. She is a generous and loving mother who is protective of her children (her initiates). However, her sweetness can quickly turn to bitterness when offended. Once she is soured, she is unforgiving. Her symbols are the fresh waters (fresh rivers, lakes, streams, brooks). In a place like Chicago, Lake Michigan is a powerful place to connect with her. She wears a coral comb in her hair and loves gold jewelry. She holds a mirror and gazes into it. Some will refer to Oshún's mirror as a metaphor for the mystery of (self)reflection.

- Saint: Our Lady of Charity of Cobre
- Colors: Yellow and amber
- Number: Five

Shango (Chango)

Shango is the energy of thunder and lightning. He symbolizes passion and virility. Shango is known as a lover of women, food, and dance. Shango is the owner of the sacred batá drum. His wives include Oyá, Oshún, and Obbá. He was once the fourth king of the city of Oyó. He was dethroned for his ruthlessness and was ordered to commit suicide by the group of wise women that brought him to power. He committed suicide with clarity of his prior actions and acceptance of his fate. This allowed him to transition from a human to a divine being. He carries a double-headed ax that symbolizes the constant state of balance between passion and calm that is necessary to navigate life. He is a master strategist and is called upon in times of war.

- Saint: Saint Barbara
- Colors: Red and white
- Number: Six

The Concept of Ache (Ashé)

Ache is an African word from the Yoruba language. It is the primordial life force or energy that lives in the universe and within every single thing; it is also the power to make things happen. *Ache* is similar to the concept of prana in the Sanskrit tradition or qi in Chinese philosophy. Our *ache* was given to us by Olodumare. *Ache* is the divine power that resides within us. It is the most precious and powerful thing we carry with us throughout our lives.

One important construct in Lucumí is the idea of good character (*iwa pele*). *Iwa pele* is a way of looking at the world. It is the idea that we do the right thing, and not out of a desire for reward or fear of retribution. *Iwa pele* is the act of doing the right thing because it is the right thing to do. As practitioners of Lucumí, our goal is to walk in *iwa pele*. *Ache* is connected to how we live our lives. Because of its sacred characteristics, there are spiritual and social ramifications to how one uses their *ache*.

We are born with a destiny. However, we have free will. This can either hinder our progress or support the elevation of our physical life as well as our spiritual selves. *Ache* is connected to one's talents, gifts, and powers. It is also connected to one's character. Everyone has their *ache*—their gifts, talents, and power. Everyone's *ache* is different and is the reason for our very existence. It makes us who we are, and it is the power and energy that leads us to our destiny.

Divination

Divination in Lucumí is the bridge between Heaven and Earth, interpreting the fall of cowry shells (*diloggun*) or using a divided coconut (*obi*). Only initiated, properly trained priests and priestesses are authorized to divine with *diloggun*. It takes years of practice and study. Santeria also includes the Yoruba divination system that is part of a priesthood called Ifa. In the Lucumí branch of Ifa, divinations can only be conducted by a male priest called a Babalawo. He uses a tool with two chains and coconuts attached called the *opele*. He can also divine by casting palm nuts (*ikin*).

The Babalawo uses these tools to communicate with the deity of wisdom/knowledge, Orunmila. This is called "casting Odu." Odu are the 256 signs that comprise the Ifa corpus to be interpreted by the priest. Divination is an essential part of the religion because it is how practitioners communicate with the Orisha and receive guidance from the Orisha and the priest or priestess, who are interpreters of the signs that are thrown on a mat.

Ebo *(Sacrifice)*

Ebo includes various types of offerings to the Orisha. Ritual sacrifice is an important part of the beliefs and practices of Orisha worshipers. It is how devotees connect with Orisha. All things have positive energy (*iré*) and negative energy (*osogbo*). If someone has digressed from their path and is "walking in *osogbo*," *ebo* can be done to correct the wrong and get them back on track. *Ebo* can also be done in honor and thanksgiving for protection that an Orisha has provided or as a way to energize or strengthen an Orisha that is doing battle on behalf of the devotee. Offerings can include fresh flowers, candles, fruit, and candy.

Divination/consultation with a priest or priestess will usually recommend the aforementioned items, along with suggestions for shifting one's behaviors. Animals are ritually sacrificed, usually different kinds of fowl. They are offered in situations such as serious illness or impending death. It is an important part of a practitioner's routine. However, it continues to be a controversial process. The process follows rites for the animal in the same way that Judaism follows the rules of shechita and Muslims follow Islamic law in the consumption of halal products.

Lucumí in the City

Traditionally, in an African village, the Chief Priest would be trained in varying practices since childhood because they would have had to "minister" to a variety of practitioners. This is a paradigm that no longer exists. The African village has extended itself to a global community. A Babalawo in one part of the world will now FaceTime their godchildren across the oceans for long-distance readings, conversations, and learning sessions. Godchildren will make the yearly pilgrimage to Africa or Cuba, New York, Florida, or Atlanta to visit their godparents and spiritual families, and to participate in ceremonies that need to be done in person.

Lucumí is no longer a centralized practice. It is diasporic, and for as much as the tradition is firmly rooted in traditional prayers, songs, and practices that are traced back to Africa, it is also ever-evolving. Technology and social media have played an extensive role in the dissemination of information and the demystification of the practices of African Traditional Religion (ATR). It has become a global spiritual community as those searching for information connect with elders from Africa to Latin America to the Caribbean. However, the easy accessibility of information becomes a forest of dense truths and falsities, with misconceptions and misinformation intertwined in the branches of the varying traditions. This is where seekers of knowledge and information need in-person practitioners to help support their learning. Even though there is a hunger to learn and learning is available via technology, Lucumí remains a closed practice—closed in that one needs to be invited into the "house" (*ile*). This allows the practitioner to undergo levels of initiation and be privy to the secrets that are only passed down through the practitioners of the lineages.

In Chicago, secrecy prevails. There are various established *iles* that have been around since the early 1990s. Many of the elders currently living in Chicago were not initiated here. They were initiated elsewhere, such as Cuba, Africa, New York, or Florida, and established their houses here, in Chicago and/or its adjacent suburbs. The diasporic and adaptive nature of this practice makes it so that other practices that trace back to religious and cultural systems from Africa are now less rigid, while maintaining the same amount of respect for the secrecy.

My own journey as priestess isn't much different than that of other practitioners from Chicago; in order to obtain access to my elders or vice versa, traveling was involved. In becoming an Olorisha, a priestess of Obatala, my initiation of Kariocha was performed in Florida. My initiation into Palo Mayombe was performed by an elder who flew in from Florida to Chicago for the ceremony. They were two different elders, in two different branches of ATRs, in two different parts of Florida. The expense of the ceremony as well as the constant need for travel to maintain my connection and community with the *ile* make it that much more of a commitment for me. It is not an easy situation to be in; I have to travel various times a year, scheduling days away from work and my personal life, to maintain my spiritual practice. But it is well worth my time and my energy. This is a commitment that extends far beyond any man-made boundaries or borders.

In conversations with various Chicago-based elders regarding the ATR scene in the area, they all said the same thing: the Chicago spiritual community is segregated. In Carl Nightingale's book *Segregation: A Global History of Divided Cities*, he discusses how Chicago was a laboratory for segregation. Tools to analyze real estate and racial data were being created in Chicago in the early twentieth century. As a result, residential segregation and housing policies have led to a racially divided city.[144] A 2020 study by the University of Califorina, Berkeley rates Chicago as the fourth-most-segregated city in the United States.[145] Hence, the spiritual community is a microcosm of the larger society. People throughout the city tend to follow the "unspoken" racial divides.

144. Nightingale, *Segregation*.

145. Menendian, Gambhir, and Hsu, "Roots of Structural Racism."

Iles on the North Side, South Side, and West Side seldom work together. There are cultural differences in the *iles* based on the ethnic identities of the groups. The Southwest and West Side *iles* are predominantly African American practitioners of Isheshe, or what is considered to be the traditional West African spiritual practice, whereas the North and Northwest Side *iles* are predominantly Latinx practitioners of Lucumí. These are not absolutes. However, the racial and ethnic divides are present, based on the way the city is divided. There are also *iles* in the Chicagoland suburbs. They also rarely work with city practitioners. Despite the segregation, sometimes relationships are built, and through those friendships, people from different *iles* do get invited to participate in ceremonies.

Chicago is a chapter city for Oloshas United, a not-for-profit religious organization with chapters across North America. Oloshas United organizes and hosts various ceremonies and celebrations that are open to the public as a way to build unity and strengthen the community. These are public events where practitioners and non-practitioners can connect and commune with Spirit as well as each other. Through these events, people from different parts of the city are able to come together in a common belief and practice.

The Personal within the Spiritual—Espiritismo and Brujeria

In Lucumí there is an understanding that all Santeros are Espiritistas, but not all Espiritistas are Santeros. Espiritismo is a practice in and of itself. At the same time, it is an integral part of the Lucumí faith. Santeria practitioners worship their ancestors (*egun*). Ancestors are a very important aspect of traditional African practices. Reverence to the ancestors is foundational to the Lucumí religion. It is important to Lucumí because often, in divination sessions with a priest or priestess, *egun* or Orisha may call for obligations to be fulfilled through work with mediums.

Espiritismo, or Spiritism, is the popular belief in Latin America, which holds that spirits of the dead can positively or negatively affect health, luck, and other aspects of human life. Spiritism is a doctrine or practice that believes communication with the spirit of a dead person is possible through a medium or otherwise; Allan Kardec, a French educator born in 1804, was the founder of this form of mediumship. He believed that human beings are Spirit within a material body and that one's true self is spiritual rather than material. His practice came to the Caribbean during the nineteenth-century explosion of interest in the supernatural and the "occult" practice of séances. He attested that Spiritism is a science and carried out investigations where he studied spirits using methods that were typical of the physical sciences at the time.

Espiritismo via *Mesa Blanca* (The White Table) is the mediumship practice where mediums congregate at the home of the lead and hosting medium. The mediums come together to call upon the Spiritual Court that exists on "the other side." The Spiritual Court is a collective group of spirits that follows each person. They work and intercede for that person. Before every ceremony, glasses of water representing different spirits, cigars, rum, flowers, different colognes, and candles are prepared. Prayers from Kardec's book, *Collection of Selected Prayers*, are carried out and songs are sung, calling the spirits to enter the space and communicate with those present. Everyone sits in a circle in front of an altar that was prepared for the welcoming of the spirits.

Spirit possession of the practitioner is common during *misas espirituales* (spiritual masses). Mediums that go into trance and are "mounted" are called the "horse" (*caballo*). During a *misa spiritual*, the entities of the participants' Spiritual Court can be called upon by the mediums (or may appear of their own accord) to give the participants insightful messages, solutions to their physical or emotional afflictions or personal problems, and messages of support and affirmation. These sessions can last for hours as different spirits and entities present themselves. It is a collective and supportive environment where all are encouraged to develop their specific abilities as a medium.

Another term that invites confusion is *bruja*. On certain occasions, I will wear my *elekes* around my neck as I run errands, my headwrap tied around my head. Some might call these symbols of my faith monikers of Brujeria. The meaning of the Spanish word *Brujeria* is "Witchcraft." The practitioners of this spiritual practice are Brujas (female), Brujos (male), or Brujix (genderqueer). Modern Brujeria is, in its essence, magic that is a blend of folklore, herbalism, African and Latin American magic and healing, and Catholicism. It usually involves charms, divination, love spells, and hexes.

The historical significance of Brujeria goes back to the early fifteenth century, before indigenous African and indigenous Latin American communities were colonized by the Europeans. Stories that are passed on from that time are filled with depictions of people—mostly women—who are portrayed as evil witches who inflict misfortune and illness, and can destroy relationships, luck, and life. This perspective came from the vilification of any non-Abrahamic spiritual practice carried out by women.

In her analysis of the Curandera-Bruja archetypal heroine, Antonia Castañeda writes that Indigenous, African, and racially mixed women were a threat. She notes that by being female, one was considered inherently evil and dangerous. These women pushed back at a time when colonizers wanted to wipe away their practices, presence, and way of life. There was a fear that the women could disrupt the status quo with their magical powers, which would be detrimental to the establishment, and so these women were made an example of how *not* to be.[146]

Within the past few years, a movement has developed where many people of color are reshaping the perception of what it means to be a Brujo, Bruja, or Brujix and acknowledge Brujeria's powerful legacy. This affirmation of the term is a rediscovery—and a homecoming of sorts—of the ability to find power in the spiritual wisdom of the ancestors. This renewed interest in Brujeria can be linked

146. Castañeda, "Engendering the History of Alta California."

to the rise of modern feminism and the historical exclusion of women of color within this movement. The idea of "La Bruja" aligns more with the Womanist movement than mainstream feminism, with Womanism focusing more on the lives and stories of women of color, especially Black women. According to the scholar Layli Phillips, Womanism seeks to "restore the balance between people and the environment/nature and reconcile human life with the spiritual dimension."[147]

When I started this path, I was not aware of the socio-political implications of my practice. I was simply looking for "more" in spirituality. Buying into the paradigm put forth by Eurocentric constructs, I was taught that people who practiced Santeria or anything other than Christianity were evil, dark, and should be shunned. I trod with caution around the images of the pentacle, tarot cards, or anything that was related to non-Christian practices. However, I was also intrigued by these things. It was not until my adult years, when I had to undergo major surgery, that I came into Lucumí. My life was in the middle of a physical, mental, and emotional shift. Lucumí offered an opportunity to believe in the power that lives inside of my body and soul through an understanding of my ancestral callings.

I do not necessarily identify as a Bruja, although many within the Latinx community will call my practices of Palo Mayombe, Lucumí, and Espiritismo "Brujeria" because, as previously stated, my practices are non-Abrahamic. Also, as an Espiritista (practitioner of Spiritism in the tradition of Allan Kardec, as brought to Puerto Rico via the elite who traveled to and from Europe), ancestor veneration and the ways of connecting to spirit are a powerful gift. The ability to access the supernatural world is also a practice that gets the side-eye. As an Afro-Latinx person, choosing to return to the ancient ways of connecting to the universe has been an act of defiance.

These alternative forms of ancestral practices are rooted in the empowerment of the marginalized. Indigenous practices are no longer hidden because they help in the reclamation of power. This world of mysticism belongs to those who are so often excluded from traditional religions that marginalize their parishioners. Practitioners of ancestral spiritualities are symbols of power outside the parameters of the status quo where patriarchy (via machismo), misogyny, and homophobia exist. We also challenge existing social constructs. Engaging in ancestral spiritual practices is an act of decolonizing one's spirit from patriarchal and Western values. It heals historical trauma. Brujeria and similar traditions reconnect practitioners to the vibrant strengths of their ancestry and culture, helping people process the embedded pain created by colonization. This allows for the creation of new historical narratives. In this context, Brujeria and other indigenous ancestral practices become revolutionary.

I am a practitioner of two separate diaspora stemming from African Traditional Religions (ATR): Palo Mayombe and Lucumí. They are different practices, although they both stem from Africa. Palo Mayombe is a religion that evolved in Cuba out of the native religious practices

147. Phillips, *The Womanist Reader*, xx.

of the Bakongo (commonly called Congo) people of Africa. In contrast, Lucumí, or Santeria, evolved in Cuba out of the traditional religious practices of the various nations who are now within modern-day Nigeria and Benin, among them the Yoruba.

The process of becoming who and what I am has not been easy. The beautiful part of these practices is that becoming a Palera, then later making Ocha and becoming a priestess of Orisha Obatala, has given me perspective and an understanding of my purpose in the universe. Going through the various ceremonies is not the end-all, as some would believe it to be. These ceremonies have been the beginning of the rest of my life. Particularly for me, Ocha designated who I am and whom I will end up being.

This ceremony was a yearlong initiation, not only into the mysteries of the Orisha but into the mystery of myself. A mirror was held up to my existence. The regulations of the initiation year (called *iyaworaje*) pushed and pulled at me. As mortal beings, there are things we believe we need. During that year, something shifted; I began experiencing the world with new eyes. It became a new reality, one in which society's perspectives of "needs and wants" did not always coincide with Lucumí's tenets of *iwa pele*.

Iwa pele is not just the paradigm of walking in good character, but the development of the understanding of the symbiotic relationship between us and the universe as a whole. The sixteen laws of Ifa are the reflections on principles given to us by nature, elders, the Orisha, and the Supreme God of the tradition. As practitioners of Lucumí, we love the Orisha. However, the intimate relationship that is developed between the Orisha and the self, the trials of life, and the tests of faith that push one to the edge are indescribable. Every day becomes a lesson in faith. Every breath is a testament to the presence of the living word that is Odu. I have the Orisha and *egun* in and around me to help navigate this journey. It is a journey I am blessed to undertake.

FIELD NOTES

The Nain Rouge

Detroit is right across from Windsor, Ontario, and the two cities have a shared history of legends and lore. One legend that seems to have filtered in from French colonists was a tale about a small reddish man who appeared in the early eighteenth century to Antoine Laumet de la Mothe Cadillac, the founder of Detroit.

Legend says that a fortune-teller had appeared at Cadillac's castle in France to tell him that he would be founding a great city, but that there was a vicious creature that must be appeased in exchange for his success. This creature was known as the Nain Rouge, or "red dwarf." (The word *dwarf* is used here in the folkloric sense rather than specifically referring to a person with the medical condition dwarfism.) Cadillac seemed to have thought it all superstitious nonsense, despite warnings from his wife, once they found some prosperity establishing a community along the Detroit River.

Then, one day, the Nain Rouge appeared to Cadillac as he was out walking. Before it could issue any demands, however, the Frenchman began whacking the creature with his cane! It scrambled away but left a chilling laugh lingering in the air—and a promise that Cadillac's life of prosperity was now at an end. Sure enough, soon after this meeting, Cadillac was taken from his luxurious and well-heeled life in Michigan and sent by his superiors to Louisiana, which he hated.

The Nain Rouge continued to appear throughout Detroit's history, usually showing up when a crisis was at hand. For example, many said they saw the Nain Rouge right before the Great Fire of 1805. More recently, during the early 2000s–era Great Recession, some reported seeing the Nain Rouge as more and more houses were abandoned or foreclosed. Some believe that he arrived with Cadillac. Others believe he represents a new form of a spirit that had been known to Indigenous peoples of the region, primarily the Anishinaabe.[148]

Despite his Mothman-like predilection for predicting disaster, the Nain Rouge is beloved by many Detroit residents. There's even an annual parade called the *Marche du Nain Rouge* featuring people dressed as various forms of the diabolical creature. During the parade, thousands pass through the city streets and finish up at the Masonic Temple, where an appointed Nain Rouge steps up and makes proclamations about the coming year.

148. See Hamlin, *Legends of le Détroit*. See also Hester, "The Spirited Afterlife of Detroit's Little Red Demon."

Roads and Rivers: Meeting Detroit Hoodoo

KENYA T. COVIAK

Let's start with me. Who am I? Where do I come from? And what do I have to do with Detroit Hoodoo?

I hail from the 7 Mile Road on the East Side, the North End, of Detroit. I've resided in every part of my city over my lifetime. My family is scattered all over the city as well as the country (in both ways). Our roots are African and Creek, and I have Sicilian paternal lineage, but in my family, we follow the waters of the maternal line for our spiritual center. I was raised by elderly fictive kin from Arkansas. "Fictive kinship" means family not by blood or marriage. My custodial parents took me in as a daughter from my biological parents. But my family, for the last few hundred years, came from Oklahoma and Mississippi. We dream true, have sight, and prophesize, as well as heal and work power. The rivers of time and magic run through us like blood, so it is only right that we settled by a river in the North.

If you stand in the middle of a Detroit Street, you can smell the river. It makes no difference if you are against the border lines of the city or downtown at the international border. You can smell the water in the air. You can feel the river in your breath, in your bones, in your skin. The Detroit River connects us. It cleanses us. It holds our secrets. It flows through all of us who practice magic here.

This city holds the spirits and workings of over seven generations of the children of Africa and their ways. The hope of the fugitive in that little room in the Second Baptist Church saw prayers and Conjure in the name of escape. The rounded tops of the cobblestones, and later the red brick, saw the passing of African American feet who lived in two worlds: the spiritual and the brutal mundane. And always, there was the river.

We follow the river down to Mexican Town to the *botanicas*. We go to E&L *supermercado* for rooster feet, tongues, and lamb's blood. We trade love with the Brujas and buy glass candles next to *lotería* card sets. Many of us grew up together, depending on what side of town you loved. We shopped, danced, cooked, and went to each other's cultural festivals. There is no real division among the magical folks, despite geography, unless imposed by those who come here from outside the city itself.

We cross the river to Belle Isle to walk the honeysuckle paths. We gather flowers for our magic there. Red berries offer themselves to us by the wild places near an abandoned zoo. They reach down to us by the river shores and lagoon. They catch in the young girls' hair and whisper that they can be used for love, and later, sex magic.

We know what roads cross backward, so we lay our tricks away from them. Our streets weave and wind like snakes on the riverbank. You may go east and west on the same road if you travel long enough. We know the small places that are dedicated and holy to the spirits. These are the spirits that traveled here on the hearts of the runaways. These are the spirits that rode in suitcases from plantations. These are the spirits residing in the carvings on the floors of the church sanctuaries.

The magics here are old, and yet they are also young and alive. They learned new tongues. Detroit was not always only English-speaking. French, German, Italian, and Greek flowed through the grasslands and ribbon farms. Anishinaabemowin (the language of the people who have always lived here, whose grandfathers knew the Manitou) flowed from wilder places, where the original instructions for this land were still observed. The mellifluous words of the Potawatomi are still spoken here, despite LaSalle. Our peoples mixed, the blood dancing together. Through the decades and cultures, the Black traditions moved like a slow ribbon, connecting our generations here to the land, the river, and our spirits.

We Are Our Stories: An Oral Remembrance of Detroit Conjure

Let me tell you about one of the oldest shops in my own memory. Goodwill Candle Shop was located on Milwaukee Street, right in front of the train tracks. This was an area known for church-mother hats and Sunday clothes. But if you knew to take a turn off Woodward, down that street, you would find a sign jutting out of the building.

A candle with an all-seeing eye blazed proudly. The building itself was painted dark so that you would not really see it if you weren't looking for it. Walking in was like passing through a rootworker's looking glass.

My friend's mother took us there when I was thirteen. The air smelled like sulfur, oil, and wax. Long glass counters contained goatskin parchments, rings with sigils, and seals of Moses. Seemingly endless rows of glass-encased candles filled every available space. We had the smell of wax in our skin. Bags were filled with skull candles and parchments; coworkers and rivals had to be handled continuously. Love magic oils were bought to place into apples. My friend's mom had an endless list. Some of the workers who looked over the counter at us then now greet us eye to eye. Those shopkeepers had children, and grandchildren, and we know all their names.

Walking through the wild places in city parks and woods, you could find anything you needed to make your own hexes. Bloodroot, blackberries, and bindweed grow freely in the abandoned places. For the young wicked witch, her apothecary was everywhere green grew or wind blew. Willow trees whispered secrets in the city for the listening ears.

I met "G" in my high school. (I use initials to protect the person's identity.) She was one of the marching band booster club mothers, and she was also a practitioner. She taught me about enemies traveling through portals created by placing mirrors in front of windows, using ammonia on candles to clean them, and burning eight candles to cast out a demon. From "G," I learned about astral projection, magical warfare, and where to buy candles after Goodwill burned down. Fuch's Candle Shop was the hub. There, reverends and rootworkers stood beside priests and pastors to purchase spiritual supplies. Skippy Candle was on the West Side, but Fuch's had three stores. Knight Light Imports and Raj's Candles always popped. Every counterperson was always a bishop, deacon, or reverend.

Suddenly, at age sixteen, magic was everywhere. Teachers in the form of necromancers, herbal doctors, witches, Wiccans, thelemites, and more seemed to have a boom in 1986. Interviews with "R," a person from the Mayflower bookstore, were on Channel 2. Auto plant workers filled the candle shops on payday. Their coveralls smelled like axle grease and Conjure oils.

It was at this time I discovered suburban shops. Riding the bus to the suburbs to explore the Mayflower bookshop was a monthly adventure. There I began to buy books on Hermetics, Theosophy, and Buddhism. "R" taught me that learning mechanics of magic meant nothing if I didn't know how it worked. I could either be a grunt or a virtuoso in my life—the choice was mine. This is also when numerology became so important to my practice. Even now, I factor it into designing my charms and creations.

Magic is in everything here. Our hairdressings have Conjure oils mixed into them. Our beauty shops play gospel songs to uplift women and hold prayer "work" for clients in distress. The mailman gets $2 bills dressed in money oil for Christmas. We face our money toward us when we pay at Coney Island. Red gardenias hang on our porches to keep the evil away, and we put brooms handle-down in our closets.

But my story is not the only story. What Detroit African American Folk Magic (AAFM) is today is living in the bodies that move through her spaces now. The root women and witches who practice here all have their own stories. We are blood; we are bone; we are living history in a moment.

In this space, it is only right to share this flow, so I reached out to three women who also live this path, this magic, this city. You have to understand, magic here does not exist in a cage—we are free. There are no competitors, only cooperative hands that lift each other up. That is how we are here.

From West to East

I reached out to my fellow Detroit African American Folk Magic practitioners for their perspectives on what Detroit Hoodoo really is. The interviews yielded soul-deep results. What follows in the next couple of sections are the actual, authentic voices of practitioners of Detroit Hoodoo. I talk to Jade Aurora and Krystal Hubbard from the West Side, and to Myisha Mastersson from the East Side, so that you can hear from four different people (including myself) what this practice is like for those who live in, work in, and fight for Detroit. Like me, some have chosen to use initials to protect the identities of specific individuals. Although we have different opinions on some issues, all of us are connected to the city and the practice, and that's what shines through.

With Jade Aurora on the West Side

I own RoxyJo Creations, which is a shop where I sell artwork and handmade accessories. I am also a model, entertainer, and author. I have been a practitioner of magic for about ten years. I am thirty-one years old, and I am a Black American.

When I was a teenager, one of my favorite films was *The Craft*. It was the first film about the occult that I had seen, that acknowledged that magic had a spiritual side and was more than just casting spells. My earliest memory of magic in the Detroit area was when I attended my first Pagan Pride Detroit event in 2010. It was my first time seeing occult practitioners at a large event. I would say that my defining moment was when I attended my first ritual. It was for the spring equinox. I immediately felt at home, like I truly belonged.

My Ancestors and spirit guides play a tremendous part in my practice. I consider my Ancestors to be my first line of defense. They're my blood, and if I can't trust them to have my best interests at heart and to protect me, who can I trust? I honestly believe that African American Folk Magic is closed. African Traditional Religions (ATRs) such as Hoodoo and Vodun were used as a tool of resistance. Vodun is what helped Haiti win their independence, and Hoodoo was used to combat white supremacy, and to help our Ancestors cope with the harsh conditions of enslavement. And Ancestor reverence plays a tremendous part in ATRs, so I can't help but side-eye non-Black people partaking in Black Ancestral Works. While Hoodoo does have European influences (i.e., the Bible), that influence was forced. It's equally infuriating that so many people assume all Black practitioners of magic practice Voodoo/Vodun. There are so many spiritual paths within African culture, and we are not one-dimensional.

With Krystal Hubbard on the West Side

I am the owner and founder of Bridging Worlds Botanica in Detroit. I am forty-eight years old with a mixture of West African, European, and Sardinian heritage. My dad was from South Carolina, and my mom was from Georgia. I am a fourth-generation rootworker and also a Lucumi aborisha. I live in my ancestral home on the West Side of Detroit.

I remember my mom always had oil lamps around. I remember her having green, red, and clear oil for said lamps. One hot summer day, she placed three lamps on the mantel above the fireplace—one had green lamp oil, one had red, and the final one had clear lamp oil. When Mom lit the lamps, I remember thinking, *The electricity isn't out. Why do we have lamps burning?* I was six years old.

When I was nine years old, I remember taking an old sock and placing a rock and a few other mementos that I needed to carry with me into the sock in order to keep the classroom bully from messing with me. I was raised in Rootwork, but it wasn't as if my mom sat me down at the kitchen table and said, "Baby, we gonna do some Rootwork now!" There was no explanation, and if you did question anything, you better be happy with the answer you received. Many of the things I witnessed and participated in as a child became incredibly clear as I grew older and firmly stepped foot on this path of Rootwork.

Honestly, the terms *Rootwork*, *Hoodoo*, or *Conjure* were not terms I heard as a child. I remember hearing things like "She worked him," or "She has gifts," etc. The most interesting information was gained by listening to grown folks' conversations and paying attention to the pauses...There was a lot of information in the pauses.

My grandmother and great-grandmother had "thangs" they would do and keep. My grandmother had a small iron doorstop at her front hallway door, as did my great-grandmother, only my great-grandmother ("AM") had an iron bulldog doorstop.

My maternal great-grandparents' house always smelled of camphor. I remember asking my mom why it smelled so weird in their home. Her reply? "To keep vermin away." Now I know that "vermin" was a loose term for things unwanted physically and spiritually!

My mom worked oil lamps and did a lot of kitchen work. When I would cook with my mom, sometimes she would tell me, "Stir this clockwise." Other times, she would tell me to stir in the opposite direction. When she knew certain folks were coming to visit, she would turn on the front right eye of the stove and heat it until it was red, then sprinkle various spices—clove, cinnamon, allspice—on the eye and let it burn off. When I asked her why, she would reply, "Makes the house smell good!" She repeated this same ritual when the company would leave.

My mom had this thing where if someone who was visiting smoked in the house after the meal (mind you, it wasn't everyone!), she would always light a candle, saying, "It cuts the smell of the smoke." It wasn't until much later that I realized my mother could see lies in the smoke.

Of course, there was the sweeping of the steps of the front porch. I would have the job of cleaning the back porch and the steps there. What I thought was just sprucing up...was serious cleaning.

• • • • • • • • • •

In my early adult years when I was married, my mom told me that if I didn't want to "be bothered with the man" to put some saltpeter in his food to keep "his nature down." I still chuckle at that tidbit.

This is why I am a strong believer in oral tradition. When information is passed down, it is usually while doing the work itself. You feel the ebb and flow of the energy, and your mentor/teacher is alongside you, advising, showing, telling what you need to know and look out for, etc. Reading and doing spells from a book by an author you don't know leaves a lot to be desired unless you already have experience in the subject. I cannot imagine being awakened by spiritual phenomena and not having my godfather/mentor/teacher to talk about it with: to get direction for what to do next, to bounce ideas off of. Oral tradition is more concrete because you are doing the work and learning at the same time. When it comes to magical workings, formalized written instruction is not like reading about anthropology. It lacks the energy, the agency, of the work. Afterall, Rootwork is work. It's what you do. Now that I know far more than what I did twenty-some-odd years ago, I can read a book on Rootwork and have a good understanding because I know what it should feel like.

Rootwork is geographically and familially unique because it is based in and on our ancestral lineage. Of course, there will be uniqueness, even in terms of the East Side and West Side of Detroit. I believe that the spirits are unique because Detroit is unique. Folks from Detroit are survivors. We have a different cadence to our walk. We have a different rhythm to our speech. Many of our ancestors moved here from the South, bringing aspects of the South with them.

Music created here changed lives and the music industry. I adore that the Detroit River is so close by and that we have some really old Catholic churches to collect Holy Water. I love that I can grow many of the herbs I use here. Detroiters know how to dance with the discord and roll with the resistance, just as our ancestors did.

I think that African American Folk Magic should be closed. It may not be a popular opinion, but it is based on African diasporic ancestral lineage. Everyone has ancestors, but not everyone has African ancestors. If you are Romani, then why would you want to practice a Folk Magic that is not of your cultural and ancestral lineage?

Rootwork/Hoodoo/Conjure are seen and practiced by different people in different ways. It doesn't mean one person is better than the next, just different. Everyone has their own history, their own experience. Just like Detroit is not a cookie-cutter city, neither is the Rootwork here.

With Myisha Mastersson on the East Side

People know me as Chef Maya. I am the chef and founder of Black Roux Culinary Collective and the founder of Black Roux Farm. I am a forty-year-old Black woman from the East Side of Detroit.

My earliest memories of magic in Detroit came from my great-grandmother. She was one of those "Christian witches" who used the Bible and hymnals in spellwork. She talked to the sky and sang to the soil. Oftentimes she would have one of her cautionary visions that would keep us (my sister and I) sequestered until she gave an all clear. She was also known by the church ladies to be someone who could help with things that the doctor and the pastor couldn't.

"LC" was my first glimpse at magic. From a very young age, I stood on a tiny stool in her kitchen and helped prepare meals and potions that healed us and her visitors, all made with her hands. I sat quietly and listened while she gave sage advice in the circle of women that she called her own. My childhood was full of magic, and she was the practitioner the neighborhood turned to. And she looked like me!

I became aware of my gift of manifestation at an early age. At that point I simply knew that if I really wanted something, all I needed to do was picture myself there, and so it was. Being raised in a household full of ritual, the incense…the candles…the music. I think that deep down, I always knew. We were the weird kids on the block, extra cultural in comparison to our peers, and we stuck out like sore thumbs.

Movies that had magical aspects always influenced me. Initially I wanted to be a vet; I believed that I could talk to the animals. As I got older, movies like *The Craft* and *Practical Magic* made me feel seen and accepted. Representations in the media made me feel normal. And then there was *Eve's Bayou*. The aunt, she always reminded me of the women in my family. She seemed to embody the maiden, the mother, and the crone, and I saw my lineage in her character.

Detroit is a special place, one whose history surpasses that of this country. The land we were born and raised on has seen battles, riots, and bloodshed and became one of the last stops of the Underground Railroad. Those spirits will always reside here. There is a fight about you when you are from the D, and it's a fight you don't see anywhere else. We are guided by those who came before us and walked this land. There isn't a place like it on earth. Our magic and our spirit intertwine and encapsulate us like Grand Boulevard circles the city. Those spirits play a major role in my practices, specifically the spirits of my direct ancestors and those that I have crossed paths with along my journey to and from home. Home will always be Detroit.

There is something to be said about cultural fusion and appropriation in Michigan specifically. It is an issue that stems from the vast divide and from the remnants of a segregated Detroit, snuggled comfortably in the palm of that big red mitten. While I do believe those issues need to be addressed, quite frankly, they just aren't the things I choose to put my energy into. Sharing rituals and magic is one thing, but appropriation is another, and sometimes the lines are so blurred that we can't tell the difference even when it's blatant and staring us directly in our faces.

What Does the Work Do?

At this point, you hopefully have a much better sense of what Hoodoo and Conjure work is in the African American Folk Magical experience. But you may also be wondering just what the spellwork is like, and how to do some of it. Following are some uniquely Detroit-based spells that the people in this area do on a regular basis.

If you're a person who comes from an African American background and has the roots to make these work (both the plant roots and the family/cultural ones), then you might find these useful too. If you are not someone with those roots, you can still learn from these spells without practicing them, and maybe understand something more about Detroit Hoodoo and the African American Folk Magic world that way.

Working No. 1: A Spell to Fix a Person for Bad Luck

Gather some bloodroot roots, blackberry root and thorns, some bindweed vines, and some willow leaf water. Let ingredients sit together in a foil pan, outside, for a week during the waning moon. Pour into a mason jar and put a broken key, an iron nail, and a photo (or name paper) of the person into the jar. Visualize all your hatred into the jar, curse the person, and bury the jar under a willow tree, in the mud. Walk away and never look back. Do not return to that tree. Take a cleansing bath.

Working No. 2: A Honeysuckle Spell

Gather honeysuckle in bloom. Bend the vine into a wreath. Place it surrounding a magenta candle and rub with vanilla extract, cinnamon, nutmeg, lavender oil, and sugar. Add a bit of your sweat from between your breasts. Write your wish for a passionate fling on the candle. Place a handkerchief under it. Burn when the hands of the clock face up. Do this on a Friday for best results. Carry the kerchief, filled with the flowers from the wreath, in your bra to attract your desire.

Working No. 3: Auto Plant Harmony Spell

Write the name of your supervisor on a small slip of paper with a red circle around it. Put it into a small half-ounce bottle with some calamus and licorice roots. Blend Bend Over oil and Domination oil, and fill the bottle up to the top. Cap it and put in front of a dressed Domination candle, reading Psalm 7 while it burns. Keep in a safe place. Take a hyssop bath. Shake the bottle periodically, when necessary, to keep people in check.

The East Side/North End/Southwest

There are moments that are part of living on the river of magic in Detroit that cannot happen anywhere else. Those times when you know that if you pick up a red stone from the water, it may be holy, so you put it back. You can taste the air on the night of the fish flies and know that it is almost time to cast your bottles into the water for banishing. You know the spirit of the lagoon on Belle Isle to be hungry, so you do nothing there that could give it a piece of your soul.

The river contains us, as we contain the river's soul. That soul runs through every ethnic enclave. It cleaves us to itself and makes us more than we are. It brews our magic like black coffee with brown sugar and every kind of creamer imaginable. But the creamers are the cultures that exchange craft with us. And that is Detroit Hoodoo—that is Detroit magic.

FIELD NOTES

Bloodstoppers and Bearwalkers

Those who look at a map of the Midlands will probably notice that Michigan is split into two pieces. "The mitten," according to colloquial terminology, is the main southern landmass of the state, housing cities like Detroit and Kalamazoo. The other is a long bowsprit of land known as the Upper Peninsula, or "UP." Inhabitants have been known as "Yoopers" (from the sound of "U-P"), and represent a fusion of numerous cultural traditions: Ojibwe, Cornish, French and French Canadian, English, Scots Irish, and more.

Early in his career, folklorist Richard Dorson spent half a year in the UP documenting folk practices in a project that would later become his book *Bloodstoppers and Bearwalkers*. In it, he documented on-the-ground folklore from a number of people, noting the prevalence of supernatural legends. (The titular bearwalkers, for example, are shape-shifting sorcerers found in Ojibwe stories, and even speaking about them or seeing them could bring bad luck and misfortune.) He also chronicled ghost stories, superstitions, and healing methods like bloodstopping, using methods found in other folk magical spaces like in Pennsylvania German Braucherei or by reciting the biblical verse Ezekiel 16:6: "And when I passed by thee, and saw thee polluted in thine own blood, I said unto thee when thou wast in thy blood, Live; yea, I said unto thee when thou wast in thy blood, Live."[149]

Dorson's documentation of these traditions was invaluable to folklore studies, but like Vance Randolph in the Ozarks, intervening years have shown that he was still very much an outsider in the area. Later folklorists like Jim Leary have pointed out that Dorson was a young scholar and much of his work was also steeped in his enthusiasm, leading to some broad generalizations about the people he studied.[150] Still, Dorson's work and the rich fusion of cultures in the UP illustrate that the Midlands region has numerous pockets of folklore and folk magic that are often overlooked.

149. Authorized King James Version.

150. Leary, "Folklore of the Upper Peninsula."

TRAVELING ON
The Midlands

As with any guidebook, there is always much more to experience than can be neatly fit into a chapter. To that end, we offer you this addendum to the map that will provide you with some tools to explore the Midlands further.

The glossary shares some keywords that might be useful. The places to visit will point you toward locations of interest that we think you might find valuable, and the reading recommendations provide you with some top-tier texts that can be used to dig in and learn more about this region.

Glossary

African American Folk Magic (AAFM): The complex of folk magical practices used, taught, and kept primarily by African American people. These often include Hoodoo, Rootwork, and branches of Conjure practice, as well as some practices derived from African Traditional Religions (ATRs).

Ashé: A force pervading all living things, as described in several African Traditional Religions, which also serves as a connection to the divine.

bearwalker: A person who can transform themselves into an animal, usually a bear, using magic or witchcraft.

bloodstopper: Someone with the power to use charms to heal and cure, especially those who can cause a wound to stop bleeding. They may also be able to charm a fever or deal with similar everyday ailments.

closed practice: A culturally bound tradition, activity, or ritual that requires one to belong to the culture of origin or receive initiation or permission from cultural tradition bearers.

diloggun: In Lucumi and other Yoruban-derived ATRs, the practice of divination using cowry shells.

dreaming true: The ability to have dreams that predict or prophesy future events, or to use dreams to influence the events of a person's life. Often this involves interpreting dream symbols using "dream books" as well as simply seeing the future in a dream.

ebo: The Lucumi concept of sacrifice as part of ritual observation.

egun: Ancestors or revered spirits of the dead in Lucumi beliefs.

Espiritismo: A religion and spiritual practice derived from nineteenth-century Spiritualism and mingled with the writings of metaphysician Allan Kardec, widely practiced in Puerto Rico and by people with Puerto Rican backgrounds.

iwa pele: In the Lucumi faith, the act of doing the right thing because it is the right thing to do without expectation of punishment or reward.

Lucumi: An African Traditional Religion based on the reverence of and work with Orishas. Practice involves initiation, ritual participation, divination, and service to the community of practitioners.

mad stones: Stones gathered from the inside of animals, notably deer, that could be used to fend off diseases like rabies.

mesa blanca (**the white table**)**:** A mediumship practice found in Espiritismo that involves a meeting with a group of practitioners and an acting medium.

Nain Rouge: A "red dwarf" figure thought to appear in Detroit during times of coming disaster or misfortune.

Olorisha: An initiated priestess of the Lucumi religion.

orisha: Spiritual forces and figures derived from African Traditional Religious beliefs. They are sometimes syncretized as saints in religions like Lucumi.

power doctor: A term found in the Ozarks and other parts of the Midwest and Upland South for a person capable of working folk magic, especially healing, protection, and anti-witchcraft charms.

Santeria: An anglicized name used to describe Lucumi, not usually used by members of the religion unless speaking with non-members.

spite doll: Figural creations that are used as a way of either cursing or removing curses within the Ozark folk magical tradition.

tonic: A strong formula, usually full of herbs, taken by a person to fortify their body or remove harmful effects. These are frequently made during the spring when they can help restore "blood" after a long winter.

witch master: An Ozark term for a person gifted in removing hexes or curses, or in dealing with malevolent witchcraft.

yarb: In the Ozarks and parts of Appalachia, the regional term for helpful or harmful plants used in folk medicine. A person gifted in using these plants might be called a "yarb doctor."

yooper: A person who lives in Michigan's Upper Peninsula (abbreviated "U. P.," which is where the "yoop" in the name comes from).

Places to Visit

Wander around Augustine's Spiritual Boutique and Lucky Hoodoo Products in Chicago, IL: These two Chicago stores are long-standing staples of the greater Chicagoland folk magical scene (Augustine's has been around since around 1995, and Lucky Hoodoo since 1993). They've inherited the legacy of the mail-order Hoodoo shops that were once very important to the preservation of Hoodoo traditions in the North (which you can read about in Carolyn Morrow Long's excellent book, *Spiritual Merchants*).

Attend the Detroit Hoodoo Festival in Michigan: This is less of a "where" than a "when," but if you happen to be in Detroit during August, you can participate in the annual Detroit Hoodoo Festival, which Kenya Coviak (whose work appears in this section) helps organize. Actual practitioners share their folk magic traditions, as well as key contemporary issues of importance to practitioners, their clients, and the larger African American Folk Magic community. If you happen to be around during the spring rather than the late summer, you could opt to see the Marche du Nain Rouge instead.

Visit (and Revisit) the Buckland Museum of Witchcraft & Magick in Cleveland, Ohio: If you're in Cleveland, this little museum is a trove of magical history and lore. It's largely the legacy of Neopagan author Raymond Buckland (famous for his "big blue book," which introduced many to Wicca in the late twentieth century). In addition to a number of artifacts inherited from Buckland and Wicca progenitors like Gerald Gardner, Aleister Crowley, and Sybil Leek, there are artifacts from folk magic practices around the world on display. The museum provides a number of educational resources about its exhibits, and its small size means that the staff is deeply knowledgeable about the items in the collection. There is a lot of rotation in the exhibits themselves as the staff rotate items from storage.

Take a Hike with a Native Plant Guide in the Ozarks: To get a real sense of just how rich and diverse the botanical treasures of the Ozark Mountains are, you might want to step into the woods with an experienced guide. They will be able to point out a wide range of plants that have been used historically for medicine (and magic) by Ozarkers, including things like bittersweet, sassafras, maidenhair ferns, and several different types of sumac. The Arkansas Native Plant Society is a good place to start (www.anps.org); they often organize these walks and tours from spring to autumn.

• • • • • • • • • •

Recommended Reading

Star Songs and Water Spirits: A Great Lakes Native Reader by Victoria Brehm
The Indigenous peoples of the Great Lakes region told a number of stories about the spirits and magic of the area, and this collection provides a good introduction to some of those tales.

Cuban Santeria: Walking with the Night by Raul J. Canizares
This is a rare but insightful glimpse into some of the traditions of Lucumi as shared by a Babalawo (priest-diviner) from the religion.

Bloodstoppers and Bearwalkers: Folk Traditions of Michigan's Upper Peninsula by Richard Dorson
This is one of the essential folklore collections of Upper Peninsula stories. It is a bit dated in some places but still offers a lot of insight into the folkways of Yoopers from the mid-twentieth century.

Folklore from Adams County, Illinois by Harry Middleton Hyatt
Hyatt drafted this collection of lore separate from his massive multivolume lore on folk magic, but it offers a great look at a number of folk beliefs and practices found in the Midwest.

Ozark Country by Otto Ernest Rayburn
As much a personal narrative of growing up in the Ozarks as a collection of lore, Rayburn's work is a snapshot of a wide range of practices and beliefs from the Ozark Mountains.

Ozark Magic and Folklore by Vance Randolph
Randolph and his wife/folklore-collecting partner Mary Celestia Parler did some of the widest recording of Ozark lore in the mid-twentieth century, and this book is a classic look at the folk magic of the region.

Ozark Folk Magic: Plants, Prayers & Healing by Brandon Weston
Weston revisits some of the folklore gathered by earlier scholars, but then explores many of the evolutions and changes in Ozark folkways. This book provides a practical introduction to the folk magic and healing traditions of the region.

CHAPTER 6

Plains West

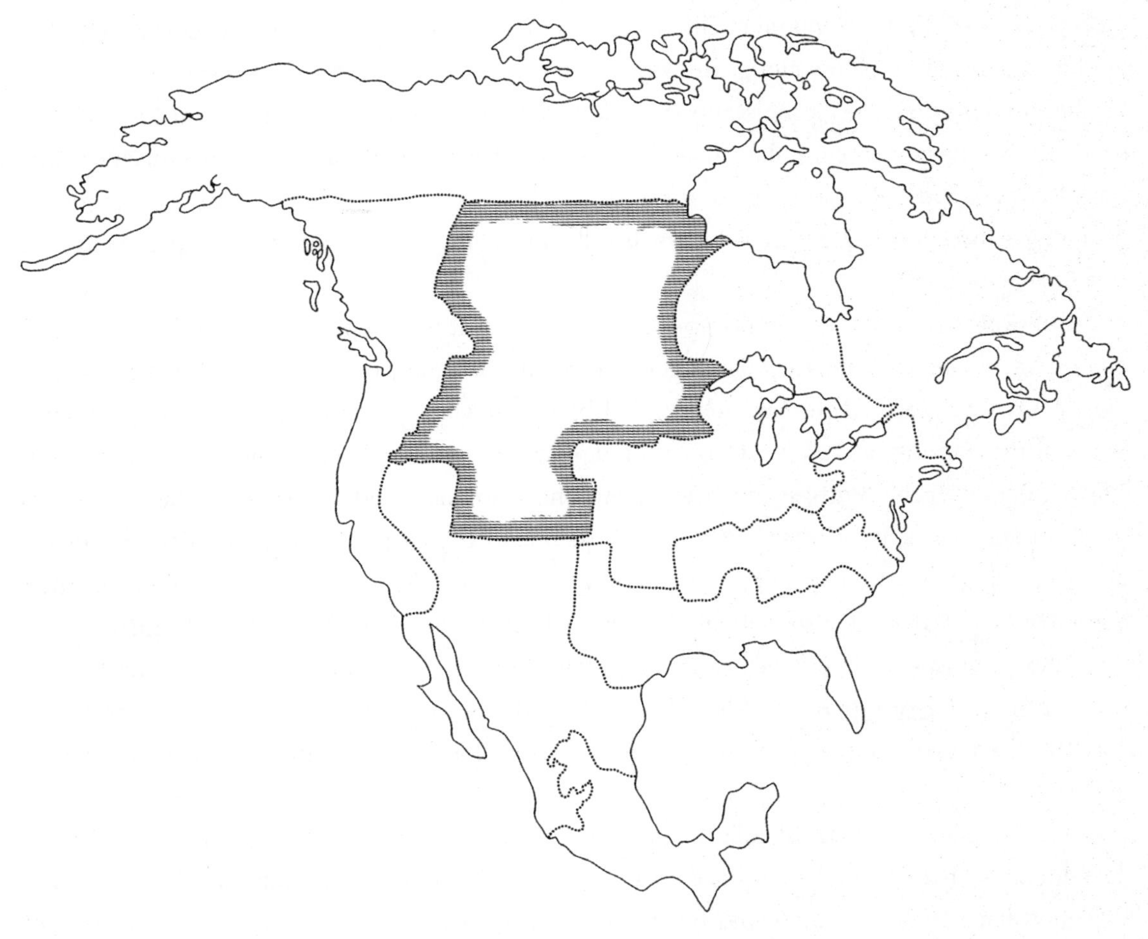

Chapter 6

Wandering with Cain in the Wilderness: An Introduction to the Folk Magic of the Western Plains

Minneapolis is a lively city full of murals and movement, transit trains that can take you where you needed to go quickly and efficiently, and funky little coffee shops with strong black brews to stir your mental cauldron as you meet a friend for conversations about folklore and magic (which is what most of my conversations are about). Minneapolis and St. Paul are "twin cities," a pair of urban expanses that have essentially merged over time, but there are pockets of magic in them ranging from the gorgeous walls of art to the playful, tongue-in-cheek affection for local pseudo–folk hero Paul Bunyan. When you spend time here, you get the feeling that you are at the edge of something—a vast expanse of westward land stretching far beyond the visible horizon.

This is a vista full of loneliness, warmth, ice, story, and magic. There's a combination of oldness and kitsch that's hard to replicate anywhere else. I've spent time driving through the Black Hills of South Dakota, stopping at the Mitchell Corn Palace—a massive house completely covered in dried ears of corn—along the way. I've seen buffalo (or rather, American bison) slowly lumbering through Yellowstone National Park only a few dozen yards from the car I was in. I've spent hours traversing the salt flats in Utah (which also has some remarkably beautiful landscapes outside of the Salt Lake basin). I spent several weeks high up in the Rocky Mountains, where I distinctly remember seeing a thunderstorm rolling in below my elevation and experiencing the awe of that moment.

All of which is to say: this landscape is dramatic. But it is also personable, and surprising in quirky ways. This is by far the largest general expanse I could point to in our journey through North American folk magic, and it's defined by a vast variety of practitioners and traditions. Some of those traditions involve deeply rooted practices that have been brought in by immigrant communities over the centuries, such as the Hmong shamans called *txiv ua neeb* (which translates as something like "spirit master"). Minnesota has one of the largest Hmong populations outside of Laos, largely due to a massive refugee influx after the mid-1970s military conflicts in their home country. There are also palpable influences from German, Slavic, and Norwegian settlers with their own folk traditions of healing and protection. To that end, in this leg of our journey I'll be introducing you to author Melissa A. Ivanco-Murray, who looks to her Slavic roots to see how they have evolved in a place like Minnesota, as well as how they maintain a connection to the past.

And there are new forms of folk magic that have sprung up here, through the migration of the adherents of the Church of Jesus Christ of Latter-Day Saints (commonly called "Mormons," although that is not their preferred terminology in most cases). The LDS colonizers brought some of their European folk traditions, of course, but a wide range of new mysticism influenced their founder, Joseph Smith, and set a new tone for folk beliefs in areas of Utah, Idaho, and parts of Colorado, Montana, Wyoming, and eastern Oregon. There, beliefs about Indigenous lore began to merge with the Christian-based mysticism of the religion, and tales of sasquatches transformed into tales of the wandering biblical figure of Cain—marked as hairy and rough-voiced when he met with travelers passing through the wild places of the Deseret Region. The LDS Church adopted the name "Deseret" as a moniker for the region of their greatest settlement and influence, deriving it from a Book of Mormon term for "honeybee." The symbol of the beehive became an emblem of the area, especially the state of Utah, and emphasized the family-oriented and hardworking society the LDS adherents wished to create. I will explore some of that folklore and folk magic as it relates to the region and its history.

The wide expanses of the plains have not always been hospitable, with terrifying storms, raging wildfires, and suffocating dust clouds passing through. The area has also seen some of the most violent massacres of the Native population in North American recorded history, such as the tragic Wounded Knee Massacre of the Lakota Sioux. That shadow-side of the land plays out in aspects of its folk traditions too. Protective charms and divining the best possible solution to a problem feature prominently in folklore collections like those of the Fifes from the twentieth century. At the same time, ghost stories and legends of strange creatures, UFOs, and secret cults also abound in the area, many of which feature extremely modern technology or occurrences at places like the Skinwalker Ranch near Ballard, Utah. Utah State University has been at the forefront of collecting digital folklore in recent years, including forms of internet-based folk belief, ritual, and even magic.

This is a vast region, one that is often envisioned as a series of wildernesses that we can get lost in, or the "wide-open spaces" of the Old West in stories, film, and television. There's some truth to that, but it's also a place where many groups have put down roots for their magic and folklore over the years, or where they have grown new forms of magic to meet the unique needs they face. Astute readers will notice that this section of the book is a bit less dense than the other sections. For one thing, there's an issue of population. While this is certainly a vast expanse of land, this also happens to be a much less densely populated region of the continent, and so with fewer folk comes fewer people to talk about their practices. Practitioners of folk magic in this region also often draw from traditions we find elsewhere and adapt those workings to the Plains environment, so some of the material could potentially be repetitive, too.

The most significant reason, though, is that in the process of seeking out practitioners to share their work, this region proved to be the most elusive. I had contacts for a number of practices and reached out to many people working in traditions ranging from Mormon mysticism to Hmong shamanism and more. Sometimes I would get some promising leads, or even a person who considered sharing their experiences, but then they would have to back away from the project for their own (often very good) reasons. That doesn't mean there's any less magic here at all! As you will see, there is still much to talk about, but the Plains West region does seem to be guarding its secrets, too, so our foray into the folk magic here must, by necessity, be a bit more limited. In the pages that follow, you'll learn a bit more about this area. It's a space that is evolving constantly, changing at a rapid pace, while still holding some achingly old pieces of tradition in its grasp.

FIELD NOTES

The Spirit Catches You: Hmong Folk Healing in Minnesota

One of the largest populations of Hmong immigrants in the world lives in Minnesota. Following a devastating civil war in Laos (and with some suspicion about the involvement of Western colonial powers), many Hmong resettled in places like St. Paul and began new lives.

The struggle to maintain some connection to their cultural past has led a number of Hmong and Hmong American people to turn to their traditional folkways, including some folk beliefs and magic. Chief among these is the community support for the *txiv ua neeb*, a term for Hmong shamanic practitioners charged with protecting the spiritual well-being of their neighbors. These shamans are specifically called to their practices through powerful trance states and can perform rituals to help bring a person's soul back to them if they seem to be lost or in spiritual danger. They may also make amulets out of red or white string to help protect those who wear them.

There are other folk magic practitioners in the Hmong community, such as the herbalists known as *kws tshuaj*. These healers do not need to have shamanic trances or visions and may pass on their knowledge to other members of the community. Folk rituals and traditions may also circulate informally in the form of house blessings or New Year's rituals.[151]

While the Hmong have largely been welcomed in America, there have historically been some conflicts between the traditional forms of Hmong knowledge and Western ideas. Perhaps the best illustration of this is Anne Fadiman's book *The Spirit Catches You and You Fall Down*. It documents a struggle between Western-educated medical doctors and a Hmong family in California as they each attempt to treat a young child's epilepsy with different approaches. In the end, the inability to effectively communicate leads to some serious consequences. The story has led to a shift in how some doctors integrate and address traditional beliefs in the diagnostic process.

151. Visit https://hmongshamans.omeka.net/ to learn more.

Rekindling the Hearth: Slavic Folk Magic in North America

MELISSA A. IVANCO-MURRAY

I no longer remember the exact moment I fell in love with mythology and fairy tales, but I do remember devouring every book about gods and legendary heroes and magic that lurked on the shelves of my elementary school library. Years before I studied Latin, I could recite the twelve labors of Heracles and bore my parents with the subtle ways in which the Roman understanding of divinity differed from the Greek. As I kept reading, I began to wonder what legends the various cultures of my own ancestors offered.

Like many American citizens, I claim several cultural heritages, but I can trace my lineage back only as far as the immigrants who brought that heritage to these shores, and I am several generations removed. From my mother's line, I have the blood of Celts and Hessians in my veins. From my father's, whose family arrived more recently, Slovak and Baltic. Information about the Pagan past and surviving folklore of Scotland and Ireland was easier to find, so at first, I turned my attention in that direction. It was only once I began to study the Russian language in college that I realized the wealth of Slavic folktales embedded in cultural memory.

And so, I fell in love again.

The Roots of Slavic Folk Magic

The phenomenon of *dvoeverie*, or dual-faith, allows us to know more about historical Pagan customs and practices among the Slavs than among other European peoples, since those practices survived, relatively unchanged, even into the twentieth century.[152] However, much of the mythos underlying those customs and practices is lost to history. No written form of Old Slavic existed until the ninth century, and for several centuries afterward, literacy was almost exclusively confined to Orthodox clergy and a handful of elites.[153] Thus, all records of historical Slavic Paganism were written by foreigners or monks, both of whom possess obvious biases. In summary, the

152. Bernshtam, "Russian Folk Culture and Folk Religion," 35.

153. Martin, *Medieval Russia 980–1584*.

forms of Slavic Pagan rituals survived, but the philosophy granting meaning to those ritual forms changed several times during the last millennium: first, with the coming of Orthodox Christianity; second, with the enforced atheism of the Soviet Union; third, with the return of religious expression during the thaw of the Cold War; and most recently, with the resurgence of interest in pre-Christian Slavic religion across Russia, Eastern Europe, and everywhere that Slavic immigrants settled.[154]

To recreate the cosmological understanding that produced these Pagan rituals, customs, and practices that survived in rural locations among the peasantry and in isolated communities in Siberia, scholars mined not only the records left by monks and travelers of the time, but also folk art, music, and lore. Still, we know more about the inner workings of Baba Yaga's chicken-legged hut than we know about the gods the early Slavs worshiped. We can name certain deities thanks to the persistence of Paganism in Lithuania and Latvia until the fifteenth century, and the names of other Slavic deities have been passed down through writings such as *The Primary Chronicle* or *The Lay of Igor's Campaign*—from these works we know of Perun, Dazhbog, Mokosh, and several others—but the Slavs left us no *Odyssey*, no *Aeneid*, no *Edda*.[155]

Instead, we have the adventures of Ivan-tsarevich and Vasilisa Prekrasnaia that endured in oral tradition. We have magical tales about prophetic birds and a deathless sorcerer. We have warnings about the *leshii*, who avenge any disrespect to their forests, and the beautiful but terrible *rusalki*, who drown the unwary. We have charms to ward away evil, to keep the hearth fire burning strong, and to placate the friendly *domovoi* lest he turn his hand to mischief. The grand Pagan liturgies, if ever they existed in any cohesive form, are lost, but the little rituals of everyday magic remain.

Renewed interest in the religion and culture of the pre-Christian Slavs has also led to renewed interest in these little rituals, and not just among scholars of Slavic languages and cultures; the presence of various Neopagan groups recreating traditions from Slavic folk magic has become so ubiquitous in Russia and Eastern Europe that they appear regularly in pop culture, such as Eastern Europe's thriving folk and Pagan metal scenes or in the fantasy series *Poka tsvetet paporotnik* ("While the Fern Blooms"). In this Russian television series that aired in 2012, a group of *Rodnovery*, or Russian adherents to Slavic Native Faith, play a prominent role, and we witness several of their rituals. It is clear in the context of the series that these *Rodnovery* are not adherents to an unbroken line of worshipers, but rather that they are attempting to recreate the historical religion.

154. Mitrofanova, "Russian Ethnic Nationalism and Religion Today."

155. English translations of these two epics can be found in Zenkovsky, *Medieval Russia's Epics, Chronicles, and Tales*.

But interest in unburying Slavic Paganism is not confined to Russia and Eastern Europe, either. In recent decades across the United States and Canada, where many Slavic immigrants and their descendants reside, a number of contemporary practitioners of what could be regarded as Slavic folk magic—for the folk magic is all that truly endured the centuries following Vladimir I's mandated Christianization of Rus'—have appeared, and that number is growing. Some of these practitioners were drawn by a desire to reconnect with their ancestors. Some grew up hearing folktales and witnessing folk magic rituals performed in otherwise strictly Christian households and wanted to learn why. And some, like myself, were lured by the rich folklore, and after devouring the stories, wanted to unbury the stories' roots.

Tens of thousands of emigrants from Poland, Czechoslovakia, Russia, and other Slavic nations came to North America during the eighteenth and nineteenth centuries. For example, sizeable Polish communities developed in and around Wisconsin, and many Yugoslav immigrants settled in Nebraska, Illinois, and Iowa.[156] Catholics and Jews comprised the majority of Eastern European immigrants at this time, and though by necessity not all their traditions and religious customs outlived the first generation, religious identity continued to play a significant role in these communities, to include the adherence to superstitions, charms, and other little magics that existed alongside their publicly observed religion.[157] However, the first immigrants to North America from the land we now think of as Russia arrived much earlier. Shared markers in mitochondrial DNA in the Native populations of Siberia and North America indicate that prehistoric humans migrated to America from Siberia and other parts of Northern Asia via Beringia during the last Ice Age.[158] Similarities between the folktales, myths, and customs of various Native peoples of Siberia and North America further support this migration theory.[159]

Contemporary Slavic Folk Magic: Slavic Native Faith and Cross-Cultural Practice

As the historical Slavs were not a single unified people, neither was their religion, and the same is true now. There is a tendency among contemporary magical practitioners to keep what works and leave the rest, which leads those who base their personal spiritual practice in part or in whole on Slavic tradition to synthesize elements from a vast array of beliefs and customs, not all of which are technically Slavic, but exist or existed in areas we now think of as part of Slavdom, such as traditional Siberian shamanism. Grounding and astral techniques as well as the use of certain

156. Leary, "Poles, Jews, and Jokes in America's Upper Midwest," 214; Roucek, "The Yugoslav Immigrants in America," 603.
157. Bodnar, "Immigration and Modernization," 47; Pula, "'A Branch Cut Off From Its Trunk,'" 45.
158. Tamm et al., "Beringian Standstill and Spread of Native American Founders."
159. Sheppard, "Population Movements, Interaction, and Legendary Geography," 154–55.

herbs, tools, and methods of communication with the ancestors all evolved, to some extent, from Siberian shamanism. For example, Yukaghir hunters perform rituals to unite their spirits with the spirits of the desired prey.[160] This wide breadth of source material, however limited in depth, has led to a loose style of contemporary North American folk magic that is rooted in historical tradition but remains deeply personal for each practitioner, informed by an individual's heritage, experiences, and intentions.

Though religious organizations dedicated to recreating historical Slavic Pagan belief systems do exist and have published guidelines and rules for their practices, they are often linked to nationalist politics and so have little involvement in North America. For example, *Rodnoverie*, or the Russian version of Slavic Native Faith, is confined to Russian borders.[161] Similarly, *Dievturi* is strictly Latvian, and so on.[162] No such religious bodies specifically govern practitioners of Slavic magic in North America, at least not in any widespread capacity. The organization Ár nDraíocht Féin: A Druid Fellowship (ADF), of which I have been a member since 2015, maintains interest groups dedicated to the individual Indo-European pantheons, including Slavic. However, since most practitioners of Slavic folk magic have no involvement with ADF and since the Slavic Kin is a special interest group, not an independent religious organization, the tenets of ADF Druidry cannot be said to govern the forms or functions of Slavic folk magic in America.

Despite the personal, and therefore variegated, nature of Slavic folk magic in the United States and Canada, common themes inherited from what we do know of the underlying mythos emerge in ritual activities and perspectives. It is commonly understood among those who study Slavic cultures that the early Slavs were strongly influenced by Scandinavian practices and religion through invasion and, eventually, integration. In short, Perun looks an awful lot like Thor. The concept of Yggdrasil, the World Tree, also finds an echo in the Slavic Pagan view of the cosmos; Perun was believed to rule from its branches, and his brother, Veles, from its roots.[163]

In contemporary practice, the overlap between Slavic and Scandinavian (and in some cases Germanic) customs is likewise apparent, with many practitioners drawing freely from either tradition for the substance of their prayers, divinations, and personal rites.[164] The most obvious manifestation of this overlap is the use of Norse runes for meditative or divinatory purposes, but parallels in grounding exercises, deity evocations, and methods of communicating with ancestors and nature spirits also exist. Since most contemporary practitioners in North America are

160. Willerslev, "Not Animal, Not Not-Animal," 629–52.

161. Aitamurto, "More Russian than Orthodox Christianity."

162. Jones and Pennick, *A History of Pagan Europe*, 175.

163. Puhvel, *Comparative Mythology*.

164. Personal communications with the author, January 2021–March 2021.

solitary, predominantly self-taught, and possess a multifaceted cultural heritage, these combined practices are a predictable development.

Bringing together elements from two or more related cultures has obvious benefits. Different methods for making offerings, taking omens, or crafting blessings can enrich the script or fill the gaps left by the magics of one of the less-accessible (at least from an English-speaking perspective) cultural practices. For example, some contemporary practitioners recite Orthodox Christian prayers to bless talismans or good luck charms of Polish, Czech, or other Slavic origin.[165] Some practitioners also use meditative techniques derived from Siberian Shamanism to commune with and seek wisdom from Russian nature spirits like the *leshii*, who, though wild and unpredictable, were said to teach a person the magic and spells of the forest if properly placated.[166]

On the other hand, whether the evocation of deities from distinct pantheons in a single ritual should be embraced or avoided is a matter of debate among contemporary practitioners. Though my ancestors of blood had reason to distrust—and, in fact, fled from—Russian expansion, when crafting my personal rites and rituals, I work exclusively with Russian deities. The reasons for this exclusivity are twofold. First, the academic in me appreciates the historical reconstructionist aspect of working within a single cultural pantheon. Second, my familiarity with the language makes sources about historical Russian Paganism more accessible than, for instance, my own Slovak heritage. I like to think my ancestors understand the necessity of my choice.

Mother Moist Earth

No treatment of Slavic folk magic, historical or contemporary, would be complete without a discussion of the centrality of the hearth and the cult of the mother. Drawn from the traditions of mostly agrarian and nomadic societies, a strong connection to the land is integral to the Slavic cosmos, and that land was and is revered as the mother from whom we come and to whom we return.[167] Slavic folktales instruct heroes to kiss their mother, and so they bow and press their lips against the earth. Offerings to Mat'-Syra-Zemlia, or Mother-Moist-Earth, are given to begin the planting as well as the harvest. The coming of new life in the spring is embodied by Vesna, and the ending of life in the winter by Marena. Vesna is usually honored by the ritual burning or drowning of a straw effigy of her deadly counterpart, a ritual that persisted alongside Catholicism and Orthodoxy until present times. (Note that I am using the Russified version of names for these deities and figures for consistency and because that is the system I am most familiar with, but these gods and goddesses are known by many names across Slavdom; for example, Marena is

165. Personal communications with the author, February 2021–May 2021.

166. Warner, *Russian Myths*, 38–39.

167. Hubbs, *Mother Russia*.

called Marzanna in Polish, Mara in Ukrainian, and Morana in Czech as well as several other Slavic languages.)

Several of the practitioners I spoke with grew up engaging in similar rituals as part of family celebrations, usually conducted before or shortly after regular church services. Others discovered and adopted such rituals after researching their Slavic heritage. Leaving a space open at the table for the beloved dead or any spirits who may wish to join the feast during holiday dinners is another common practice. I witnessed the latter tradition during my time in Russia in 2009, and it is a tradition I have since incorporated into my own practice to honor my ancestors and the spirits of place during family celebrations. Even the Soviet government, vehemently opposed to any kind of religion, failed to eradicate these little magics.

Figure 6-1: Straw Effigy. Straw effigy of the winter maiden, also known as Maslenitsa or Marena, to be either drowned or burned in celebration of the return of spring.

The importance of hearth and home can be seen in folklore and folk art alike. The stove, or *pech'*, stood at the center of the Slavic peasant household as both the means of feeding the family and a vital source of heat in winter. The *domovoi*, a protective household spirit that some scholars suggest is a remnant of the primordial Slavic god Rod, is said to reside under the stove, and the space on top of the stove was traditionally a coveted sleeping location occupied by the eldest member of the household or reserved for honored guests. With the evolution of modern kitchen appliances, the *pech'* is obsolete, but contemporary folk magic often incorporates domestic acts as ritual to preserve the essence of the *pech'*. Cooking dinner for one's family becomes a symbolic feeding of the ancestors, especially when cooking traditional Slavic meals or recipes handed down through the generations. Similarly, the simple act of keeping the fireplace swept and free of ash placates the household *domovoi*.

In the tale of Vasilisa Prekrasnaia, or "Vasilisa the Beautiful," the heroine's stepmother and stepsisters commit the ultimate crime: they let the hearth fire burn out, which necessitates Vasilisa to fetch fire from Baba Yaga. The image of Baba Yaga persists in Slavic cultural memory across the globe, perhaps better than any other folkloric personage besides the firebird, and a plethora of articles—academic and otherwise, and exploring many of her aspects—have been devoted to this complex figure. I even wrote my undergrad honors thesis about Baba Yaga, framing her as a symbol of initiation into adulthood. Often linked to a dark mother, a primordial death goddess, or a keeper of the underworld later transformed by Orthodoxy into a simple witch, Baba Yaga's voracious appetite provides the central conflict of many folktales.[168] However, as the story of Vasilisa Prekrasnaia demonstrates, Baba Yaga possesses a dual nature: she is the hag who consumes all and makes way for growth, testing the hero or heroine with seemingly impossible tasks in the process. If they pass, she rewards them; if they fail, she consumes their flesh, and her hearth consumes their bones.

Another important facet of Slavic folk magic that descends from the centrality of the hearth—and one that, as an artist, drew me deeper into my studies in this area—is the prevalence of handcrafts like weaving and woodwork as spiritual acts. Like domestic tasks, these seemingly small magics carry greater significance. Weaving, sewing, and other textile crafts were integral aspects of historically feminine spiritual expression in Slavic folk practice, as they honored the goddess Mokosh, usually incorporating goddess symbols and iconography.[169] Blessings of health and wealth were woven into decorative wall hangings, prayers for safe travels into shawls and cloaks, and symbols of fertility into the patterns on quilts. Handcraft as an expression of spirituality is one activity many contemporary practitioners of Slavic folk magic have reclaimed. For example, with over twenty-five years of experience as a weaver, Cathy J. creates new patterns based on traditional Polish and Ukrainian motifs to honor her heritage through her art.[170] Though not nearly as skilled at traditional crafts, I have similar motivations in the creation of my own art, drawing inspiration from folklore for my paintings and illustrations, like those I created when developing the *Slavic Tarot*.

The importance of observing seasonal changes is another remnant from the agrarian and nomadic roots of Slavic societies. Thanks to *dvoeverie*, many contemporary holiday traditions are little more than Pagan rituals repackaged with Orthodox Christian names. Observation of the solstices and equinoxes are most popular, but many also observe the quarter days in between, which in Slavic tradition are usually tied to worship of a specific deity such as Mokosh or Veles. Since largescale gatherings of Slavic folk magic practitioners rarely occur outside of Russia and Eastern Europe, most of these seasonal observations are solitary affairs and, ergo, subdued in comparison. After all, there is little point in jumping over a bonfire alone during the rites of Ivan Kupalo (the summer solstice).

However, the frying of multitudes of butter-slathered *blini*, a slightly thicker version of crêpes, to honor the sun's shining face and the return of warmer days during the spring equinox remains equally popular among solitary practitioners. When I lived in Russia, my host served *blini* not only during Maslenitsa, the week-long celebration of spring during which *blini* are traditionally prepared in bulk, but every Sunday for breakfast. While my schedule does not support this level

168. Warner, *Russian Myths*, 73.

169. Kelly, "Goddess Embroideries of Russia and the Ukraine," 11.

170. Personal communication with the author, March 28, 2021.

of pancake devotion, my husband can attest to the quantity of *blini* I have forced him to consume over the years.

A Solitary Ritual to Observe the Changing of Seasons

This ritual is a simplified version of one I performed to observe the spring equinox. I usually conduct my personal rites in accordance with the ADF core order of ritual, so some elements of that structure, such as the offerings and taking of omens, are included here. ADF is not considered a closed tradition, though members of the organization do have access to additional resources and ritual outlines not readily available to the public; thus, this ritual is open for anyone to perform, whether you identify as a Druid or not.

Additionally, certain phrases are inspired by prayers and chants I've absorbed over the years from multiple traditions, Slavic and otherwise, but the words as written are my own. During this particular ritual, I initially offered scotch rather than the usual vodka to my ancestors. According to the runes I drew that day, they were not pleased, so I gave another offering of vodka to placate them. My ancestors have received exclusively vodka ever since.

1. First, prepare your offerings. I usually offer vodka to the ancestors and deities, milk or honey to the spirits, and oats to the earth, but you can substitute other offerings according to your ritual preferences. Any divinatory aids (tarot, runes), candles, incense, or other ritual tools should be gathered at this time as well. This ritual is best conducted outside, but you can easily modify it for indoor use by collecting your offerings in a bowl so they can be given to the earth once complete. On particularly windy days I resort to this method.
2. Begin by grounding, feeling your connection with the roots of the World Tree, then extending your consciousness to its branches. When you are ready, present your offering to Mat'-Syra-Zemlia and say the following:

   Mat'-Syra-Zemlia, I honor you.
   You are the damp soil in the fertile field.
   You are the tangled roots at the heart of the forest.
   You are the one who nourishes and sustains all.
   From you we spring, and to you we return.
   Mother-Moist-Earth, accept my offering!
3. Ready the offerings for your ancestors, for the spirits of nature and place, and for any deities with whom you wish to work. If honoring any specific deities associated with the holiday, such as Vesna for the spring equinox or Jarilo for the

summer solstice, ready an offering for them as well. The example below honors Vesna.

Ancestors, mighty and beloved dead,
Those who stood where I now stand
And walked the pathways I now tread, I honor you.
My blood is your blood; my bones are your bones.
Ancestors of blood and ancestors of spirit,
Accept my offering!

Nature Spirits, friends of feather and fur,
Of skin and scale and hoof and horn,
Leshii, Firebird, Vili, Rusalki, I honor you.
You walk beside me, sometimes as friends,
Sometimes as foes, but always as teachers.
Nature Spirits, accept my offering!

Shining Ones, rulers of all, I honor you.
In Perun's rumbling thunder,
In Mokosh's gentle hand,
In Devana's swift arrows
And Svarog's bright forge,
You weave the threads of life
Into a tapestry no mortal can see.
Gods and goddesses of the heavens and earth,
Accept my offering!

Vesna, goddess of the blooming spring,
You who plant the seeds of beauty
Across the warming land, I honor you.
In the awakening of spring, we remember
That times of dark and sorrow always end,
And that love and life will survive and return.
Vesna, accept my offering!

4. At this point I usually take an omen, using either runes or the *Slavic Tarot*, to determine whether my offerings were accepted, and if so, what blessings or wisdom the ancestors, spirits, and deities wish to offer me in exchange.
5. For seasonal celebrations, now is a good time to enact one of the small magics of folk practice, such as tying ribbons on a tree branch for spring or summer observances, dancing around a bonfire if you feel so inclined, or lighting a log in the hearth at the winter solstice.
6. Lastly, close out the ritual with some final words of thanks and celebrate with a meal. No Slavic celebration is complete without a hearty feast.

Slavic Faith and Practice Around the World

Slavic folk magic practices in North America are steadily growing and evolving as more and more people seek to reconnect with their ancestral roots, though not as swiftly or prominently as in Russia and Eastern Europe. Additionally, new translations of traditional Slavic folktales and other primary sources are becoming increasingly available outside of scholarly circles, allowing a greater audience to discover the small magics hidden within their pages. For those curious about the tenets and practices of contemporary Slavic Native Faith in Eastern Europe, www.Rodnovery.ru offers numerous introductory publications in Russian, English, and several other languages.

Perhaps such an organization might take root in North America one day, but as it currently stands, North American practitioners of Slavic folk magic remain too isolated for a coherent, governing community to be practical, as much as I would love a space to gather and perform group rituals centered on Slavic traditions. Especially in light of ongoing political struggles in the region, it is now more important than ever to preserve cultural heritages. Incorporating Slavic folk traditions into one's personal spiritual practice is only one such way.

FIELD NOTES

Lumberjacks, Paul Bunyan, and Folk Magic on the Job

Plenty of North American children grow up hearing tales of an enormous lumberjack named Paul Bunyan. With his faithful big blue ox named Babe at his side, the giant Bunyan—whose size seems to grow and shrink at alarming rates, depending on the story—does everything from stamping his boots to create Minnesota's "ten thousand lakes" to piling up Pike's Peak in Colorado.

Bunyan's story is legendary, and even as children, many understand that his tales cannot be taken as infallible truth. At the core of many stories, though, we often find a hint of something real. In Bunyan's case, that winds up being roots in the stories of a well-known Quebecois lumberjack named Fabian "Saginaw Joe" Fournier, alleged to be six feet tall and bearing an extra set of teeth. Known for his rough lifestyle, incredible strength, and tendency to brawl, lumberjacks passed around Saginaw Joe tales in the latter half of the 1800s. These became Bunyan stories when an ad writer for the Red River Lumber Company named William B. Laughead decided to coopt the Saginaw Joe stories and attach them to a fictitious giant named Paul. This intentional rewriting of the lore being passed around among loggers felt inauthentic to some, such as folklorist Richard M. Dorson, who called such revisionist tale-telling "fake lore."[171]

Part of what got Dorson's dander up about Bunyan was that there was no need to create a story of a giant with a big blue ox because lumber workers already *had* stories, beliefs, and other folklore of their own. Indeed, dangerous occupations like logging often had enormous stockpiles of lore, since danger often required special protection or precaution, including forms derived from superstition. For example, in the early part of the twentieth century, workers in a number of dangerous industries including steel mills, lumber, and coal mining all had taboos about allowing women into their workspaces. Other lore discusses beliefs about when you should work: working too hard on a Monday means you'll work too hard all week and be worn out by Friday, while Friday is generally a very bad day to begin work in the first place (as is a Sunday).[172]

Virtually all fields of work have their own folklore and beliefs, and it should be noted that those change over time. Many women currently work in the logging industry, so the beliefs about women bringing bad luck have largely transformed, while starting a new job on a Friday is still considered to have a taint of misfortune to it.

Some additional folk beliefs based on occupation:

171. Dorson, "Folklore and Fake Lore." See also Blum, "Paul Bunyan and the Myth of the American Lumberjack."

172. Hand, *The Frank C. Brown Collection of North Carolina Folklore*, 460–61.

- Some electricians carry marjoram and feverfew as a way to deflect potential electrocution.
- Nurses and public safety service workers often swear that full moons bring out the wildest, strangest, and most intense cases (or at least the largest quantity of imperiled people each month).
- Coal miners will burn the hat of someone who has recently become a new parent to provide protection and blessing to their family; there are also sexist beliefs similar to those found at racetracks about keeping women away from the mines/workplace.
- Pilots—like racers—won't take photos right before a flight, and they usually don't allow their spouse or significant other to watch them take off to prevent any accidents or crashes.
- Seamstresses and tailors won't do repairs on their own clothes, especially not while they are wearing them, for fear of bringing bad luck (even death).
- Most cooks and chefs won't keep parsley growing indoors because it can invite death into the kitchen or restaurant.[173]

In the end, the Bunyan legend is entertaining as a story about a giant and his enormous blue bovine companion, but it's always worth digging a little deeper to find out what rich folklore is circulating among any given group of people.

173. Penrod, "Folk Beliefs about Work, Trades, and Professions from New Mexico"; Yronwode, *Hoodoo Herb and Root Magic*.

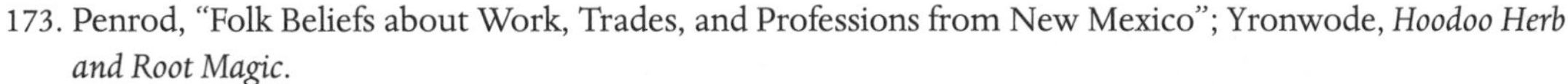

The Salamander and the Shew-Stones: Traditions of Folk Mysticism in the Mormon Cultural Region

CORY THOMAS HUTCHESON

A desperate woman with a sick child prays every day for her child's recovery. After three months, a mysterious stranger shows up and offers to pray with her. His prayer is unlike anything she's ever heard, and immediately afterward, the child gets up and begins singing, fully healed. The stranger is gone.

A young couple with a sickly child is struggling to make ends meet. One night a stranger shows up at their door asking to warm himself by their fire. They let him in and one by one, everyone dozes off. The mother awakens in the night to see the stranger sitting at a table with a white tablecloth and a loaf of bread that radiates light, then falls back asleep. When they all awaken the next day, the father goes to walk the man out of the house, only to find he disappears once they cross the threshold. Their child, it turns out, is now healthy and well.

In 1944, a man and his wife are driving a truck down a stretch of highway when they pick up a hitchhiker. He rides with them for a ways, tells them about his faith, and asks about current events, including the ongoing war. Then he asks to be let out on a desolate spot of the road. Despite their misgivings, they pull over. As the stranger leaves, he tells them they will return carrying a dead man, and that the war will be over in August. The truck driver and his wife continue, but on their way back they are stopped at a bad roadway accident. The police ask if the driver can use his truck to transport one of the deceased victims back to town. And, of course, the war does in fact end.[174]

These tales of mysterious strangers with miraculous powers of healing and prophecy all appear as a part of the Mormon series of narratives known as "The Three Nephites." The story has its origins in the Book of Mormon, the gospel narrative and religious texts collection assembled and allegedly translated from divinely inscribed sources by Latter-Day Saints' founder, Joseph Smith. In the Book of Mormon's scripture, Jesus established a set of twelve apostles through the

174. These three tales paraphrased from Dorson, *Buying the Wind*.

course of a North American ministry after fulfilling his ministry in and around Jerusalem. As they reached the zenith of their work, nine of the apostles asked to enter heaven when their earthly mission was finished (i.e., upon their deaths), but three of these apostles belonging to the Nephite tribe (a tribe descended from the tribes of Israel) asked to remain on earth preaching until the return of Jesus. He granted their desire, giving them extended life so that they could continue to do good works (3 Nephi 28).

The legend of the Three Nephites has been a central pillar of LDS folklore for well over a hundred years. It has been told hundreds of times, with Nephite sightings by members of the LDS Church all over the world. It has been studied by folklorists for nearly as long as versions of it have been in print circulation, and it appears in records collected by Austin and Alta Fife, William A. Wilson, and Richard Dorson, among others. In some ways, it is the central defining tale of Mormon folklore studies, yet as Eric A. Eliason and Tom Mould point out in the introduction to their collection *Latter-Day Lore: Mormon Folklore Studies*, "The Three Nephites provide one way to narrate the origins of Mormon folklore studies, but such a story leaves much unexamined."[175]

The examination of the story of the Three Nephites is a glimpse—and only a glimpse—into a rich mystical tradition within the LDS worldview, but getting inside that worldview can be extremely tricky for those who are outside the church. Even those with strong connections within the LDS church can wind up ostracized or excommunicated for digging too deeply. Joseph Smith biographer Fawn Brodie learned this after publishing her book *No Man Knows My History* in 1945; the church officially cast her out the following year for her portrayal of Smith as something of a genius huckster.

In my own experience, I have very limited knowledge of official Mormonism. I had several family members who converted to the faith during a tumultuous period in my teens, and I attended a few services with them. I have also had teachers, friends, and colleagues from within the church, and as a folklorist I spend more than my fair share of time working with materials collected by and about Mormon people. (LDS lore has been some of the best documented and recorded, given the tremendous amount of support that the Latter-Day Saints community throws behind things like folklore and genealogy.) None of that scant experience gives me a true insider's perspective, though, so what I write here should be understood as a window into what is publicly known and available, not an invitation to go digging for false gold in someone else's backyard.

Still, we cannot tell the story of North America's magic and mysticism without at least looking at the role Mormonism plays in that narrative. To that end, this section will address a few key elements of LDS lore related to the experience of what we are calling "folk magic" in this book. Crucially, magic is a very taboo concept in the official LDS Church, and most of what is described

175. Eliason and Mould, *Latter-Day Lore*, intro.

here would likely be cast in a positive light as mysticism, divine miracles, or prophecy—and in a negative light as mere superstition and not representative of Mormon thought as a whole. Additionally, throughout this essay, I will be referring to "Mormons," "Latter-Day Saints," and "LDS" fairly interchangeably. It should be noted, however, that the colloquial descriptor of "Mormon" is not the preferred choice among those who are members of the Church of Jesus Christ of Latter-Day Saints. It is primarily used here for the convenience of its recognizability and its brevity.

I will begin with a very brief peer into the past to see how some of the roots of Mormonism are entangled with the roots of other magical practices. I will touch on some well-known elements—such as Smith's family history of magical treasure hunting—as well as some of the misrepresentation around those practices. However, this will not be an extensive history of the history of Latter-Day Saints as a religious group or of Smith himself, as that would be well beyond the scope of this book.[176] Instead, I will be keeping my aim firmly set on the issues of the magical and mystical. Following the history, I will turn toward the broad expression of folk culture in Mormonism, then present an assortment of specifically mystical or magical folklore derived from LDS culture. I also address contemporary concerns about the use of folklore and Mormon history, and the representation of Mormons more broadly as well.

In the end, this is not an attempt at an exposé on some "secret Mormon magic," but rather an effort to recognize just how much enchantment is embedded in and growing from LDS roots in North America.

A Brief Latter-Day History

Joseph Smith grew up near Palmyra, New York, within what was known as the "Burned-Over District" of the state. It had earned that nickname because of the sheer number of religious revivals that had come through, burning with holy fire and sparking what was to be known as the Second Great Awakening. This religious zeal would also be a part of Smith's life, but not until the 1820s, when he received visitations from the angel Moroni that led him to discover buried golden plates inscribed with the text of the Book of Mormon. Prior to this revelation, however, Smith and his family were treasure hunters who employed a "seer stone" (sometimes called a "peep stone" or a "shew stone") to locate underground caches of treasure and help bring them to the surface. Much of what they hunted came from legends, and there were often spirits associated with protecting or guarding the treasures.

The hunt for these treasures often involved extensive purification rituals and had deep roots in Western Hermeticism and alchemy. The treasure-digging process represented an alchemical

176. For those interested in general Mormon history, I highly recommend Richard Lyman Bushman's *Mormonism: A Very Short Introduction* and Fawn M. Brodie's *No Man Knows My History: The Life of Joseph Smith*.

transformation of the soul, and a treasure chest surfaced at the wrong time might magically be transformed into nothing more than a large boulder. Historian John L. Brooke notes that "these volatile treasures reflected a continuing, if truncated, belief in the Hermetic concept of metallic growth" and links much of the treasure-hunting practices of Smith's family to similar rituals and procedures found in German alchemical rites and writings.[177]

In addition to the practice of treasure-hunting magic, Smith had some connections to Freemasonry. His brother Hyrum was a Mason, and Smith joined the Nauvoo Masonic Lodge (which became controversial among the broader Masonic community and was discontinued). By 1842, he had apparently achieved a "sublime degree" among the Masons, but his fascination with them also led to suspicion and, later, condemnation of Masonry among early church leaders.[178] The order and structure of Masonry, along with the power of divine revelation, buried treasure (read metaphorically), and transmutation all became essential components of Smith's early cosmology in establishing the Mormon religion. But Smith also had a more personal interest in folk magic; religious scholar Catherine L. Albanese goes so far as to say, "Joseph Smith himself was, by any standard, a cunning man," referring to the English tradition of diviners, folk healers, charmers, and curse-breakers.[179] Beyond his seer stones, Smith appears to have owned a number of magical objects, including a silver Jupiter talisman (derived from Hermetic tradition) that was supposed to bring him wealth, as well as elements of "astrology, talismans, a dagger for drawing magic circles...and magic parchments for purification, protection, and conjuring a spirit."[180]

By the time of Smith's assassination in 1844, the church he established was moving away from both Masonry and Western Hermetic traditions in any official capacity, although even Brigham Young—who inherited leadership of the LDS church after Smith's death—still endorsed the use of seer stones. Smith's youthful enthusiasm for treasure hunting and magic had itself been transmuted and transformed into a more religious form of alchemy, and the early Mormon church attempted to put some space between itself and the burnt-over, magical past of the Palmyra days.

All of that distance collapsed with the introduction of something called "The Salamander Letter" in the 1980s. A rare documents dealer named Mark Hoffman produced the letter, even going so far as to have an eminent Mormon historian verify its authenticity. The letter, reportedly written by Martin Harris (who paid for the first printings of the Book of Mormon), claimed that Smith had been engaged in a treasure-digging episode and encountered a fire spirit (called a salamander after the European elemental creature, not the amphibian). The spirit demanded that

177. Brooke, *The Refiner's Fire*, 30–32.

178. Albanese, *A Republic of Mind and Spirit*, 136–50.

179. Albanese, *A Republic of Mind and Spirit*, 145.

180. Quinn, *Early Mormonism and the Magic World View*, 78–79.

Joseph bring his brother (who was deceased) to receive the treasure, which turned out to be the golden plates that became the Book of Mormon.

The problem, of course, is that the letter was an utter fraud and forgery. Hoffman was producing numerous counterfeit documents. He appealed to gross sensationalism about the connections between Smith's history in treasure hunting and folk magic and more overtly occult phenomena like the salamander spirit and the hints of necromancy involving Alvin. For example, rumors circulated that Alvin's grave had been dug up for occult rites, although there is no evidence of such events. It's also important to note that the connection between treasure hunting and folk magic would not have been particularly controversial in the early 1800s.[181]

To attempt to cover his tracks, Hoffman bombed the owner of the letter (and another woman). He was caught, and the truth of the letter's falsity came out. In the intervening years, many scholars have pointed out that the Salamander Letter is still used as though it were an authentic source by many lay historians of the church and those who wish to paint it with a sensational brush. There is no doubt that the young Joseph Smith did indeed have involvement in folk magic and treasure hunting, but making too much of that point can distract from the richer folk practices that grew from those early Mormon roots.

Temple Garments and Vision Tales: Mormonism and Folk Mysticism

Focusing too much attention on Smith and his magical experiences reveals much less about LDS folk mysticism than looking at the stories they tell about and among themselves. As noted earlier, the enthusiasm for folk culture among Mormons tends to run very high, not least because they have spent a long time defining themselves as a cultural group within their own cultural region (commonly referred to as "Deseret," meaning "honeybee," and leading to a lot of folk associations with bees, hives, and honey among Mormons). The folkloric connection also has to do with the efforts made by many LDS adherents to trace their genealogy, as part of the official church doctrine allows for the baptism of the deceased into the Mormon faith, thus ensuring that even if someone was Catholic, Jewish, or Hindu in life, they can be a Latter-Day Saint in death and join their family. (This practice is not without its own intense controversies.)

There are several well-known bits of Mormon folklore that circulate. For example, one widespread bit of lore discusses the use of "Mormon underwear." These items, more properly called "Temple Garments," are a set of white underclothes that many LDS wear when entering the most sacred spaces of the church, referred to as "the Temple." The whiteness of the clothes represents a state of spiritual purity because they can only be worn by those who have undergone a very rigorous ceremony known as "endowment" to verify their faith and devotion to the church.

181. Eliason, "Seer Stones, Salamanders, and Early Mormon 'Folk Magic'"; Hall, *Worlds of Wonder, Days of Judgment*.

While they are regarded as official ceremonial garb (although garb not displayed for anyone, importantly), they are sometimes also treated as magical talismans, and stories circulate about Latter-Day Saints wearing their Temple Garments and being saved from near-death experiences like car accidents.[182] Many members are also buried wearing their Temple Garments.

The Temple itself is endowed with a great deal of mystical importance. Not every LDS church building is a Temple, as they are specially constructed in areas where there are large concentrations of Mormon people (the best-known and largest one being in Salt Lake City, Utah). Once a Temple is consecrated and officially opened, only members of the LDS Church in good standing are allowed to enter one. Within the Temple, there are places that are even more sacred, such as a series of rooms that follow the path of the fall and redemption of humanity, beginning in a Creation Room and ending in the Celestial Room. There are also "Sealing Rooms," in which Latter-Day Saints can be married or "sealed" to one another. The Sealing Room is almost entirely white—again representing purity—and contains mirrors that reflect one another, creating an "eternity" effect, as Mormon marriage is believed not to end with death but to continue forever.

The Temple and its related garments have elements of official church culture to them, even if they sometimes get used in folk ways (such as with the protective undergarments). Of more interest to those studying folk magic and mysticism are the numerous unofficial ways that Mormon culture gets expressed. Perhaps the strongest element of LDS folk culture is the use of narratives, which often have deeply embedded mystical elements. For example, most Mormon missionaries have stories they tell among themselves about temptations that nearly pulled them from their path while on their mission. (Most young Mormons go on a mission after high school and work in pairs at locations around the world.) Similarly, stories of the Three Nephites and their miraculous rescues often serve to reinforce the sanctity of the church, but they also make those who share the stories feel like part of a prophetic tradition.

There are also tales that represent the flip-side of the Mormon experience, darker tales that indicate the presence of curse figures or divine judgement. Stories recalling the tragic Mountain Meadows Massacre of 1857—in which Mormon settlers killed a party of travelers they had promised to safely lead through their land—involve figures like the Devil.[183] Other stories tell of the biblical Cain—who slew his brother Abel and was cursed with the "mark of Cain" in Genesis—roving the wilderness as nothing less than the folk creature known as Bigfoot![184] Still other tales feature the antisemitic figure of the "Wandering Jew" found in a number of European narratives, who was cursed with lasting life but an inability to rest for refusing to help Jesus during the crucifixion.[185]

182. Eliason and Mould, *Latter-Day Lore*, intro.

183. Dorson, *Buying the Wind*, 509–11.

184. Bowman, "A Mormon Bigfoot."

185. Dorson, *Buying the Wind*, 507–8.

The belief in cursing features heavily in personal narratives, too, and not just those associated with the past or biblical figures. Just as Temple Garments might save someone's life, the violation of a taboo in Mormon folk culture can lead to disaster. Since Latter-Day Saints are supposed to use Sunday as a day of rest (only attending church and spending time with their family or in religious service), any activity that violates that rest can bring harm. Stories of those who decided to go out to eat after church (even to a drive-through) or tried to do work at home often end with harrowing experiences like car crashes or house fires. Crucially, most of those stories are shared by those who lived them, and they are usually not seriously harmed, but take the events of the story as a warning against violating the interdiction on Sunday labor again. Similarly, not acting in the hospitable way expected of Latter-Day Saints can result in a curse, although that curse can take some truly strange forms, as when one woman refuses to help a "tramp" and finds that her yard is then overrun with Bermuda grass.[186]

Perhaps the most potent form of folk mysticism, however, aligns with Smith's: visions and dreams. While most Mormons are discouraged from engaging in active forms of divination (such as tarot cards), visions that appear through no action of the seer are thought to be divine in origin and potentially prophetic. The official LDS Church may investigate some visions to establish veracity, but on the whole visions are circulated in stories among Latter-Day Saints as a way of reinforcing their faith or carrying messages to one another about crucial issues like the death of a loved one, the potential of a future marriage prospect, or a spiritual danger. Even more common are the dreams that guide and shape Mormon life through the revelation of divine purposes. One of the best examples of such dreams are those experienced by Latter-Day Saints mothers. Because family is so central to the values of the church, large families are encouraged, but some women hesitate to have many children. Often, these women will have two or three children and then consider stopping, only to then be visited in a dream by either Heavenly Father (a name for God), Jesus, or a future unborn child. This then affirms the need to have more children to the mother, and many stories about meeting unborn children also state that the next child the mother has looks exactly like they did in the dream.[187] These "vision narratives" or "visionary narratives" are a way of connecting with the divine and understanding one's role or purpose better, and in many ways, they are part of a long tradition in Mormon history dating back to Smith himself.

Funeral Potatoes and the Folkloresque: Toward a Conclusion

The broader reach of Mormon folk culture is vast. It is impossible to cover all the various folk rituals of faithful Latter-Day Saints, ranging from serving a plate of "funeral potatoes" to the

186. Fife Folklore Collection, FMC Ser. I, v. 1, n. 31.

187. Brady, "Transformations of Power."

elaborate performances associated with creative dating proposals, which can involve flash mobs or campaign-style signs and slogans to ask someone to prom, homecoming, or other social events. The role of missionary selection and receiving one's missionary letter could merit its own extensive study; missionary letters can develop a talismanic quality of their own. There are highly symbolic aspects of Mormon city planning and architecture, and I feel almost entirely remiss about skipping over the folkloresque romanticization of the past found in the Pioneer Day celebrations. There are dark sides left unexplored in this essay as well, such as the church's racist past. (It largely excluded Black members from any sort of official power or even membership until the 1970s, and its treatment of Native Americans has been patronizing and domineering at times.) Much more can be said on the history of Mormonism, and much more can be found by spending time exploring Mormon culture.

In the end, this essay has only briefly introduced you to the complex world of the Latter-Day Saints. While there are historical roots in folk magic that resemble what you will find elsewhere in this book, LDS members downplay any connections to magic or mysticism in their history or today. This likely stems from the fact that LDS followers have had to fight for over one hundred years to establish their identity, and outsiders have often focused on superstition or controversy to discredit Mormon culture. But the folk magic is there; it's just perhaps a little hidden, like the Temple Garments. Folk magic is a living, breathing tradition of Mormon folk mysticism, nonetheless.

FIELD NOTES
Fearsome Critters

Around the campfires of loggers, trail rangers, ranchers, and even RVers in the West, a newcomer might settle in for a meal after a long day to hear one of the older, more experienced hands start a story with something like, "It was the damndest thing I ever saw: a bird flying backward!" or, "Did you hear that? Something's moving out there in the trees." Another old-timer might join in and put a name to it, one that sounds nonsensical—at first. Words like "fillyloo" or "hidebehind" come up, and the novice might let a half-smile run across their lips before noting everyone else's dead-serious expressions. Slowly but surely, tales come out about beasts that sound more mythical than natural, with countless horns, devilish howls, and bizarre habits. Senior campfire attendees might even lead an expedition, with the camp acolyte in tow, to catch a wampus cat or a snipe.

They might as well be chasing a wild goose, though. In fact, they'd have a much better chance of catching the goose—because it actually exists. These are tales of what have come to be known as "fearsome critters," legendary creatures that are used to pull one over on those too wet behind the ears to know any better. Getting someone new to believe in the story or to participate in a chase is a hazing ritual for many folks. I remember being led on a snipe hunt (a sort of wild goose chase) at a summer camp when I was young, and I even heard rumors about an escaped Tasmanian devil running loose near the campgrounds.

So, what are some of these fearsome critters? Here's a handful of examples found in oral lore spread by migrant workers of the western plains:

Axehandle Hounds: Hairy, wolflike beasts that eat the unattended ax handles of errant loggers.

Belled Buzzards: Large vulturelike birds that have a bell around their neck, which portend doom and disaster if you hear them.

Cactus Cats: A type of wild bobcat that is covered in spines and is thought to get drunk on cactus milk.

Fur-Bearing Trout: A type of trout found in glacial streams said to grow a thick coat of fur to stay warm in winter.

Hidebehinds: Shadowy, narrow creatures that lurk just behind trees in dim forests, waiting to snatch away unwary travelers and lumber workers.

The Hodag: A horn-covered ferocious beast with huge fangs found in the woods of rural Wisconsin (and eventually revealed to be a hoax).

Hoop Snakes: A venomous serpent that rolls itself into a wheel to chase down its prey; you can only escape one by jumping through the gap in its center, supposedly.

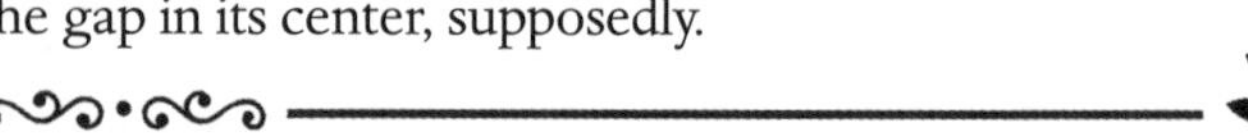

Jackalopes: Rabbits (or sometimes hares) with the antlers of deer protruding from their heads.

Skinwalkers: A creature from southwestern Indigenous lore such as that of the Diné (Navajo) people, usually thought to be a witch taking on a monstrous, animallike form. To even say or write its name is taboo; the name is only given here as an identification. The word is often written without vowels in printed contexts: sk*nw*lk*rs.

Splintercats: Large wildcats that have thick skulls they use to smash trees down in order to get at prey in the branches.

The Squonk: A lumbering warthog-like creature that is said to dissolve into a puddle of tears if anyone looks at it.

Upland Trout: A trout that leaves streams to make its nests in trees.

Wampus Cats: Large catlike creatures found in dense forests (or sometimes even in desolate areas, like deserts or decaying urban zones). They are sometimes said to be transformed women, and they can walk upright and scream and cry with a woman's voice.

Wendigo: Another creature whose name is not to be spoken, based on Algonquin-language lore about a carnivorous or cannibalistic spirit of the woods.[188]

Most of the stories are good-natured practical jokes, designed to break the ice for someone new to the group. Plenty of the fearsome critters seem to be made up entirely, but a few do have roots in older mythology and folklore, and even get magical attributes ascribed to them. The belled buzzard, for example, is an omen that may be based on Indigenous and Colonial descriptions of a mythic creature known as the Thunderbird (which may have been an actual species like the California condor). The jackalope has become something of a mascot for many parts of the West, and some places sell taxidermied creations that you can take home with you. Some of these creatures are deeply tied to lore about witchcraft and magic, as is the case in the sk*nw*lk*r stories in Indigenous contexts.

These creatures also belong to a wider phenomenon known as cryptids, short for cryptozoological creatures, which include Bigfoot and many lake and river monsters. Cryptids frequently represent an outgrowth of regional or local beliefs associated with particular legends and place-based spirits.

So go on that snipe hunt if they ask you to. You'll probably be plenty safe and end up the butt of a joke or two. But remember there may be a little more to the story than even the old-timers know.

188. For more on these, see Fee and Webb, *American Myths, Legends, and Tall Tales*; Tryon, *Fearsome Critters*; Randolph, *We Always Lie to Strangers*; Cohen, *The Encyclopedia of Monsters*.

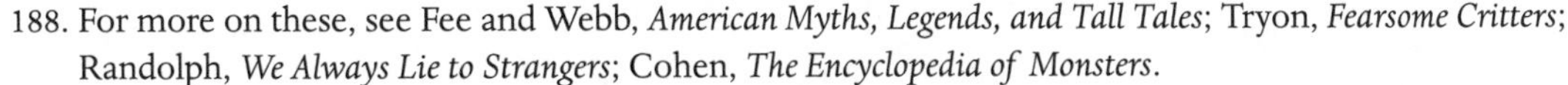

FIELD NOTES

Don't Touch My Hat, and Other Cowboy Superstitions

While many people may associate the cowboy figure with the Southwest, the Plains is one of the primary places where roping and riding are a part of everyday life. While cowboys, cowgirls, and cowfolk have a reputation for being no-nonsense and practical, they also have their fair share of superstitions. These beliefs have the patina of magic, as they often have to do with issues of luck or money (and even love). Some examples include:

- A cowboy should never set his hat on a bed, or else it will instantly cause a run of bad luck (or possibly even death).
- If one does put their hat on the bed, they must stomp the hat with their boots on in order to get rid of any bad luck. If that fails, they should burn the hat and get a new one.
- Some consider it unlucky to wear yellow, particularly when competing in rodeos or other dangerous activities. It's thought to signal cowardice.
- Eating chicken before a rodeo is a taboo. This may stem from the idea that a person doesn't want to be "chicken" in the arena (similar to the taboo about wearing yellow to avoid associations with fearfulness).
- Shave before going out on a trail ride, doing a rodeo for money, or meeting a possible love interest for the first time. (This makes you presentable to Lady Luck.)
- Some cowfolk burn their hats upon the birth of their first child in order to provide it with good luck throughout its life. (This is lore shared by other groups, like miners.)
- A cowboy shouldn't wear a new hat to a rodeo, nor should they use a new rope in competition.
- A cowboy will have one hat that is a "lucky" hat. If that hat is lost or unavailable, it's a sign that it's bad luck to ride without it that day.
- A hat should be put down upside down, with the brim up and the head-hole exposed, so that your luck won't run out.
- Never touch another cowboy's hat. It's bad luck and it can get you punched, kicked, or worse!
- Never give an open knife to another person. Always pay at least a penny for a knife. Also, never give a knife as a gift or you will sever a friendship or luck.

- Don't ride in a rodeo with change in your pocket or else that will be all the money you get. Similarly, don't carry around fifty-dollar bills or you won't win anything.
- Put on your right pant leg and right boot first so that you will always be starting off on the right foot.
- If snakes come out of their holes and head to high ground, watch for rain to follow soon.
- A thick swarm of butterflies or "heel" flies on cattle indicates rain is coming soon.
- A number of cows lying down on the ground indicates a big storm on the way.[189]

189. Dobie, "Weather Wisdom of the Texas-Mexican Border," 87; Dewey, "Many Riders Proudly Go Against Common NFR Superstitions"; Penrod, "Folk Beliefs about Work, Trades, and Professions from New Mexico," 180–83.

TRAVELING ON *Plains West*

As with any guidebook, there is always much more to experience than can be neatly fit into a chapter. To that end, we offer you this addendum to the map that will provide you with some tools to explore the Plains West further.

The glossary shares some keywords that might be useful. The places to visit will point you toward locations of interest that we think you might find valuable, and the reading recommendations provide you with some top-tier texts that can be used to dig in and learn more about this region.

Glossary

Baba Yaga: A witch figure found in a number of Central and Eastern European folktales. The Baba Yaga is helpful in some stories, but she can also be extremely dangerous to those who do not know how to interact with her.

cryptid: A legendary creature that some believe exists, usually tied to a particular region or cultural group.

domovoi: The Slavic household spirit(s) that often protect or aid a family. They are frequently placated with household offerings to avoid rousing them to mischief.

dvoeverie: A Slavic term for "dual-faith," representing the frequent mixture of both pre-Christian and Christian customs in many aspects of Slavic folklife.

fake lore: A term coined by folklorist Richard Dorson for folklore that doesn't originate from its purported group, but is created by outsiders about that group (e.g., Paul Bunyan and lumber workers).

fearsome critters: Legendary creatures, usually comical or absurd, used to haze newcomers to migrant work camps of the American West.

Ivan-tsarevich: The "little Tsar Ivan" who features as the hero of many Slavic folktales.

kws tshuaj: Practitioners of herbal-based folk healing within Hmong tradition.

leshii: In Slavic lore, the *leshii* are forest spirits that can be provoked by those trespassing in or harming their woodlands.

runes: A system of markings that operates as an alphabet in some contexts and a ritual form of writing or divination in others.

Rusalka: A Slavic siren figure that lures people into bodies of water to drown them.

The Salamander Letter: A forged document created by Mark Hofmann that alleged deep mystical connections between the Church of Jesus Christ of Latter-Day Saints founder Joseph Smith and magical treasure hunting. While Smith and his family did have a history with magical treasure hunting, the letter's contents were false and overstated the occult nature of Smith's work.

seer stones: A set of stones (also sometimes called "shew stones" or "peep stones") used by Latter-Day Saints' founder Joseph Smith to find and translate the golden plates that would become the bases for the Book of Mormon and subsequent articles of faith. Smith apparently used similar stones in earlier endeavors while treasure hunting in New York, but he associated the stones used in religious service with the biblical divination tools known as Urim and Thummim.

Slavic Native Faith: A Reconstructionist faith built on the reverence of pre-Christian Slavic deities, the use of a Slavic cultural calendar cycle and rituals, and the practice of Slavic-based divination and folk magic. It also has regional variants, such as *Rodnoverie* in Russia or *Dievturi* in Latvia.

txiv ua neeb: Hmong shamanic practitioners charged with protecting the spiritual well-being of their neighbors.

Temple Garments: Clothes and/or underclothes, usually white, that are reserved for special ceremonial occasions in the LDS church. They are sometimes believed to have spiritual powers or carry a divine blessing to those who wear them.

vision narrative: Originally, a vision narrative referred to one of the divine visions received by Joseph Smith when visited by the angel Moroni or the figures of God and Jesus. They can also refer to stories shared by members of the LDS church, especially women, who receive dreams regarding their future; these dreams often involve future children or a role within the church.

Places to Visit

Plan a Trip to "Paganistan," Minnesota: Because of the high concentration of magical folk, as well as a cosmopolitan community of immigrants from places like north-central Europe and Laos, the Twin Cities is home to a very diverse population. That includes diversity in beliefs, as this city boasts one of the largest Neopagan populations in the country, and thus has earned the nickname "Paganistan." There are lots of occult shops, and the headquarters of renowned new age publisher Llewellyn is just a few miles away in Woodbury, Minnesota.

Tip Your Hat to the National Cowboy & Western Heritage Museum in Oklahoma City, Oklahoma: If you're drifting across the plains, you might as well pull up to this museum, which showcases Western and Plains history. It provides a backdrop for Indigenous, Mexican American, African American, and European American peoples in the landscape, and it also features art, artifacts, and historical photographs exploring the wide range of behaviors and beliefs that influenced them all. If you keep your eyes open, you'll find discussions of luck, folk belief, weather lore, and more.

Walk the Garden of the Gods in Colorado Springs, Colorado: The grand red sheets and spires of the Garden of the Gods have impressed since at least the time of the Indigenous Ute people, who carved petroglyphs into the rocks. It's thought to be a place of power, used by the original inhabitants as a meeting place and neutral ground. It is currently a National Natural Landmark as well.

Watch the Skies near Skinwalker Ranch in Utah: If you're in the Ballard, Utah, area, you might want to keep an eye or two looking up because you are close to a UFO hotspot. While UFOs may not seem like they have a lot to do with folk magic, in this case there are a number of other supernatural legends associated with the 500+ acre ranch named after Indigenous shape-shifter myths. Some people report seeing beasts with red eyes at night or weird magnetic phenomena. At the very least, it is a good place to break out a protection amulet or two!

Peruse the Fife Archive at Utah State University: Austin and Alta Fife were giants in the area of early Mormon folklore research. As such, their massive collection of folk materials includes photos, texts, objects, recordings, and so much more related to Mormon culture (including beliefs that involve mysticism and magic-adjacent superstitions). If you can coordinate a visit to the archives at the Utah State University, you'll find lots of layers to the magical stories of this region. Stop by the William A. Wilson Folklore Archive at Brigham Young University for even more lore and materials!

Recommended Reading

Seasons of the Slavic Soul: A Quest for an Authentic Polish Spirituality by Claire M. Anderson
This short book is a personal examination of the Wisconsin-based author's Polish roots and a search for a spiritual (and occasionally folk magical) connection to her family history.

A Treasury of Western Folklore by B. A. Botkin
This is a hearty collection of folklore ranging from strange creatures and local legends of the West to cowboy poetry.

Latter-Day Lore: Mormon Folklore Studies by Eric A. Eliason and Tom Mould
A very academic book, but one that assembles a number of essays on a variety of LDS folklore topics, including vision narratives and Temple Garments.

Legends and Tales of the American West by Richard Erdoes
An excellent collection of folklore and legends from the West.

The Spirit Catches You and You Fall Down: A Hmong Child, Her American Doctors, and the Collision of Two Cultures by Anne Fadiman
This is a heartbreaking but valuable tale about what happened when the beliefs of the Hmong community in California were not listened to by established Western medicine, and vice versa.

Demystifying Hmong Shamanism: Practice and Use by Hmong Americans Across the Lifespan by Linda A. Gerdner and Shoua V. Xiong
An academic case study collection rooted in ten years of research, this text provides insight into the practices and cosmology of Hmong shamans and their communities.

Baba Yaga's Book of Witchcraft: Slavic Magic from the Witch of the Woods by Madame Pamita
This book primarily focuses on Slavic-rooted folk magic traditions and practices. Contemporary revisions bring those beliefs into the twenty-first century.

Early Mormonism and the Magic World View by D. Michael Quinn
While slightly dated, this is one of the first and best looks at the magical and folk history of the LDS cultural region.

CHAPTER 7

El Norte

Lechuzas y Barrancas: An Introduction to the Folk Magic of Mexico and the American Southwest

My father grew up in El Paso, and for many years my grandfather lived there as well. ("Big Daddy" was originally from Alabama, as the name probably indicates.) When we would visit him, we'd frequently look out across the basin of the Rio Grande and see Ciudad Juárez, the Mexican settlement on the other side of the river border. There were contrasts, of course, but there was also a sense that these were less two distinct cities than a single metropolitan unit with a strange divide forced between them. Gloria Anzaldúa, a Chicana poet, author, and activist, once noted that being a member of these border zones meant having a fluency in nearly a dozen different dialects and languages because you connected to so many different cultures in one space.[190]

Beyond the space around the Rio Grande, there are a variety of landscapes: deserts in Arizona, snow-capped mountains in New Mexico, and rich farmland in Chihuahua. Not to mention the crackling electric neon of a place like Las Vegas, which has likely been home to more magic than most would guess (and not just of the Siegfried and Roy variety).

The history of the lands that make up the El Norte region—including large sections of Mexico (Baja California, Durango, Chihuahua, Coahuila, Sinaloa, Nuevo León, Tamaulipas, and Sonora)—is one of violent conflict, annexation, invasion, settlement, resettlement, and division. Yet it is also a history of movement, migration, family, connection, and exchange. Culture on both sides of the official border is often remarkably similar. The specter of La Llorona—the weeping woman aching for her children while also threatening to drown any others she finds—haunts the *barrancas* (canals or waterways) of both Mexico City and Austin. Mothers tell their children to be wary of the *lechuzas*—owl witches—coming to their windows at night to summon them from their beds (with firm warnings to never go outside at night when something is calling their name).

The magic here has commonalities on both sides of the border as well. We may not immediately see how a *limpia* cleansing done by a *curandero* is like an apple-headed doll, but both are often used to help pull evil influences from a person (such as the dreaded *mal de ojo*). There are also strong connections to family and tradition, and a desire to carry forward the work of the past. Celebrations like *Día de los Muertos* invite connections to ancestors for those within Mexican and Mexican American culture, while household shrines and talking to the spirits of one's grandparents can make those connections for others.

On the road through this region, you'll be meeting practitioners who emphasize both the similarities and differences we can see among the magical work found in places like west Texas, New Mexico, Arizona, Southern California, and Nevada, as well as the Northern Mexico states. First, we will visit Fresno (by way of Northern Mexico) as we meet contemporary *curandera* Ixotii

190. Anzaldúa, *Borderlands/La Frontera*, chap. 5.

Paloma Cervantes, who discusses some of the ways that her traditional Mexican healing practices have evolved in the lands of sunny California. We'll also encounter Eliseo "Cheo" Torres and Mario Del Ángel Guevara, two scholars and practitioners of traditionally rooted but contemporarily practiced Curanderismo who offer some broader regional history as well as a closer look at the hallmarks of their practice.

In both of these essays, the emphasis is very much on seeing how magical components fit into the greater worldview around them. For Paloma, that involves connecting the traditions she learned in Mexico to the contemporary needs of her Southern California community (which sometimes has a messy relationship with those traditions). For Cheo and Mario, this means looking to cultural expressions of folk ailments, such as *susto*, to understand why the magical practices fit the way they do. Along the way I'll share some Southwestern stories and even a few lucky charms, just in case you stop by the glittering wonderland of Las Vegas.

This region is vast and full of life, energy, and magic—we can hardly capture it all in these few pages. As we pass through these borderlands, I hope you will remember that borders are artificial, man-made, and political, and seldom stand in the way of magic. The enchantment of El Norte moves freely, like a *lechuza*, and finds its home on either side of the Rio Grande.

FIELD NOTES

La Guadalupe, Compassionate Mother of the Americas

One of the most revered figures in all of folk Catholicism—and a figure deeply associated with Curanderismo, Hechiceria, and Brujeria—is the figure known as La Virgen de Guadalupe (or sometimes simply "La Guadalupe" or "La Guadalupana"). She is an apparition of the Virgin Mary who appeared to a Chichimec peasant named Cuāuhtlahtoātzin (later called Juan Diego in Spanish) in the late fifteenth century. She asked him to get the local priest to build her a chapel on the site where she appeared, and after two failed attempts, she filled his *tilma* (cloak or apron) with roses. When Juan Diego went to show the priest the roses that had bloomed in December, they spilled out and left an image of the Holy Virgin on his clothes.

La Guadalupe is one of the "dark Madonnas," images of the Virgin Mary with black, brown, or bronze skin. She may have some roots in Aztec mythology, although she is largely understood to be the primary product of Catholic folk belief. She is considered the patroness of the Americas, offering miraculous intercession to any who come to her and especially favoring the poor and oppressed. La Guadalupe is invoked to provide compassion and comfort to anyone in need and is thought to be able to provide miracles even in the direst of circumstances. Many people offer her medals, candles, rosaries, acts of devotion and pilgrimage, and even tattoos to show their love and devotion to her.

The *tilma* of Juan Diego is still on display in the Basilica of Our Lady of Guadalupe in Mexico City on Tepeyac Hill (where she had asked for the chapel to be built), and while it is woven of natural fibers, it has not significantly degraded over the years.[191]

191. Illes, *Encyclopedia of Mystics, Saints & Sages*, 329–32.

Curanderismo: Latinx Spiritual/ Energetic Rituals that Heal

ELISEO "CHEO" TORRES AND
MARIO DEL ÁNGEL GUEVARA

We define Curanderismo as the practice and belief of Latinx, especially Mexican, traditional medicine. The word *Curanderismo* is derived from the Spanish word *curar*, which means "to heal." What makes Curanderismo unique is that it is a holistic approach to healing a person's body, mind, and spirit. When we mention spirit, we are also including the term *energy* that some healers use. Others may use the word *soul*, and in certain treatments they refer to soul retrieval, which means that a person has lost their soul and the rituals are intended to return the soul to the body.

How does one become a *curandero/a*? A *curandero/a* is a person who practices Curanderismo, traditional medicine. They have apprenticed under a senior healer for several years and have learned to use herbs, rituals, and other elements to bring balance to a person's health. At times, a person is considered to have a *don*, a gift to become a healer. Nowadays, there are schools that prepare healers for their profession, such as *El Centro de Desarrollo Humano hacia la Comunidad* (The Center for Community Human Development), located in Cuernavaca, Morelos, Mexico. The authors of this essay have spent time in the Center and have met a number of instructors and attended some of their classes.

History and Influences of Curanderismo

In the year 1519, the Spaniards arrived in Mexico, bringing with them a knowledge of medicinal plants and rituals that they had learned from the Moors from northern Africa, who had control of Spain for about eight hundred years. Unfortunately, the Spanish culture clashed with the Indigenous people in a number of areas, such as religion, medicine, art, etc. By the year 1521, Tenochtitlan, the capitol of the Aztec empire and what is now known as Mexico City, was destroyed by the Spaniards, including knowledge of some three thousand medicinal plants.

In the year 1552, a short time after the conquest of Mexico by the Spaniards, an Aztec doctor named Martin de la Cruz wrote the first medical journal on medicinal plants, listing 251 herbs.

The natives of Mexico during this time were brilliant in their knowledge and research of medicinal plants. This book was called *Codex Badiano* because a scribe of Martin de la Cruz translated it from the Native language of Nahuatl to Latin, the language of the school. A codex is an ancient manuscript that was handwritten before the modern book was invented. The *Codex Badiano* was written on Amate bark in lieu of paper.[192]

A number of cultures have contributed to the rich practice of Curanderismo. Here are seven influences of Curanderismo:

1. The first influence is a blend of Native American and Spanish roots, as mentioned previously. The natives of Mexico had a vast knowledge of medicinal plants and wrote the first medicinal journal, *Codex Badiano*, about herbal plants. They experimented and researched a number of medicinal herbs. The Spaniards learned medicinal plants and rituals from the Moorish North African culture that controlled Spain for several hundred years. When the Spanish arrived in Mexico, both cultures blended their knowledge of medicinal plants and ritual, creating what we refer to nowadays as Curanderismo.
2. The second influence is a Judeo-Christian influence that the Spaniards introduced to the natives. In this influence, the *curandero/a* believes they have a gift from the almighty and that God helps during their treatments. They may say "It's not me doing the healing; I am just an instrument of God performing this treatment."
3. The third influence is the Greek humoral belief in a balance of hot and cold within the body. When the body is out of balance, a person becomes sick. In order to treat a hot illness, cold remedies are used, and vice versa.
4. The fourth influence is Arabic. It was brought by the Spaniards, who were influenced by Moorish culture. The belief is that there is a direct psychic energy projected by one person onto another that causes illness. For example, in the belief of the evil eye, a person can stare at a baby and make the baby ill. The infant may suffer from diarrhea, irritability, or fever.
5. The fifth influence is a blend of Catholic saints and African orishas that are used during healing ceremonies. This practice is evident in areas of the United States that practice Santería (also known as Regla de Lucumí), such as Florida, Louisiana, and other states and countries that have a large number of Afro-Latino Caribbean populations.

192. Chavarría and Espinosa, "Cruz-Badiano Codex and the Importance of the Mexican Medicinal Plants."

6. The sixth influence is a spiritualist and psychic influence where a *curandero* may channel spirits and communicate with them during the healing process. We believe that this influence comes from a Frenchman by the name of Allan Kardec, who wrote his first book on Spiritism in the mid 1800s.
7. The seventh and last influence is scientific. *Curanderos/as* have studied and possibly apprenticed under a nurse or a physician and know germ theory, biomedicine, and psychology, and will be able to refer some patients to modern allopathic physicians.

Spiritual and Energetic Cleansings (*Limpias*)

The definition of a *limpia* in Spanish means a cleansing. You can clean a home by sweeping and mopping, or you can do a cleansing of a negative or evil spirit in a home by using certain elements, such as burning plants in different parts of the home and allowing the smoke to cleanse the air, causing evil spirits to vanish. You can also use what is common in Mexico: copal incense.

Copal is a resin that is derived from the copal tree found in certain regions in Mexico. The copal can be found in different types such as white copal, brown copal, and black copal. The most common is white copal, which comes in a resin form. This custom has been used for centuries in Mexico and is even burned in churches during certain ceremonies, including funerals. The copal is usually burned in an incense burner, called *sahumerio* or *popoxcomitl* in the Native language of the Aztecs, Nahuatl. During the smoke-cleansing of the person, there is continuation of a prayer, chant, or song that asks the smoke to carry the unwanted energy to the universe.

You can cleanse a person who may be experiencing certain symptoms such as headaches, nervousness, irritability, and insomnia. In performing a *limpia* on a person, sage, copal, or sweetgrass can be burned to allow the smoke to cleanse the energy and negative vibrations of the person receiving the *limpia*. The belief is that during a traumatic experience, the person lost their spirit or soul, and the process of the *limpia* will allow the spirit to return to the body.

Another element that can be used in a cleansing is an egg. An egg is considered the largest living cell; therefore, it is being sacrificed during the *limpia*. The egg absorbs negative energy or vibrations from the body. It is rubbed on the person from head to toe, doing small crosses on the joints of the person. This is done along with a prayer, chant, or the sounds of the chakras. It is common belief that the egg represents the element of wind and pulls and absorbs energy. There is no correct way to do a *limpia*; the most important thing to remember is the positive intentions one has in doing the ritual. At the conclusion of a *limpia*, the egg is broken in a glass of water and the contents are buried outdoors, thrown in a river, flushed down the commode, or thrown on the form of a cross at a road crossing.

Water can be considered a spiritual drink and has been used as such by *curanderos* for years, such as the famous Don Pedrito Jaramillo, who lived in South Texas and is considered one of the most famous *curanderos* in history. Some *curanderos* take water into their mouth and spray it on the patient's back, in front of the neck, into open hands, and onto the navel and feet; others use a spray bottle for sanitary and safety reasons. This practice is called "the breath of life" because when the water is sprayed, there is a surprise and shock element from the person receiving the *limpia*. Some *curanderos* use bathwater on the person, called Florida water, and others prepare their own scented water spray using rosemary or lavender oil.

Aromatic plants such as sage, lavender, rosemary, and basil can be used to sweep the body during cleansing rituals. You can use a single plant or a combination of plants for the cleansing. The plants contain positive energy that comes from the earth, and the aroma of these plants impact the person's energy. Some healers soak the plants in water during the sweeping process of the body. The person's legs are lightly hit with the bundle of aromatic plants on the back all the way to the feet as the *curandero/a* asks the spirit of the person to return to its body.

Another element is a candle offered by the healer, who tells the person that the candle is a symbol of light that destroys all negative vibrations including fear, anger, insecurity, and anxiety that could be causing the illnesses and problems that are to be discarded by the *limpia*. All of these negative emotions and feelings will be burned when the candle is lit at home before going to bed. (This candle should be put out before falling asleep.)

To perform a *limpia*, one can use only the plants, egg, water, candle, and incense, or a combination of these elements, or all five elements. There is no right way to perform the *limpia*. This ritual can be done once, or it can be repeated two or three days in a row, depending on the severity of the problem. People receiving the *limpia* feel much better afterward, and testimonials have indicated that many have been cured of a traumatic experience after this healing process is performed on them. Some healers say, "The *limpia* does not harm you, but it can help you."

Folk Illnesses and Their Treatments in Curanderismo

The rituals already discussed can be used in a variety of settings, but there are specific applications for some rituals that arise when facing certain folk illnesses. These illnesses are not necessarily seen as purely medical diagnoses, but holistic ones requiring an understanding of a person's mind, body, and spirit in conjunction. Two of the most common of these folk illnesses and their particular treatments are listed here.

The Evil Eye (Mal de Ojo)

One of the problems that can be treated with a *limpia* is the *mal de ojo*, or evil eye. Generally, there is nothing evil in the cause of the evil eye. It is when a person stares at another, especially an infant, and fails to touch the person, which would neutralize the negative vibration that may cause *mal de ojo*. The symptoms of *mal de ojo* can be a headache, irritability, fever, insomnia, or vomiting. In treating *mal de ojo*, one can use a *limpia* technique and one element, usually the egg that was described earlier. Aromatic plants, copal incense, water, or a candle could also be used for the *limpia*.

Fright and Shock (Susto)

In the publications *Healing with Herbs and Rituals: A Mexican Tradition* and *Curanderismo: The Art of Traditional Medicine without Borders*, *susto* is defined as "a loss of spirit or even loss of soul or shock."[193] Some sociologists refer to it as "magical fright."[194] *Susto* could also be caused by a traumatic experience that brings about stress, nightmares, insomnia, anxiety, and fear. For some, it is akin to what some might be labeled post-traumatic stress disorder (PTSD). These experiences can lead to other serious illnesses if not treated in a timely fashion.

There are professions that experience *susto* on a frequent basis, such as law enforcement, firefighters, health professionals such as physicians and nurses, religious personnel such as priests and pastors, and soldiers returning from active duty. Receiving shocking news, experiencing a robbery or burglary, or witnessing a shocking event could be other causes of *susto*. It should be noted that the belief is that the spirit leaves the body during a traumatic experience, and a *susto* ritual will allow the person's spirit to return.

Some *curanderos* believe that, if not treated in a timely fashion, *susto* could lead to a serious illness or even death. The term they use is *susto pasado*, or a past *susto*, and a more intensive ritual will have to be performed on the person, such as a treatment for *espanto*.

Susto involves a number of different ritual techniques. The *limpia* is a universal technique used to treat the malady of *susto*. Aromatic herbs used for this treatment can be rosemary, rue, basil, and rose. A well-known *curandera* from Mexico City places the petals of roses in a glass container and fills it with rubbing alcohol in order for the plant to release its properties. The container is kept in a dark, cool environment for about two weeks before being poured into a spray bottle. The person receiving the *limpia* is asked to lie facedown with a warm white sheet covering the body and is sprayed with the fragrant herb potion.

This ritual is usually done outdoors when the sun is at its hottest point. Along with a prayer or soothing song, the body is swept with fresh aromatic plants and sprayed with the fragrant rosewater. Some spray the rosewater on the plants and brush the body with the wet plants from head to toe while reciting the prayer or the song. The healer may ask the patient to remember the incident that caused the *susto* and continuously reminds the person to take deep breaths and to

193. Torres, *Healing with Herbs and Rituals*; Torres, *Curanderismo*.

194. Gillin, "Magical Fright."

exhale slowly as the body is brushed with the plants. The bundle of plants is then used to lightly tap from the person's back all the way to the legs while the *curandero* calls out the person's name and requests that their spirit returns to the body. This process is repeated faceup.

The final step is to place copal incense in an incense burner (*sahumerio*) and cleanse the person's body with the copal smoke, continuing with the prayer or song. The belief is that the copal smoke will take the negative vibrations of the person to the universe and cleanse the body of any negative energy still remaining from the *susto* experience.

After the ritual is completed, the patient is given a hot cup of herbal tea for relaxation. The tea used by most healers is passionflower tea. Other the types of tea that can be given are chamomile, peppermint, or linden flowers.

This treatment takes approximately one hour and can be repeated for three to four consecutive days if the trauma is serious. Many times, families or partners are invited to observe and/or participate in the rituals. If relatives are not present, neighbors or friends can also be invited. This is a holistic approach to healing the body, mind, and spirit with support from loved ones.

Day of the Dead (*Día de los Muertos*): A Example of Ritual in Healing Grief

In recent years, many American cities with large Hispanic/Latinx populations have begun to celebrate the Mexican Day of the Dead (*Día de los Muertos*). The celebration includes altars to remember loved ones, parades with many dressed as skeletons, a number of traditional foods such as *pan de muerto* (sweet bread in the form of a skeleton) and sugar skull candy, and Mexican traditional drinks such as *champurrado*, a thick chocolate porridge made with cornmeal or corn *masa* (dough). This tradition is borrowed mostly from Mexico but is also celebrated in other Latin American countries around the world.

In Mexico, this celebration is believed to have started with the Mesoamerican cultures. The belief was that there were two worlds, one where the earth is located and the second one with thirteen skies and nine hells. The Aztec culture believed that death was actually another stage of life and that during the year, the spirits would return to earth and join their families for a few hours before returning to one of their worlds. Therefore, grief was dealt with as a celebration when the spirit would return to their families. Nowadays, the tradition continues with some modifications, such as the creation of an altar. An altar may include three levels, with photos of the loved ones on the first level, food that was enjoyed by the deceased, flowers, candles, and incense on the second level, and a path of yellow or orange marigold flowers and candles on the third level that would indicate to the spirits the path back to their loved ones.

In the Southwest, Latinx and other cultures are understanding how to use the Day of the Dead rituals to honor their deceased loved ones and to better grieve their loss by celebrating the memories of their loved ones once a year for a few hours. This celebration has healed many families that have difficulty grieving and remembering those that have left for the spirit world.

It should be noted that all of us experience grief during our lifetime and many people are unable to cope with it. That is why the Day of the Dead celebration is borrowed by many Americans in the Southwest: it offers them a yearly opportunity to celebrate and remember their loved ones and to celebrate their contributions while they were alive.

Ancient and Modern: Conclusions about Curanderismo

In this essay we have shared that Curanderismo is a holistic approach to healing mind, body, and spirit. In order to appreciate this topic, we have offered a brief history of Curanderismo and its influences. A unique aspect of Curanderismo is the healing of the spirit, soul, or energy using the ritual of a *limpia*, or an energetic/spiritual cleansing. Three rituals were discussed, with two involving *limpias*: *mal de ojo* (evil eye) and *susto* (magical fright). We also discussed healing grief through an ancient belief system and *Día de los Muertos*. A deep understanding of many effective rituals in Curanderismo can keep us healthy and offers a holistic approach to wellness.

FIELD NOTES

A Coyote Tale: Trickster Witches in the Southwest

There's a reason that the *Looney Tunes* cartoon character Road Runner always got away from his nemesis, and a reason that his rival was named Wile E. Coyote. The figure of the coyote has been present in the El Norte region since at least the time of the Aztecs, and likely long before. The animal's name comes from *Huehuecóyotl*, a Nahuatl word for a mischievous god of debauchery and trickery. In folktales that have been passed down, the coyote figure has been a trickster to both humans and gods.

In one Caddo story, he argues that Death should be allowed to keep human beings forever and manages to get his way by closing a door before spirits can return from the underworld. He is usually not the winner, however, as in one Apache story where he is tricked into fighting with a lump of tar-like pitch until he gets stuck.

Because of the coyote's ability to work both sides of the moral coin and the fact that he has associations with shape-shifting, trickery, and the underworld, he has also figured into stories about witchcraft and magic. Stories from the southwestern United States tell of sorcerers who would use a series of special hoops to transform back and forth into coyotes to go on raids in local villages, and one particularly feared shape-shifting ritual involves wrapping oneself in the pelt of a coyote to transform into a fast-moving monster.

Despite his propensity to be outwitted by an oversized roadrunner, the coyote's tales are the stuff of folklore and witchcraft in their Native contexts. That's a point worth remembering the next time you see him pause to hold up a little sign after running off a cliff.[195]

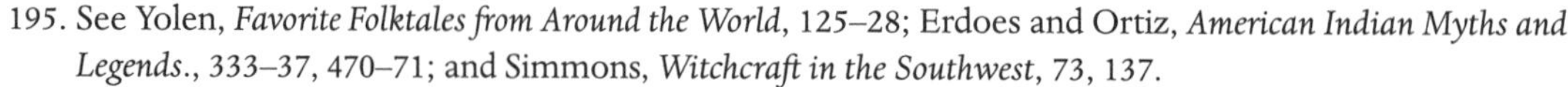

195. See Yolen, *Favorite Folktales from Around the World*, 125–28; Erdoes and Ortiz, *American Indian Myths and Legends.*, 333–37, 470–71; and Simmons, *Witchcraft in the Southwest*, 73, 137.

Tradicion, Salud, Energía: Principles of Curanderismo

IXTOII PALOMA CERVANTES

Hola! My name is Ixtoii Paloma Cervantes and I am a Curandera and a Mexican Shaman. I would like to share the Curanderismo tradition in the way that I was told to teach: in story form. Hidden in my story, you will find tons of information about this tradition. Enjoy!

What is Curanderismo? Or more specifically, Mexican Curanderismo? If you asked me a couple of years ago, I would have given you a different answer than today, and that is because Curanderismo is changing all the time. When I was invited to participate in this book, I felt so happy to share what Curanderismo is about because I consider this practice a beautiful way to live and improve our lives. My deep desire is for each person on this planet to have tools to improve their lives regardless of whether they follow Curanderismo or not. With that said, take what resonates with you in this essay and give it a try. Knowledge is nothing if we don't put it into practice.

Curanderismo is the ancient spiritual and healing tradition that is practiced in Mexico and in other parts of America. Nowadays it is extending and being practiced almost anywhere in the world. The Curanderismo that I am describing goes back to the ancestral people and culture of the Anahuac. Mexico is the cradle of the Anahuac civilization. The Anahuacas are the inhabitants of the Anahuac, and among these are the Mayans, Aztecs, Chichimecas, Olmecas, etc. The Curanderismo way of life is very old—thousands of years old. It has never died. It has never been rescued. It goes through changes all the time. It evolves. In fact, *that is its beauty and its secret for such a long life*. Unfortunately, in some areas, this tradition has been wiped out.

I wrote that Curanderismo is a "spiritual and healing tradition." That means that Curanderismo is a tradition in which spiritual and healing practices are performed as one thing. It is based on the observation of the Universe and nature and how they relate to each other in harmony. We call it *Mexican cosmology* or *cosmovision*. With the knowledge acquired from this observation, we work on describing, interpreting, and reproducing what we see in the cosmos and nature to understand life, and to bring healing and harmony back when things are not going well for us.

We should also look at the roots of the word *Curanderismo*. It comes from the Spanish word *curar*, which means "to heal." A person that heals with Curanderismo techniques is a Curandero for a male and Curandera for a female. In modern times, the terms *Curanderx* or *Curander@* are also used, although the *x* is preferred because it's not gender-exclusive.

When I was growing up, Curanderos were called *Tatich*, which translates as "master." We also have the *Nahual* or *Brujo*, which can be translated as a Mexican Shaman. A Nahual is more of a wizard; they're very knowledgable and powerful. Some people fear them—it's as if they were sorcerers. The name for sorcerers is also, unfortunately, Nahual.

When I was a child, the roles of a Curandero and a Curandera were different. Now things have changed, although there are one or two roles that are still assigned according to gender. For example, a *partera* (midwife) is for women and a *tiempero* (weather controller) is mostly for men. A *tiempero* is a person that helps when we need rain or we need to stop the rain if it is too much, like a storm or hurricane that may damage crops. Nowadays, most of the specialties in Curanderismo can be performed by anyone.

Becoming a Curandera

Curanderismo is not a religion. I am not an anthropologist, nor a historian, nor a researcher; I do not hold a title about Latin culture. I didn't learn this tradition from reading books or ancient codices. I learned in the old-fashioned way, and that is by oral tradition. That means having a mentor that also learned by oral tradition from his or her mentor. I can tell you that the Curanderismo practiced in Mexico is different than the one in the US. Whichever country I'm in, I work accordingly. I will explain the differences a little later.

In the old ways, when someone wanted to know if they could become a Curandero or Curandera, the first thing they would do is search for an experienced Curandero (or, preferably, an elder Nahual) to perform a special ceremony in which they asked the spirits if the person had what it took. Then the person would go through a series of trainings and tests until one day, their main mentor/maestro took them under his or her wing.

It is believed that a Curandero or Curandera is chosen by the spirit and that his or her abilities arise with events like a near-death experience or sickness. Other ways to become a Curandero are by coming from a family of Curanderos, or if a Curandero has a dream about someone having what it takes and the abilities. Curanderos must master the abilities to heal, overcome obstacles, and take care of negative energies. Having the *don,* or "gift," comes with a big responsibility for working on ourselves and on other people. Today, some Curanderos also go by will. That means someone feels the call and goes through an extensive training.

In some cases, when a person is born in a family of Curanderos, it is believed to be because the family was meant to teach the future Curandero. In fact, there is a ceremony to "see" what the baby is going to be when they become an adult. Traditionally, this is one of the first ceremonies we do in order to guide the child on their destiny.

Another way to learn is to find a Curandero or Curandera that you like and be persistent in asking to be taught. That is what I did with a couple of mentors that I had. Now, in modern times, we even have online classes. My advice to you is that if you are learning online, make an effort to practice and have private mentoring by a Curandera that you feel connected to. There are so many ways to be successful in the training of Curanderismo, and everything depends on both the teacher and the student.

In some areas, a weekend, a week, or a two-week training is enough for someone to be a Curandera. I believe there is nothing wrong with a two-week training as long as it is taken as an introduction and as an opportunity to start walking the path of Curanderismo and not as the end of the learning process. It takes years of learning and practice to become a good practitioner, so never stop learning; Curanderismo is a way of life.

I was trained in the old-fashioned ways. I can say that my training and my life as a Curandera was not my priority, nor was it my conscious choice. My mom used to say to me, "Do whatever you want because at the end, you will be working on this." So, I did. I was trying to prove her wrong, and in the process I learned so many things not related to Curanderismo.

I was also trained by different Curanderos. My main teacher is a Nahual. He is my dear maestro, Don Manuel Flores. (I changed his name in order to protect him and his family.) He came when I was in my thirties and already working as a Curandera. He looked for me because spirit told him that he needed to teach me the things I didn't know about Curanderismo. That is how the long and beautiful relationship between us started. Little did I know he was my relative, which was later discovered by a DNA test! At that time, he barely spoke Spanish, and to this day he doesn't know how to read or write.

From my mom, I learned ancient and modern ways that are used in Mexico in the healing techniques. We call this Curanderismo, *Medicina Tradicional Mexicana* (MTM), or Traditional Mexican Medicine. From her teachers, I learned ancient traditional ceremonies, initiations, and different ways of healing with energy and spirits. From Don Manuel, I learned more healing techniques that are very traditional, as well as the challenges that a strong Curandero faces in the spirit world in order to bring health to a client.

What a Curandera Does

Curanderismo is now practiced all over the world, but not so long ago it was only practiced in the Americas and Spain. We can consider it a complementary practice to allopathic medicine (often called "Western medicine"). For the best results, we combine both, depending on the problem to treat. Ideally, we use Curanderismo as preventive medicine, which means we use Curanderismo techniques to keep our immune system and ourselves strong, including the spirit, mind, and emotions.

In the Curanderismo world, there are different areas or types of practitioners. Because this is a healing modality, you can find Curanderos or Curanderas that work on the body like a *sobador* (masseuse), *huesero* (chiropractor), and *partera* (midwife). The ones that work with counseling and healthy habits are *consejeras* (counselors). The ones that work with things related to other realities and energy are *Chimanes*, *Nahuales*, and/or *Brujos* (Mexican Shamans).

The foundation of the Curanderismo practices is love and respect for everything and everyone. This is very important to remember at all times. When you are experiencing a moment of doubt, go back to this foundation of love and respect. From there, make your decision, and you will always be right and in alignment with the Universe.

We believe that everything is alive and has a soul and inner intelligence; that we are connected with everything by invisible lines of energy. We all pulse as one big heart, including the sun, the moon, the stars, and the whole Universe. We can charge the pulsing energy with different vibrations. As Curanderos, we work diligently to develop the ability to raise our energy to a high vibration. Love is the highest vibration; that is why Curanderismo's foundation is love. Take great note of this. When we are sick or out of alignment, the cause is a lack of love. Once the Curandera establishes a loving connection again, the immune system is stimulated to invite in healing.

A little note here before I carry on. In Mexico, we call the people that come to be treated by a Curandera "patients." Sometimes, besides calling us a Curandera, Chaman, Bruja, Nahual, etc., patients refer to us as *doctors* or *doctoras*. In the US, for legal purposes (depending on which state we live in), we call them "clients," and they call us a Curandera, Shaman, or Curanderismo practitioner.

Curanderismo is a very complex system used to bring the body back to health. In Mexico, you can find clinics and hospitals dedicated only to Curanderismo or to *Medicina Tradicional Mexicana* (MTM). Recently, it has been offered as a bachelor's degree at some universities. So, as you can see, it is as I said in the beginning: always changing and evolving.

I would like to be clear about the word *Curanderismo*. Although it is a Spanish word and the Spaniards used it to describe our practices when they came to Mexico, it refers to our ancient ways. In order to survive when the Spaniards came to Mexico, some of the practices merged with the Catholicism they brought. You will find Curanderismo practiced with Catholic prayers and saints as well as Curanderismo practiced with ancient spiritual tools like rattles and feathers.

Traditionally, when something happened, like when someone was sick or had a twisted ankle, the first choice was to go see a Curandera. If there was a missing object or person, a dying person, childbirth, a snakebite, depression and mental problems, emotional problems, family or love problems, indigestion, etc., you would visit a Curandera. Especially in my town, where there were no clinics or hospitals, you would go see a Curandera.

A Cautionary Tale

I remember when I was a child, there were some tourists in the ruins of Tulum in the Yucatán Peninsula. Their kid was bitten by a *cuatro narices* ("four noses") snake (*Bothrops asper*). That is a deadly venomous bite. At that time, the closest hospital was two and a half hours away. Even if the hospital had been nearby, the problem was that medical staff didn't know the remedy to treat a bite from a *cuatro narices*. In those times, the hospital staff came from big cities like Mexico City and were not familiar with local problems like snakebites, dengue fever, etc. Reliable and traditional remedies had been used effectively for thousands of years, so you can see why the first choice would be to go to the Curandera. At that time, the Curanderas were the only ones that knew how to prepare the remedy for a bite from a *cuatro narices*. If a bite from a *cuatro narices* snake is not treated within thirty minutes, the person will die. And that is exactly what happened. The parents did not trust a folk healer or Curandero and took a taxi, trying to rush to the hospital. Even with today's highways and faster cars, it would be impossible to make it in time. And so, the child died.

That story left a deep impact on me. In my own child's mind, I could not understand why they allowed their child to die. It was only then that my mom explained that some people don't believe or trust Curanderas. That was when I learned that outsiders did not believe in our ways. I thought to myself, *One day I would love to share what Curanderismo is about with the rest of the world.*

This is how life and the Universe work…Here, many years later, that is exactly what I am doing: I am practicing and teaching Curanderismo away from my homeland Mexico to outsiders. But don't think it has been easy. For years, I was bullied and a victim of hate crimes. I live in the US near so many people that are afraid of Curanderas.

An oddly wonderful thing that the pandemic of 2020 brought to my life is that Curanderismo is now more accepted because more people want to learn about natural ways of healing. Sadly, this also came with increased cyberbullying about if something is the "right" way to practice Curanderismo. With everything I've already explained, you know that there is no right or wrong way in Curanderismo because it is a tradition that evolves all the time. For me, what matters is the result. If a person feels better after receiving a *limpia con huevo* (energy cleansing with an egg), it does not matter if the eggs come from the supermarket or from someone who raises hens in the backyard.

My advice to you is to never believe anything until you experience it. This book is your opportunity to learn how many things there are to be experienced.

Learning the Many Ways of Curanderismo

From Don Manuel Flores, I learned things like *ventosas* (cupping); different Mexican massage techniques; *tomas*, or herbal potions; how to make amulets and *resguardos* (protections); different kinds of energy cleansing, or *limpias*; Mexican acupuncture with obsidian points; psychic surgery to boost the immune system after a physical surgery to speed the healing; *susto*, or recovering the lost soul; how to remove dark entities and energies from a person; and *levantamientos*, or how to remove a soul of a dead person that is trapped in someone's body. This last one, by the way, I was not looking forward to learning. I used to hide from my teacher so that I wouldn't have to learn it. He would knock at my door and I would pretend I wasn't home. Hours later, I would peer through the peephole to make sure he was not there before going outside. When I opened the door, he would be sitting on the floor, waiting. He would say "Ayyy, señora!" while shaking his head. He is the typical mentor: persistent, strong, loving, and cruel sometimes. Plus, being a Nahual, Don Manuel always knew where I was hiding and what exactly I needed to learn. We believe that a Nahual has special abilities, like reading your mind and traveling between realities and through time.

In these days, people interchange the term *Nahual* with *Brujo* as if it were the same thing. In the old days, a Nahual was a person that was educated and had a deep knowledge of the spiritual and healing practices, and a Brujo was a person that leaned the techniques and ceremonies without having a deep understanding or knowledge of the subject.

Don Manuel is the one that initiated me in the deepest parts of Nagualismo, which is the art of improving ourselves, managing energy, and working in different realities. In this part of Curanderismo, the art of dreaming is very important. Here is where we learn to control our dreams and also receive teachings through them. Don Manuel also taught me other things, like how to make rain, stop the wind, make things invisible, and bring animals back into places where civilization has changed so much that the animals went away. Let's say there is a new housing development being built and the construction company wipes out the trees and plants that animals use for feeding and living. Once the new houses are ready, the land around usually feels inert, with no life. As Curanderos, we have some ceremonies to bring back animals like hawks, eagles, and other wildlife.

I am sharing all these techniques to give you an idea of how interesting and broad Curanderismo can be. Although they might sound impossible, they are possible. Mastering the techniques only requires dedication and practice.

As a Curandera, I went through and am still going through initiations, healing ceremonies to align my body to be a better Curandera, more teachings, and tests that take me to my limits. In the end, what I can share with you is that although my life is crazy with so many challenges (just like everyone else—being a Curandera makes me no less human or more special), the overall feeling is of internal peace, wholeness, and a feeling of being alive and connected with the Universe, Mother Earth, my spiritual guides, ancestors, and helpers. Not to mention all the magical things that happen due to my connection with spirit! And this is what Curanderismo is about. I never feel alone or left behind because this connection is so strong. My wish for you is that you do not stop looking until you find something similar. No matter what the tradition is, Curanderismo or not, as long as you can feel what I just described, you will understand. I think a good beginning is this book, because you can have a little taste of so many things that are practiced these days.

Tea with the Curandera

I would like to finish by giving you the opportunity to see for yourself what Curanderismo is about. Here is an herbal tea and a personal ceremony for you to try.

In a traditional Curanderismo consultation in Mexico, the first thing the Curandera does is give the client tea. This tea is usually for relaxing because people are nervous when consulting a Curandera. After all, a consultation is usually about something super important to the client. When the consultation is over, we give a little bit of the herbal mixture to the client so they can prepare it at home.

In the US it is different. Depending on what state you live in, you most likely cannot give the client something homemade to drink. The main reason you should not serve tea or anything to eat/drink is because most people that come to experience a Curanderismo ceremony have not experienced anything like it before. They are not used to energy work, and the energies can be so intense that people feel dizzy, tired, hungry, and drained. These symptoms are sometimes taken as one of two things:

1. That the healer "added something" to the tea: some kind of plant that had effects like a hallucinogenic.
2. That the healer "did something" to bewitch or hex the person. This is what happens: people come for healing and cleansing of negative energies, and they leave feeling good. Then, they usually do not follow instructions like drinking plenty of water, not drinking alcohol, and things like that. As a result, they go back to the way they were before. Then they blame us when they get sick again. Some people are in difficult situations or in a lot of pain, and their way of acting can be very hurtful and even revengeful against the Curandera or Curandero who was trying to help.

So, I would not recommend offering homemade tea to a client. This is a preventive way to protect yourself. As a result, sadly, I always skip this step in my consultations. But I can share the tea recipe with you here!

Please remember this is not a medical recommendation, only a traditional preparation of a tea used in Curanderismo. The traditional tea is a mixture of equal parts dried lavender (*Lavandula angustifolia*), lemon balm (*Melissa officinalis*), and any kind of mint (*Mentha* spp.). Sometimes we add chamomile (*Matricaria chamomilla*) or rose petals. Add the herbs to a container and shake it to mix them. Choose a container that can keep the herbs dry, and keep them away from the light because some herbs lose their properties when exposed to light for a long period. We use equal parts, but you can play with the proportions until you find a flavor that you love.

When it is time to serve the tea, grab the container with your hands and bring it to your chest (heart chakra). Say a prayer asking the spirits of the herbs to bring their medicine to this tea. Remember, the foundation of Curanderismo is *love*. Think about something that produces love in you and transfer that love from your heart to your hands, and from there to the container with the tea, until you feel the container vibrating with love.

To prepare the tea, bring one cup of water to a boil. Turn the heat off and add a pinch of the tea mixture. For us, a small pinch is whatever amount three fingers can grab (less than a quarter of a teaspoon). Cover and let it steep for a couple of minutes.

To serve the tea, pour it in a cup. You can add honey, or sugar, or nothing—whatever you prefer.

You can use this tea at home to relax before going to sleep. Drink it at least an hour before going to bed. It is safe and does not create any dependency.

Some people have allergies to certain herbs, so feel free to change the ingredients. If you don't know if you are allergic to these herbs, you can make a separate tea for each herb. Then measure a teaspoon of one of the teas and apply it to the inner part of your arm and wait twenty minutes. If the skin becomes red, you may be allergic to that herb.

A Curandera's Cleansing, *Una Limpia con Vela*

This is a ceremony to cleanse ourselves from negative energies. Usually, a Curandera does this ceremony for her clients when many things are going on in the client's life. The negative energy can come from our own thoughts and emotions or from outside ourselves; it is the energy we may "grab" from our surroundings. If the ceremony is performed correctly, we should feel light and peaceful when it's done.

You will need to set up an altar in the same way you usually do. If you have never set up an altar or you would like to try a Curanderismo-style altar, then get a red bandanna and set it on a flat surface. In the center, put a white candle; it represents the energy of the divine.

Align the altar to the directions north, south, west, and east. You can use a compass for this, or open a compass app on your phone.

In the east, you are going to add something that represents the element of fire. An incense burner, another candle, a piece of resin, or an incense stick will all work.

In the west, you are going to add something that represents the earth element, like seeds, flowers, or fruits.

In the north, place the element of wind. You could use a flute, a feather, or something similar. Traditionally, we use a conch to represent the wind. It can be played by blowing into it.

In the south, we have the element of water. This could be a bowl filled with water.

You can also add anything that you feel will increase the power of the altar, like rocks, crystals, rattles, or any special thing you have.

Next, take another white wax candle in a clear glass, separate from the white candle on the altar. This is the one you are going to use for the cleansing, or *limpia*. You will also need a lighter or matches and something pointy to write on the wax of the candle; a pen or the tip of a knife will do.

When you have all the materials set up on your altar, put on some inspiring music, turn your phone on silent mode, and take a moment for yourself. Then you may begin the *limpia*.

1. Light the candle that is in the middle of the altar.
2. Close your eyes and breathe several times, as deep as you can, to reset yourself and be present in your ceremony. Try to breathe deeply until you feel relaxed.
3. Generate the energy of love by thinking about something that produces feelings of love. Then grab the glass white candle with both hands and hold it close to the center of your chest. Do a prayer asking the spirit guardians of Curanderismo to help you release all negative energies. Address the prayer to spirit helpers and ancestors, introduce yourself, say what you want to remove and what you want to attract, and always finish your prayer with gratitude. Here is an example of such a prayer:

   > Grandfather Creator, Grandmother Creator, Spirit Guardians of all directions, Spirits of the elements Fire, Earth, Wind, and Water, my Spirit Guides, my Ancestors, Spirit animals, and Protectors, it is me, [full name]. I am coming this day with good intentions and respect. I have offerings on my altar for you. I am sending this prayer asking for assistance in releasing all the negative energies that I may be carrying.
   >
   > Please help me release and transform the negative energies due to my thoughts, negative emotions, sickness, and anything that I may have grabbed that does not serve me.
   >
   > I ask that this candle turns into a magnet to grab all my negativity, and as I burn the candle, this negativity is transformed in *love*.
   >
   > Also, I ask that the space that this negative energy leaves is filled up with blessings of health, peace, love, abundance, and happiness.
   >
   > Thank you for all the blessings, and I pray that these blessings also reach anybody that needs them as I do.

4. After you say your prayer, keep your eyes closed and try to feel the energies coming from the divine into the candle. Stay there until you feel the vibration or

energy of love is very strong. It might feel like a tingling sensation, a change in temperature, a vibration, etc. If you don't feel anything, that is okay; remember, you are learning something new and the only way to master it is to practice. So, keep going. You may want to try repeating this ceremony on another day.

5. Once you feel the energies, allow a moment for these energies to charge the candle. When the candle feels like it is vibrating, grab your sharp object (a pen or the tip of a knife) and write your name, date of birth, and the city where you were born on the wax. Write over your words if there is no space. The candle is ready.
6. Set down your sharp object and grab the candle. Rub your body with it as if it was bar soap, starting with the head and working your way down to the feet. Try to be very precise and cover as much of your body as you can. (It will be very tricky on the back.)
7. Once you are done, put the candle on the west part of the altar. This is the direction that helps get rid of what we no longer need. Make sure the candle is in a safe position, then light the candle and go and take a shower.
8. Allow the candle to burn at the altar for as long as you can. If you're worried about the placement of your candle, find a safe place where it can keep burning. It could be in a fireplace. If you don't have a safe place, you can light your candle for a couple of hours each day so you can supervise the candle to avoid any accidents.
9. When all the wax is gone, the ceremony ends. This may take days, depending on the size of the candle and how many hours a day you can leave the candle to burn. Each time you light the candle, say the same prayer.
10. A successful ceremony has occurred when the candle glass is clear. If yours is not like that, then get another candle and start all over. Repeat this ceremony until you get a clear glass.

La Vida de una Curandera

This is my life and my experience as a living example of this tradition. I carry my ways, which I call my medicine, everywhere I go. Prejudice against Curanderos has helped me develop a strong, compassionate, loving heart. I hope you learn something new from this book that you are willing to try and learn for yourself. Live your life as if it was your last day. Always give thanks to the Great Creator and to Mother Earth for the precious opportunity to be a part of this beautiful Universe. Remember, we are all connected and beating together, with love, as one big heart. Enjoy it.

FIELD NOTES

Baby Needs a New Pair of Shoes, or Lucky Charms in Sin City

If you're heading to Las Vegas and planning to play the slots while you're there, you might want to take along a gambling charm or two! Here are some examples of lucky charms found in North American folk magic:

- A horseshoe.
- A four-leaf clover.
- A two-dollar bill dressed with money oil.
- A rabbit's foot dressed with lucky oil, preferably a back foot.
- A red flannel bag filled with a lucky coin, collard seeds, and some tobacco, dressed with the urine of a woman (preferably pregnant).
- A racoon's baculum (penis bone).
- A badger's tooth.
- A buckeye carried in your right pocket.
- An image of a frog or a frog bone.
- A *maneki-neko*, or "lucky cat" figure.
- A dried alligator foot holding a silver dime, wrapped in red thread.
- A High John the Conqueror root.
- A sprig of cinquefoil (five-fingered grass) carried in your wallet.
- A prayer card of Saint Cajetan.

One well-known lucky charm for gambling is a nutmeg filled with mercury and sealed with wax. Mercury is poisonous and evaporates quickly in air, so this is not a charm one should mess around with today—at least not in its original form. However, it's easy to adapt this by simply drilling a hole in a whole nutmeg, slipping a bit of silver or a silver dime into it, and sealing it up again. You could substitute other lucky charms, like a four-leaf clover or a two-dollar bill dressed with money oil, to update this old charm.

Additionally, gambling can be fun, but it can also become a serious problem for those who face gambling addiction. If you or someone you know is struggling with gambling, please call 1-800-522-4700 to reach the National Problem Gambling Helpline (or visit them on the web at www.ncpgambling.org).

TRAVELING ON
El Norte

As with any guidebook, there is always much more to experience than can be neatly fit into a chapter. To that end, we offer you this addendum to the map that will provide you with some tools to explore El Norte further.

The glossary shares some keywords that might be useful. The places to visit will point you toward locations of interest that we think you might find valuable, and the reading recommendations provide you with some top-tier texts that can be used to dig in and learn more about this region.

Glossary

Brujeria: A word that translates as "witchcraft" but involves a wide complex of magical practices. Brujos can do many of the tasks a curandero can do, but they may also do work for love, lust, revenge, or justice that are beyond the typical scope of their healer counterparts.

Curanderismo: The folk magic healing practices associated with traditional Mexican American culture. These can involve the treatment and removal of both physical and spiritual diseases, as well as cultural functions such as blessings or honoring the dead.

Día de los Muertos: A mid-autumn celebration that translates as "Day of the Dead." It honors ancestors and the deceased in Mexican and Mexican American culture. It frequently involves skeletal symbolism, feasting, dancing, visiting family plots in the cemetery, and making offerings to the dead.

folk saint: A holy figure that has not been officially recognized by the church. Santa Muerte and other folk saints often have very devoted followings, despite attempts to eradicate their reverence.

Hechicería: The practice of using folk magic to accomplish day-to-day needs within Mexican American folk tradition. Hechiceras use spoken charms, spells, and prayers as well as some physical objects (like red thread or certain herbs or roots) to help with problems related to love, luck, money, justice, and more.

hierbera: Term for someone specializing in herbal remedies and plant medicine in Mexican and Mexican American healing practices.

lechuza: A folkloric creature known as a "witch owl" that frequently terrorizes children. It can roost in the branches outside of a home and call people out by name to catch them.

levantamientos: A Curanderismo ritual for freeing a soul trapped in a body after death.

limpia: A ritual cleansing found in Curanderismo (and to some extent within some forms of Brujeria). It frequently involves sweeping a person with an object like an egg or herbs in order to remove harmful influences.

mal de ojo: The evil eye. A type of curse that can be inadvertently cast through jealousy or anger, as well as intentionally placed on someone to make them lose their luck or waste away.

Nahaules: Also spelled Naguales. The term for a prophetic seer or shamanic counselor in Mexican and Mexican American folk belief who also provides spiritual and personal guidance.

Nahuatl: One of the Indigenous languages of Northern Mexico, and one from which many terms in Curanderismo derive.

partera: Term for a midwife in Mexican and Mexican American healing practices.

sobadora: Term for someone specializing in massage in Mexican and Mexican American healing practices.

susto: A folk medical condition that involves conditions like stress, sleeplessness, anxiety, or nightmares. Curanderos treat it as a shock or fright to the soul that needs to be remedied.

ventosas: The use of cupping massage techniques in Curanderismo.

Places to Visit

Browse the Witchy Wares at the Sonora Marketplace in Mexico City, Mexico: This is one of the largest vending locations in the world for folk magic. You can browse dozens of stalls selling charms, talismans, amulets, animals, plants, statues, dolls, and more. Some of the items are mass-marketed things you could find anywhere, but some are esoteric and unusual components you'd be hard-pressed to find anywhere else! While you're in the area, you can also stop by the Museo Guadalupano to learn more about the patroness of the Americas, La Virgen de Guadalupe, or you can stop by to visit the highly revered (if somewhat feared) skeletal saint at the shrine at the Santa Muerte Sanctuary. If you're feeling really brave, you could also visit La Isla de las Muñecas (Island of the Dolls), located in the canals around the city.

Dig the Best Holy Dirt at Chimayo, New Mexico: For over two hundred years, a little folk shrine housing a relic of a traveling priest has been the site of a massive pilgrimage. During Holy Week, tens of thousands of visitors arrive in Chimayo, New Mexico, to pay their respects to the last resting place of the priest and his crucifix depicting a Black Jesus. Beyond being a site of religious awe, the dirt found in a hole where the crucifix was originally buried is thought to have miraculous healing properties. Those who come to pay their respects bring offerings of money, food, or other objects and can leave with a bit of the magically empowered dirt, which is sometimes eaten or kept as a talisman against harm.

Seek the Lost Dutchman Mine in the Superstition Mountains of Arizona: A famous story from the southwest notes that a German immigrant once found an astounding lode of gold in a secret mine hidden in the spooky Superstition Mountains. His find became known as the "Lost Dutchman Mine" (German language was called Deitsch, which is where the "Dutchman" comes from). Supposedly the passage to the mine is cursed and guarded by protective spirits. But proceed with caution—people frequently go missing in pursuit of the secret site, and some wind up being found days or even weeks later with no memory of where they have been or what happened to them.

Try Your Luck in Las Vegas, Nevada: Stop by this glittering city in the desert to see if your gambling charms are working! Las Vegas has had its share of grifters and those who have tried to game the system, but as far as we know, anyone with a lucky charm or a bit of magic on their side is still welcome to give it a go here. Of course, there are numerous little oddities tucked away in a city like this, where time loses all meaning. You might stop by the collection of haunted artifacts at Zak Bagans' The Haunted Museum (named after the television ghost hunter who owns it) or visit the third-largest gold nugget in the world at the Golden Nugget Casino. You can also check out perhaps the quirkiest spot, the Office of Collecting and Design, full of lots of broken, lost, and cast-off objects.

Recommended Reading

Magia Magia: Invoking Mexican Magic by Alexis A. Arredondo and Eric J. Labrado
A slim little book by two Texan folk magicians drawing on the traditions of Curanderismo, Hechicería, and Brujeria.

Woman Who Glows in the Dark: A Curandera Reveals Traditional Aztec Secrets of Physical and Spiritual Health by Elena Avila and Joy Parker
This book explores the practices of Curanderismo through the eyes of a practitioner who connects it to the Indigenous history of Mexico and the Southwest.

Border Lore: Folktales and Legends of South Texas by David Bowles
Bowles retells a wide range of fantastic stories rooted in Mexican and Mexican American folk culture, including stories of the witch-owls (*lechuzas*) and more.

Feathered Serpent, Dark Heart of Sky: Myths of Mexico by David Bowles
Another work by Bowles, this time attempting to weave a variety of historical codices together into an epic mythic history of Mexico and Central America.

Cleansing Rites of Curanderismo: Limpias Espirituales of Ancient Mesoamerican Shamans by Erika Buenaflor
Buenaflor's book is a focused, scholarly look at the rituals and history of Mesoamerican healing and spiritual practices.

Brujerías: Stories of Witchcraft and the Supernatural in the American Southwest and Beyond by Nasario García
This excellent collection of firsthand interviews and stories tells all sorts of magical lore, including narratives about brujas and curanderos, ghosts and devils, and much more.

Curandero: A Life in Mexican Folk Healing by Eliseo "Cheo" Torres and Timothy L. Sawyer
Torres and Sawyer look at a few of the better-known curanderos and curanderas throughout history and also discuss the practice as it exists today.

CHAPTER 8

The Left Coast

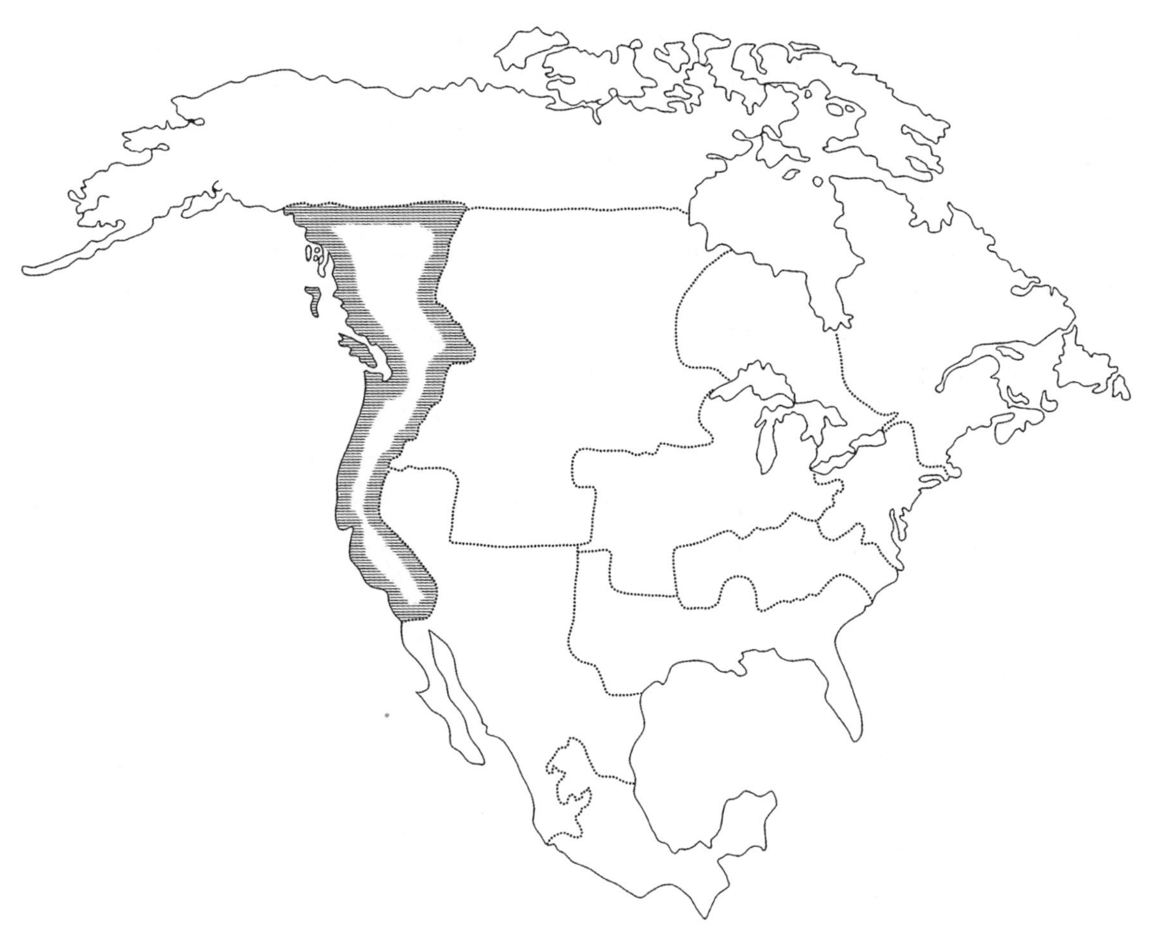

Clay Hearts and Paper Lanterns: An Introduction to Folk Magic on the Left Coast

A few years back, I wound up visiting San Francisco with a group of friends, a few of whom shared my interest in folk religious traditions. One afternoon, one of those friends and I ventured into Chinatown—mostly in search of something to eat, I think, as I am always hungry, but we also knew there was a Daoist temple somewhere along that stretch of street. It turned out to be tucked away behind an unimposing door and up a few flights of stairs, but once we were inside something rather remarkable happened. Despite the busy nature of San Francisco at large and Chinatown specifically, everything hustle-and-bustle fell away. The room was set up with a number of Daoist statues, as well as some Buddhist ones and some bits and pieces of Confucian literature and iconography. Paper scrolls and lanterns hung about the room. Incense was burning in a peppering of censers and pots, and people were quietly sitting with their respective ancestors or deities in prayer and meditation. It was like entering another world at that moment, and my friend and I quietly made an offering of incense at the main altar and then just quietly sat for a bit. No one paid any attention to us, and a few people wandered in and out during the time we were there, but that stillness and calm pervaded the large room the entire time.

When we left, we made our way down the street and found a little shop with hundreds of carved statues in the windows, ranging from Hindu and Roman gods to Christian angels and even dragons and unicorns. Most were carved out of deep red wood, with a good number made from plaster or stone or bronze. They offered discounts for buying multiple statues or statues in bulk, and they sold all sizes. The till rang and rumbled as they made sale after sale and did a brisk trade in the effigies of the divine (or at least divine-adjacent). I recalled interviewing Cat Yronwode, proprietress of the Lucky Mojo Curio Company based out of Northern California, who once told me about a spiritual shop owner in Oakland. When she asked why he, like the shop in Chinatown, carried so many different icons and statues, he simply responded "Oh, I carry *all* the popular gods!"[196]

In my visits to the West Coast, I've often felt that this sort of whiplash experience is a part of the nature of the folk magic there. It's still, quiet, ancient; you might wander the redwoods or hunt for mushrooms in the Emerald Triangle of Northern California or the dense deciduous rainforests near Portland and Seattle. Yet it also has a hum of novelty and innovation—a bustle to it that makes places like Los Angeles, San Francisco, and Portland hubs for magical shops of all stripes. Numerous paths cross here, bringing influences like Chinese folk sorcery, Baja California Brujeria, and the esoteric practices of contemporary Neopaganism into contact.

196. Hutcheson, "Episode 14 – Interview with Cat Yronwode."

The folk magic found on the "Left Coast" is full of that exchange and energy, while also remaining deeply rooted. In the sections that follow, you'll be meeting folk diviners, magicians, and—well, witches, who live those intersections and connections. We'll begin by swinging through San Francisco to spend time with Benebell Wen, who has written extensively on Chinese folk sorcery, such as the use of *fu* talismans, and the deeper symbolism of the Western Hermetic tradition. (And she has even created her own astoundingly well-researched tarot deck to boot.)

Then we'll head up to Portland, where we'll meet with J. Allen Cross, who explores the way that Brujeria evolves in a setting like the Pacific Northwest. He makes the point that brujos and brujas are not just found in Mexico and its adjacent borderlands, but rather are part of virtually every place within the broader reach of North America.

Finally, we will visit Via Hedera, a multiethnic practicing folk magician in Seattle who crafts clay hearts and effigies from the mud of her local Duwamish River to work her magic and also spends hours in the library doing extensive research on North American folklore and folk magic.

In meeting these three, I think you'll find that still, quiet place that looks back in time and draws on ancient trees and the lifeblood of the Pacific Ocean and the Columbia River. You'll also find a powerful, vibrant group of people who are helping shape the folk magic of the future, carving out a place for experiences that aren't neatly boxed up and categorized and delivering a living world of enchantment to all who travel up the coastal highways.

Descendants of the Dragon: Chinese Americans and Taoist Magic

BENEBELL WEN

As early as the Zhou Dynasty (1046–256 BCE) in Chinese history, secret societies formed by rebels, insurgents, revolutionaries, and dissidents against the occupying seats of government tapped into ceremonial magic for their sources of subversive power. During the Han Dynasty (206 BC–220 CE), the first magical Taoist lineage, the Tian Shi, led the Yellow Turban Rebellion against the emperor, sending China into anarchy during the Three Kingdoms Era (220–265 CE). Tian Shi priests performed healing magic for the poor and peasant classes for free in exchange for their pledges of loyalty and for joining the revolt. Warlords sought alliances with Taoist sorcerers. When China came under the foreign rule of the Mongols during the Yuan Dynasty (1271–1368 CE), underground resistance organized by Taoist secret societies invoked the old gods of the Taoist pantheon and integrated the shamanism of China's antiquity into their occult orders.[197]

The White Lotus was a secret religious and political organization formed with the mission to overthrow Mongol rule and reinstate the Han. The society venerated the Queen Mother of the West, Xi Wang Mu, also known as Wujimu, or Infinite Mother, a dark goddess who blessed her adherents with magical abilities. Secret societies organized under the Manichaean religion—a medieval faith originating from Persia that syncretized Zoroastrian angelology, Gnosticism, Islam, and esoteric Buddhism, with strong emphasis on alchemy, astrology, and ceremonial magic—also opposed foreign rule.[198]

One common thread among the different secret societies was the trinitarian worldview that power is harnessed through an alchemical and mystical mastery over Heaven, Earth, and Man, also expressed as *Shen*, *Qi*, and *Jing*. The alchemical triangle became a popular emblem of these secret societies. That concept of the triangle evolved into the modern term for all Chinese secret societies: the Triads. Among native Chinese, though, the term for these groups is the *Hak Sh'e Wui* (Cantonese) or *Hei She Hui* (Mandarin): the Black Societies. Their patron god was Guan Di, the

197. Wen, *The Tao of Craft*.

198. Wen, *The Tao of Craft*, 330, 332–33, 399.

immortalized divinity of the legendary Guan Yu from the Han Dynasty and featured prominently in the *Three Kingdoms*, a fourteenth-century text that has profoundly influenced East Asian culture. The legendary Guan Yu was a warrior renowned for his bravery and honor. The immortalized god Guan Di is a god of war, the military, brotherly loyalty, vigilante justice, and martial arts.

In the 1800s, China was marred by rebellions and revolts. Once again the country was ruled by foreigners—the Manchurians. Different revivals and reincarnations of the White Lotus led the resistance, often under the banner "kill the rich and help the poor." Ethnic groups that had historically been suppressed by the Han Chinese and the Qing Dynasty also rose in revolt. Riots to overthrow the growing power of Christian missionaries and Chinese resistance against Western imperialism in their own country intensified native Taoist mystical practices. As if in reactive defiance against Christianity, Taoist mysticism grew more zealous and ideological. Government crackdown on these dissidents resulted in widespread arrests and subjugation of Triad members.[199]

When China and the US signed the Burlingame-Seward Treaty of 1868, members of these Triads saw an opportunity. To both escape capture and to chase the American Dream, these Triad dissidents fled to the United States and entered through Angel Island. For safety in numbers, Chinese immigrants huddled together in enclaves that came to be known as Chinatown. Triad leaders from the mother country formed the tongs—Chinese American secret societies.

Tong subculture was steeped in Taoist mystical traditions, from blood oaths during initiation and pacing rituals rooted in Taoist ceremonial magic to honoring Guan Di as a patron god and ancestor veneration. Taoist-Buddhist temples have become key fixtures in the Chinatown landscape. Fortune-tellers and psychic medium operations run by the tongs doled divinatory advice to the enclave's residents. Inadequate medical care meant that faith healers and Taoist priests who could provide magical talismans grew in importance within Chinatown.

Characteristics of Chinese American Folk Magic

Now that you have a sense of how Taoist mysticism became part of California's quilt of magical cultures, what are some of the key elements of Chinese American folk magic in practice? While much of what I'll cover here is more enclave-specific than region-specific, meaning that these magical traditions are found in any of the Chinatowns across North America, I'll be focusing my insights on the Left Coast. Old Chinatown in the San Francisco Bay Area was formed when the first significant wave of Chinese immigrants entered California in 1848 through Angel Island, in

199. For social, cultural, and political context on North American Chinatowns, I recommend Kwong, *The New Chinatown*; Yuan, *The Magic Lotus Lantern and Other Tales from the Han Chinese*; and Ni, *From Kuan Yin to Chairman Mao*.

search of *Gam Sann*, "Gold Mountain."[200] They brought with them their folk magic, superstitions, gods, and initiatory traditions of secret societies rooted in blood oaths and Taoist rituals.

In addition to my genetic and familial connections to Taoist folk magic, during my university years, I focused my academic research on studying tong subculture and the history of Chinese Triads. I now practice law in California, and the pro bono legal work I do is devoted to Chinatown residents. I often get a close-up view of tong subculture and, more significantly, how Taoist folk magic is featured in the Chinese diaspora.

I was born into these magical traditions, though growing up, I would not have known to describe the practices as "magical." It was just everyday life. It was my grandparents' lived experience in Taiwan, using faith healing and talismans in lieu of modern medicine, talking to ancestors, feeding the hungry ghosts, fortune-telling, and daily offerings of incense. It was my mother's knowledge of feng shui, her accounts of journeying through the underworld to talk to the dead, and her ability to read auras. Dreams and flashbacks of past-life memory were taken very seriously. I learned how to craft talismans from my mother, and I grew up hearing old wives' tales about Taoist sorcery and spirit mediums only to later—as an adult researching historical and anthropological literature—validate the truths behind these tales.

It's being taught, from an early age, all the ways to protect myself and my home from poison arrows, demons, hexes, and curses. It's hearing about how black vinegar wards off evil, or how wood ear mushrooms and red dates help improve a woman's *qi* (life force). I was forced to eat particularly large quantities of goji berries as a child because, allegedly, they would improve my bad eyesight and help with my asthma. Food was blessed before you ate it; that way there was both physical and spiritual nutritional value.

Heirlooms from my grandmother included bronze and gold amulets, a way of passing ancestral powers from generation to generation. I learned about the metaphysical correspondences of herbs and spices in a piecemeal way as my mother narrated her cooking methods to me. While sitting at the kitchen table, I'd learn how to integrate numerology into the number of garlic cloves or pods of star anise to drop into the pot. She'd tell me to recite certain mantras while I tore the cabbage leaves from its head and collected them in a basket—and yes, tear with my hands; never cut or chop with a knife if you don't want to accidentally cut away healthy *qi*, or the auspices of good health. Did that make any rational sense to me? No. Did I do it anyway out of fear of not living another day if I disobeyed Mom? Yes.

The main altar was an important fixture in our home. Mom had the ornate statuaries blessed at a temple in Tainan and held them in her lap for the entire plane ride. The altar would get rearranged depending on whether she was blessing our schoolbooks so we'd excel in academics or for the Lunar New Year (usually late January or early February), the winter solstice, Ghost

200. Danico, *Asian American Society*, 216.

Month (the seventh month in the Chinese calendar, usually around August), or a close relative's wedding or funeral.

There was a bronze bell, a wood block used during rites and rituals, divination tools, incense that she burned every day, red candles, fresh flowers, and weekly offerings of five different fruits that correspond to the Wu Xing, the five changing phases of Taoist metaphysics. Drawers concealed by the gold altar cloth contained sacred texts, like sutras. When Mormons and Jehovah's Witnesses came knocking on our door and insisted that Mom take their Bibles, she didn't quite know what to do with the books, so she tucked them reverently into those drawers, next to her sutras.

My journey of magical studies is not unlike my journey of learning how to cook: You grow up surrounded by family members cooking for you. You observe it. Mom tells you about how Grandma used to do it. Grandma visits and tells you that Mom does it all wrong. You're ordered by the adults to help with the preparation. You're given the simplest tasks at first. Eventually you graduate to being allowed near the stove. And then one day you leave home, and as you try to stand on your own two feet, you find yourself calling Mom to ask how this is done, how to do that, and what this means, and what was the recipe for that again? After years of experience, you venture away from tradition and develop your own signature style. And just as Grandma did to Mom, Mom tells you that you're doing it wrong.

Walking on Many Paths at Once

As with many other Chinese American families in the Bay Area, I visit a Buddhist temple before the Lunar New Year to receive messages from the gods and ancestors about what's in store for me, to read my karma. When it is Tomb Sweeping Day, my family, along with other Chinese Americans who still observe folk traditions, will take the day off to venerate our ancestors. This means setting up an ancestor altar just for the occasion, leaving out dinner plates of food for the dead, and burning incense and offerings. It's using red *jiaobei* divination moon blocks to talk to the spirits. And then it's energetically clearing and consecrating the home afterward.

Growing up in this tradition is growing up with two calendars on the kitchen wall: the familiar Gregorian calendar, so Mom could keep track of our school and community activities, and the lunisolar calendar based on moon phases and solar terms, a calendar system dating back to the third millennium BCE, anchored by the equinoxes and solstices.[201]

The fourth solar term of the Chinese lunisolar calendar system is the spring equinox, when sun cakes are eaten in honor of Tai Yang Gong, or Grandfather Sun. If on the day of the spring equinox you can make an egg stand on its own upright, then you'll be blessed with prosperity

201. Wen, *The Tao of Craft.*

and abundance during the upcoming harvest season. The season of the autumnal equinox coincides with the Moon Festival, when mooncakes are eaten and children are retold the myth of Chang'e, the moon goddess.

In California there are both closed, secret magical Taoist traditions and more open, accessible folk practices. The closed traditions are not talked about and are never shared, and their existence is not even acknowledged when speaking to outsiders. Any written records are kept closely guarded and inaccessible. It's common for a closed tradition to have established their own written language system or code that initiates would be required to memorize. Then any written materials would be written in that proprietary language system.

Yet open, accessible folk practices of Taoist magic welcome noninitiate Chinese and non-Chinese alike. Taoist magic is historically syncretic, meaning that it fuses together deities, sacred texts, prayer invocations, and ritual practices from different belief systems. Throughout the dynasties, Taoist magicians have grafted Buddhism, Hinduism, Jainism, forms of Indigenous shamanism from the various ethnic groups resident in China, and even Christianity and Islam onto native Taoism. Depending on the reigning philosophy of the time, the moral codes and principles of magic that initiated Taoist magicians adhered to were influenced by Legalism, Mohism, or Confucianism.

There is no convenient Chinese equivalent to the Western Neopagan concept of witchcraft. Rather, there are five primary, but distinctly separate, branches of metaphysical practices: faith healing, ancestor veneration, pacts with gods or spirits, spirit mediums and fortune-tellers, and Taoist ceremonial magic.

An Oakland Chinatown faith healer might be a middle-aged man with leathery brown skin and missing teeth, wearing "Coke bottle" glasses and claiming to descend from seven generations of healers. You'd go to his apartment, he'd sit you down in a dimly lit room filled wall-to-wall with statues of gods and Buddhas, burn so much incense that your eyes tear up, beat on a wood block, and chant over you. Then he'd hand you a rice-paper talisman with instructions to dissolve it in your bathwater. He'd consult the lunisolar calendar, cross-referenced to your natal chart, to pick the most auspicious date for your bath. In exchange, you'd hand him a red envelope thick with cash.

Meanwhile, ancestor veneration might be a grandfather's urn, a framed grayscale photograph of him, fruits, flowers, and incense in the corner of a living room. On special occasions, Grandpa's favorite dishes and a bowl of rice would be set out on the altar, chopsticks planted vertically into the rice. The children of the house would be tasked with sitting around the dining room table and folding origami ingots out of gold and silver paper, to be burned later as offerings.

A pact with Guan Di, a god of war and vigilante justice, to rectify an unfair judgment from the US legal system might require a visit to a temple. With hands in prayer, you would beg him to bring justice and tell him that if he did, you would donate money to the temple, or you agreed to give up something precious to you. Then you threw the divination moon blocks before Guan Di's feet to get your answer—how the moon blocks landed would let you know whether Guan Di had accepted your pact.

Spirit mediums enter a trance state and channel a particular deity. They speak the prophetic words of that deity or, embodying that deity, now possess the power to heal your ailments and bless you with prosperity. The most popular method of fortune-telling in Chinatown might be *kau chim* (Cantonese) or *qiu qian* (Mandarin), a form of drawing lots where you shake a container of sticks while praying to the gods. The sticks that fall out or are chosen are interpreted as an oracle. More advanced practitioners and diviners will study the I Ching.

Taoist ceremonial magic is premised on a trinitarian principle (hence the emblem of the triangle used by the historic Triads). Heaven is the celestial kingdom above, and a master practitioner of magic must be in good standing with the gods. Astrology and divination are connected to the Heaven branch of magic. Earth is symbolic of both the natural world around us and the underworld; the magus must have a working knowledge of plants, herbs, alchemy, demonology, and the realm of ghosts and hungry ghosts. Ritual practices of transmutation are covered under the Earth branch. The third, Man, is embodied by the tension of free will and karma. This is also the power of emotion and analytical reasoning that a magus brings to the craft.

While ritual instructions will differ depending on lineage, generally, to prepare a space for ritual, the four directions must be acknowledged in some way. The north is guarded by the black tortoise, the south by the red phoenix, the east by the azure dragon, and the west by the white tiger. The black tortoise (or its equivalent) is petitioned to endow those in ritual with clairaudience, or the power to hear the voices of the spirits while in ritual. The red phoenix will bless those in ritual with supernatural abilities to create and to bring about growth—this is the blessing of your spells being effective. The azure dragon brings power and control over extenuating events, and the white tiger brings the power of clairvoyance, which is being able to see beyond the capabilities of physical sight.

Any form of transmutation in Taoist magic is premised on the five changing phases called *wu xing*, often translated into English as the "five elements." They are wood, fire, earth, metal, and water, which represent the five basic states of material change or transformation. All forms of spellwork and alchemy are rooted in the elemental theory of *wu xing* because the *wu xing* is about the energy of change.

The better correspondence to the Western alchemical four elements (fire, water, air, and earth) would be the Taoist eight trigrams, or *Ba Gua*: Heaven, lake, fire, thunder, wind, water, mountain, and earth. The eight trigrams are the elemental building blocks of life, while the *wu xing* describe the transformative processes of the eight trigrams. Taoist alchemy is premised on the synthesis of both the changing phases and the trigrams.

Descendants of the Dragon: A Story and an Identity

In the myth of how the Chinese civilization came to be, the Yellow Emperor (who is more of a legendary figure than historical) was one of the civilization's founding shamanic kings during the Bronze Age. When a great war broke out that threatened the very existence of the civilization, Heaven sent a celestial spirit, a protégé of Xi Wang Mu, the Queen Mother of the West. The celestial spirit, whom people called the Lady of the Ninth Heaven, taught the Yellow Emperor the art of war and the art of magic. As part of the magic he learned, the emperor could transform into a yellow dragon, and with that power, he defeated his nation's enemies. The Chinese people call themselves his descendants, and thus we are the descendants of the dragon.

FIELD NOTES

Hell Money

During a number of Chinese festivals, bundles of brightly colored paper inscribed with images of people, animals, buildings, and more are frequently burned as offerings to spirits or ancestors. These paper slips are known as "hell money," or *míngchāo*, and are designed to look like real money, but they are in fact printed on a scented paper called joss. Usually, they are used to ensure that the spirits of the dead are provided for in the afterlife, with the assumption that the burned notes become legal tender in the otherworld, to be used by ancestors for particular debts. They might be used to pay for passage or cover unresolved debts that the deceased left in life.

"Hell money" is largely a descriptor applied by non-Chinese, and it's not something that Chinese people typically call them. While there are concepts similar to hell in Chinese cosmology, it is seldom as clear-cut as it is in Western myth.

Many of the denominations are quite large, reaching up to millions or even billions of yuan (or dollars, in the United States). Some hell money is modeled on Western currency as well, and the notes are sold frequently outside of China in places like Malaysia and Singapore, as well as in Chinese communities in North America. Different locations may have different designs. For example, the bank notes in Singapore sometimes depict a boy holding a carp, while notes produced in the United States may be green to more closely resemble American currency.

Hell money is frequently burned or scattered at funerals, as well as during events like the Hungry Ghost Festival in late summer/early autumn.[202]

202. Feuchtwang, *Popular Religion in China*, chap. 5.

Saints with Scissors: American Brujeria

J. ALLEN CROSS

I found God in the back corner of a Mexican convenience store off SE Powell in Portland, Oregon. Even if you've never been there, I'm sure you know a place just like it: flypaper hanging from the ceiling, rosaries of every color displayed by the cash register, and a five-hundred-year-old woman sitting behind the counter. *Tiendas*, much like churches, all seem the same after a while. I found what I was looking for on a shelf in the back, behind the cleaning supplies. That's where they kept the novena candles with the images of saints, right between the bottles of bubblegum-pink Fabuloso and the bathroom you needed a key attached to a big wooden spoon to get into.

To this day, I'm not exactly sure what drew me there, other than a curious sort of longing. I could feel something calling to me from that shelf. I had been looking for it forever, I just hadn't known until I was in the process of finding it. What I found there, in the back of that little grocery store, was God. Are you surprised? Because I sure was. But God will always be found in honest places where believers go, and the people who were going to the back corner of that *tienda* were true believers. The power of this belief was stronger than any other magic I had come across. When people are in need and they have nowhere else to turn, their magic will be at its strongest, and the Mexican people know this more than most. God was there, in that little store, far from any church, because there were believers. In fact, I felt the presence of God stronger in this place than I had in any church in my life. This was a holy place, flypaper and all.

I had always been a witch's witch. You know, all Pagan all the way, anti-Christianity, and anti-anything that resembled my Catholic upbringing. That lasted me a good long while, until I got reconnected with my ancestors. Once that happened, I found myself reconnecting with my culture on a deeper level, and I could feel them asking me to work a form of magic they could understand. In that *tienda* I could feel their hands on my back, pushing me forward. After I purchased that first saint candle (Saint Martha, the only saint I thought might understand me), I was faced with the enormous task of restructuring my entire magical system to form something my ancestors could understand and take part in. It forced me to come face-to-face with God, make new spirit allies, and basically relearn everything I thought I knew about religion and spirituality.

This path led me back to my culture, my crooked faith, and eventually to writing my first book, *American Brujeria*.

Setting the Scene

I was born and raised on stolen land, and still inhabit it to this day. Oregon is the homeland of Indigenous people such as the Umatilla, Cayuse, Chinook, and Kalapuya, just to name a few. This land is complicated, like its history. Sometimes Oregon is soft and mossy; other times it's dry as a bone. The people are the same way, and range anywhere from transactivist art students to gun-toting, Confederate-flag-waving men in red caps, though if we are being honest, the latter is more common. Oregon's history is deeply racist, and this history contributes to its sociopolitical climate to this day. Though people have continued to fight for over a century to keep Oregon as white as possible, they forgot to factor in one important thing: immigration.

Mexican immigration is a powerful subversive act that chips away at even the whitest of communities. According to the American Immigration Council's website, one in ten people living in Oregon is an immigrant. In 2018, 432,410 members of the Oregon population were counted as "foreign-born," and of those immigrants, 36 percent had "Mexico" listed as country of origin.[203] The state of Oregon is home to a great deal of farming, and the agriculture industry often employs migrant laborers and draws the Mexican population to the area for seasonal work. Beyond that, we see immigrants settling in Oregon to open small businesses, join the workforce, and/or seek education and opportunities for their children (as of 2018, nearly half a million American-born residents of Oregon have at least one immigrant parent).[204] With immigrants comes culture, wisdom, and a different understanding of how the universe works.

Within a spiritual practice as closely rooted to people and culture as American Brujeria is, it is crucial we start by figuring out where it is we actually live and who is around us. For most of us, this is fairly easy now, thanks to the internet. To set your own scene, first try to find out who originally kept the land you live on by using search words like the name of your state and "Indigenous peoples" or "Native American tribes." Who were these people? What did they call themselves? In your searches, you may come across a Canadian project called "Native Land" that is attempting to map the borders and boundaries of tribal land across the United States.[205]

Look up things like immigration statistics or recent census records. Who are the people who live where you do, or who have lived there before you? What do they do? What do they believe? Where are they coming from, and what are they bringing with them? Find out what percentage

203. "Immigrants in Oregon."

204. "Immigrants in Oregon."

205. Visit https://native-land.ca/ for more.

of your area is immigrant and where they originally came from. Ask yourself, *How do I see their presence in the world around me?*

What Is American Brujeria?

I know what you are thinking: *Why is this Oregonian trying to tell me about a practice that clearly belongs in the Southwest near the border?* While this is a valid question, it fails to take something important into consideration, and that is Mexicans (and Latinos in general) will always defy categorization. Many things we think we know about this population are stereotypical at best and racist at worst. Things like the exact shade of *café con leche* our skin is "supposed" to have, even though the colors of the Latinx population range from pasty white to black as night and all of them are valid. We as a people are not purely Indigenous, and while we must have respect for Indigenous people and culture, it is incorrect to assume that is the end of the road for Mexican identity. We are also Spanish, African, Jewish, German, Irish, and many other colors and cultures. Our diversity makes us powerful. More than that, we also exist outside of the American Southwest. *We are everywhere.*

When people immigrate from Mexico to the United States, we bring with us valuable culture, including a great deal of folklore, recipes, superstitions, and cures for all kinds of things. Where we come from, these things have value. They can mean the difference between life and death. In Mexico the people have access to powerful spiritual workers, such as Curanderos (the folk healers of Mexico and other Latin American countries), who do this work for us. When we immigrate to the United States, we leave these people behind. Don't get me wrong, Curanderos do exist in the United States, but they are few and far between. Same with Brujas and Brujos. This means Mexican immigrants must take the work of concocting remedies, doling out justice, and shooing away evil spirits into their own hands. These powerful works see them through and get passed down to their descendants, who become more and more American with every generation. The current generation is reclaiming these spells, recipes, and prayers and weaving powerful magic with them. We call this "American Brujeria."

Old Practices and New Tools: *Limpias* "Oregon Style"

In celebration of powerful Mexican wisdom being found all throughout the United States, I would like to propose something that I have affectionately been calling an "Oregon style" *limpia*. A *limpia* is a form of spiritual cleansing that is used to not only get rid of spiritually unfavorable energies in or around a person or place, but also to clear old unhealthy patterns or open a path to the things we want to accomplish in this life.

There are many different types of *limpias*, but for this we will focus on something called a *barrida*, which means "sweep." During a *barrida*, an item (in this case, a bundle of herbs) is swept from head to toe to clear bad energy from a person, as well as impart good vibrations that may aid the recipient in living a better life. For this you'll want to pick a common Oregon plant ally to assist you. Any one of these will do the job, but pick the one that has what you need most. You may choose:

Yarrow: Imparts bravery and helps seal holes in the aura where energy is escaping.

Lilac: Removes ghosts and helps lift the spirit.

Huckleberry: Helps cool anger and grounds the person's energy.

Juniper: Removes evil spirits, as well as malefic magic, and promotes healing.

Cedar: Helps to heal and strengthen the spirit and imparts protection.

Once you've picked your plant ally, you'll want to gather red string, a white candle, and some holy water. (You may substitute Florida water or a floral water such as rose or orange blossom water.) Begin by lighting the white candle and saying a prayer, asking your guardians, guides, and/or deities to be with you. Use the red string to bind the fresh plants you've gathered into a small broom and cut a separate piece of string to wrap around the palm of your dominant hand; this prevents the unfavorable energy being removed from reentering your body through your hand. You may do this on yourself or someone else. Either way, the person being cleansed should stand or lie down flat on their back.

Sprinkle the plants with the holy water and pray over them, blessing and asking them to assist you in removing any unhealthy, dense, or negative energies. Then bring the plants to the top of the head and sweep down the body on all sides. (If the person is lying on their back, just do the front.) Pay special attention to the head, neck, and shoulders area; the reproductive areas (if appropriate); and the palms of the hands and soles of the feet. As you do this, continue praying that they be cleared of any unfavorable energy and that they are blessed by the spirit of the plant and by your higher power.

Once you're done, thank the plants, then bend or snap the little broom in half to neutralize the energy. Throw it in the trash immediately, at which point you may bring your prayers to a close. I then like to wash my hands in salt water or Florida water to cleanse them, and I take the trash outside.

The Magic Is Like the People: Getting to Know the Saints with Scissors

Like all kinds of folk magic, this work reflects the people it comes from. In this case it's the Mexican American folk, who are hardworking, industrious, and utilitarian. So is our magic. We have spells to topple just about every obstacle you can think of, from healing a scrape to finding a husband. This magic must adapt to new places, new resources, new languages. It has to bend depending on what we have access to and what we can afford. This is not fancy magic; it's gritty, and you're more likely to find tin cans and household cleaners than you are to find ceremonial daggers and crystal wands. Remember, this is magic by and for marginalized communities with limited access. At the end of the day our power comes from three main places: faith (in a higher power, whether that is God, La Virgen, the saints, or even the devil), family tradition (when we do it the way our family taught us, then we have the power of the ancestors behind us), and last but not least, nature (which supports us, feeds us, and provides powerful allies such as plants, stones, and animal guides). These three elements empower and influence our culture and, therefore, our magic. Remember, folk magic is an extension of the folk.

This is not Catholicism the way you know it, and the Christian God you may be familiar with cannot be found here. Our God is much bigger, older, and more complicated. What we do in this work—with our saints, our prayers, and our scissors—is nothing the church would approve of. In fact, we subvert the church as an institution with the point of every needle and the flame of every candle. We call this "Folk Catholicism" where, yes, we believe in God the Almighty, Jesus, the angels, and of course, the saints. Still, that's just the beginning. We know two important secrets. First, there is more out there than just angels and demons; the spirit world is rife with creatures the way our world is filled with a wide array of flora and fauna all our own. Second, the "spirit world" is not its own separate thing. It's here, in our world. There is no separation, these things are very real, and they are here with us right now. Some of them are friendly; others are not. The trick is to ally yourself with the friendly ones, be they angel, saint, demon, or devil, and then guard yourself against the rest.

If you think this work has anything to do with "the church" as an institution, think again. This adventurous form of Catholic magic is completely unauthorized by "the church" and often flies directly in the face of its authority. For instance, Mexican people seem to care very little for who "the church" recognizes as a saint. We have our own saints, beatified by the people, for the people. The most identifiable example of this is La Santa Muerte, our holy saint of death. She is not canonized, and the church vehemently discourages any veneration of her spirit, yet the Mexican people flock to her loving, protective embrace by the thousands. We know as a people that the church as an institution is not here to protect us or provide for us, so we aren't afraid to find that elsewhere. La Santa Muerte is only one of the saints brought forth by the people regardless of the church's approval. There are others, such as Juan Soldado, Jesús Malverde, Teresa Urrea, San Simón, and more. These are what we call "folk saints," or people who were heroes or remarkable in some way, who continued to help people even after death. To this day, you can go to the grave of Juan Soldado and make a petition for his help.

But what about the Catholic saints? This is where a lot of folks think that Brujeria is the same as Santeria/Lucumí, but they are very different. When I talk about working with saints, I don't mean African spirits in disguise, I mean the Catholic saints…more or less. We have our own understanding of them, and our own lore and ways of working with them that are both Catholic and heretical. The saints are much more than just some nice Christian folk. They are mighty and will curse your enemies just as quickly as they will heal the sick. Show them respect and kindness, and they'll show you the same.

A St. Michael Novena and the Power of Vicks: Some Examples of a Folk Catholic Magic

St. Michael is a powerful, protective spirit that is called on to shield us in times of danger. During the height of the COVID-19 pandemic of 2020, I found myself calling upon him almost daily, to either protect myself and my loved ones against sickness, or to bring swift justice to help those in need. I was even able to continue doing house cleansings from a distance with the aid of St. Michael, using a novena candle and prayer. This is a candle spell you can do yourself to protect you and your home.

You'll need…

- 1 St. Michael novena candle (or a plain red novena)
- St. Michael oil (or olive oil)
- Rue (dried)
- Garlic (dried and granulated)
- Angelica root (dried and chopped)

Begin by cleansing the candle by passing it through some smoke or wiping it down with Florida water. Then say the prayer to St. Michael:

> Saint Michael the Archangel, defend us in battle. Be our protection against the wickedness and snares of the devil; may God rebuke him, we humbly pray; and do thou, O Prince of the Heavenly Host, by the power of God, thrust into hell Satan and all evil spirits who roam the world seeking the ruin of souls. Amen.

Pour a little oil into the candle, just enough to lightly coat the top. Add a small pinch of each herb, then hold it in both hands and repeat the St. Michael prayer.

Then hold the candle in your right hand and cross yourself with it (forehead, solar plexus, left shoulder, right shoulder). Hold it up to the sky and say the St. Michael prayer for the third and final time.

When you are done, light the candle in your home and return to it every day it burns and pray for protection. It is best to let these candles burn uninterrupted, but safety should be our first priority. Please extinguish candles when leaving home or going to bed, or make a ritual of burning a certain amount of the candle each day. These safety practices do not impact the success of the spell.

Not everything is saints and rosaries, of course. Much of this practice has to do with what the people themselves do with the tools around them. For example, if you grew up in a Mexican American household, you have undoubtedly experienced the miraculous healing powers of Vicks VapoRub. While it may seem silly at first, that small jar of potent medicine also carries strong magical power, which is part of why it's remained a household staple for so long. Here is a spell to bring healing to a sick person through the magic of Vick's.

You'll need:

- Vicks VapoRub
- A small bowl
- A spoon
- Holy water (optional)
- A white candle
- A statue of La Virgen de Guadalupe (optional, you can also substitute the white candle for a white Guadalupe novena)

Light the white candle beside the statue and say a prayer to La Virgen for healing. Scoop a spoonful of the Vicks into the small bowl and add in three drops of holy water, then stir it up good. Apply the Vicks mixture in your usual manner while saying the traditional magic words: *"Sana sana, colita de rana. Si no te alivias hoy, te alivias mañana."*

Repeat as necessary.

The Rules of the Game

All magic comes with rules. Whether they are spiritual laws or cultural taboos, it's important to be aware of the "dos and don'ts" of this work. For example, by now you're probably wondering, *Do I have to be Catholic?* and the answer is no, you do not. Or, at least not in the traditional sense. You don't have to call yourself Catholic or go to church on Sunday. You also don't have to approve of "the church" as an institution. But you do have to believe in the holy forces behind this work, and you do have to put aside your personal issues and humble yourself enough to ask sincerely. If you have major religious baggage or simply cannot wrap your head around working with Catholic spirits such as saints, Jesus, God, Mary, etc., then this work may not be for you. That being said, it's important to realize this is an unorthodox and unauthorized form of Catholicism that is more pliable than what you hear about in church. If you'd like to pare it down to just working with Guadalupe, that is acceptable as well. Folks turn their backs on this work thinking it will be like their childhood experience of Sunday school, but that couldn't be further from the truth.

You may also be wondering, *Is this a closed practice? Aren't all practices closed now and forever?* and the answer is also no, this is not considered a closed practice. You can practice this even if you don't speak Spanish, or if your family is from a Latin American country other than Mexico. You can practice this even if it wasn't handed down in your family, or if someone has told you you look "too white" or "too black" to claim your Latino/a/x heritage. People confuse the ideas of "deserves respect" and "closed practice." Just because a practice comes from somewhere and has history, tradition, and culture tied to it doesn't mean it's closed—it means it deserves our respect. There is a difference. If you've come to this work hungry to be given spells and aren't at all curious about the people this work comes from or our history and culture, then you need to do some work.

Which brings us to the third most-asked question: *What if I'm not Latino/a/x?* We must remember that when we use magic from someone's culture, we must also learn their history, and we have to engage with the community. So, get some academic texts. Learn about Mexican history and the history of this magic. Inspect your relationship with Mexican and Mexican American people. You should be supporting them with how you speak, how you spend your money, and how you vote. If your actions begin to damage the Mexican and Mexican American communities around you, you've put yourself in direct opposition to the magic you are using, and that never goes well. Give back, respect the culture and traditions, and remember, you are a guest in this space. Taking the magic and leaving the people, the history, and the culture is what we call misappropriation.

Meeting Our Lady of Guadalupe

If you spend time in Mexican American neighborhoods, stores, or online spaces, you're likely to bump into a familiar image of La Virgen de Guadalupe, the young woman with hands in prayer and eyes cast down, watching over her people. La Virgen de Guadalupe is a sort of cultural crossroads spirit, a liminal space, and a spirit that—like her people—defies tidy categorization. Is she the Indigenous earth goddess we call Tonantzin? Or is she the colonizers' imported and superimposed Virgin Mary? The answer is, both and neither. Folks try to label her as solely one or the other, but the truth is that she is a reflection of her people. It is said that if you view her famous image from one side of the room, she looks Indigenous, and if you view her from the other side, she looks European. Our people are similarly varied, and regardless of how you choose to view her origins, the simple truth is that she is here for us.

Guadalupe is quite different from the other forms of Mary she's often grouped with. Her coloring, symbols, and style of veneration set her far apart. In fact, her odd liminal nature means you can work with her from many angles, and some folks throw out the rest of the Catholic symbols and spirits and simply follow her. They call themselves *Guadalupanos*. Since the beginning, people have worked with her in a style that is more Brujeria than it is Catholic, and she's accustomed to our candles and cords and secret spells. She understands the language of our magic, and she wants us to ask her for things. In the story of Juan Diego, she asks for the temple to be built on Mount Tepeyac so that the people may come to her and she may help them.

If you'd like to have a place for Guadalupe to hear your prayers as well, you may create your own space for her in your home. Begin by cleaning off a surface. On top of it, place a white novena candle, a glass of water, incense, and an image of her, which can be on the candle, a prayer card, or even found online and printed in your home. You may add other decorations as you see fit. When you are ready, light the candle and the incense and say a prayer inviting her into your home and your life.

La Futura

In order to fully understand the power of the Mexican American people, you must embrace the wild diversity of our people. We are Indigenous, and we are African, and we are Spanish, and we are Jewish, and so much more. Our colors extend to every edge of the rainbow. Our power is in our diversity. We grow and expand beyond our borders, and we live outside Mexico, Arizona, Texas, and other southern states that toe the border.

As a people, we must learn to stop thinking of our heritage as roots that keep us stationary in one place, but instead see our heritage as a compass that guides us as we venture into the world beyond. We cannot chain our identity and power to geography or social constructs. We must rise and move into the future unafraid, because we have the ancestors and the spirits with us wherever we go. We can reclaim our magic and our power and our culture and our traditions wherever we are. It's up to us to decide what happens next and where we go from here.

FIELD NOTES

La Santa Muerte, Devotion to the Bone

Among the many folk saints revered by practitioners of folk Catholicism, none seems to garner as much controversy as La Santa Muerte. Represented as a skeletal figure in holy garb, this depiction of death incarnate makes many outsiders fear her as a harbinger of doom, but for those who work with her, that is almost entirely contrary to what they know of her. Instead, she is invoked as someone who can protect people in vulnerable situations (including people involved in illicit trades such as drugs or sex work) and offer favors and benefits to those without many resources. She is seen as a *padrina*, or "godmother," figure and treated with reverence and respect. (She is Death, after all.) But she is also a figure who treats everyone who comes to her with fairness and compassion (because, of course, Death takes all people equally, regardless of station, skin color, or creed). While her adherents are quick to note that she can be temperamental, they also talk about how readily she comes through for those who keep their devotions to her.

La Santa Muerte is a target of official reprobation by the Catholic church, who emphatically deny her role within any sort of orthodox canon, but that has not stopped people from expressing deep devotion to her and asking for her intercession in times of need. She has been called upon by those facing immigration trials, those in the LGBTQIA+ community, and those who have disabilities. A number of spells have also grown up around her, including the use of different color robes on her statuary or imagery to petition different needs: white for forgiveness, protection, and exorcism; red for lust and love; black for witchcraft and hexing; rainbow for multiple needs or for work with queer people; gold or yellow for luck, money, and wisdom. She is, of course, found in virtually any place that Mexican and Mexican American people are, but she does have strong devotional ties in places like Mexico City and Los Angeles. In fact, religious scholar R. Andrew Chesnut has noted that her following is one of the fastest growing in North America.[206]

Working with La Santa Muerte requires establishing an altar with her representation and keeping it in good order. She can be picky about sharing space with other saints or spirits, and anything you promise to her, you are obligated to fulfill. You can offer her water, service, candles, incense or cigarettes, flowers (they must be fresh), rum, tequila, rosaries, and candy, fruit, or other foods.[207]

206. Chesnut, *Devoted to Death*, 6–12.

207. See Cross, *American Brujeria*; Arredondo and Labrado, *Magia Magia*; and Illes, *Encyclopedia of Mystics, Saints & Sages*.

In the Shadow of the God Mountains: Multicultural Folk Magic

VIA HEDERA

This is a land ruled by old mountain gods, sacred rivers, and endless green. A place where the compass winds were said to battle and where fire was stolen by tricksters. The marine air and old-growth forests have nursed the Northwest's ecological strength, and the magic that grows here has been nurtured on this sacred landscape as well. Haunted and green, flowing with rivers and teeming with life, this corner of the land is made for magic and medicine, and for those who practice those green arts. In summer as the rivers rush down the mountains, it is "the white water streaming from their slopes [like] milk pouring from their glacial breasts. They make fruit ripe, animals pregnant, and they call the salmon to spawn."[208]

Despite the area's reputation for rainy wilderness, the territory is vast, carved into different ecological systems and bioregions by mountain ranges and rivers. Shaped by glaciers and volcanos and time, the terrain has inspired and encouraged countless stories, tales, and legends, giving this place a sense of magic and majesty that is felt in the bones.

This noticeably lush edge of the country is still considered a somewhat wild place, a region rich in trickster heroes, natural phenomena, hauntings, and even witches. Reflected in the great many animistic myths and humorous stories of the First Peoples, there is a common theme of dangerous otherworldly beings and their power over people, their health, and their livelihoods.

West of the Cascades, this witch finds comfort and community in the ghosts, demons, animal allies, and restless old gods who share this space. It is a territory heavily populated by people who have immigrated and migrated from every corner and bring their own histories here, to a land rich in history and mystery.

The cycles and tides of the seasons in any given place shape my faith, and the stories of my heritage, of my community, shape my ever-present spiritual values that place connection between spirits—of the living, dead, and otherworldly—above all things. My work takes me hexing by the riverside because the river is a transformer and life giver/taker, or my work takes me hunting for

208. Buerge and Rochester, *Roots and Branches*, 9.

healing in the undergrowth, calling on the winds and the haunting, whispering dead to guide my hand.

The old gods of this land are elk-gods and sea-kings and mountain grandmothers, and they have become my own divinities, teaching me how the cycles and shapes of a place can introduce a spiritual rhythm to our lives. Where I grew up, the sea was the domain of Mary and Yemanja and La Sirena, and the hills were haunted by bloodsucking devils and dead celebrities. But in the Cascade region, the Sound is domain to ancient serpent demons and hidden oceanic kingdoms, and the hills are haunted by tribes of wooly ogres. I honor them all, all those otherworldly things in league with the ways of witches. It is they who join in my crossroad sabbats, ecstatic dreams, and night flights.

Colossal Claude and Hungry Witches: Meeting and Naming the Otherworldly Folk of the Sound

Logging, hunting, camp-haunting, mining, and maritime superstitions once abounded in the Northwest, coming together from different cultures and peoples sharing their environment (the breeding ground of folklore). When combined with Indigenous folktales and legends, the Northwest begins to take on a terrifying and magical spirit—one that stirs up magic. Great serpents of the waters are no uncommon sight, made famous in the folktales of Lake Quinault and Lake Chelan and referred to by settlers as "dragons"—ones they claimed to encounter.[209] Artifacts found in the Skagit River dated to 200 CE have depicted the image of what appears to be a ferocious serpent on an atlatl.[210]

These kinds of great serpents were reportedly witnessed by quite a few non-natives as well: fishermen, sailors, pastors, judges, and passersby have described sighting all kinds of massive, serpentine creatures with reptilian features like a serrated back or protruding humps. One such sea-serpent beast, the famous Colossal Claude of the Columbia River, was sighted frequently in the early twentieth century, found slinking through the waters of the river that divides Oregon and Washington, and still occasionally haunts the imaginations and superstitions of residents along these bodies of water. They haunt my practice as well; my hexes and defensive charms can involve calling on devouring sea-beasts of all kinds: those in my local waters, as well as those who can be conjured from worlds away.

Often, these old stories shape the folk knowledge and superstition surrounding particular places. There is much magic to be found in our corpse- and monster-inhabited lakes and the sea-serpent-infested waters of the Sound, and in the woods that are supposedly haunted by tribes of

209. Hackenmiller, *Ladies of the Lake*, 157.

210. LeBlond, "Sea Serpents of the Pacific Northwest," 47.

wooly woodland giants (including the famed Sasquatch) and great child-eating ogresses.[211] The mountains themselves were temperamental kings and grandmothers of the sky, interconnected in Pacific Northwestern storytelling branches with the other numerous peaks as warring brothers, giving deities, or star-crossed lovers, depending on who told the tale.

Even the mountain meadows, valley wetlands, and swamps are said to be filled with otherworldly mysteries, as local historian Ella E. Clark reported: "The spirit of swamps and thickets could be heard but never seen, it did no harm except that its voice sometimes caused people to become lost, because it kept them from knowing the right direction."[212] Those who wander near the darkest parts of the forests know how easy it is to be led astray by the whispers. The spirits are no laughing matter, and their powers are far-reaching—good company for a folk-witch like myself who dances with both the living and the dead. Witchery and wild magic root in the imagination wherever they can, and they grew along the Puget Sound long before colonizers came.

Figure 8-1: Rabbit Spirit. Image by Andrew Jimenez, used with permission

Not too unlike the ghostly witches and boo-hags of the South, here we have our own rumored witches throughout Puget Sound folktales and mythology. They were not night-riding succubae atop horses and butter-dashers, but terrifying devouring-witches, snake-basket witches, bug-eyed snail women with carnivorous appetites.[213] Children were warned not to wander too close to a witch and her basket, to distrust the nocturnal hags and spirits that haunted the woods in winter, who would pick off those naughty children who did not mind their duties and stay close to home: "Away back in the past, Snail was a powerful woman who used to carry people off, putting them in a basket on her back. She cooked them for her food."[214]

These cannibal-hags who carried pitch-lined baskets and devoured witless children were, by all accounts, dangerous creatures. The hags were explicitly related to witches and cannibalism in these old legends, and much like their East Coast counterparts, symbolized the wild, death, and danger. As historian David M. Buerge described, "The snail shell

211. Clark, *Indian Legends of the Pacific Northwest*, 8; Bragg, *Washington Myths and Legends*, 13, 15–23; Hilbert, *Haboo*, 9, 17, 49, 108.

212. Clark, *Indian Legends of the Pacific Northwest*, 9.

213. Buerge and Rochester, *Roots and Branches*, 9.

214. Ballard, *Mythology of Southern Puget Sound*, 104.

and the basket are symbolic of the womb, but the hag's is a carnivorous womb, devouring life instead of producing it."[215] Magic and those who wield the most fearsome of powers find roots wherever they go, and in the shadow of the mountains, they still haunt the water and woods. I am partial to the lore of the ogresses of the mountains; they remind me that the Witch Queen wears many forms and is personified in many ways around the world, always present, always devouring.

All manner of otherworldly beasts and demons, and the souls of our living and our dead, coexist with us, as ever-present as the evergreens. Every animal, plant, stone, mountain, and river was and is capable of song, sacred healing, and secret magic—and the power they could have over us is a fearsome thing. We share in these gifts together, in the kinship of being part of life and death. There's a deep root of animism to the lore of the land, so those who worship the green and the bones that rest within it may find themselves easily adapting their practices to the terrain, flowing with the rivers of change, as all things must in time.

Where Medicine Grows Magic

Most of the folktales and fables of the Northwest are Indigenous in origin, reflecting the vast array of cultures, tribes, language groups, and territories. Along the Green-Duwamish River and the Puget Sound, this is especially true. The river I work along is descended from the Cascade volcanic arc that bridges the West Coast together, and it feeds the bay and relishes life in the estuaries and wetlands of the area. It is these mountains that were once believed to be as great and destructive as gods, and the rivers that come from them were symbolic of the life they give. Rivers everywhere are truly a symbolic representation of merging life, and that's part of what makes magic in wild green places.

Puget Sound storytelling and Coast Salish artistic culture are an integral and inseparable part of the identity of the landscape. And yet, as more people have come to live here, there come new folktales and fables, new superstitions and magic, and they merge with the mysteries of the old to make something entirely new. Coexisting alongside one another in the folklore of the Pacific Northwest are the introduced legends and superstitions of the many settlers who have established themselves here, notably Scandinavian, East Asian, Latin American, Russian, and African American communities—many populations that settled around the area during the boom of development and trade. The founding of some of the first churches, fisheries, logging camps, and railways of the Northwest supported industry towns that brought people the world over for work opportunities in the late nineteenth century, and they brought their superstitions with them. Over a short period of time, the sea monsters, logger-camp heroes, and fireside ghost stories of elsewhere

215. Buerge and Rochester, *Roots and Branches*, 9.

found themselves sewn into the blanket of the Northwest, where the monsters of the woods and waters inspired fear in Indigenous people and settlers alike.[216]

Making Mud-on-the-Feet Magic: A Love Dolly

The ethnobotany (the study of the plants utilized in the traditional medicinal and spiritual wisdom of the people) of Western Washington tells a story of love magic, of bulbs and roots and branches that conjure up storms of love—their purported medicinal values mirroring their spiritual natures. One of the oldest and most widely used magics in the world is image magic. A love-draw dolly can be made in the image of a person or can conjure and house those imps and incubi who ride in the night. It smells of summer and sex, and it is intended to draw romance to the one who stitches, stuffs, and feeds it (a little drop of blood or prayer here and there). The following project is meant to sit upon the altar as an ensouled idol, housing spirits of love and beauty who inhabit the plant-spirit world and will now inhabit the doll's form.

The material used to make the pattern ought to be from a natural fiber: cotton, flax, silk, bamboo, or other natural fibers. Cut out the shape of a person from two pieces of cloth, which will be stuffed and sewn closed. Use red or pink thread for stitching. Sew the doll on days of Luna and Venus—Monday or Friday—during a moon near-full and bright in the sky.

Stuffing examples:

Dried Wild Rose Petals (*Rosa nutkana*): An herb of love and healing. Grows along roadsides and riversides throughout the region. Readily found mid-to-late summer in radiant reddish-fuchsia and pale pink tones. This herb will guard one's heart with sincerity and bring purity to the intention of the work.

Cottonwood Fluff (*Populus* spp.): In mid-to-late spring, the balsam poplar trees expel massive clouds of sticky, sweet-smelling fluff that gathers in every nook and cranny of the cities and forests. Easily collected and stored, this is a perfect stuffing for dollies, one that is readily found come spring. The sensual, sexual scent of the downy fluff will bring a sense of passion to the dolly.

Dried Vetch Flower (*Vicia* spp.) or Seeds: Hairy and common, vetch grow infectiously in meadows and along riversides in palest white, buttery yellow, and deepest rouge. They tangle and choke, grabbing hold of all that they can. Their pods snap loudly in the high summer winds and their seeds, often infected with burrowing beetles, rattle in the shells. They will tangle the steps of a lover or get them tangled up in you.

216. Bragg, *Washington Myths and Legends*, 12–23.

Black Locust Flower (*Robinia pseudoacacia*): When dried to papery thinness, these powdery, fragrant flowers are an excellent stuffing, giving a sweet and dangerous spirit to the doll, haunting it with their thorny beauty.

Seeds of Fruit-Bearing Trees: Apple seeds or cherry stones symbolize the heart and sexual organs. Meant to represent sexuality and fertility in whoever makes the stitches. Seeds are potential, they are expectations, and they provide this energy wherever they go.

Personal Concerns: The byproducts of our body have a distinct magical value that create a bridge of connection in a spell and bind the living to an object. This is known as *contagious magic*, whereby one holds power over another by holding possession of that person's very self. Personal concerns are hair, teeth, skin, blood, eyelashes, spit, fingernails, sexual fluids, and even excrement. Hair will do just fine for dolly magic, as hair carries a great deal of power; it will give the soul of the dolly a little piece of the one who it is meant to inspire. If not, spit will seal the spell just as well.

Keeping this dolly on the altar and feeding it sweet nothings, prayers, and oils, perfumes, or fragrant smokes is meant to keep the dolly spirited and fed. Speak your prayers and needs quietly to this doll, like a lover would, and let it be the vessel you call the spirits or gods of love into during your work. A house for a spirit is an important thing; it needs no higher details, only to be filled with meaning and with purpose.

The River's Journey: Where My Magic Comes From

Wherever there are legends of haunted woods and magical monsters, there you will find those who come to live with the mysteries and add their own sense of magic to the place. The witchcraft of the Old World may not have had much time to root in the Pacific Northwest, but it grows with all who come to live here, bringing the magic of their ancestors with them on migrations across land and sea.

Spiritual and magical beliefs adapt to people and places—to the land, sky, and sea and the natural things that develop there—and witchcraft does this wherever it goes, changing to fit necessity as it arises. In the evergreens, otherworldliness just seems to grow with the blackberries and flow with the river. Maybe that's what makes magical faith so fearsome in the first place: its power to transform.

Having moved up the West Coast, migrating along with my family, being passed from relative to relative, I learned to set roots down quickly, make connections with the land immediately, and absorb the lifestyles of the friends and family who formed the village that raised me. We are, all of us, shaped by our experiences as we move through life, and while I make my home in the emerald hills of Western Washington, my roots were first planted in the dry desert heat of Southern California.

It was in California that I learned to hear the whispers of spirits in swampy places, and to be wary of the wild spirits who haunt groves and grottos. Most of my relatives in California had originated from Florida, and with them came the spirits and stories that had haunted their worlds, brought here to mingle with the ghosts and ghouls who dwelled in the hills and desert places. From their point of view, the devil and his conjury were in the land, rooted like some eternal weed, and we were meant to be wary but respectful. When I moved to the Northwest, these tools served me well and gave me a sense of familiarity with this new land, whose mythological identity is wrapped in the ways of the otherworldly, the elements, the cosmic.

Magic is a migrating force, as am I. In the Southwest, surrounded by the folk Catholic magic of my *tía* and her family and of my community, I felt the world was inhabited by the magical and spiritual and never assumed otherwise. I was born into a belief in the supernatural, and it was natural to me to participate in the superstitious rituals around me.

It was the rituals, little and large, that struck me: feeding food to the dead as though they still taste; the stringent avoidance of ill-speaking the dead; the pouring of fine liquor libations. These rituals crossed cultural boundaries and were a normalized practice in my family regardless of their culture, as if ensuring the spirits of the deceased were appeased was simply a facet of the life cycle process. Sometimes it was a horseshoe over a garage door or a spirit plate at the head of the table, and sometimes it was a bowl of smoke that filled the air and the bellies of the dead.

When we moved to the Northwest, the values of the spirit-connected world were paralleled in the mythology of the land, and the surrounding greenery deepened my faith in the divinity of things that grow from the land, that dwell in the wild—and our inherent connection to them. It's a staple of storytelling in the Northwest, the power of connection between man and beast, between beast and cosmos, and creation. I became enamored with the haunted beauty of the woods, rivers, and mountains of places—especially after I began to sit with the storytellers while attending Indigenous curriculum programs in the early 1990s and spending more time with my relatives and community within Coast Salish cultures. It was different here; the sacred smokes were from cedars and spruces rather than copal and tobacco, and the spirits here often wore the skins of the local flora and fauna and the skins of stars, winds, and thunder. The Northwest is, like all the places I've ever known, inhabited by the spiritual and unseen forces, and no matter what form these mysteries take, they can be approached, they can be connected to, and they can be honored with magic.

The community of people around me as I grew up all seemed to hold a deep faith in a world inhabited by the spirits. I am multiracial and from a largely adoption-based and collective family that extends in all directions; most of my relatives had migrated west from the South, Southeast, or beyond the sea, and they certainly brought their superstitions and spiritual values with them wherever they went. I was taught to see the world as one filled with souls, whether kind or dangerous or somewhere in between—beings once living, those that died, and the altogether otherworldly. Honoring one's dead, fearing evil influences, blessing homes, amulets of luck, and little healing sorceries were just a normal facet of life for me as a child and were reflected in the people around me as we all moved up and down the Coast.

How many of us grow up in the midst of magic unseen, ritual unrecognized? How many of us hold rituals for the dead? Open windows to let the soul free? Light candles to guide the beloved in their final hour? Cover house mirrors so that the souls won't wander through the looking glass? We can live by simple and meaningful rituals without recognizing the magic there. I was taught to watch what ill words I spoke into being, to value the dead on their days, and to hold space for ancestors on an altar. Even as my family and I moved up the Coast, these beliefs did not change because they were present wherever the river of life took us. There are always spirits to feed, herbs to be enchanted by, and hauntings to fear.

Like ivy, I can grow anywhere and carve a niche in any space I find. Every place has its spirits, its allies, its old gods, those sleeping and those still wandering. I look for the parallels, for those kindred spaces of familiarity: love roots, haunted places, the cryptid kings and legendary beasts—I look to these places and find a familiar thread and adapt my ways to what I have around me. Instead of eucalyptus for my purification baths, I turn to cedar. Instead of calling on the dead that haunt the orange groves, I call to the dead that lurk in the nurse logs. Adaptation is rooted in my animism, and it doesn't take theft or intrusion to accomplish—it only takes trusting intuition and forging our own respectful, personal relationships with the spirit-inhabited world around us.

Anywhere I set down my life, shed my blood and tears, and take from the green, I am sure to make the acquaintance of the spirits there, their stories, and their story-keepers. Sometimes we can't know the names or the rituals of these old gods; sometimes we have to forge our own independent relationships with the forces we encounter in the world. We have to find their names and seek their essences using nothing more than our cunning, our sight, our will. That journey is what I love most about animistic magic; we draw on our own interactions with the spirits we find, develop our own practices based on our own experiences, and let life shape our path. One can carve a place for their magic anywhere they go if they nurture their roots and those around them.

Green Witchery by the Green River

The magic that develops in one place is never quite like another because the spirits shape the landscape, and the landscape shapes the spirits. Folk magic practices anywhere are generally centered around some basic necessities meant to be addressed by charms, rituals, and incantation.

These rituals, by their mystical and spiritual virtues, could alter the path of our fate or reveal hidden wisdom. The charms I've most encountered in the collections of regional North American folklore show a pattern of addressing basic needs and wants:

- Funeral rituals and grieving rites.
- Agrarian and domestic protection.
- Appeasing or averting of the dead (or otherworldly).
- Divination and fortunes.
- Romantic and erotic charms.
- Minor and major healing.

Herbs do much of the magical heavy lifting in these parts. Witches must be innovative and adaptive to the environment. It's on us to adapt to the landscape and shape our magic to work with the spirits here, and that starts with looking for the right tools and allies to work one's craft with them.

The magical roots and materials that grow in the Northwest are unique but find parallels with magical herbs elsewhere in the world. Like the witching roots of the Old World, ours have a history of traditional spiritual and medicinal use, and they are defined by their own kind of Doctrine of Signatures. There is a magical signature to every animal, fungus, plant, and natural feature: gardens of powerful purgatives, mineral-rich roots, weather-conjuring trees, and forbidden flowers still believed to call down the rain when plucked.[217] The love roots common to the Sound are not mandrakes and High John, but trillium, false hellebore, and oxalis.

There is healing in the clay of some of these old-growth creeks if one knows where to look. It is from this soil, packed with the carcasses of the dead insects and fish and the nutrients of the flora that grow along the creeks and root in the clay, that I draw the mud that makes my effigies of the woodland deities, of the Witch Gods, of my familiar shapes. Love potions come easy when there are sugar-sweet saps and nectars hidden inside every creeping honeysuckle and bitter cherry blossom, and I craft my love charms with these herbs: honeysuckle wands that ensnare and enchant; cherry blossom dew that adds a touch of innocence to any elixir. Practical and powerful, the natural magic and medicinal materials of Pacific Northwest witching are found in the land itself.

217. Gunther, *Ethnobotany of Western Washington*, 18–19; Turner, *Ancient Pathways, Ancestral Knowledge*, 315–16.

A Little More Mud-on-the-Feet Magic: A Footprint Charm

One of the more commonly practiced folk magics from the lore of the Southern United States (and principally represented in Afro-American magical-spiritual traditions) is footprint or "track magic": the power of enchanting or conjuring over the footsteps of another for the purposes of love, protection, aversion, or hexing. This magic is basic contagion: this-effects-what-it-touched magic. Either by gathering the footprints left by another in the dirt and conjuring over them, or by sprinkling hexing elements into their footsteps, the idea was that what affected the footprints would affect the person they belonged to. This concept of magical contagion was popular throughout world folklore, reflected in Hoodoo, Conjure, witchery, and folk magic alike.[218]

Track magic is almost exclusively geared toward retaining a wandering lover, slowing a thief, or protecting oneself from a bad influence. Like detritus and muck on the bottom of a shoe, sometimes we pick up people or entities in our lives that get stuck to us and need diverting. When we find ourselves followed by people or entities that cause us stress or distress, we may practice these comforting little charms to treat this spiritual illness.

To banish or avert a lingering and unwanted presence, a footprint charm or "track trick" is a way to ask the land itself to help ground, banish, and block the path of those who wish you harm. My banishments reflect my adaptation of Southern diaspora to the land on which I now live.

I recommend performing track tricks on a moon that is growing dark, on the days that serve hexes and witches, Mars, and Venus (Tuesday or Friday), at a liminal hour, either dawn or eventide. Perform with clean hands and careful fingers—gloved is best.

This witching calls for the use of the thorny herbs of the riverside hedgerow. Pluck prickly plants, preferably from dead or dying bramble branches. Take thorns from a vine that once choked others but is now lifeless and unmoving—a fitting symbol for the charm at hand. Briars are boundary markers by virtue, defensive and repelling.

Shake loose from the earth the soils of erosion and decay, the slimy ones where the rock is withering away. Even the ash from a violently erupted volcano is useful for this dust magic, adding a sense of finality to the work, of settling the charm.

Carefully seek out old spikes from abandoned and overgrown train tracks, or nails from railroad ties (track planks), and chip a little rust from them. Abandoned railroads are commonplace around the Northwest; they exist in stasis, stuck in time, and can no more be the nexus of transport they once were, bringing with them a sense of inertia in travel.

Place these together on your altar in a bowl or in a vessel, one preferably made from elements of the land: clay, carved wood, concave stone, woven reeds/bark, etc. Call to those spirits that guard you: your familiars, your family and ancestors, your other-self, your patron deity, your star

218. Frazer, *The Golden Bough*, 209–11; Prahlad, *The Greenwood Encyclopedia of African American Folklore*, 636.

of influence, your very Will—whomever is your guide and sits with you in your work. Ask them to do exactly what the herbs and needles will do by their very nature: guard you from whoever is so unfortunate to find this dust mixed with their footprint.

When you are ready to use the track dust, sprinkle a little around the footprints of the person you wish to avert. Or covertly pour in a circle around the enemy's shoe if it's handy so that their steps will be tacky and tedious as they seek the one who poured the dust. Additionally, if you have collected the dirt from their footprints, this can be mixed with your averting dust and tossed downstream, where the footprints will be carried away in a symbolic act of separation.

Like the river muck, let the virtues of the track dust be caught on them to pain their steps if they come your way, to bring their travel to a halt like a ruined old railroad.

River, Wood, and Mountain

River magic means spells of removal, banishing, and offering: a place to rinse off the impurities gathered during everyday life. Riverbeds and creek beds in some of these older forests are rich with soft mud and rock clay that can be shaped into idols and offering bowls; cattail reeds easily braid into baskets, and decayed cedar makes for spirit-pleasing smoke. The solitary riverside witch may find all the kinship they need in the sacred landscape, in every hemlock, borage, and butterfly bush that shades the riverside.

Woodland work means charms of familiar magic, spirit wandering, and crossroads magic. It means communing with old gods at cold, rocky creeks and at the base of hollow nurse logs. There are medicinal plants and dreaming fungi to aid those kinds of magics, and plenty of haunted places to conjure and indulge in necromancy. Imbued with all the devilish power of the volcanic forge is one of the more useful mountain gifts: St. Helens' ash, our own protective and averting dust that does the job as good as any red brick or black salt. I light my tapers with the pitch of mountain pines and count owl pellets among my favorite sources of ethical bone collection—and I steer clear of the swamps that whisper, and the disappearing meadows.

There are few laws in nature; things live, change, devour, and die at some point, and we belong to that cycle—it does not belong to us. If one chooses to take to the "crossroads" places (hilltops, graves, caves) and renounce their old faith, dedicating themselves to spiritual service in exchange for mysterious gifts, then the first step may be sitting with the otherworldly beings, meeting them at their liminal space to learn from their wildness.

Those who work with otherworldly things should honor those beings before their work *and* after. This can mean simple prayers of acknowledgment, singing a song, or making a gesture. This can mean feeding water to the dry bush who offers a seedpod or leaving food for the insects who feed the nurse log that offers so much. The old laws of witchery still abide: all magic has a cost; familiar spirits must be fed. All connections come with that balance, and part of the balance—the cycle of life—includes feeding the souls.

The spirits here are ancient, secretive, and quiet. And they get restless, the hungry dead—much like the living. They need comforting, they need feeding one way or another, whether that's exorcising perceived devils from one's home to placate the living or appeasing ancestors to respect our beloved dead. This animistic thread is familiar territory here. One informant I spoke with regarding the role of spirits in her family and life as a Pacific Northwest woman of Cowichan heritage shared with me that the spirits, much like us, grow hungry and need feeding: "We believe that there are certain things you shouldn't do, such as eat outside after dark, because it brings the hungry spirits out."[219] Those who work in service to the otherworldly in their craft may recognize this concept well. By witch's teat or by witch's hand, that is part of the cost of magic work with the living or the dead.

The Community Garden

Honoring the spirits includes respecting the boundaries of their legal status by leaving minimal trace and avoiding protected species. Honoring the spirits and land also means taking only what you need from it, and nothing more. When studying the plant and animal spirits who play such a prominent role here, no resource can be more valuable than experience.

Though a lot can be learned from the ethnographies of the area and from local history collections, no teacher will be more valuable than the experience gained from service to the community, sitting with storytellers, volunteering to maintain the landscape and restore local rivers and wetlands, dedicating time and resources to sustainable indigenous horticulture, and, importantly, supporting local tribes in their effort to steward their traditional territories. If we listen, the people, the spirits, the land, the sea, and the sky have spiritual—even magical—wisdom to teach us all.

219. A. D., personal communication with author, April 2017.

FIELD NOTES

Folk Magic at the Movies

Hollywood glitz and glam is not exactly known for telling true stories (even the ones that are "based on a true story" get a bit of the Tinseltown treatment). Many people think that magic is all wands and sparks and lightning bolts hurled by bearded wizard-types because of portrayals in films like *Lord of the Rings* or *Harry Potter*. Yet every once in a while, Hollywood makes a movie that gets it a little bit right when it comes to folk magic. I've put together a coven of films that bring in folklore and folk magic with a bit of a realistic touch.

***Spitfire* (1934):** An early Katharine Hepburn film sees her playing Trigger, a woman who is believed to have supernatural healing abilities. As the story progresses, however, those around her begin to question whether her gift is truly divine, or if she's secretly a witch in disguise.

***Resurrection* (1980):** Ellen Burstyn accidentally gains healing powers following a car accident. Once her abilities become known, her role as a folk healer becomes a magnet for a wide range of the "faithful," including some who take their zealotry too far.

***The Craft* (1996):** While this film has a lot of sensational elements, including a fictitious witch god that apparently hates sea creatures, it also manages to get a few things right about folk practices within the tradition of Wicca. (The filmmakers had a Wiccan consultant advise them.) The movie left a lasting impact on several stars, as Fairuza Balk eventually purchased an occult bookshop in LA and Rachel True went on to design and release her own tarot deck.

***The Witches of Eastwick* (1987):** In this dark comedy, a group of women in the little New England town of Eastwick become involved with a diabolical new arrival (played by Jack Nicholson). The lore under the story is loosely connected to other New England witch tales, but some of the folk spells—such as the infamous cherry pits scene or the use of wax dolls—are based on principles of sympathetic magic.

***Like Water for Chocolate* (1992):** This Mexican film, based on a book by Laura Esquivel, tells the story of a young woman named Tita (Lumi Cavazos) and her sisters, as well as their struggle to get out from under the thumb of their mother, Elena (Regina Torné). Along the way, Tita winds up creating accidental spells out of the foods she makes by adding things like tears to the recipe, which has a strong element of folk magic about it.

***Eve's Bayou* (1997):** The story of family betrayal, heartbreak, and love within this Black-led film is powerful, as is the character of Mozelle (Debbi Morgan), a woman with clairvoyance and a knack for working Hoodoo charms for her neighbors. Add to that the cursing and hexing undertaken by Elzora (Diahann Carroll), and you've got a movie with plenty of magic.

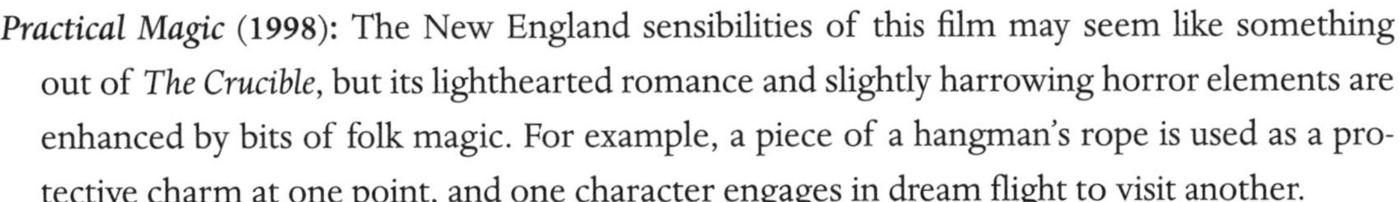

Practical Magic (1998): The New England sensibilities of this film may seem like something out of *The Crucible*, but its lighthearted romance and slightly harrowing horror elements are enhanced by bits of folk magic. For example, a piece of a hangman's rope is used as a protective charm at one point, and one character engages in dream flight to visit another.

The Gift (2000): In this story of a Southern woman with the titular gift of clairvoyance, a murder can only be solved by connecting with the spirit of her great-grandmother. When Annie (Cate Blanchett) begins to unravel a dark web of abuse and intrigue, she finds herself targeted by a killer and aided by spirits from beyond the grave.

The Skeleton Key (2005): This film is a supernatural thriller/horror, but it also features a tremendous amount of Hoodoo and folk magic in it. This makes sense, as one of the consultants for the film was the owner of the Lucky Mojo Curio Company, Cat Yronwode, who specializes in Hoodoo products and information.

The Witch (2015): Billed as "A New England Folktale," this dark and brooding film is constructed from actual records of New England witch stories and trials.[220] Thomasin (Anya Taylor-Joy) struggles as her family is torn apart by religious zealotry and witchcraft. This is portrayed with a mix of sensationalism and some very real folk charms, spells, and practices woven together.

The Love Witch (2016): An atmospheric nod to '70s filmmaking, this movie features the titular love witch Elaine (Samantha Robinson) and her freewheeling search for love and sex. She does several spells, such as the creation of a witch bottle, that are rooted in real folk magic.

The Lighthouse (2019): This is a strange mix of folklore, mythology, tragedy, horror, and comedy. Two lighthouse keepers, played by Willem Dafoe and Robert Pattinson, find their monthlong isolation together slowly drives them mad. (Or were they mad all along?) Maritime folklore abounds, including lore about seabirds and mermaids (none of which is particularly pleasant).

The Witches (2020): This is an adaptation of Roald Dahl's beloved children's book, but the 2020 version of the film featuring Octavia Spencer also incorporates a few elements of folk magic. Spencer's character, for example, maintains a room in her home full of folk charms and protective magical items similar to those used by Hoodoo practitioners. While this version does attempt to be more inclusive, it still maintains some of the antisemitic imagery from Dahl's book.

The Old Ways (2020): This film presents the story of a Mexican American woman named Cristina (Brigitte Kali Canales) who goes home to Veracruz only to become the target of a local bruja, who believes Cristina has a demon that needs to be purged from her. While it is brutal to watch, there are elements of Brujeria within the film that reflect some actual practices.

220. O'Falt, "How Robert Eggers Used Real Historical Accounts to Create His Horror Sensation 'The Witch.'"

TRAVELING ON
The Left Coast

As with any guidebook, there is always much more to experience than can be neatly fit into a chapter. To that end, we offer you this addendum to the map that will provide you with some tools to explore the Left Coast further.

The glossary shares some keywords that might be useful. The places to visit will point you toward locations of interest that we think you might find valuable, and the reading recommendations provide you with some top-tier texts that can be used to dig in and learn more about this region.

Glossary

Ba Gua: A series of eight trigram figures in Taoist folk belief, representing the elemental building blocks of life in the form of heaven, lake, fire, thunder, wind, water, mountain, and earth.

Brujería: A word that translates as "witchcraft" but involves a wide complex of magical practices. Brujos can do many of the tasks a curandero can do, but they may also do work for love, lust, revenge, or justice that are beyond the typical scope of their healer counterparts.

Chang'e: The Taoist moon goddess revered at the autumnal Moon Festival.

Curanderismo: The folk magical healing practices associated with traditional Mexican American culture. These can involve the treatment and removal of both physical and spiritual diseases, as well as cultural functions such as blessings or honoring the dead.

dollies: Figures made from corn husks, rags, apples, or other household items, used to focus magical intention.

ethnobotany: The study of—and sometimes practice of—ecological and botanical relationships and human culture.

God Mountains: Grandfather Mount Rainier (also known locally as Tacoma), lonely Mount Adams (Pahto), shining Mount Baker (Kulshan), and fiery Mount St. Helens are rulers among the mountains that shape the Pacific Northwest, overlooking the region and dominating the horizons.

I Ching: A Taoist book of divinatory and philosophical poems associated with geomantic figures. Sometimes also used to refer to a divination system based on the book, which is more properly called *kau chim* (Cantonese) or *qiu qian* (Mandarin).

jiaobei: A geomantic divination system that uses half-moon-shaped blocks or inscribed shells to provide messages from the gods in Taoist folk magic.

limpia: A ritual cleansing found in Curanderismo (and to some extent within some forms of Brujeria). It frequently involves sweeping a person with an object like an egg or herbs in order to remove harmful influences.

nurse log: A fallen tree whose decaying corpse provides essential nutrients, growth area, and protection for a vast array of new life. From its death, thousands of organisms are fed and the forest floor is replenished.

old-growth forest: Aged, undisturbed, or minimally impacted forests that are rich in indigenous plant life and ecologically valuable to the biology of coniferous forests.

qi: The life force, sometimes also spelled or pronounced "chi," that pervades all things in Taoist folk belief.

Tai Yang Gong: The Taoist "Grandfather Sun," revered at the spring equinox.

Taoism: A Chinese religious and philosophy system with a number of sects and branches, including several involving magic and sorcery.

tongs: The term for Chinese secret societies in North America, often very tightly interwoven with mysticism and ancestor veneration, as well as the reverence toward warrior-god Guan Di.

track magic: The use of footprints for magical influence.

Triads: A term referring to secret societies in China, sometimes also called *Hak Sh'e Wui* (Cantonese), *Hei She Hui* (Mandarin), or Black Societies, that revere legendary warrior god Guan Di.

Wujimu: The colloquial name for Xi Wang Mu, a dark goddess also known as Infinite Mother who gave adherents like those in the White Lotus society magical gifts or abilities.

Wu Xing: The system of transformation in Taoist thought that represent five states of material change: wood, fire, earth, metal, and water.

The Yellow Emperor: A legendary shaman-king in Chinese folklore and mythology with the reputed power to transform into a yellow dragon.

Places to Visit

Make Magic Beyond the Movies in Los Angeles, California: Los Angeles is a nexus of people from all over the world, not to mention a land of innovation, dreamers, disappointment, and despair (probably due to the traffic). It's no wonder that there are lots of occult shops like House of Intuition and The Green Man dotting the landscape, not to mention the bizarre but witch-friendly shop called Soap Plant / Wacko. Similarly, a number of botanicas fill the city blocks, offering supplies to folk magic practitioners. You can visit the massive occult book collection at the Philosophical Research Society or peruse the vast offerings at The Last Bookstore. You should check events calendars before you visit because there are tons of magic-friendly gatherings happening at any given time, from the *Día de los Muertos* event on Olvera Street to the Krampusnacht festival that celebrates the yuletide devil-figure of Krampus on Torrance Boulevard.

Find Taoism or Hoodoo in and around San Francisco, California: If you're visiting "The City by the Bay," you are likely to find all sorts of wonderful magical options to explore. The Chinatown district is full of wonderful things to see and do, including getting your fortune told by a practitioner of traditional *qiu qian* stick readings. There are also shops selling spiritual supplies from around the world, including statuary from a variety of beliefs and "hell money" used for offerings. If you head just a bit north of the city proper, you can also visit Forestville, California, home of Lucky Mojo Curio Company. This shop has been offering Hoodoo and folk magic supplies for years, and there is always a staff member ready to direct you to the magical components you might need, from good luck amulets to oils like "Court Case" (to help with legal troubles) and "Do As I Say" (to compel others to obey).

Explore the Weirder Side of Folk Magic in Portland, Oregon: The City of Roses has a reputation for being more than a little odd. You could get a Voodoo Donut and stab it with a pretzel stick for some sweet-treat poppet magic, or you could visit the haunted stone structure in Macleay Park known as "The Witch's Castle," associated with tragic murders and ghostly goings-on. Up until recently, there was also a major shrine to the American folk saint Elvis Presley, although that is now defunct.[221] For a bit of occult history, you can stop by the Theosophical Society or visit the Hotel deLuxe (formerly the Mallory Hotel), a site of many séances and Ouija sessions during the early twentieth century. For a final bit of weird history that touches on a few of the folkloric bits of the city's past, you can take a historical or ghost tour that discusses the Shanghai tunnels, an underground network of passages used for almost one hundred years to move both legal and illicit goods.

221. For more on why Elvis is considered a folk saint, I highly recommend Illes, *Encyclopedia of Mystics, Saints & Sages*.

Wander Between the Worlds in Seattle, Washington: The stars-to-subterranean nature of Seattle has several interesting occult elements. For example, you can visit one of the strangest secret libraries on the continent, housing over ten thousand books on magic, the occult, and other paranormal topics, if you head to Northwest Market Street. There, you'll see a red-outlined building with a sign saying Kress, and a little glass door to one side. If you head down into the basement, you'll find the As-You-Like-It Library, also known as the Seattle Metaphysical Library. (They aren't allowed to advertise their business, so finding the library is part of the magical adventure.) For more secret spaces, you can visit the halfway-hidden Kubota Garden, a Japanese-inspired park full of native Northwestern plants. It would hardly be Bigfoot country without some oddity shops, such as Big Top Curiosity Shop or Ye Olde Curiosity Shop (which has objects like Jenny Hanivers and mummy parts in their inventory). And, of course, don't forget to visit the troll living under the George Washington Memorial Bridge. (He's just a sculpture—we think—but maybe keep your distance if you're a billy goat.)

Recommended Reading

Mythology of Southern Puget Sound: Legends Shared by Tribal Elders by Arthur C. Ballard
The best way to know an area is to know its stories, and Ballard's collection of Salish, Duwamish, and other Indigenous tales gives narrative voice to the people and landscape of the Pacific Northwest.

Cleansing Rites of Curanderismo: Limpias Espirituales of Ancient Mesoamerican Shamans by Erika Buenaflor
Buenaflor's book is a focused, scholarly look at the rituals and history of Mesoamerican healing and spiritual practices.

The Woman Warrior: Memoirs of a Girlhood Among Ghosts by Maxine Hong Kingston
This astounding autobiography explores the author's life as a Chinese American woman growing up with the stories her mother told from Chinese folklore, and how those stories had a lasting impact on her for the rest of her life.

Ancient Pathways, Ancestral Knowledge: Ethnobotany and Ecological Wisdom of Indigenous Peoples of Northwestern North America by Nancy J. Turner
This tome looks at the Indigenous knowledge of, and uses of, plants in the Pacific Northwest and also incorporates scientific understanding about local ecologies.

Chapter 8

American Brujeria: Modern Mexican American Folk Magic by J. Allen Cross
Cross looks at the way that Brujeria has grown and evolved in the US landscape, providing a guide that is both informative and practical.

Folkloric American Witchcraft and the Multicultural Experience: A Crucible at the Crossroads by Via Hedera
The slim size of this book belies its incredibly well-researched and thorough contents, which chronicle a wide variety of folk magic practices from North America.

From Kuan Yin to Chairman Mao: The Essential Guide to Chinese Deities by Xueting Christine Ni
This whirlwind tour of Chinese spiritual figures covers both ancient and contemporary spirits that are revered by people in China and people with Chinese heritage in North America.

The Tao of Craft: Fu Talismans and Casting Sigils in the Eastern Esoteric Tradition by Benebell Wen
Wen's hefty book is a motherlode of information on the practice of crafting Chinese *fu* talismans, as well as a guide to how some of the principles of those talismans can apply to other forms of magic.

The Magic Lotus Lantern and Other Tales from the Han Chinese by Haiwang Yuan
This book offers a handful of valuable folktales drawn from the Han Chinese storytelling tradition that are still influential today.

ROADS LESS TRAVELED: A (SORT OF) CONCLUSION

We stop at the Puget Sound. Or maybe at the base of Mount Rainier. Possibly we pull off the road and stretch our legs in Vancouver, looking out over the gray-blue waters of the Northern Pacific. We watch the sun sink down below the horizon, and the first twinkling of stars appear in the sky as we pull our sweaters tighter around us in the chilly breeze.

This isn't the end, however. In our pocket, we carry a little packet spell we picked up somewhere down south to help us wing our way west safely. We remember our stop with Dr. Coelacanth and how he twisted sieve and shears to let us see what the trip might have in store for us, and we still smell the scent of herbs in our hair from when an Olorisha in Chicago gave us a blessing to watch over us. Our car is stuffed with lucky coins, a packet of hell money, a few small jars of bloodroot and rabbit tobacco, a *himmelsbrief* from Pennsylvania, and a Bible, which sits next to the dime-store reprint grimoire and almanac lining our rearview window, all absolutely crammed with notes on the various practices we've met along the way.

But there's still more. Even as the sun sets in the west, it's shining on someone doing North American folk magic somewhere else. As much as the enchantment in North America is a product of this place, this land, it is also a product of the people. There are people who have always been here, and those who came here from distant lands—willingly or not. Those who came here brought magic with them, and that magic has found North America to be a fertile place to root and grow. If there's one thing we've learned from meeting all these magic-keepers on our trip, it's that magic doesn't stay still. It moves, changes, blooms, fades, and renews itself generation after generation. It goes beyond what we think of as the boundaries of the continent, stretching into places we haven't visited.

When the contributors set out to make this journey, and to write this book, we hoped to bring in as many authentic, traditional voices as we could to talk about the many, many forms of folk magic here. We call this a "complete book," but it would be impossible to make anything truly complete when the enchantment we're writing about is still thriving and growing. Inevitably, we have missed so many aspects of folk magic here. We could not get to every iteration of ethnic folk magic, for example, and so we are missing the rich traditions of Filipino American and Italian American spell-casters, which are incredibly robust and worth exploring. Jewish, Hmong, and Cajun folk magic traditions have been squeezed into a few sentences or paragraphs. At one point, we considered including an "islands" section to cover the Caribbean, Hawaii, and even Alaska and the Northern Territories, but in the end we had to make tough choices and consider just how much we could cover in one book.

Together, reader, we have covered much ground. But there is still more. There will always be more. Which means it is time to hand the map and compass over to you.

This book has let you visit with two dozen magical practitioners, and it's taken you to stop-offs of sorcery or witchcraft that were slipped into the itinerary as we passed through the land. There are still so many more people practicing folk magic in North America, though. It's your turn to go out and meet them.

The best way to learn folk magic is to talk to the folk. You have seen how so many of these practitioners work with their traditions by listening to their elders and partaking in their communities. That is a good next step for you. If you take the trip back home, you'll find what I said at the beginning of the book is true: magic is right outside your front door. Now that you know the magic of Vicks VapoRub and chain letters, the stories that haunt the northern lights and the hills of the southern Appalachians, and the history of crossroads deals and love dollies, you know what you're looking for. You can go back and look at the books we've recommended along the way. You can visit the roadside stops (or even just seek them out online if you can't go in person) and delve deeper into the folklore. You can talk to your neighbors and ask them why their porch roof is blue, or whether they think it's a good time to plant potatoes based on their almanac. You can watch the parades at *Día de los Muertos* or the Lunar New Year and get to know the people who weave the magic. And you can look at your own practices, the things you've grown up doing or learned from those around you. You can share those right back, and you may find that you've been right in the thick of enchantment all along.

I'll share with you a final bit of folk magic, one I learned from Southern Conjure and adapted to my own needs. All you need is a penny—one of the US pennies with an image of a shield on the back. Hold it in your hands and whisper a protective prayer over it. (I like Psalm 23, but any shielding or protective incantation will work.) When you finish, breathe on the penny, paying it one breath of your life to do its work, then place it shield-side up on your dashboard to protect you on all your journeys. Like so much of folk magic, it is simple and cheap and practical, but it gets the job done. And with that, I can send you safely on your way.

This isn't the end; it's just another stop on the journey. You have the map now. Where will magic take you next?

• • • • • • • • • •

BIBLIOGRAPHY

Introduction

Dorson, Richard M. *Buying the Wind: Regional Folklore in the United States*. Chicago: University of Chicago Press, 1964.

Glassie, Henry. *Pattern in the Material Folk Culture of the Eastern United States*. Philadelphia: University of Pennsylvania Press, 1971.

Mood, Terry Ann. *American Regional Folklore: A Sourcebook and Research Guide*. Santa Barbara, CA: ABC-CLIO, 2004.

Woodard, Colin. *American Nations: A History of the Eleven Rival Regional Cultures of North America*. New York: Penguin Books, 2011.

1. New England and the Maritimes

Agrippa, Heinrich Cornelius. *Three Books of Occult Philosophy*. Translated by J. F. London: 1651.

———. *The Vanity of Arts and Sciences*. London: 1676.

Aubrey, John. *Three Prose Works*. Edited by John Buchanan-Brown. Carbondale: Southern Illinois University Press, 1972.

Barbeau, C.-Marius. "Anecdotes populaires du Canada." *The Journal of American Folklore* 33, no. 129 (July–Sept. 1920): 173–297. https://www.jstor.org/stable/534891.

Barone, Fran. "Luck of the Irish: Folklore and Fairies in Rural Ireland." Human Relations Area Files, March 12, 2020. https://hraf.yale.edu/luck-of-the-irish-folklore-and-fairies-in-rural-ireland/.

Blagrave, Joseph. *Blagrave's Astrological Practice of Physick*. London: 1671.

Bower, Edmond, ed. *Doctor Lamb Revived, or, VVitchcraft Condemn'd in Anne Bodenham*. London: 1653.

Boyer, Paul, and Stephen Nissenbaum. *Salem Possessed: The Social Origins of Witchcraft*. Cambridge, MA: Harvard University Press, 1974.

Boyko, John. "Company of One Hundred Associates." The Canadian Encyclopedia. Last modified January 25, 2022. https://www.thecanadianencyclopedia.ca/en/article/compagnie-des-cent-associes.

Butler, E. M. *Ritual Magic*. London: Cambridge University Press, 1979.

Butler, Gary R. *Histoire et traditions orales des franco-acadiens de terre-neuve*. Quebec: Les Éditions du Septentrion, 1995.

Butler, Jon. "Magic, Astrology, and the Early American Religious Heritage, 1600–1760." *The American Historical Review* 84, no. 2 (April 1979): 317–46. https://doi.org/10.1086/ahr/84.2.317.

Choquette, Leslie. "French Canadian Immigration to Vermont and New England (1840–1930)." *Vermont History* 86, no. 1 (Winter/Spring 2018): 1–8. https://vermonthistory.org/journal/86/VH8601FrenchCanadianImmigration.pdf.

Cummins, Alexander. "Transatlantic Cunning: English Occult Practices in the British American Colonies." In *Prophecy and Eschatology in the Transatlantic World, 1550–1800*, edited by Andrew Crome, 151–86. London: Palgrave Macmillan, 2016.

———. "'In the Manner of Saint Cyprian': A Cyprianic Black Magic of Early Modern English Grimoires." In *Cypriana: Old World*, edited by Alexander Cummins, Jesse Hathaway Diaz, and Jennifer Zahrt, 83–116. Tumwater, WA: Revelore Press, 2017.

———. *The Starry Rubric: Seventeenth-Century English Astrology and Magic*. Keighley, UK: Hadean Press, 2012.

Davies, Owen. *Popular Magic: Cunning-Folk in English History*. London: Hambledon Continuum, 2003.

Davies, S. F. "The Reception of Reginald Scot's *Discovery of Witchcraft*: Witchcraft, Magic, and Radical Religion." *Journal of the History of Ideas* 74, no. 3 (2013): 381–401. https://doi.org/10.1353/jhi.2013.0021.

desRuisseaux, Pierre. *Croyances et pratiques populaires au Canada Français*. Montréal: Éditions du Jour, 1973.

———. *Magie et Sorcellerie populaires au Québec*. Montréal: Triptyque, 1976.

Dorais, Louis-Jacques. "La Vie Traditionnelle Sur La Côte de Beaupré, au Début du XX Siècle." *Revue d'Histoire de l'Amérique Française* 19, no. 4 (March 1966): 535–50. https://doi.org/10.7202/302511ar.

Dorson, Richard M. *Bloodstoppers and Bearwalkers: Folk Traditions of Michigan's Upper Peninsula*. 3rd ed. Madison: University of Wisconsin Press, 2008.

———. *Buying the Wind: Regional Folklore in the United States*. Chicago: University of Chicago Press, 1964.

Evans-Wentz, W. Y. *The Fairy-Faith in Celtic Countries*. Charleston, SC: BiblioLife, 2009.

"The Explorers: Jacques Marquette 1673." Canadian Museum of History. Accessed January 25, 2021. https://www.historymuseum.ca/virtual-museum-of-new-france/the-explorers/jacques-marquette-1673-1694/.

Fraser, Mary L.. *Folklore of Nova Scotia*. 2nd ed. Nova Scotia: Formac Pub, 2009.

"The French (1673–1763)." Illinois State Museum. Accessed January 18, 2021. http://www.museum.state.il.us/muslink/nat_amer/post/htmls/soc_french.html.

Gifford, George. *A Dialogue Concerning Witches and Witchcraftes in which Is Laide Open how Craftely the Diuell Deceiuth not Onely the Witches but Many Other and so Leadeth Them Awrie into Many Great Errours*. London: 1593.

Glanvill, Joseph. *A Philosophical Endeavour towards the Defence of the Being of VVitches and Apparitions*. London: 1666.

Gordon, Stephen. "Domestic Magic and the Walking Dead in Medieval England: A Diachronic Approach." *The Materiality of Magic*, edited by Ceri Houlbrook and Natalie Armitage, 65–84. Oxford: Oxbow, 2015.

Gouvernement du Québec. "Compagnie des Cent-Associés." Répertoire du Patrimoine Culturel du Québec. Accessed February 1, 2021. https://www.patrimoine-culturel.gouv.qc.ca/rpcq/detail.do?methode=consulter&id=9104&type=pge.

Hadass, Ofer. *Medicine, Religion, and Magic in Early Stuart England: Richard Napier's Medical Practice*. University Park: Penn State University Press, 2019.

Hall, David D. *Worlds of Wonder, Days of Judgment: Popular Religious Belief in Early New England*. Cambridge, MA: Harvard University Press, 1990.

Heydon, John. *Harmony of the World*. London: 1662.

———. *Theomagia, or the Temple of Wisdom*. London: 1664.

Hodson, Christopher. *The Acadian Diaspora: An Eighteenth-Century History*. New York: Oxford University Press, 2012.

Hufford, David J. "Ste. Anne de Beaupré: Roman Catholic Pilgrimage and Healing." *Western Folklore* 44, no. 3 (July 1985): 194–207. https://doi.org/10.2307/1499835.

Karlsen, Carol F. *The Devil in the Shape of a Woman: Witchcraft in Colonial New England*. New York: W. W. Norton, 1987.

Klaassen, Frank, ed. *Making Magic in Elizabethan England: Two Early Modern Vernacular Books of Magic*. University Park: Penn State University Press, 2019.

Klaassen, Frank, and Sharon Hubbs Wright. *The Magic of Rogues: Necromancers in Early Tudor England*. University Park: Penn State University Press, 2021.

Landry, Nicolas. "History of Plaisance." Newfoundland and Labrador Heritage. Accessed January 18, 2021. https://www.heritage.nf.ca/articles/exploration/placentia.php.

Larson, Denise R. *Companions of Champlain: Founding Families of Quebec, 1608–1635*. Baltimore, MD: Clearfield, 2008.

Legard, Phil, and Alexander Cummins, eds. *An Excellent Booke of the Arte of Magicke: The Magical Works of Humphrey Gilbert & John Davis from British Library Additional Manuscript 36674*. London: Scarlet Imprint, 2020.

Lilly, William. *Christian Astrology*. London, 1647.

———. *William Lilly's History of His Life and Times: From the Year 1602 to 1681*. London: 1715. https://www.gutenberg.org/files/15835/15835-h/15835-h.htm.

MacDonald, Michael. *Mystical Bedlam: Madness, Anxiety, and Healing in Seventeenth-Century England*. New York: Cambridge University Press, 1981.

Mather, Cotton. *The Wonders of the Invisible World*. London, 1693.

Norton, Mary Beth. *In the Devil's Snare: The Salem Witchcraft Crisis of 1692*. New York: Vintage Books, 2003.

Ó hÓgáin, Dáithí. *Irish Superstitions*. Dublin: Gill Books, 2002.

Ó Súilleabháin, Seán. *Nósanna agus Piseoga na nGael* [Irish folk custom and belief]. Dublin: Three Candles, 1967.

Pearl, Jonathan L. "Witchcraft in New France in the Seventeenth Century: The Social Aspect." *Historical Reflections/Réflexions Historiques* 4, no. 2 (Winter 1977): 41–55. https://www.jstor.org/stable/41298699.

"Population: Pays d'En Haut and Louisiana." Canadian Museum of History. Accessed January 18, 2021. https://www.historymuseum.ca/virtual-museum-of-new-france/population/pays-den-haut-and-louisiana/.

Quinn, E. Moore. *Irish American Folklore in New England*. Washington, DC: Academica Press, 2009.

Rankine, David, ed. *The Grimoire of Arthur Gauntlet: A 17th Century London Cunning-man's Book of Charms, Conjurations, and Prayers*. London: Avalonia, 2011.

Rawlinson Manuscripts. Bodleian Library, Oxford.

Reynolds, Samuel Harvey, ed. *The Table Talk of John Selden*. Oxford: Clarendon Press, 1892.

Rousseau, Madeleine, and Jacques Rousseau. "Charmes et merveilleux." *Archives de folklore* 4 (1949): 77–89. http://www2.ville.montreal.qc.ca/jardin/archives/rousseau/publi/Charmes_et_merveilleux.pdf.

Roy, Carmen. *Litterature orale en gaspesie*. 2nd ed. Ottawa: Ministère du Nord Canadien et des Ressources Nationales, 1962.

Scot, Reginald. *The Discovery of Witchcraft*. London, 1665.

Sloane Manuscripts. British Library, London.

Sneddon, Andrew. *Witchcraft and Magic in Ireland*. New York: Palgrave Macmillan, 2015.

Stratton-Kent, Jake. *Geosophia: The Argo of Magic*. Encyclopædia Goetica. London: Scarlet Imprint, 2010.

———. *The Testament of Cyprian the Mage*. Encyclopædia Goetica. London: Scarlet Imprint, 2014.

———. *True Grimoire*. Encyclopædia Goetica. London: Scarlet Imprint, 2009.

Thwaite, Annie. "What Is a 'Witch Bottle'? Assembling the Textual Evidence from Early Modern England." *Magic, Ritual, and Witchcraft* 15, no. 2 (Fall 2020): 227–51. https://doi.org/10.1353/mrw.2020.0018.

Timbers, Frances. *The Magical Adventures of Mary Parish: The Occult World of Seventeenth-Century London*. Kirksville, MO: Truman State University Press, 2016.

Verney, Jack. *The Good Regiment: The Carignan-Salières Regiment in Canada, 1665–1668*. Montreal: McGill-Queen's University Press, 1991.

Wilby, Emma. *Cunning Folk and Familiar Spirits: Shamanistic Visionary Traditions in Early Modern British Witchcraft and Magic*. Brighton: Sussex Academic Press, 2005.

2. New Holland and Deitscherei

Bilardi, C. R. *The Red Church or the Art of Pennsylvania German Braucherei*. Sunland, CA: Pendraig Publishing, 2009.

Bird, Stephanie Rose. *The Healing Power of African-American Spirituality: A Celebration of Ancestor Worship, Herbs and Hoodoo, Ritual and Conjure*. Newburyport, MA: Hampton Roads, 2022.

———. *Sticks, Stones, Roots & Bones: Hoodoo, Mojo & Conjuring with Herbs*. St. Paul, MN: Llewellyn Publications, 2004.

———. *365 Days of Hoodoo: Daily Rootwork, Mojo & Conjuration*. Woodbury, MN: Llewellyn Publications, 2018.

"Born in Slavery: Slave Narratives from the Federal Writers' Project, 1936 to 1938." Library of Congress. Accessed June 13, 2022. https://www.loc.gov/collections/slave-narratives-from-the-federal-writers-project-1936-to-1938/about-this-collection/.

Breslaw, Elaine G., ed. *Witches of the Atlantic World: A Historic Reader & Primary Sourcebook*. New York: NYU Press, 2000.

Chisholm, James. *Groves and Gallows: Greek and Latin Sources for Germanic Heathenism*. Smithville, TX: Runa-Raven Press, 2002.

Donmoyer, Patrick. "Hex Signs: Sacred and Celestial Symbolism in Pennsylvania Dutch Barn Stars." Kutztown, PA: The Pennsylvania German Cultural Heritage Center, 2019. Published in conjunction with an exhibition of the same title, organized by and presented at the Glencairn Museum, March 1, 2019–November 3, 2019. https://www.glencairnmuseum.org/newsletter/2019/3/19/hex-signs-sacred-and-celestial-symbolism-in-pennsylvania-dutch-barn-stars.

Fortson, Benjamin W., IV. *Indo-European Language and Culture: An Introduction*. 1st ed. Oxford: Blackwell Publishing Ltd, 2004.

"Fortune Telling Frauds Stir State Hexerei Probe." *Reading Times* (Reading, PA), February 19, 1932. https://www.newspapers.com/newspage/47723352/.

Franklin, Benjamin. "Observations Concerning the Increase of Mankind, 1751." *Founders Online*. Accessed June 23, 2022. https://founders.archives.gov/documents/Franklin/01-04-02-0080.

Franklin, Chris. "'It Was a Part of All Our Lives': 600-Year-Old Oak Tree Will Get Final Send-Off in Memorial Service." *NJ Advance Media*, June 19, 2019. https://www.nj.com/salem/2019/06/it-was-a-part-of-all-our-lives-600-year-old-oak-tree-will-get-final-send-off-in-memorial-service.html?outputType=amp.

Free, Shane, dir. *Hex Hollow: Witchcraft and Murder in Pennsylvania*. New York: Shane Free Productions, 2015.

Giangrosso, Patricia. "Charms." *Medieval Germany: An Encyclopedia*, edited by John M. Jeep, 114–14. New York: Routledge, 2001.

Griffiths, Bill. *Aspects of Anglo-Saxon Magic*. 3rd ed. Little Downham, England: Anglo-Saxon Books, 2003.

Grimassi, Raven. *The Cimaruta and Other Magical Charms from Old Italy*. Springfield, MO: Old Ways Press, 2012. Kindle.

Hand, Wayland D. "The Evil Eye in Its Folk Medical Aspects: A Survey of North America." *The Evil Eye: A Casebook*, edited by Alan Dundes, 169–80. Madison: University of Wisconsin Press, 1992.

Herr, Karl. *Hex and Spellwork: The Magical Practices of the Pennsylvania Dutch*. Newburyport, MA: Weiser Books, 2002.

Hyatt, Harry Middleton. *Hoodoo, Conjuration, Witchcraft, Rootwork: Beliefs Accepted by Many Negroes and White Persons, These Being Orally Recorded Among Blacks and Whites*. 5 vols. Hannibal, MO: Western Pub, 1970.

Jennings, Francis. "Glory, Death, and Transfiguration: The Susquehannock Indians in the Seventeenth Century." *Proceedings of the American Philosophical Society* 112, no. 1 (Feb. 1968): 15–53. http://www.jstor.org/stable/986100.

Kao, Audiey. "Medical Quackery: The Psuedo-Science of Health and Well-Being." *Virtual Mentor: American Medical Association Journal of Ethics* 2, no. 4 (April 2000): 30. https://journalofethics.ama-assn.org/article/medical-quackery-pseudo-science-health-and-well-being/2000-04.

Kriebel, David W. "Medicine." *Pennsylvania Germans: An Interpretive Encyclopedia*, edited by Simon J. Bronner and Joshua R. Brown. Baltimore, MD: Johns Hopkins University Press, 2017.

———. *Powwowing Among the Pennsylvania Dutch: A Traditional Medical Practice in the Modern World*. University Park: Penn State University Press, 2007.

List, Edgar A. "Frau Holda as the Personfication of Reason." *Philological Quarterly* 32 (Jan. 1953): 446–48.

Long, Carolyn Morrow. *Spiritual Merchants: Religion, Magic & Commerce*. Knoxville: University of Tennessee Press, 2001.

McGinnis, J. Ross. *Trials of Hex*. Fawn Grove, PA: Davis/Trinity Publishing Company, 2000.

Mitchell, David. "The SATOR Square." *Bright Morning Star* (blog), August 12, 2021. https://brightmorningstar.org/the-sator-square/.

Orsi, Robert A. *The Madonna of 115th Street: Faith and Community in Italian Harlem, 1880–1950*. 2nd ed. New Haven, CT: Yale University Press, 2002.

Paxson, Diana L. "Matronæ and Dísir: On Ancestresses." Hrafnar. Accessed June 23, 2022. https://hrafnar.org/articles/dpaxson/asynjur/matronae/.

Pennick, Nigel. "The Goddess Zisa." *TYR: Myth—Culture—Tradition*, edited by Joshua Buckley, Collin Cleary, and Michael Moynihan, 107–10. Atlanta: Ultra, 2002.

Peterson, Joseph H., trans. *Egyptian Secrets of Albertus Magnus*. Twilit Grotto: Archives of Western Esoterica. Accessed June 13, 2022. http://www.esotericarchives.com/moses/egyptian.htm.

Phoenix, Robert. *The Powwow Grimoire*. Self-published, CreateSpace, 2014.

Rouvalis, Cristina. "Psychics Have Trouble Foretelling When a State Law May Be Used Against Them." *Post-Gazette*, January 19, 1999. https://old.post-gazette.com/magazine/19990119psychic1.asp.

Russell, James C. *The Germanization of Early Medieval Christianity: A Sociohistorical Approach to Religious Transformation*. Oxford: Oxford University Press, 1996.

Schreiwer, Robert L. *The First Book of Urglaawe Myths*. Bristol, PA: Distelfink Sippschaft, 2014.

Shyrock, Richard H. "The Pennsylvania Germans in American History." *The Pennsylvania Magazine of History and Biography* 63, no. 3 (July 1939): 261–81.

Soderlund, Jean R. "Women in Eighteenth-Century Pennsylvania: Toward a Model of Diversity." *The Pennsylvania Magazine of History and Biography* 115, no. 2 (April 1991): 163–83. https://www.jstor.org/stable/20092603.

"State Official Here Concerning Death of Fredericksburg Child." *Lebanon Semi-Weekly News* (Lebanon, PA), December 24, 1928. https://www.newspapers.com/newspage/13850734/.

Taumaturgo, Agostino. *The Things We Do: Ways of the Holy Benedetta*. Self-published, CreateSpace, 2007.

Tirabassi, Maddalena. "Why Italians Left Italy: The Physics and Politics of Migration, 1870–1920." *The Routledge History of Italian Americans*, edited by William J. Connell and Stanislao G. Pugliese, 117–31. New York: Routledge, 2018.

Trachtenberg, Joshua. *Jewish Magic and Superstition: A Study in Folk Religion*. New York: Meridian Books, 1961.

Wallace, Paul A. W. *Indians in Pennsylvania*. Harrisburg: The Pennsylvania Historical and Museum Commission, 1991.

Wenger, Diane, and Simon J. Bronner. "Communities and Identities: Nineteenth to the Twenty-First Centuries." *Pennsylvania Germans: An Interpretive Encyclopedia*, edited by Simon J. Bronner and Joshua R. Brown. Baltimore, MD: Johns Hopkins University Press, 2017.

Weslager, C. A. *The Delaware Indians: A History*. New Brunswick, NJ: Rutgers University Press, 2008.

Z. "A Short History of Tichels and the Modern Resurgence." Jewitches, June 24, 2021. https://www.jewitches.com/post/a-short-history-of-tichels-and-the-modern-resurgence.

3. The Upland South

Albanese, Catherine L. *A Republic of Mind and Spirit: A Cultural History of American Metaphysical Religion*. New Haven, CT: Yale University Press, 2008.

Appalachian Melungeon Heritage Cookbook. Kearney, NE: Morris Press, 1995.

Aswell, James, Julia Willhoit, Jeannette Edwards, E. E. Miller, and Lena E. Lipscomb. *God Bless the Devil!: Liars' Bench Tales*. Chapel Hill: University of North Carolina Press, 1940.

Ballard, H. Byron. *Staubs and Ditchwater: A Friendly and Useful Introduction to Hillfolks' Hoodoo*. Asheville, NC: Silver Rings Press, 2017.

Bible, Jean Patterson. *Melungeons: Yesterday and Today*. Signal Mountain, TN: Mountain Press, 1975.

Butler, Jon. *Awash in a Sea of Faith: Christianizing the American People*. Cambridge, MA: Harvard University Press, 1990.

Cavender, Anthony. *Folk Medicine in Southern Appalachia*. Chapel Hill: University of North Carolina Press, 2007.

Covington, Dennis. *Salvation on Sand Mountain: Snake Handling and Redemption in Southern Appalachia*. New York: Da Capo Press, 2009.

Cross, Tom Peete. "Witchcraft in North Carolina." *Studies in Philology* 16, no. 3 (July 1919): 217–87.

Davis, Hubert J., ed. *The Silver Bullet and Other American Witch Stories*. Middle Village, NY: Jonathan David Publishers, 1975.

Dorson, Richard M. *Buying the Wind: Regional Folklore in the United States*. Chicago: University of Chicago Press, 1964.

Dromgoole, Will Allen. "The Malungeons." Melungeon Heritage, October 14, 2016. http://melungeon.org/2016/10/14/the-malungeons-by-will-allen-dromgoole-1891-article/.

Duke, James S. *Handbook of Medicinal Herbs*. 2nd ed. Boca Raton, FL: CRC Press, 2002.

Foxfire Fund. The Foxfire Series. 12 vols. Edited by Eliot Wigginton. New York: Penguin Random House, 1972–2004.

Gainer, Patrick W. *Witches, Ghosts, and Signs: Folklore of the Southern Appalachians*. Morgantown: West Virginia University Press, 2008.

Genovese, Eugene D. *Roll, Jordan, Roll: The World the Slaves Made*. New York: Vintage Books, 1976.

Groover, Mark D. "Creolization and the Archaeology of Multiethnic Households in the American South." *Historical Archaeology* 34, no. 3 (2000): 99–106. https://www.jstor.org/stable/25616835.

Halpert, Herbert. "The Devil and the Fiddle." *Hoosier Folklore Bulletin* 2, no. 2 (Dec. 1943): 39–43. https://www.jstor.org/stable/i27655455.

Hashaw, Tim. *Children of Perdition: Melungeons and the Struggle of Mixed America*. Macon, GA: Mercer University Press, 2006.

———. "MALUNGU: The African Origin of the American Melungeons." *Eclectica*. Accessed June 30, 2022. https://www.eclectica.org/v5n3/hashaw.html.

Hazzard-Donald, Katrina. *Mojo Workin': The Old African American Hoodoo System*. Champaign: University of Illinois Press, 2013.

Hyatt, Harry Middleton. *Folklore from Adams County, Illinois*. New York: Alma Egan Hyatt Foundation, 1935. https://archive.org/details/folklorefromadam00hyat.

lcbudd14. "The Witch of Pungo Statue." *Atlas Obscura*, January 25, 2016. https://www.atlasobscura.com/places/the-witch-of-pungo-statue-virginia-beach-virginia.

McAtee, W. L. "Odds and Ends of North American Folklore on Birds." *Midwest Folklore* 5, no. 3 (Fall 1955): 168–83. https://www.jstor.org/stable/4317532.

McMillan, Hamilton. *Sir Walter Raleigh's Lost Colony: An Historical Sketch of the Attempts of Sir Walter Raleigh to Establish a Colony in Virginia, with the Traditions of an Indian Tribe in North Carolina, Indicating the Fate of the Colony of Englishmen Left on Roanoke Island in 1597*. Wilson, NC: Advance Presses, 1888. https://digital.lib.ecu.edu/13413.

Milnes, Gerald C. *Signs, Cures & Witchery: German Appalachian Folklore*. Knoxville: The University of Tennessee Press, 2011.

Morrison, Toni. *Sula*. New York: Vintage Books, 2004.

Oberon, Aaron. *Southern Cunning: Folkloric Witchcraft in the American South*. Winchester, UK: Moon Books, 2019.

Olson, Ted, and Anthony P. Cavender, eds. *A Tennessee Folklore Sampler: Selections from the Tennessee Folklore Society Bulletin [1935–2009]*. Knoxville: The University of Tennessee Press, 2009.

Paredes, James Anthony, ed. *Indians of the Southeastern United States in the Late 20th Century*. Tuscaloosa: University of Alabama Press, 1992.

Pezzullo, Joanne. "The Malungeons According to Joanne." The Melungeon Indians. Accessed June 30, 2022. http://historical-melungeons.com/joannesmalungeons.htm.

Price, Sadie F. "Kentucky Folk-Lore." *The Journal of American Folklore* 14, no. 52 (Jan.–Mar. 1901): 30–8. https://doi.org/10.2307/533104.

Raboteau, Albert J. *Slave Religion: The "Invisible Institution" in the Antebellum South*. New York: Oxford University Press, 2004.

Randolph, Vance. *Ozark Magic and Folklore*. New York: Dover Publications, 2003.

Richards, Jake. *Backwoods Witchcraft: Conjure & Folk Magic from Appalachia*. Newburyport, MA: Weiser Books, 2019.

———. *Doctoring the Devil: Notebooks of an Appalachian Conjure Man*. Newburyport, MA: Red Wheel/Weiser Books, 2021.

Steiner, Roland. "Superstitions and Beliefs from Central Georgia." *The Journal of American Folklore* 12, no. 47 (Oct.–Dec. 1899): 261–71. https://doi.org/10.2307/533053.

Taylor, J. P. "Oil Testimonial." Oil & Gas Prospecting. Accessed December 20, 2022. https://www.prospectingoilandgas.com/oil%20testimonial.html.

Thomas, Daniel Lindsey, and Lucy Blayney Thomas. *Kentucky Superstitions*. Princeton, NJ: Princeton University Press, 1920. https://archive.org/details/kentuckysupersti00thomuoft/.

White, Newman Ivey, ed. *The Frank C. Brown Collection of NC Folklore*. Vol. 6, *Popular Beliefs and Superstitions from North Carolina, pt. 1*. Durham, NC: Duke University Press, 2013.

———. *The Frank C. Brown Collection of NC Folklore*. Vol. 7, *Popular Beliefs and Superstitions from North Carolina, pt. 2*. Durham, NC: Duke University Press, 2013.

Woodard, Colin. *American Nations: A History of the Eleven Rival Regional Cultures of North America.* New York: Penguin Books, 2011.

4. The Deep South

Alston, Bailey M., Thomas R. Rainwater, Benjamin B. Parrott, Philip M. Wilkinson, John A. Bowden, and Charles D. Rice. "Quantifying Circulating IgY Antibody Responses against Select Opportunistic Bacterial Pathogens and Correlations with Body Condition Factors in Wild American Alligators, *Alligator mississippiensis*." *Biology* 11, no. 2 (2022): 269. https://doi.org/10.3390/biology11020269.

Anderson, Annye C. *Brother Robert: Growing Up with Robert Johnson*. New York: Hachette Books, 2020.

Bird, Stephanie Rose. *365 Days of Hoodoo: Daily Rootwork, Mojo & Conjuration*. Woodbury, MN: Llewellyn Publications, 2018.

Casas, Starr. *The Conjure Workbook Volume 1: Working the Root*. Sunland, CA: Pendraig Publishing, 2013.

———. *Old Style Conjure: Hoodoo, Rootwork & Folk Magic*. Newburyport, MA: Weiser Books, 2017.

Chireau, Yvonne P. *Black Magic: Religion and the African American Conjuring Tradition*. Berkeley: University of California Press, 2006.

Congdon, Kristin G. *Uncle Monday and Other Florida Tales*. Jackson: University Press of Mississippi, 2001.

Dorsey, Lilith. *The African-American Ritual Cookbook*. Self-published, 1998.

———. *Orishas, Goddesses, and Voodoo Queens: The Divine Feminine in the African Religious Traditions*. Newburyport, MA: Weiser Books, 2020.

———. *Voodoo and African Traditional Religion*. New Orleans: Warlock Press, 2021.

Dorson, Richard M. *Buying the Wind: Regional Folklore in the United States*. Chicago: University of Chicago Press, 1964.

Dunham, Katherine. *Island Possessed*. Garden City, NY: Doubleday, 1969.

Fee, Christopher R., and Jeffrey B. Webb, eds. *American Myths, Legends, and Tall Tales: An Encyclopedia of American Folklore*. 3 vols. Santa Barbara, CA: ABC-CLIO, 2016.

Hazzard-Donald, Katrina. *Mojo Workin': The Old African American Hoodoo System*. Champaign: University of Illinois Press, 2013.

Hurston, Zora Neale. *Mules and Men*. New York: Harper & Row, 2008.

———. *Tell My Horse: Voodoo and Life in Haiti and Jamaica*. New York: Harper & Row, 2008.

Hyatt, Harry Middleton. *Hoodoo, Conjuration, Witchcraft, Rootwork: Beliefs Accepted by Many Negroes and White Persons, These Being Orally Recorded Among Blacks and Whites*. 5 vols. Hannibal, MO: Western Pub, 1970.

Kail, Tony. *A Secret History of Memphis Hoodoo: Rootworkers, Conjurers & Spirituals*. Charleston, SC: The History Press, 2017.

Lee, Michele E. *Working the Roots: Over 400 Years of Traditional African American Healing*. Oakland, CA: Wadastick Publishing, 2017.

"The Legend of the Crucifix Fish." Florida Memory. Accessed February 16, 2022. https://www.floridamemory.com/items/show/269847.

Lewis, Alex. "Krewe Du Kanaval Honors the Haitian Roots of New Orleans." *NPR*, February 12, 2020. https://www.npr.org/sections/world-cafe/2020/02/12/804873908/krewe-du-kanaval-honors-the-haitian-roots-of-new-orleans/.

Long, Carolyn Morrow. *Spiritual Merchants: Religion, Magic & Commerce*. Knoxville: University of Tennessee Press, 2001.

Martinié, Louis, and Sallie Ann Glassman. *The New Orleans Voodoo Tarot*. Rochester, VT: Destiny Books, 1992.

Núñez, Luis Manuel. *Santeria: A Practical Guide to Afro-Caribbean Magic*. Thompson, CT: Spring Publications, 1992.

Oberon, Aaron. *Southern Cunning: Folkloric Witchcraft in the American South*. Winchester, UK: Moon Books, 2019.

Rhodes, Kalie. "The Native Roots of the French Market." New Orleans Historical. Accessed July 8, 2022. https://neworleanshistorical.org/items/show/1641.

Sexton, Rocky. "Cajun and Creole Treaters: Magico-Religious Folk Healing in French Louisiana." *Western Folklore* 51, no. 3/4 (July–Oct. 1992): 237–48. https://doi.org/10.2307/1499774.

Yronwode, Catherine. *Hoodoo Herb and Root Magic: A Materia Magica of African-American Conjure*. Forestville, CA: Lucky Mojo Curio Company, 2002.

5. The Midlands

Bilardi, C. R. *The Red Church or the Art of Pennsylvania German Braucherei*. Sunland, CA: Pendraig Publishing, 2009.

Blevins, Brooks. *Arkansas/Arkansaw: How Bear Hunters, Hillbillies, and Good Ol' Boys Defined a State*. Fayetteville: University of Arkansas Press, 2011.

———. *A History of the Ozarks, Volume 1: The Old Ozarks*. Urbana: University of Illinois Press, 2018.

Canizares, Raul J. *Cuban Santeria: Walking with the Night*. Rochester, VT: Destiny Books, 1999.

Castañeda, Antonia I. "Engendering the History of Alta California, 1769–1848: Gender, Sexuality, and the Family." *California History* 76, no. 2/3 (July 1997): 230–59. https://doi.org/10.2307/25161668.

Dorson, Richard M. *Buying the Wind: Regional Folklore in the United States*. Chicago: University of Chicago Press, 1964.

Frazer, James George. *The Golden Bough*. New York: Dover Publications, 2019.

Hamlin, Marie Caroline Watson. *Legends of le Détroit*. Detroit: Thorndike Nourse, 1884.

Harper, Kimberly. *White Man's Heaven: The Lynching and Expulsion of Blacks in the Southern Ozarks, 1894–1909*. Fayetteville: University of Arkansas Press, 2012.

Hester, Jessica Leigh. "The Spirited Afterlife of Detroit's Little Red Demon." *Atlas Obscura*, October 28, 2019. https://www.atlasobscura.com/articles/nain-rouge-detroit.

Hyatt, Harry Middleton. *Folk-lore from Adams County, Illinois*. New York: Alma Egan Hyatt Foundation, 1935.

Leary, James P. "Folklore of the Upper Peninsula." *Festival of American Folklife*, edited by Ed Brown, 51–54. Washington, DC: Smithsonian Institution, 1987. https://folklife-media.si.edu/docs/festival/program-books/FESTBK1987.pdf.

Menendian, Stephen, Samir Gambhir, and Chih-Wei Hsu. "Roots of Structural Racism." Othering & Belonging Institute, October 11, 2021. https://belonging.berkeley.edu/roots-structural-racism-2020.

Milnes, Gerald C. *Signs, Cures, and Witchery: German Appalachian Folklore*. Knoxville: University of Tennessee Press, 2007.

Mooney, James. *James Mooney's History, Myths, and Sacred Formulas of the Cherokees*. Fairview, NC: Bright Mountain Books, 1992.

Nightingale, Carl H. *Segregation: A Global History of Divided Cities*. Chicago: University of Chicago Press, 2012.

Parler, Mary Celestia. *Mary Celestia Parler Folklore Collection*. 1950.

———. *Folk Beliefs from Arkansas*. Self-published, 1962.

Phillips, Layli. *The Womanist Reader: The First Quarter Century of Womanist Thought*. New York: Routledge, 2006.

The Pluralism Project. "'Santeria': La Regla de Ocha-Ifa and Lukumi." Harvard University. Accessed May 20, 2021. https://pluralism.org/%E2%80%9Csanter%C3%ADa%E2%80%9D-the-lucumi-way.

Pompey, Sherman Lee. *Granny Gore's Ozark Folk Medicine*. Self-published, 1961.

Randolph, Vance. *Ozark Magic and Folklore*. New York: Dover Publications, 2003.

Rayburn, Otto Ernest. Papers. Special Collections Department, University of Arkansas Libraries.

———. *Ozark Country*. New York: Duell, Sloan & Pearce, 1960.

Weston, Brandon. *Ozark Folk Magic: Plants, Prayers & Healing*. Woodbury, MN: Llewellyn Publications, 2021.

Wilson, Charles Morrow. *Backwoods America*. St. Clair Shores, MI: Scholarly Press, 1979.

6. Plains West

Aitamurto, Kaarina. "More Russian than Orthodox Christianity: Russian Paganism as Nationalist Politics." *Nations under God: The Geopolitics of Faith in the Twenty-First Century*, edited by Luke M. Herrington, Alasdair McKay, and Jeffrey Haynes, 126–32. Bristol: E-International Relations Publishing, 2015. https://www.e-ir.info/wp-content/uploads/2015/08/Nations-under-God-E-IR.pdf.

Albanese, Catherine L. *A Republic of Mind and Spirit: A Cultural History of American Metaphysical Religion*. New Haven, CT: Yale University Press, 2007.

Bernshtam, T. A. "Russian Folk Culture and Folk Religion." *Russian Traditional Culture: Religion, Gender, and Customary Law*, edited by Marjorie Mandelstam Balzer, 34–47. Armonk, NY: M. E. Sharpe, 1992.

Blum, A. A. "Paul Bunyun and the Myth of the American Lumberjack." *Contemporary Review* (1996). https://www.thefreelibrary.com/Paul+Bunyon+and+the+myth+of+the+American+lumberjack.-a019139592.

Bodnar, John. "Immigration and Modernization: The Case of Slavic Peasants in Industrial America." *Journal of Social History* 10, no. 1 (Autumn 1976): 44–71. https://www.jstor.org/stable/3786420.

Botkin, B. A. *A Treasury of Western Folklore*. New York: Random House, 1990.

Bowman, Matthew. "A Mormon Bigfoot: David Patten's Cain and the Conception of Evil in LDS Folklore." *Journal of Mormon History* 33, no. 3 (2007): 62–82. https://digitalcommons.usu.edu/mormonhistory/vol33/iss3/1.

Brady, Margaret K. "Transformations of Power: Mormon Women's Visionary Narratives." *Latter-Day Lore*, edited by Eric A. Eliason and Tom Mould, 215–23. Salt Lake City: University of Utah Press, 2013.

Brodie, Fawn M. *No Man Knows My History: The Life of Joseph Smith*. New York: Alfred A. Knopf, 1966.

Brooke, John L. *The Refiner's Fire: The Making of Mormon Cosmology, 1644–1844*. Cambridge: Cambridge University Press, 1996.

Bushman, Richard Lyman. *Mormonism: A Very Short Introduction*. New York: Oxford University Press, 2008.

Cohen, Daniel. *The Encyclopedia of Monsters*. New York: Avon Books, 1991.

Dewey, Todd. "Many Riders Proudly Go Against Common NFR Superstitions." *Las Vegas Review Journal*, December 13, 2013. https://www.reviewjournal.com/sports/rodeo/national-finals-rodeo/superstitions-common-on-the-rodeo-circuit-but-many-proudly-go-against-them/.

Dobie, J. Frank. "Weather Wisdom of the Texas-Mexican Border." *Publications of the Texas Folk-Lore Society, Volume 2*, edited by J. Frank Dobie, 87–99. Austin: Texas Folk-Lore Society, 1923.

Dorson, Richard M. *Buying the Wind: Regional Folklore in the United States*. Chicago: University of Chicago Press, 1964.

———. "Folklore and Fake Lore." *The American Mercury* (March 1950): 335–42. https://www.unz.com/print/AmMercury-1950mar-00335.

Eliason, Eric A. "Seer Stones, Salamanders, and Early Mormon 'Folk Magic' in the Light of Folklore Studies and Bible Scholarship." *BYU Studies Quarterly* 55, no. 1 (2016): 73–93.

Eliason, Eric A., and Tom Mould, eds. *Latter-Day Lore: Mormon Folklore Studies*. Salt Lake City: University of Utah Press, 2013. Kindle.

Erdoes, Richard, ed. *Legends and Tales of the American West*. New York: Pantheon Books, 2018.

Fadiman, Anne. *The Spirit Catches You and You Fall Down: A Hmong Child, Her American Doctors, and the Collision of Two Cultures*. New York: Farrar, Strauss & Giroux, 1998.

Fee, Christopher R., and Jeffrey B. Webb, eds. *American Myths, Legends, and Tall Tales*. 3 vols. Santa Barbara, CA: ABC-CLIO, 2016.

Fife Folklore Collection. Utah State University.

Green, Garry, ed. "Slavic Pagan World: Slavic Pagan Beliefs, Gods, Myths, Recipes, Magic, Spells, Divinations, Remedies, Songs." Rodnovery. https://www.rodnovery.ru/attachments/article/526/slavic-pagan-world.pdf.

Hall, David. *Worlds of Wonder, Days of Judgment: Popular Religious Belief in Early New England*. New York: Alfred A. Knopf, 1989.

Hand, Wayland, ed. *The Frank C. Brown Collection of North Carolina Folklore: Popular Beliefs and Superstitions from North Carolina*. Durham, NC: Duke University Press, 1961.

Helvin, Natasha. *Slavic Witchcraft: Old World Conjuring Spells & Folklore*. Rochester, VT: Destiny Books, 2019.

Hubbs, Joanna. *Mother Russia: The Feminine Myth in Russian Culture*. Bloomington: Indiana University Press, 1993.

Jones, Prudence, and Nigel Pennick. *A History of Pagan Europe*. New York: Routledge, 1995.

Kelly, Mary B. "Goddess Embroideries of Russia and the Ukraine." *Woman's Art Journal* 4, no. 2 (Autumn 1983–Winter 1984): 10–13. https://www.jstor.org/stable/1357939.

Koppana, K. M. *Over Nine Forests: Folk Beliefs and Practices from Lithuania to the Urals*. Loughborough, UK: Heart of Albion Press, 2006.

Leary, James P. "Poles, Jews, and Jokes in America's Upper Midwest." *Western Folklore* 71, no. 3/4 (Summer and Fall 2012): 213–37. https://www.jstor.org/stable/24550725.

Martin, Janet. *Medieval Russia 980–1584*. Cambridge: Cambridge University Press, 1995.

Mitrofanova, Anastasia. "Russian Ethnic Nationalism and Religion Today." *The New Russian Nationalism: Imperialism, Ethnicity, and Authoritarianism 2000–2015*, edited by Pål Kolstø and Helge Blakkisrud, 104–131. Edinburgh: Edinburgh University Press, 2016. https://www.jstor.org/stable/10.3366/j.ctt1bh2kk5.

Penrod, James H. "Folk Beliefs about Work, Trades, and Professions from New Mexico." *Western Folklore* 27, no. 3 (July 1968): 180–83. https://doi.org/10.2307/1498103.

Propp, Vladimir. *Morphology of the Folktale*. 2nd ed. Translated by Laurence Scott. Edited by Louis A. Wagner. Austin: University of Texas Press, 2015.

Puhvel, Jaan. *Comparative Mythology*. Baltimore: Johns Hopkins University Press, 1987.

Pula, James S. "'A Branch Cut off from Its Trunk': The Affects of Immigration Restriction on American Polonia." *Polish American Studies* 61, no. 1 (Spring 2004): 39–50. https://www.jstor.org/stable/20148692.

Quinn, D. Michael. *Early Mormonism and the Magic World View*. Salt Lake City: Signature Books, 1998.

Randolph, Vance. *We Always Lie to Strangers: Tall Tales from the Ozarks*. New York: Columbia University Press, 1951.

Roucek, Joseph S. "The Yugoslav Immigrants in America." *American Journal of Sociology* 40, no. 5 (March 1935): 602–11. https://www.jstor.org/stable/2767923.

Ryan, W. F. *The Bathhouse at Midnight: An Historical Survey of Magic and Divination in Russia*. Phoenix Mill, UK: Sutton Publishing, 1999.

Sheppard, William L. "Population Movements, Interaction, and Legendary Geography." *Arctic Anthropology* 35, no. 2 (1998): 147–65. https://www.jstor.org/stable/40316494.

Tamm, Erika, Toomas Kivisild, Maere Reidla, Mait Metspalu, David Glenn Smith, Connie J. Mulligan, Claudio M. Bravi, et al. "Beringian Standstill and Spread of Native American Founders." *PLOS ONE* 2, no. 9 (Sept. 2007). https://doi.org/10.1371/journal.pone.0000829.

Tryon, Henry H. *Fearsome Critters*. Cornwall, NY: Idlewild Press, 1939.

Warner, Elizabeth. *Russian Myths*. Austin: University of Texas Press, 2002.

Willerslev, Rane. "Not Animal, Not Not-Animal: Hunting, Imitation, and Empathetic Knowledge among the Siberian Yukaghirs." *The Journal of the Royal Anthropological Institute* 10, no. 3 (Sept. 2004): 629–52. https://www.jstor.org/stable/3803798.

Zenkovsky, Serge A., ed. *Medieval Russia's Epics, Chronicles, and Tales*. New York: Meridian, 1974.

7. El Norte

Anzaldúa, Gloria. *Borderlands/La Frontera: The New Mestiza*. San Francisco: Aunt Lute Books, 1987. Kindle.

Arredondo, Alexis A., and Eric J. Labrado. *Magia Magia: Invoking Mexican Magic*. Mobile, AL: Conjure South Publications, 2020.

Avila, Elena, and Joy Parker. *Woman Who Glows in the Dark: A Curandera Reveals Traditional Aztec Secrets of Physical and Spiritual Health*. New York: Jeremy P. Tarcher/Putnam, 1999.

Bowles, David. *Border Lore: Folktales and Legends of South Texas*. Beaumont, TX: Lamar University Press, 2015.

———. *Feathered Serpent, Dark Heart of Sky: Myths of Mexico*. El Paso, TX: Cinco Puntos Press, 2018.

Buenaflor, Erika. *Cleansing Rites of Curanderismo: Limpias Espirituales of Ancient Mesoamerican Shamans*. Rochester, VT: Bear & Company, 2018.

Chavarría, A., and G. Espinosa. "Cruz-Badiano Codex and the Importance of the Mexican Medicinal Plants." *Journal of Pharmaceutical Technology, Research, and Management* 7, no. 1 (2019): 15–22. https://doi.org/10.15415/jptrm.2019.71003.

Davidow, Joie. *Infusions of Healing: A Treasury of Mexican-American Herbal Remedies*. New York: Fireside, 1999.

de la Portilla, Elizabeth. *They All Want Magic: Curanderas and Folk Healing*. College Station: Texas A&M University Press, 2009.

Erdoes, Richard, and Alfonso Ortiz, eds. *American Indian Myths and Legends*. New York: Pantheon Books, 1984.

García, Nasario, trans. *Brujerías: Stories of Witchcraft and the Supernatural in the American Southwest and Beyond*. Lubbock: Texas Tech University Press, 2007.

Gillin, John. "Magical Fright." *Psychiatry* 11, no. 4 (1948): 387–400. https://doi.org/10.1080/00332747.1948.11022704.

Hudson, Wilson, ed. *The Healer of Los Olmos and Other Mexican Lore*. University Park, TX: Southern Methodist University Press, 1975.

Illes, Judika. *Encyclopedia of Mystics, Saints & Sages: A Guide to Asking for Protection, Wealth, Happiness, and Everything Else!* New York: HarperOne, 2011.

Moore, Michael. *Los Remedios: Traditional Herbal Remedies of the Southwest*. Santa Fe, NM: Red Crane Books, 1995.

Simmons, Marc. *Witchcraft in the Southwest: Spanish & Indian Supernaturalism on the Rio Grande*. Lincoln: University of Nebraska Press, 1974.

Torres, Eliseo. *Curanderismo: The Art of Traditional Medicine without Borders*. Dubuque, IA: Kendall Hunt Publishing Company, 2009.

———. *Healing with Herbs and Rituals: A Mexican Tradition*. Edited by Timothy L. Sawyer. Albuquerque: University of New Mexico Press, 2014.

Torres, Eliseo, and Imanol Miranda. *Curandero: Traditional Healers of Mexico and the Southwest*. Dubuque, IA: Kendall Hunt Publishing Company, 2019.

• • • • • • • • •

Torres, Eliseo, and Timothy L. Sawyer. *Curandero: A Life in Mexican Folk Healing*. Albuquerque: University of New Mexico Press, 2005.

Yolen, Jane. *Favorite Folktales from Around the World*. New York: Pantheon Books, 1986.

8. *The Left Coast*

Adamson, T. *Folk-Tales of the Coast Salish*. New York: The American Folk-Lore Society, G. E. Stechert and Co., 1934.

Arredondo, Alexis A., and Eric J. Labrado. *Magia Magia: Invoking Mexican Magic*. Mobile, AL: Conjure South Publications, 2020.

Ballard, Arthur C. *Mythology of Southern Puget Sound: Legends Shared by Tribal Elders*. Whitefish, MT: Literary Licensing LLC, 2011.

Boas, Franz, James Alexander Teit, Livingston Farrand, Marian K. Gould, and Herbert Joseph Spinden. *Folk-Tales of Salishan and Sahaptin Tribes*. New York: American Folk-Lore Society, 1917.

Bragg, L. E. *Washington Myths and Legends: The True Stories Behind History's Mysteries*. 2nd ed. Lanham, MD: Rowman & Littlefield, 2015.

Buenaflor, Erika. *Cleansing Rites of Curanderismo: Limpias Espirituales of Ancient Mesoamerican Shamans*. Rochester, VT: Bear & Company, 2018.

Buerge, David M., and Junius Rochester. *Roots and Branches: The Religious Heritage of Washington State*. Seattle: Church Council of Greater Seattle, 1988.

Chesnut, R. Andrew. *Devoted to Death: Santa Muerte, the Skeleton Saint*. New York: Oxford University Press, 2012.

Clark, Ella E. *Indian Legends of the Pacific Northwest*. 1st ed. Berkeley: University of California Press, 2003.

Cross, J. Allen. *American Brujeria: Modern Mexican American Folk Magic*. Newburyport, MA: Red Wheel/Weiser Books, 2021.

Danico, Mary Yu, ed. *Asian American Society: An Encyclopedia*. Thousand Oaks, CA: SAGE Publications, 2014.

Daniels, Cora Linn. *Encyclopedia of Superstitions, Folklore, and the Occult Sciences of the World*. Vol. 3. Ann Arbor: University of Michigan Library, 1903.

Feuchtwang, Stephan. *Popular Religion in China: The Imperial Metaphor*. London: Curzon Press, 2001.

Frazer, James George. *The Golden Bough*. New York: Collier Books Publishing, 1985.

Gordon, Lesley. *Green Magic: Flowers, Plants & Herbs in Lore & Legend*. New York: Viking Press, 1977.

Gunther, Erna. *Ethnobotany of Western Washington: The Knowledge and Use of Indigenous Plants by Native Americans*. Revised ed. Seattle: University of Washington Press, 1973.

Hackenmiller, Tom. *Ladies of the Lake: Tales of Transportation, Tragedy, and Triumph on Lake Chelan*. Manson, WA: Point Publishing, 1998.

Hedera, Via. *Folkloric American Witchcraft and the Multicultural Experience: A Crucible at the Crossroads*. Hampshire, UK: John Hunt Publishing, 2021.

Hilbert, Vi, trans. and ed. *Haboo: Native American Stories from Puget Sound*. Seattle: University of Washington Press, 1997.

Hutcheson, Cory Thomas. "Episode 14 – Interview with Cat Yronwode." *New World Witchery*, August 31, 2010. Podcast, MP3 audio, 1:40:18. https://newworldwitchery.com/2010/08/31/episode-14-interview-with-cat-yronwode/.

Illes, Judika. *Encyclopedia of Mystics, Saints & Sages: A Guide to Asking for Protection, Wealth, Happiness, and Everything Else!* New York: HarperOne, 2011.

"Immigrants in Oregon." American Immigration Council, August 6, 2020. https://www.americanimmigrationcouncil.org/research/immigrants-oregon.

Kwong, Peter. *The New Chinatown*. New York: Hill and Wang, 1996.

Lau, Theodora, and Laura Lau. *The Handbook of Chinese Horoscopes*. 40th anniversary ed. Berkeley, CA: North Atlantic Books, 2019.

LeBlond, Paul H. "Sea Serpents of the Pacific Northwest." *Montana: The Magazine of Western History* 43, no. 4 (Autumn 1993): 44–51. https://www.jstor.org/stable/4519621.

Ni, Xueting Christine. *From Kuan Yin to Chairman Mao: The Essential Guide to Chinese Deities*. Newburyport, MA: Weiser Books, 2018.

O'Brien, Suzanne Crawford. *Coming Full Circle: Spirituality and Wellness among Native Communities in the Pacific Northwest*. Lincoln: University of Nebraska Press, 2013.

O'Falt, Chris. "How Robert Eggers Used Real Historical Accounts to Create His Horror Sensation 'The Witch.'" *IndieWire*, February 19, 2016. https://www.indiewire.com/2016/02/how-robert-eggers-used-real-historical-accounts-to-create-his-horror-sensation-the-witch-67882/.

Prahlad, Anand. *The Greenwood Encyclopedia of African American Folklore.* 3 vols. Westport, CT: Greenwood, 2005.

Thompson, M. Terry, and Steven M. Egesdal, eds. *Salish Myths and Legends: One People's Stories.* Lincoln: University of Nebraska Press, 2008.

Turner, Nancy J. *Ancient Pathways, Ancestral Knowledge: Ethnobotany and Ecological Wisdom of Indigenous Peoples of Northwestern North America.* Montreal: McGill-Queen's University Press, 2014.

Wang, Jun. *Cultivating Qi: An Introduction to Chinese Body-Mind Energetics.* Berkeley, CA: North Atlantic Books, 2011.

Wen, Benebell. *The Tao of Craft: Fu Talismans and Casting Sigils in the Eastern Esoteric Tradition.* Berkeley, CA: North Atlantic Books, 2015.

Yuan, Haiwang. *The Magic Lotus Lantern and Other Tales from the Han Chinese.* Westport, CT: Libraries Unlimited, 2006.

INDEX

C

D

H

I

J

K

L

M

Q

R

S

T